Gilding the Acorn

Gilding the Acorn

Behind the façade of the National Trust

Paula Weideger

S I M O N   &   S C H U S T E R

LONDON · SYDNEY · NEW YORK · TOKYO · SINGAPORE · TORONTO

First published in Great Britain by Simon & Schuster Ltd, 1994
A Paramount Communications Company

Simon & Schuster Ltd
West Garden Place
Kendal Street
London W2 2AQ

Simon & Schuster of Australia Pty Ltd
Sydney

A CIP catalogue record for this book is available from
the British Library.

ISBN 0–671–71129–6

Typeset in 11.5/13.5pt Garamond by
Hewer Text Composition Services, Edinburgh
Printed and bound in Great Britain by
Butler & Tanner Ltd, Frome and London

Contents

Credits

Photographs:

Sir Robert Hunter, Post Office Archive; Canon Hardwicke Rawnsley by Rupert Potter, Brandelhow Park by Rupert Potter, Beatrix Potter, her father Rupert Potter and Hardwicke Rawnsley by Rupert Potter, kindly lent by Rosalind Rawnsley; Octavia Hill, Elliott & Fry Ltd; Trevelyans at Wallington with the kind permission of the Trustees of the Trevelyan family papers; Alan Clutton-Brock, © *The Times*; James Lees-Milne used with his kind permission; Lord and Lady Scarsdale by Robin Laurance © *The Times*; Lord Rothschild and Mrs James de Rothschild, with the kind permission of Lord Rothschild; Castle Coole, A. F. Kersting; Cdr Conrad Rawnsley with his kind permission; Enterprise Neptune Appeals Brochure, NT Archive; George Elliott © Roger Bamber; Lady Emma Tennant and Graham Stuart Thomas, the National Trust; Nigel Nicolson with his kind permission; Jimmy Hancock, David Gepp; Dave Mason, John Ferris; Stan Emondson, Tony Greenbank; Sir Francis Dashwood, Long Crendon Courthouse, the Pin Mill at Bodnant, Hill Top farmhouse, A la Ronde and Mr Straw's House by the author.

Documents:

My thanks to Miss Felicity Ashbee for permission to quote from the Journals of C. R. Ashbee; to Lord Crawford for permission to quote from a letter written by the 28th Earl of Crawford and Balcarres; to Cdr Conrad Rawnsley RN (ret'd) for permission to quote from his papers and to Janette Harley, the National Trust's archivist.

Introduction

'Why are you, *an American*, writing a book about the National Trust?' people have asked. They weren't belligerent; several were reassuring and said they thought it was good that someone for whom the class system has no place, and who votes in another country, was going to look at this very English institution. Still they were puzzled. What had given me the idea?

It was the Englishness of the National Trust that first attracted me. In 1979 when I came to stay in London, it was my way of getting to know the country in which I was living. I could have visited the law courts or watched a lot of television; instead I went to look at the houses of the National Trust.

I was lured by their inlaid marble table tops, the tapestries, canopied beds, the carved panelling, even the cavernous kitchens, though they never smelled of butter and sugar or roasting meat. And all that gilt: at the time I didn't think about what it cost and what might be bought with the money instead; the longer I lived in a grey world, the more enticed I was by things that shone. I wanted to be be dazzled, and I was. Then too, we have no eighteenth-century palaces where I come from.

A time came when gardening possessed me. I ought to move to the country and make a garden, I thought, seeing myself as a Bronx Vita Sackville-West. By train and bus I travelled to Sissinghurst. Later came a car and Hidcote.

Though I was beginning to know London, when I looked at a map of all that surrounds it, I saw only names and lines

[1]

connecting them. Joining the National Trust was a way of finding out what Buckinghamshire looked like, and Norfolk, Sussex and Berkshire.

'Why not ask them to put you on the press list,' a friend, who was, generously suggested. It was the booming 1980s when the Trust's policy was especially open-handed with the press. There was not too much scrutiny of what was written after a jaunt; in fact there seemed to be none. A year or more passed during which I went on every trip I could, saw a lot and produced not a published word. But then I started writing about its houses and gardens and the cast of characters: titled folk who live on as tenants in mansions that had been owned by their families for generations; the landlord's middle-class staff, who often looked as if they'd prefer the aristocrat-in-residence to say 'hallo' than for him to hand over the rent cheque. (I hadn't yet learnt that usually there was no cheque because there was no rent.)

Why was there no book about the Trust? I wondered. By a person who was not of it, that is. I wanted to know more. I wrote a proposal, then put it in a desk drawer. While I mulled it over, an invitation arrived to join the Trust on a visit to its new garden at Biddulph Grange. I accepted, and early one morning took the train to Staffordshire with the rest of the party. As we headed north I overheard a bit of gossip about an old woman that made me look nonchalantly out of the window and concentrate hard so as to not miss a word. It seemed that she had reneged on a promise to give her house to the Trust and without warning had put it on the market. 'Everyone at the office is terribly upset . . .'

I enjoyed High Victorian Biddulph and wrote about it. But the titbit about that elderly woman's promise not kept went on tugging at me and I followed. I found myself drawn into the story of Chastleton House: a saga in which a great deal was at stake and everyone was wrong. Everyone means the National Trust too, though it did not concede there had been any mistakes – on its part. Publicly it never does.

The Trust had begun to look more like a secret kingdom than a charity supported by the contributions of millions of people. Facts are exceptionally hard to prise out of most of those who work at its Queen Anne's Gate headquarters. For instance, ask its Press Office, as I did, what a recruiter is paid and they are 'unable to provide' the information. The answer is that like those who work in its tea rooms and shops, they earn £3.20 an hour.

Or ask its lawyer what the procedure is when people with country houses want to give them to the charity as a way of settling inheritance tax bills and the answer is, 'There haven't been any since I've been here, so I can't say.' Hundreds and hundreds of other items are treated as if they, too, were highly confidential. Surely the National Trust was too big, too important, too influential and too good a thing to carry on as if it were Japan before the arrival of Commodore Perry?

Just who were these people? What does the National Trust actually do? The proposal came out of my drawer.

Ten days later, I had my first lesson in how things work in the lap of the English establishment, where the National Trust so snugly nestles. A phone call came from the Trust's press and public relations manager.

'I hear you're writing a book about the National Trust,' he said jovially.

I mumbled and stalled. (I mean my agent had only just sent out the proposal.) He went on to quote a couple of phrases I'd written, followed by some flattering remarks to sugarcoat the shock. The fax of my pages was sitting there on his desk!

My agent was furious. Publishers are not supposed to do such things. What could I do but smile and feel that my education had begun. I call it being underhand; they call it the old boy network.

I've now travelled the National Trust's empire from top to bottom and side to side and talked to literally hundreds of people. I hadn't grasped before how enormous and varied it is, how spread out its properties and how far from straightforward the relation of any one of its assorted parts is to the others. I came to understand that I couldn't attempt to tell the whole story.

The Trust produces its own guides and celebratory albums. And me? I've approached the National Trust as a stranger in a strange land, which is after all what I am. This book is a traveller's account. I'm the sort of person who likes to read up before a journey and study *en route*, but the perceptions, like the opinions, are my own. The reason I mention this is that the National Trust enquired (sometimes it seemed more as though they leaned hard): would it be possible to see my manuscript when it was complete? It was not.

There must have been times when I seemed as much an oddity to the natives as they to me. Often I'd drive up to a garden, a saw-mill, a cottage or, in the case of Waddesdon Manor, a French château, in the company of my navigator, and dog: a poodle, a white one, worse yet. But weighing five stone at least he wasn't a lap dog and was able to look the many labradors he met straight in the eye.

For a social climber the National Trust does provide scope. If I wrote a list acknowledging all those who were good enough to talk to me about the charity, it would go on for pages, and while the majority of names on it would not be found in *Debrett*, the litany of lords would be quite long enough to be embarrassing. So let me here thank all who shared their time and thoughts with me; those willing to speak for the record and those asking for anonymity instead. There were, as as I went along, a few people at Queen Anne's Gate who, within the confines of what they saw as their duty to withhold, were generous and genuine in their attempt to help – the historic buildings secretary especially; the archivist, eventually. I thank them, too.

I found the grandees whose extravagant mansions have gone to the Trust less glamorous and more sympathetic than I'd imagined they would be, and on the whole their heirs too. Even the vainest and most pompous of them deeply loves and honours his ancestral home. Being so house-proud and having such powerful family feeling seemed touching rather than egomaniacal. (Though to this there were one or two exceptions as the reader will see.)

But the greatest privilege and my real reward was even more unexpected.

Born a city girl, I did not grow up a rambler; as a sufferer from altitude fever, I would not wish to climb a fell or walk a coastal path unless it was set well back from what I regard as the edge of the end of the world. Even my gardening ambitions have shrunk to fit my patch. Neither as a member of the National Trust nor as a journalist had I much experience of its countryside property, by choice. So it was a revelation and an education as well as a big pleasure when I met the wardens, gardeners, foresters and farmers.

They work fifty and sixty hours a week and more, using all their gifts and their guile. They are often proud of the results, and they should be. They are often insufficiently appreciated by their employer, and they shouldn't be.

But it isn't only the grand job done by these people that's so impressive. It's also a matter of character. There's nothing furtive about them; they do not seem complacent.

My heart went out to more than one of the men who work on the ground; and to all of them I dedicate this book.

In the Nick of Time

'Octavia Hill?' The woman paused. 'Yes I know the name . . . An open space in Kent somewhere, isn't it?' These words were overheard in 1938 at the centenary celebration of Miss Hill's birth. The woman's ignorance was forgiveable. Octavia Hill had been a well-known figure in 1895 when she, along with Hardwicke Rawnsley and Robert Hunter, founded the National Trust, as they had been too. But within decades the three of them were pretty well forgotten. Their creation, however, was on its way to becoming the largest, richest charity in the land.

Admittedly for many years the advance of the National Trust was more like that of a tortoise than a gazelle. But today the Trust is the largest 'private' landowner in England, Wales or Northern Ireland. (Only the Forestry Commission owns more.) Among landlords of rural property, possibly only the Crown outstrips it. The Trust's membership has grown from only eight when it started to more than two million today. And if the names of the trio that conceived the charity are obscure, they are not altogether disregarded.

'The Founders will be turning in their graves!' outraged subscribers bellow when the Trust has been judged to be taking a wrong turn. It's the NT version of 'To the barricades!' The cry is not heard very often. The members, on the whole, are a pacific group and usually seem sufficiently pleased with what the National Trust is doing. Not that they know much about it. Quite a few, for instance,

have the idea that the Trust may be part of the government.

There is a perhaps understandable lack of curiosity about
what the National Trust actually does. It's enough that its
goals seem wholly admirable and it appears to be meeting them.
The tea rooms are bright and clean (the cakes often tasty), the
shops fully stocked, the houses impressively glittering. In the
countryside, fences are where they're meant to be and upright,
car parks conveniently placed (though more could be planted
with trees around the perimeter to protect dogs when it's hot!).
Ramblers – members or not – seem to be more inquisitive, and
not coincidentally, more vigilant. If they come upon fences
where there should be none and gates with barbed wire on
top they make a stir.

When an issue does draw the attention of members to it – and
it might be anything from nude bathing to hunting – the spirit
of *laissez-faire* is abandoned, however. The founders are taken
down from the shelf on which they otherwise rest gathering ever
more dust. The memory of Octavia Hill, Sir Robert Hunter and
Canon Hardwicke Rawnsley is being betrayed, it is asserted,
by the pygmies now standing where those nineteenth-century
giants once stood.

With an equal display of piety but in voices that are softer and
less high-pitched, the men who are responsible for the policies
of the National Trust can also be heard summoning up the
venerable threesome. But from these lips, the founders are not
brought out of storage to be used as an offensive weapon; but to
serve, instead, as an amulet warding off attack. They, of course,
know all three founders' names – usually. ('Don't know much
of the early history,' Lord Chorley, the chairman, confesses
when trying to recall who they were.) And if in reference to
them one name is singled out, it's always the same person.

'This is exactly what Octavia Hill had in mind,' the people
running the National Trust insist, when a new and possibly
controversial plan, or merely a change in emphasis, is being
presented. Presumably, with such an upright and selfless spinster's seal of approval on it, how could anyone object to the
policy – for long.

[7]

Just who were these founders? What was it they hoped to accomplish in establishing the National Trust? Is what they set out to achieve being honoured or traduced? Does it matter? Can what Hill, Hunter and Rawnsley struggled towards at the end of the nineteenth century have any bearing on what the National Trust is doing a hundred tumultuous years later?

Yes, certainly the National Trust has changed since its beginnings: in its emphasis, its focus and even what could be called its style. It has shifted its direction more than once, as I intend to show. And if people really do turn in their graves, there have been periods when the founders would have been three subterranean whirling dervishes. (This very moment would be one of them.) But, given all that has changed in society as well as at the National Trust, the touch of the founders' hands and the preoccupations of their hearts are still in evidence. Though sometimes only just. This isn't altogether surprising, however. They were mavericks whose views seem almost conventional today.

While the British Empire was expanding, most people in England were convinced that growth was a synonym for progress. Octavia Hill, Hardwicke Rawnsley and Robert Hunter were among the minority who did not. 'Each year these public grounds of recreation and health are narrowed and invaded by private greed, miscalled enterprise,' Rawnsley wrote in one of his many communiqués on the subject.[1]

For all three of them, unrestrained industrialization and the unrestricted building-up of cities that went with it was clearly dangerous. There was plenty of evidence all around them. People were being crushed together in the towns, breathing air blackened by the smoke from factory chimneys. London, yellow with fog, had 2 million residents in 1851 and 4 million in 1890. The city expanded its boundaries of course, but that didn't make Londoners feel less pinched. In 1801 there were 20.9 people per acre in the city; by 1900 the population density, as well as the population, had doubled. As for the countryside into which people might escape to revive their health and their spirits, it was being cut into bits and paved over. The National Trust led the way in attempting to protect what is now called the environment.

Rebels with a cause

In 1895 the founders of the National Trust were well into middle age. Rawnsley, the youngest, was forty-four; Hill was fifty-six and Hunter exactly in between. Yet all of them were feisty campaigners and had already achieved a great deal.

Hardwicke Rawnsley, a canon of Carlisle Cathedral, made his home and his crusade in Westmorland and Cumberland. 'King of the Lakes', some people called him.

Robert Hunter, an astute lawyer, had been knighted for his work as chief solicitor to the Post Office. But for decades before he went to work for the government, he'd successfully fought to keep common land open to all. Like Miss Hill, he lived near London.

Octavia Hill, certainly the most eminent of the three, had been a formidable housing reformer for thirty years with a mission to provide healthier, more attractive living conditions for the poor. Comparisons have been made with Florence Nightingale and Elizabeth Garrett Anderson and, when she died, Westminster Abbey was offered as a place of burial. (Her family, following her wishes, buried her in a Kent churchyard next to the grave of Miranda, a favourite sister.)

Early in their lives these three individuals became passionate about the need to save open spaces in order that working people would have a chance to breathe clean air, walk, daydream and explore. And each grew up to fight their different battles successfully to achieve this end. But however good at defending his glorious patch Canon Rawnsley was, however skilfully Sir Robert argued his cases, however expert Miss Hill could be at persuading and rallying her troops, it was their separate but common experience that fighting one skirmish and then another was exhausting without being exhaustive – even if their battles were won. The pressure from greedy landowners and expansionist developers was too great. Another fight always seemed to be there waiting. What was needed was a way to make their victories stick.

The National Trust which came into existence in January 1895 would acquire places 'of historic interest and natural beauty'. Once owned by the Trust, these properties would remain unspoilt and people, particularly the poorer ones, would be able to benefit from them for generations to come.

'A somewhat woolly idealist' is the way Rosalind Rawnsley describes Octavia Hill, while Robert Hunter, she thinks, must have been a rather 'dull lawyer'. Her conclusion is that 'without the up front PR chap that Hardwicke Rawnsley was, they never would have got it off the ground'. The canon's great-granddaughter is not only demonstrating family pride. He was a gifted publicist. Just the same, she is not exactly accurate about the contributions, or attributes, of the other two.

Without Hill and Hunter, the canon's ability to draw attention to his campaigns – to make people see that what they loved and took for granted soon might be for ever lost – all this would have lacked a solid yet at the same time expandable frame to support the public's response when it came.

Robert Hunter, who had drafted the Articles of Association that gave the National Trust its legal existence in 1895, twelve years later created the Act of Parliament which has been its Constitution ever since. The charity had only 550 members and 2,000 acres of land at the time, yet this armature, though rusted and creaky now, has managed to carry the Trust through all its enormous subsequent growth. (See Chapter 5.)

Octavia Hill wrote the early appeals that brought in the money to buy the Trust's first and crucially important acquisitions. Rawnsley for all his love of words didn't have her touch. He drafted appeals; she rewrote them. 'I thought it perhaps would be well', she tactfully began when explaining some changes she'd made in what he'd written about eighteen acres in Cornwall which the Trust was hoping to buy, 'to dwell a little on the breeze & beauty of the space as well as on its historic & poetic side.'[2] Every one of Octavia Hill's appeals was successful.

A family album

For three people who were so prominent in their time, very little original material about their lives remains; there's even less about their practical contribution towards running the National Trust. No volume has been devoted to the life of Sir Robert Hunter; the one solid biography of Octavia Hill[3] has only a solitary chapter about Hill's involvement with National Trust; the biography of Hardwicke Rawnsley was written by his second wife, Eleanor, who seems to have been of the 'if you don't like what they say, ignore it and then destroy the documentary evidence' school of image-making.

As for the National Trust itself and its approach to keeping an archive: 'They must have had a big bonfire,' says Rosalind Rawnsley, 'and burnt all the papers.' And according to Robin Fedden, the Trust's historic buildings secretary when he wrote his history in 1967, this is what they did just before the Second World War. There was 'a conflagration shrouded in mystery as deep as that which attended the burning of the Alexandrian library,' he writes. Or, as an overwhelmed Samantha Wyndham, the staff member the National Trust charged with producing a booklet of facts about itself for its Centenary remarked, 'the Trust seems to have spent all its time looking after other people's property and very little on looking after its own.'

In 1992, the Trust finally hired a fulltime professional archivist. Janette Harley was shocked by the archaic and inefficient way the charity kept its papers. Despite all that was for ever lost, she reckoned it would take her at least five years to discover just what was in its central files. And then there were the sixteen regions offering further mystery, yet more chaos, and, in Wessex alone, a Matterhorn of paper. Beginning in 1955, Wessex, perhaps in a guilty overreaction to house cleanings past, began saving every single scrap of paper that came into, or was produced by, the Regional Office, however trivial its nature.

When it began taking on inhabited country houses and the families who had owned them offered to give the National Trust their papers, too, the charity's recommendation was to deposit them with their County Council's Record Office instead. If only the Trust had taken its own advice. From its earliest days, snapshots and snippets are all that's left.[4]

The more avant-garde of Hill, Hunter and Rawnsley's contemporaries were young women who went in for loose and flowing dresses; there was a vogue for naked bathing, too, and for Oscar Wilde's plays. The elegant visited the zoo while 'common folk' packed circuses and music halls. Yet among the founding trio, only the clergyman looks as if he ever found life a treat. Both Robert Hunter and Octavia Hill seem so sober and constrained. 'Hard and shrivelled' is the way one colleague described Sir Robert and he found Miss Hill a woman with 'a stern' self-control.[5] It is not perhaps irrelevant that Hardwicke Rawnsley was the only one of the three who is said to have had a reasonably carefree childhood; though he, as well as the others, had bouts of blackness when he grew up.

On 1 December 1898, as a gift for her sixtieth birthday, Octavia Hill was presented with the portrait which 200 of her admirers had commissioned from John Singer Sargent. It shows a woman with grey hair, plump cheeks and a placid expression. Miss Hill, who was not of tranquil disposition, disapproved of the extravagance. As for the work itself, the artist, perhaps, had not captured his subject's character.

'Sargent matched the Edwardian age to a nicety . . .' Osbert Sitwell later wrote about this painter to whom his own family had sat for an enormous group portrait. 'He was so plainly more interested in the appurtenances of his sitters . . . than in their faces.' Sitwell acerbicly describes Sargent as a man who pictorially exalted the dessert called Pêche Melba 'to the rank of an ideal'.[6] And in fact there is something confectionery about Octavia Hill as Sargent portrayed her. This woman whom her biographer describes as 'inflexible, dogmatic and harsh' looks more like a lusciously iced bun – sweet, smooth and doughy.

Miss Hill was an unpretentious soul; she was also an ambitious and tenacious woman. She flattered others with her protestations of her own inferiority; meek apology, often repeated, was characteristic, too. But then she'd go in for the kill, frequently in the form of asking for help (especially financial) for some good cause.

This combination of submissiveness, thought to be typically female, and ferocious determination in action was not rare among the ambitious, campaigning spinsters of the Victorian era. And sadly, her pattern – of being extremely energetic, followed, periodically, by breakdowns – was not an uncommon one in the lives of the exceptional people among whom she lived.

Charles Darwin and John Ruskin as well as Hill, Hunter and Rawnsley all showed this same curve of prodigiously productive work followed by dives into neurasthenia. Whatever drove each of them to push so very hard propelled them unrelentingly. They seemed to lack the ability to slow down and therefore stopped only when mentally or physically exhausted.

Octavia Hill was born in 1838 in Wisbech, Cambridgeshire, where her father was then a prosperous banker. Their house was on the Brink, an all too prophetic address. James Hill took to backing radical schemes he thought might help the working class with the same hapless conviction other men demonstrate at the races. His money went into numbers of ambitious but financially unpromising projects, among them the bank rolling of a Utopian community – a money loser with a proven track record. By the time Octavia Hill was two years old, her father was bankrupt.

A nomadic life began as he travelled England looking for a way to become solvent again. He tried and failed until he had a breakdown and didn't or couldn't make the effort any more. James Hill then permanently retired from the responsibility of supporting his brood. His wife Caroline, and her doctor father, became responsible for the wellbeing of the family.

Dr Thomas Southwood Smith was gifted and distinguished. Initially a Unitarian minister, both Byron and Wordsworth were among those who thought highly of his religious writing.[7] When he became a doctor and wrote a text on the Philosophy of Health, it went into ten editions. It was intended to be of both practical and spiritual value, being subtitled: 'An exposition of the physiological and sanitary conditions conducive to human longevity and happiness'.[8] The intended audience was everyone from mothers to soldiers and politicians. But it was when he switched from the practice of medicine to the politics of prevention, or Sanitary Reform as it was then called, that the physician had his greatest influence. Sadly, Caroline Southwood Smith's father, so successful in other ways, eventually had financial problems, too, and she had to take on the entire burden of raising her family.

When Octavia Hill was thirteen, her mother took a job that changed both their immediate circumstances and her future course. In 1851 Caroline Hill went to work as the manager of the Co-operative Guild, a charity housed in Fitzroy Square. It contained a school as well as an arts and crafts workshop.

Before this move into the centre of London, the Hills had lived only a couple of miles away in Finchley, which was still countrylike in 1852. Octavia Hill was depressed by the dirty, noisy city. But her mother kept her busy, an approach that seemed to work.

The following year, John Ruskin came to the Guild scouting for attractive crafts. Octavia Hill had read, and revered, his book *Modern Painters* and saw her chance. Could he help her, she asked him. She wanted to learn to draw and paint.

John Ruskin clearly took to having acolytes and knew how to attract them. Within two years the artistic education of Octavia Hill was firmly – not to say rigidly – in his hands. He put this eager would-be artist to work copying old masters – sometimes for as much as six hours every day of the week. Creativity, inspiration, self-expression: Ruskin gave her room for none of this. Very briefly, Octavia Hill balked. She soon settled down.

Later in her teens Octavia Hill became a Christian Socialist. The ambition, sometimes obsessive, to restore the family's fortunes is one well-known reaction to a childhood experience like Octavia Hill's yet the only way she could have done that was through marriage. She remained a spinster; but she had a powerful ambition to make good just the same. And though she retained artistic ambitions well into her twenties, eventually she carried forward her father's and her grandfather's ideals with great success and never a hint of financial disgrace. She called it her 'human work' and for it she eventually became celebrated. That, in retrospect, her greatest success proved to be the National Trust – now sometimes known as a Society for the Preservation of the Aristocracy – is an irony as comfortable as the proverbial old shoe. And just like a worn-out slipper it both fits and keeps falling off. (More on this subject will follow.)

Octavia Hill was personally allergic to materialism as a result of her family's experiences, or, rather, she felt that accumulating money or the objects it could buy was not a worthy goal. But she became adept at chasing contributions for her various causes and an alert, even avid, keeper of accounts. Her early history also provided Octavia Hill with a tendency towards melancholy and a skittish disbelief that stability could last.

All her life, Octavia Hill remained devoted to Ruskin. Yet from the time she was a teenager what he'd offered her was a peculiar mixture of poison and ambrosia. Ruskin became her guiding star and a competitive, cruel critic.

Was it a coincidence that just at the point Octavia Hill had become sufficiently proficient and confident to be offered portrait commissions that Ruskin made it plain he didn't think she had the gift to be an artist? Or that when he came into a substantial inheritance on his father's death (£175,000 plus land and houses) John Ruskin offered Octavia Hill a loan of £800 to buy some rundown houses and rehabilitate them for the poor? But perhaps it was just a fortuitous meeting of a generous impulse on his part and the chance it gave her to, as it were, make good the family name.

Octavia Hill was twenty-six years old. She accepted the money and bought three wretched houses in Paradise Place, Marylebone. She was launched on the enterprise that became her life's work. Yet in this 'human work', too, the more she achieved, the less Ruskin liked it. He also had ambitions in that department. (In 1855 Ruskin began brooding about starting a Utopian brotherhood based on his conception of

medieval social life; in 1871 it took shape as the Guild of
St George.)

Miss Hill went on to buy and rehabilitate more houses.
The interiors of what had been slum tenements were cleaned;
windows were cut to let in more light and air. As she conceived
it, a bed of flowers as well as a tidy rent roll were important to
the success of these schemes. And sometimes Ruskin's gardener
landscaped bits of land that surrounded some of the houses she
bought.

For all her activity in London, Octavia Hill never completely
converted to city life. She was among those who believed that
the countryside was not only a source of beauty and healthier
than town, but that it was also healing. People with money and
leisure had easy access to all this. Her concern was for those
who did not.

The parks and gardens she provided for her tenants were
Octavia Hill's attempt to try to bring some of the country
into town. Her wish was to provide as she put it – and the
National Trust loves to quote – 'open air sitting rooms for the
poor'. This was not an idiosyncratic notion. William Morris too
believed that 'every child should be able to play in a garden close
to the place where his parents live'.[9] The idea certainly was not
a new one. Town gardens can be seen in early Egyptian wall
paintings; Epicurus created them in Athens; the inhabitants of
palaces from ancient Rome to Marrakesh have enjoyed the scent
of flowers, the sound of splashing water, the murmur of the
wind in the trees. But it wasn't until early in the nineteenth
century that providing gardens in cities for the enjoyment of
everybody – the poor especially – began to be a preoccupation
in England.

A tree grows in London

Like Hill, in the years before she helped create the National Trust (though unlike the Trust as it evolved), nineteenth-century landscape designers dreamed of the country, without scorning urban life. And while their preoccupations didn't shape the policy of the National Trust when it came into being, their aims and, even more, the obstacles they met as they tried to realize them, played a part in its creation just the same. Had it been possible to bring more of the countryside into town, the desperation felt about saving the rural landscape might never have become so great.

'We in London have to share our gardens,' Octavia Hill was to say in a speech to the students at Newnham College, Cambridge, in 1898 in explanation of the aims of the National Trust which she had helped to found three years earlier. 'Perhaps England itself will learn to share some of its gardens.'[10] (The sharing in the years since has amounted to 600,000 acres.)

In 1800 the population of London was 750,000. It was twice that by 1830. In 1833 (five years before Octavia Hill was born), John Claudius Loudon, the landscape gardener and influential writer, published a paper called 'Breathing spaces for the Metropolis'.[11]

Loudon was among the people who felt that crowding people together in cities caused asphyxiation of the spirit as well as of the lungs. In response he proposed a solution in the form of an imaginative town plan for the capital.[12]

As a model, Loudon took the target, with St Paul's Cathedral as its bull's eye. He proposed that London's development take the form of a series of concentric bands in which rings of park land would alternate with built-up belts until the last of the green circles merged with open country. Even in the very centre of the city a person could be in countryside – simply by taking a good brisk walk.

Loudon's plan remained just that. But a few years later, Joseph Paxton had more success with a less radical but still audacious scheme. In 1823 Paxton had become head gardener to the 6th Duke of Devonshire at Chatsworth in Derbyshire; a quarter of a century later he brought the grandee's landscape into town. In 1847 at Birkenhead, outside Liverpool, Joseph Paxton created a landscaped park of the sort that might envelop a great country house – complete with artfully 'natural' lake. (Octavia Hill was nine years old.)

It's true that the Duke of Devonshire's Chatsworth Park was open to the public, but the park at Birkenhead was not only open to everyone, it was their property. (A century later, quite a few of the country-house parks on which Paxton had patterned Birkenhead themselves became everyone's property when they were acquired by the National Trust.)

The notion of what these green spaces could – and should – accomplish was evolving. Parks like Birkenhead not only provided fresh air and leafy spaces but they were conceived as a kind of green social engineering. At this time such a grand open space as the zoo in Regents Park was open only to members and those paying 'strangers' whom they recommended. But city parks were there for everybody. Because the poor strolled through them in proximity to those far better off, it was imagined that this would have the same sort of effect on their manners as cleaner air would have on their lungs.

Given all that the do-gooders had in mind, any old square was better than none of course. But some sharp-eyed and creative designers saw that even open spaces can be constricting and depressing. For instance, after the American landscape architect Frederick Law Olmsted visited Britain in 1850, he made acid remarks about Hyde Park with its 'lines of repellant iron work and hot-house plants between which the public pass like hospital convalescents, who have been turned into the yard to walk about while their beds are making'.[13] Paxton's park at Birkenhead was the inspiration Olmsted took with him when he returned to New York and set to work creating Central Park.

'Openness is the one thing you cannot get in buildings,' he said in 1870. 'Picturesqueness you can get . . . the beauty of the park should be the other. It should be the beauty of the fields, the meadow, the prairie, of the green pastures, and the still waters.'

Five years after Olmsted had written the above words, Octavia Hill was fighting to save the meadows which stretched north from Swiss Cottage to Parliament Hill in Hampstead. Here, right on the edge of London, was beauty in abundance of just the kind Olmsted had described. There was no need to fabricate it. Yet Swiss Cottage Fields had been sold to a builder!

As far as Octavia Hill was concerned, the Fields belonged to the public. London must have it. And because Robert Hunter was then very successfully fighting cases for the Commons Preservation Society, she went to him for advice. But Hunter explained that there really wasn't a legal case he could fight and expect to win. Her only hope, he told her, was to raise the money to buy the fields back.

The builder asked £10,000. Ruskin was among those approached when Octavia Hill launched her appeal. 'While your work is only mitigating of mortal pain,' he wrote back, 'mine is radically curative—.'[14] Ruskin had already begun pouring his fortune, and his fanaticism, into the Guild of St George.[15]

'London is an utterly doomed Gomorrah,' he went on to inform his devoted disciple. She was, therefore, wasting her time.

One of Ruskin's schemes for his Guild was to bring spinning back into the cottages of the Isle of Man. (The women had been put out of work by machines.) Another would turn thirteen derelict acres on the edge of Sheffield into a fruit and berry farm. He was not focused and he certainly wasn't practical. And while Ruskin felt everyone should give his notions their complete attention he could be offhand, even slack. One enthusiast, for instance, gave the Guild twenty acres in Worcestershire; Ruskin couldn't even be bothered to go to see the land. Yet he found it in himself to become outraged because Octavia Hill's supporters weren't giving the Guild sufficient backing.

(In 1877 his jealousy led him to turn on his old pupil and publicly denounce her.)

Ruskin's refusal to contribute to Octavia Hill's campaign was a personal slight, nothing more. It took only a few months for the appeal to approach the £10,000 mark. With its goal in sight – and because of that – the builder backed out. He'd feigned a willingness to sell to her because he thought that in doing so he could look public-spirited without having to act it. He'd assumed Miss Hill never would come up with the money. A very great deal more could be made if the land was developed. And it was. The long stretch of Fitzjohn's Avenue lined with now sought-after brick villas cuts through the meadows she had hoped to save.

Octavia Hill was enraged and desolated. She continued to attend to her houses and to provide green places for her tenants to rest. And she became a member of the Commons Preservation Society in the hope that by working together they would, in future, be able to keep such tracts of open land safe.

Sir Robert Hunter had been solicitor to the Post Office for twelve years when he was knighted in 1894. But from the 1860s until he went to work for the government, he'd been applying his talents to the fight to keep common land open. As a result of his diligence and gift for strategy, the Commons Preservation Society had fought and won most of its battles to ensure that people had access to common land.

For all his long involvement in saving land in the countryside, Hunter was a city boy: born in Camberwell, South London, on 27 October 1844 where his father was a successful though not wealthy merchant. Apart from short holidays, the family continued to live in the capital.

Outside the law courts Robert Hunter was an introvert. This tendency to be more comfortable when alone than when among other people may have been a side-effect of his childhood, during which he was often isolated. Having succumbed to enfeebling cholera when he was three, he seemed to be either ill or recuperating for many of his boyhood years.

With an honours degree from University College London in

1864, Hunter went to work for a firm of Holborn solicitors. This made his ambitious parents happy but Robert Hunter was bored.

Like a lonely lass scouring the personal columns in hopes of finding Prince Charming or at least some excitement, Robert Hunter must have read even the tiniest notice in the newspapers thinking that he'd find something, someday, that would lead him out of the trap he was in. On seeing an announcement that the newly formed Commons Preservation Society was offering £400 in prizes to the winners of an essay contest he decided to enter it.

The CPS was running the contest as a publicity device. It wanted people to understand that they were not only a protest group but had theoretical interests, too. The notion that such a group could attract interest by appearing intellectual seems as dated as those pre-First-World-War ads hawking a secret formula which promises to make women more beautiful by making them fatter.

Contestants were asked to give an analysis of the best way to make common land available for public use. And Robert Hunter set about this so diligently that he spent the entire winter working on the essay each evening and at weekends. He was thoughtful, thorough and ambitious; by the spring he had finished and sent in a 15,000-word treatise. It was picked as one of the six top entries. His work was so much admired, in fact, that a few months later when the Society's honorary solicitor left to work in the government, Hunter was offered his job. He accepted. He was not quite twenty-four.

Hunter began the fight to open wrongfully enclosed lands and to insure that those commons to which the public did have access weren't fenced in or developed. And he had some astonishing victories. The first of these was a case which began on 29 June 1874 against sixteen separate lords of the manor. It lasted twenty-two days. Epping Forest was being destroyed piecemeal as the Crown sold off land and various lords of the manor enclosed it. The battle to convince the government and Gladstone to stop this wasn't making substantial progress and the Commons Preservation Society decided to take it on.

As a result of Hunter's arguments and the persuasive testimony given by witnesses bought forward by the preservationists, 6,000 acres of Epping Forest were saved from developers and became common land open to everyone. This was an enormously popular victory and thousands of people cheered when, in 1882, Queen Victoria rode into the forest to dedicate it to public use. An equally impressive campaign masterminded by Hunter secured the New Forest for the public in 1877.

Hills and Hunters

They might not believe that industrial growth meant progress, but these high-minded Victorians certainly seemed convinced that, as the number of groups dedicated to reform multiplied, the chances for social progress increased too. They must have thrived on going to meetings.

No sooner did a couple of people come up with an idea about how things could be improved than a new committee or a society was formed to do something about it. The energy used in establishing one apparently augmented rather than depleted the energy it needed to establish the next. (Something very like this took place almost exactly a century later when the women's movement was revived and every day seemed to produce a half a dozen new groups.)

A year after Octavia Hill lost her battle to save the fields at Swiss Cottage, her sister Miranda and Dorothy Hunter, sister of Robert, came up with a solution of their own. The Kyrle Society came into existence in 1876, not to fight battles nor to save open spaces, but to beautify.

Hospitals and halls would be decorated and musical performances encouraged. William Morris gave lectures on art. Not that every single Kyrle Society scheme was aesthetically ambitious. It didn't have to be; nature after all was an unending source of loveliness. Excursions into the countryside were organized so that poor girls could gaze at the hills and collect posies to take back to their 'umble 'omes. (It is easy to mock the organizers; and they do seem to have been both naïve and condescending. But it requires only a minute's reflection to remember the cocky pride of a city childhood; the thrill that came when a bunch of wild flowers picked during an outing to the country sat in a jug of water on the kitchen table.)

Once set up, these societies gave scope for subdivision into groups for those with yet more specialized interests and, in 1879, Octavia Hill organized an Open Space committee for the Kyrle. What with his interests – and the close family connection – Robert Hunter became the honorary legal adviser of Octavia Hill's committee. (Such a title seems comically grandiose but these inspired do-gooders routinely took their associations very seriously and behaved as if each of them would last for many, many years.)

Octavia Hill and Robert Hunter's committee now tackled the problem of how to create more open space in a city that seemed to have none left. They soon concluded that putting burial ground to use for the living was the answer. The churches they approached did not often agree to open their land for use as public parks. But at St George's in the East, 24,000 spring bulbs were planted; at St John's Waterloo, clematis and wisteria were soon climbing the ornate cast-iron fence.

Not only did they have common interests and inclinations as well as respect for one another's gifts, by working together in their sisters' society, Robert Hunter and Octavia Hill built up an easy confidence in one another on which within a few years they began to build.

Hardwicke Rawnsley's childhood has been called idyllic. And the middle-class little boy's early years at Shiplake-on-Thames do seem to have been a rural romp – chasing rabbits and learning about wild flowers and so on. But an idyll? Not when Father was around. The Reverend Drummond Rawnsley seemed to have had such abundant high expectations for his brood that even spread among his eleven children there was enough to oppress. This, however, didn't become obvious, in the case of Hardwicke, until he was eleven and sent to public school, at Uppingham.

The boy seemed to freeze from the fear that he might not be able to live up to what his father expected of him. Fortunately Edward Thring the headmaster was able to thaw him out. And soon Hardwicke Rawnsley had discovered poetry. He developed a passion for writing sonnets and though he never much improved, this did nothing to cut back on his prodigious output.

At Oxford, Rawnsley met John Ruskin who was then Slade Professor of Art. Ruskin, whose social and aesthetic theories were intertwined, developed a scheme for improving the road from Oxford to the nearby village of Hinksey. His art students would be the labourers; the work would benefit these priviliged young men as well as the working people of Hinksey.[16]

Clearly Ruskin was a charismatic character and among those who laboured on the road were Arnold Toynbee, Oscar Wilde and Hardwicke Rawnsley. (In later years this enterprise was looked back upon and mocked, but never by Rawnsley. For him, as for Octavia Hill, Ruskin remained an influential figure; Rawnsley always believed that the Hinksey road scheme had been a successful way of educating young men to help the less well off.)

At Oxford, Rawnsley did not show any signs of great intellectual devotion. Nor even of being intellectual. In 1874 he received a Third in Natural Science and decided to go into the Church. And though he was made a canon of Carlisle Cathedral when he was forty-two, for several years after university there was good reason to think he might never succeed as a clergyman or even become one.

When he came down from Oxford, Hardwicke Rawnsley went to London and became a lay chaplain in Soho at the Newport Market Refuge for down-and-outs. With him when he set off for London was a letter of introduction from Ruskin addressed to Octavia Hill.

Rawnsley's enthusiasm was fired by the housing work for which Octavia Hill had already become well known. When he went to see her, she arranged for him to help collect rents for her colleague Emma Cons, who was running a scheme similar to her own, in Covent Garden. But in 1875, after being in London for only a few months, Hardwicke Rawnsley collapsed with a nervous breakdown.

He went to spend some time in the Lake District with cousins at Wray Castle. Octavia Hill arranged for him to stay with her friends the Fletchers, on Lake Windermere. This was all of a piece with the conviction that pure air and beautiful scenery were therapeutic. Meeting Edith, one of the Fletchers' daughters, also helped. She later became Mrs Rawnsley.

After the Lakes (and Edith) had completed Rawnsley's recovery, his old headmaster and mentor Edward Thring helped him find work in a mission for the poor on the edge of Bristol. Hardwicke Rawnsley was ordained a deacon in 1875.

Rawnsley was shepherd to an obstreperous flock: an assortment of rough and tumble lads who were not always kept under what other people considered sufficient control. Two years of their acting up were more than the sponsors of his mission chose to sanction. The deacon was given the boot.

Thring was there to help Rawnsley yet again. And so were his cousins in the lakes who had the church of St Margaret, Wray-on-Windermere in their gift. By the end of 1877, Hardwicke Rawnsley had become a priest and, in the New Year, he married and began ministering to his tiny rural parish.

Rawnsley lived the rest of his life in the Lake District. He was not, however, a man who had run away into the hills to hide. On the contrary. Hardwicke Rawnsley was by far the most outgoing of the trio who founded the National Trust. Though their activity centred in London and he lived in a small community in a remote corner of England, Rawnsley gained considerably more knowledge of the wider world than either Hill or Hunter.

Whenever he could arrange it, Hardwicke Rawnsley was off abroad: once a year to the Alps with Edith, the Middle East, Russia, the United States. He became a keen reporter (he covered the Coronation of the Tsar), a lecturer and a writer of travel books and a children's book, as well as poetry, always.

No one could call Hardwicke Rawnsley's many journeys rest cures, but they may have given him the breaks he needed to keep his obsessiveness in check. And even with his travels, he suffered more than one collapse. It was as if he could operate only at one speed: full steam ahead. Perhaps the fear that once had paralysed him had transformed itself into an unrelenting goad.

Vigorous, attention-loving, impulsive, active rather than reflective, Hardwicke Rawnsley enjoyed being combative in the service of a cause. The Lake District Defence Society, the Cumberland County Council, the Keswick Footpath and Commons Society all eventually became the beneficiaries of his zealous sense of mission, manic energy and winning delivery.

In 1883 Hardwicke Rawnsley became the vicar at Crosthwaite outside Keswick. That year, too, he embarked on his career as the Lake District's protector. As soon as he found out that there was a plan to run a railway from Buttermere to Braithwaite he was committed to stopping it. The railway would cut through Newlands; a long, opalescent bowl of green; an untouched, exquisite valley.

The vicar began a letter-writing campaign. While the owners of the quarries up on the fells of the northern lakes calculated that the railway would be the most profitable way of transporting green slate to the market town of Keswick, he reckoned it was the crudest destruction. The Borrowdale and Derwentwater Defence Fund was formed and down in London the Commons Preservation Society, where Robert Hunter was then struggling to keep the railway out of Epping Forest, gave its support. All over England people joined in the campaign. The Lakeland campaigners were in the national spotlight and, only two months after their protest began, the quarry owners dropped their plan.

Soon yet another railway scheme was launched. This time the line was to hug the edge of Lake Ennerdale. Rawnsley fought again. And again the preservationists were victorious.

Hardwicke Rawnsley became a nationally known figure as a result of his effort to keep the Lake District unspoilt. He was launched on a new career but it wasn't as a preservation politician.

At least one of his parishioners called Canon Rawnsley 'the most active volcano in Europe'.[17] Unlike Hill and Hunter, committees were not his natural habitat. Though a popular local hero and elected to the first Cumberland County Council he was not voted into office twice. His genius was as a crusader.

A National Trust

Octavia Hill, Robert Hunter and Hardwicke Rawnsley were none of them idle; they had more to do than they themselves sometimes could cope with. In between their often successful campaigns to better the lives of poor people and preserve the countryside, each experienced bouts of melancholy – or, for Hill and Rawnsley, complete nervous collapse. Why in the world did they dream up yet another organization for the improvement of society?

To them this question would have been puzzling. What else could they do? For years they had recognized a danger which in spite of attempts to limit it was only getting worse. Examples would have been all too easy to give. There was, for instance, the Evelyn affair.

In 1884 a descendant of the diarist John Evelyn wrote asking Octavia Hill to help him save their Deptford family home, Sayres Court. But developers bought it before it was possible to raise the money to preserve it.

Disappointment and frustration of this kind continued to hound Octavia Hill. She went to Robert Hunter and they began to talk about setting up an organization that would not just fight to save land but would have the power actually to hold it. Not only would such a society be in a position to raise money and then buy properties but people might chose to make gifts of their land or houses to such an enterprise.

Robert Hunter brooded about the possibilities of this idea and later wrote to Octavia Hill with his solution: they should set up a joint stock company. Miss Hill, demonstrating the combination of subtlety and realism that led her to be such a successful fund-raiser, wrote back commenting: 'You will do better, I believe, to bring forwards its benevolent rather than its commercial character.'[18] Were it to be called a trust rather than a company, she mused, people would be more likely to forgive it its blunders. A hundred years and more of evidence has accumulated to prove how shrewd – and right – she was. For the very reason Octavia Hill gave, the National Trust today – with all its 123 tea rooms, 200 holiday cottages and 199 shops – is anxious to be seen never as a commercial enterprise but always as a preservation charity.

'?National Trust' Robert Hunter jotted in a note to himself at the top of Octavia Hill's letter. That punctuation mark is positively cherished by the Trust's staff today. Though doubtful to Sir Robert then, it is hard to imagine a more effective name today. If only he'd made it an exclamation point, NT Enterprises might be selling silver-plated facsimiles.

A decade passed before the National Trust was actually created. The main reason for the delay seems to have been George Shaw-Lefevre, head of the Commons Preservation Society. Not everyone, it turns out, was such an enthusiast for starting up a new organization every time someone identified a new need.

Like Ruskin who had earlier been against Octavia Hill's efforts in this line, Shaw-Lefevre was opposed to the formation of the trust being proposed because he felt it would attract support that otherwise would go to his own organization. Shaw-Lefevre in fact turned out to be both misguided and prescient. A hundred years later the CPS had 2,000 members; the National Trust more than 2 million. But the Commons Preservation Society, a campaigning organization with no ability to own property, could never have achieved what the National Trust has, no matter how much money or publicity it got.

Ruskin's anxiety that Octavia Hill's work would detract from the Guild of St George was fed by emotions that were deeper, more personal and nastier than Shaw-Lefevre's. And Ruskin, of course, was the single largest contributor to the failure of his own enterprise. But he was right when he suspected that her efforts would prosper and his would not. The Guild of St George still exists, chiefly in the form of the Ruskin Museum in Sheffield on the site where he'd dreamed of setting up a fruit and berry farm. According to its current master, the Guild owns 'a lot of land'. When asked for a somewhat more exact figure, the answer was 'about a hundred acres'.

It was only when the fight to save the land surrounding and including the spectacular Falls of Lodore in the Lake District was lost that Shaw-Lefevre capitulated. The price of resistance to Hill and Hunter's scheme had clearly become too high. Neither the Commons Preservation Society nor local governments had been able to stop the sale. Some successful way to preserve the landscape had to be found.

This account of the genesis of what today is the largest non-governmental preservation organization anywhere follows the generally agreed-upon facts. Canon Rawnsley, however, constructed a different version of the Trust's conception.

While Octavia Hill was modest and Hunter downright self-effacing, Hardwicke Rawnsley was a forthrightly egotistical man and his account of the Trust's origins is entirely in character. According to Canon Rawnsley, the idea for starting the National Trust was his own.

By the time Canon Rawnsley published his account in 1914, there was no one with first-hand knowledge to dispute it. Octavia Hill had died in 1912. (It seems unavoidable to mention this, though just what one thing has to do with the other is obscure, but Octavia Hill who had given so much of her energy and time trying to provide poor people with more access to clean air, died of lung cancer herself.) Late in the following year Sir Robert Hunter died of blood poisoning. Indeed it was on the occasion of Hardwicke Rawnsley's homage to Sir Robert, that the canon gave this version of the National Trust's natal history in the *Cornhill Magazine*:

'Circumstances had made the writer feel,' Rawnsley recorded, 'that it was imperative that some association be formed for the securing and the permanent holding of places of historic interest and natural beauty. The first person consulted was Robert Hunter. He threw himself into the scheme at once, but begged that Miss Octavia Hill might be consulted. When consulted, not ten minutes elapsed before she said, "If Sir Robert

Hunter will help us and the Duke of Westminster will allow us to meet in Grovesnor House, the scheme will go forward.'"[19]

Dorothy Hunter, Sir Robert's daughter, in her later synopsis of 'The Genesis and Foundation of the National Trust' seems to be sticking closer to the facts (while at the same time defending the memory of her father) when she notes that 'between 1885 and 1893 ... when Miss Hill and Robert Hunter were seeking to win adherents to their idea of a "Land Company" or "National Trust" they seem to have had no communication with Canon Rawnsley.'[20] Though in 1893 when things finally started moving, Hardwicke Rawnsley most certainly was there.

As the National Trust developed, Octavia Hill unquestionably believed that Rawnsley's contribution to it was invaluable, as did the Duke of Westminster.

When, in 1900, the canon was offered the Bishopric of Madagascar his admirers encouraged him to turn it down. 'I quite agree with those of your friends who hope that you will not undertake the Bishopric,' wrote the Duke, 'as we want you at home!'[21] Octavia Hill pressed even harder and at greater length. 'The Trust owes & must owe, much of its special character to your influence,' she wrote to the canon. 'If it is to gather in the givers, if it is to seize on the important opportunities for good, if it is to retain some element of poetry & of hope, it seems to me as if it must depend on you ... I really should be *most* discouraged about the Trust if you were to leave us.'[22] Pages more on these lines followed. This was one of the unbroken string of successful appeals written by Octavia Hill on behalf of the National Trust. The canon stayed at home.

Date of birth?

In the early 1990s, the buzzing of busy bees got louder and louder at the offices of the National Trust throughout its domain. It was approaching its hundredth birthday and the centenary promised to produce a bumper crop of honey.

This was an extraordinary opportunity to encourage people to notice all that the NT had achieved since it came into the world – and to what a high standard – without at the same time appearing to brag. It was only natural that there should be celebrations and huge amounts of publicity. Not to mention a massive fund-raising campaign. After all, in 1945 the National Trust launched its Golden Jubilee Appeal, for the first time seeking contributions not for the purchase of a property but for its General Fund. (With the government matching the public, pound for pound, a total of more than £122 million was raised.) And, of course, there would have to be a lunch of the Great and the Good to mark the anniversary. But just what was the National Trust's official birthday? It turned out there were quite a few dates to chose from.

Whoever had thought of it first, Hill, Hunter and Rawnsley, all believed the idea was a good one and in November 1893 they met at the offices of the newly sympathetic Commons Preservation Society in order to begin working on setting up their 'National Trust for Historic Sites and Natural Beauty'.

The Duke of Westminster was already the president of the Kyrle Society. He knew about and respected Octavia Hill's achievements and agreed to become the Trust's first president. He lent such a steadying hand as it took its baby steps that looking back on those early days, John Gaze, its long serving land agent and author of an official history of the charity in the 1980s, touchingly – if eccentrically – said thank you, by insisting that the Duke be given credit as the National Trust's fourth founder.

On 16 July 1894 the inaugural meeting of the National Trust was held at the Duke's London town house. *The Times*, on 17 July, duly announced the meeting. The paper took the opportunity to open an anti-litter campaign and it had an aesthetic dimension, too. It warned the new organization to be vigilant and take care that neither 'orange peels and sandwich wrappers' nor 'statues, fountains and allegorical memorials' be allowed to deface its properties. The *Daily News*, on the same day, showed more restraint and simply welcomed this 'healthful sign of the new interest taken in the finer things of life'. All this said, 16 July 1994 was not selected as the Trust's hundredth birthday. That, it decided, would be celebrating prematurely.

What about 12 December 1894 then? On that day Sir Robert Hunter finished drafting the Memorandums and Articles of Association for the National Trust. That document after all gave the Trust its form. But 12 December was not held to be the natal day either.

The twelfth of January 1895 was picked as the National Trust's date of birth. It was on that day that the Articles of Association of the National Trust written by Sir Robert Hunter were registered under the Companies' Acts. Once this occurred, the Trust had an official existence. But 16 January might have served as its birthday instead, because that is when the first meeting of the National Trust's Provisional Council was held at 1 Great College Street, Westminster.

The eight founding members were present. As noted on the register they were: two peers of the realm (one of whom was the Duke of Westminster, its president); one Member of Parliament; two privy councillors; one knight (Sir Robert Hunter); one J.P.; one clerk in holy orders (Hardwicke Rawnsley) and one spinster (Octavia Hill).

Sir Robert Hunter became the Trust's first chairman. Octavia Hill was in charge of appeals and Canon Rawnsley became the Trust's honorary secretary which he remained until he died in

1920. It was at this meeting that the National Trust was able to officially accept its first acquisition – though in fact the property had been offered the year before.

An early birthday present

During the spring of 1894 Canon Rawnsley had travelled through western Britain and written a book about his trip. In it he recorded, and this time reliably, how its very first property came to the National Trust, though of course it hadn't officially been created quite yet.

One of Rawnsley's stops had been on the Welsh coast where he was the guest of Fanny Talbot at her house, Tyn-y-Fynnon, just above Barmouth.

Mrs Talbot had earlier given six cottages built into the walls of the cliffs below her house to John Ruskin for his St George's Guild. But she had become disenchanted with Ruskin's inadequate management of them. When, during the canon's visit, he received a copy of the Trust's proposed articles of association, she was galvanized. Dinas Oleu, 'the Fortress of Light', five acres rising up out of the Irish sea at Barmouth, was given to the National Trust before it was technically in a position to accept it.

'I have long wanted to secure to the public for ever the enjoyment of Dinas Oleu,' she told the canon. 'But I wish to put it into the custody of some society that will never vulgarize it, or prevent wild Nature from having its own way.' She didn't leave her idea of vulgarity to his imagination.

It was all right for paths to be made for the public – provided they were grassy. Stone seats could be built so that visitors could have a place to sit and rest to look out on to the sea. 'But,' she stressed, 'I wish to avoid the abomination of asphalt paths and the cast-iron seats of serpent design which disfigure so largely our public parks. It appears to me,' she concluded,

[33]

'that your organization has been born in the nick of time to be my friend.'[23]

'We have just received our first property,' Octavia Hill later wrote to her mother when Hardwicke Rawnsley proudly brought this gift to the attention of his co-founders. 'Five acres overlooking Cardigan Bay. I wonder,' she added, 'if it will be our last?'

I wonder, was Octavia Hill being coy? Given her lack of belief in the lasting power of anything she deeply cared about, probably not. And, after all, even if its name made it sound big and important, the National Trust was only one of several tiny groups with which the founders were connected. Its 'work might grow,' she wrote to a friend the year after its birth, 'but then it might not'.[24]

Why did it? And why did it grow so very, very large and so very, very rich?

Fanny Talbot, the National Trust's first donor, had probably articulated one of most fundamental answers to these questions, if not the only one with merit. 'I feel so indebted to the National Trust,' she wrote in May 1895, 'for taking my little bit of favourite cliff under their protection for ever.'

The Trust came into existence at a time when people on both sides of the Atlantic were becoming aware that their beloved countryside might not be inviolate. Hill, Hunter and Rawnsley were visionaries because they were among the small group who perceived clearly that if the landscape were taken for granted it could be lost. They had the imagination, the intelligence and the experience to see the threat and to know it would probably get worse. And, crucially, they had the desire, the drive and the courage to do something about it.

Green dreams

'The English are a rural-minded people on the whole,' wrote
Vita Sackville-West,[25] who grew up in Kent and was given to
generalizing from her own experience. But it is a truism that
England has a country-favouring population. As the nineteenth
century advanced, however, this began to be more a matter of
memory and fancy than of fact.

England, which had led the world into the Industrial Revolution, had, as a result, led it into being citified. By the middle of
the nineteenth century, and for the first time anywhere, more
of England's people lived in towns than in the country; by
the beginning of the new century more than seventy-five per
cent of the population lived an urban life. (There had been
only six towns in England and Wales with more than 100,000
people in 1841, but by 1901 there were five times that number.)
Nostalgia for rural life grew as the number of people living it
shrivelled.

People longed for and increasingly idealized what they were
only able to have a taste of during their holidays, if at all. To
quite a few intelligent people with lofty principles the cities –
with their slums, crowds, crime and bad air – were seen as evil;
grass and trees and bubbling brooks were good. But as more
than one writer has pointed out, life in the country hadn't been
quite good enough to offer people the means of surviving in it
and so the enormous urban migration occurred.

The story is, of course, more complicated. Factories put
cottage industries out of business (something Ruskin thought
he could reverse with his scheme for women on the Isle of
Man). And there were hovels among the hedgerows just as bad
as those in London's East End. But those who disdained city
life and were seduced by birdsong paid little attention to this.
George Macaulay Trevelyan was such a man. The historian who
played an important part in the development of the National

[35]

Trust later on (see Chapter 9) and was author of *English Social History* obviously knew better. But he was blinded by his love of country life. It *was* England. In his bestselling history, GMT observed that among all the terrible consequences of the long agricultural depression that began in 1875, the most terrible had been 'the general divorce of Englishmen from life in contact with nature, which in all ages had helped to form the mind and the imagination of the island race'.

But some people forced to move into town took to city life with enthusiasm – even those who were crowded together in damp, dark houses. While public parks were only alleged to be 'civilizing', they most certainly were an opportunity for one class to see what the others were wearing. At least one or two of the girls Octavia Hill and her sister Miranda coaxed out for a walk in the grass probably had no longing to follow in the footsteps of Dorothy Wordsworth. Instead they may have yearned for a pair of fabulous silk shoes with star-studded, teeter-totter nine-inch heels that were in vogue. The years of the National Trust's birth and infancy were the Gay Nineties after all. But not for Hardwicke Rawnsley, Robert Hunter and Octavia Hill.

For the high-minded, England passed through the late nineteenth century in a fever of earnest attempts at reforming and improving. As the century ended, the idealistic new National Trust was created to protect countryside and historically important buildings and preserve them for ever – as they then were.

However radical they were (or are), conservation makes people conservative. And from its beginnings the National Trust seems to have been involved in stopping the clock. (Later it started trying to run it backwards.) But that is only a part of the story.

[2]

Gentlemen's Agreements

Alfriston Clergy House in Sussex, with gaps in its thatched roof and its ancient, sagging half-timbered walls, became the first historic building to be acquired by the National Trust. It was bought for £10 in 1896 and then made sound again. Four years later the charity acquired another half-timbered house, this one at Long Crendon in Buckinghamshire. It had been used as a manorial court since the time of Henry V. From the very beginning, then, the Trust was engaged in trying to save historically important buildings.

The three founders of the National Trust, being followers of John Ruskin and William Morris, valued medieval architecture above all else: both Alfriston Clergy House and the Courthouse at Long Crendon had been built in the fourteenth century.

Hill, Hunter and Rawnsley were in the Ruskin/Morris tradition but they were neither purists nor fanatics. When, for instance, Barrington Court in Somerset was offered to the National Trust in 1904, this shell of a handsome mansion wasn't rejected, even though it was Tudor. And while Ruskin created his Guild of St George in an attempt to recreate the harmonious, non-hierarchical society which he imagined had existed in the Middle Ages and Morris, looking forward as well as to the past, came to believe that only through a Marxist revolution would such a society come about again, the National Trust could be said to have had a more modest goal. It was created to preserve buildings and countryside so that people, especially the poor, could take pleasure in using it all, both in the present and in future generations.

During the first years of the charity's existence the question of what to do about its countryside properties was easily answered: list them. People could then visit them if they wished. But what about its old buildings? What was to be done about them?

Octavia Hill felt that the National Trust's houses ought to be lived in. Perhaps she reckoned that such questions as: how? by whom? for what purpose and whose benefit? would answer themselves. She soon discovered she was wrong. And so did C.R. Ashbee, architect and craftsman, who unwittingly took part in what turned out to be an unhappy National Trust experiment, though it started off cheerfully enough.

Ashbee became a member of the Trust's Council in 1896. When he married two years later, he and his wife Janet were given the use of Alfriston Clergy House for their honeymoon. Then, following a period in 1900 which they spent in America where the architect lectured about the National Trust and tried to raise money for its preservation projects, he and his wife began staying at the Courthouse in Long Crendon. It became their weekend home. Soon apprentices from Ashbee's Guild of Handicraft in London's East End came, too. That is when the trouble began, though the Ashbees weren't aware of it at once.

The 'boys', as Ashbee called these lads, quickly became attached to the picturesque house close to the church in the pretty, dozy village of Long Crendon. All of them began to feel increasingly at home. They began to talk about bringing in Guild-made furniture for the large room on the first floor of the house. Octavia Hill heard about this and was alarmed.

It may have been because she disliked the idea of mixing periods in the decoration of the Courthouse, or, more probably, of having so many Cockney young men living in this aged building and racing around its small but lovely garden, though of course her reason could have been one she actually gave: if Ashbee and the apprentices filled the first floor with their furniture, the public would find it difficult, maybe impossible, to visit. She objected vigorously.

Miss Hill and Mr Ashbee rowed. To Ashbee it was a question of principle. For Octavia Hill it may have been one also but as Ashbee saw it it seemed more like a demonstration of the exceptional force of her will. Octavia Hill would not budge. Her attitude, he wrote, was 'something akin to an English Govt. Department & a seaside lodging house landlady'.[1]

The Ashbees and his disappointed apprentices left the Court-house at Long Crendon; Ashbee resigned from the National Trust's Council.

'. . . The beautiful Court House is of the present at least to remain a mere dead lumber house with no humanity in it just to be looked at by Tourists,' he noted in his diary. 'No more singing by the Ingle, no more buzz of life & living links with the past. . . . I'm really sorry for the boys because they had got to love the place & they would have given it such a soul as no dead museum in the Trust's charge can possibly have.'

The subject of the National Trust's houses and their function went into hibernation. It was more than thirty years before it became an issue again. And when it did, the matter of houses and their purpose was to alter the direction of the National Trust, its conception of itself and the public's perception of the charity. It also had an impact on the Trust's popularity because as it turned out people love visiting other people's houses. Though it will soon be seen that pleasing the public was not the motive when acquiring mansions really got underway.

In the three decades between Octavia Hill's dispute with C.R. Ashbee and the inauguration of the National Trust's Country Houses Scheme, the charity altered little except in one important if technical-sounding respect – the document that set down its responsibilities and powers, its Articles of Association, was changed.

The founders had quickly discovered that the Articles weren't a sufficiently potent document. In 1896, the same year the National Trust bought Alfriston Clergy House, the charity had succeeded in raising the money to buy its first piece of England's coast from the Earl of Wharncliffe. He attached only one condition to the sale of Barras Head in Cornwall, which was 'the right of pre-emption at any future time should the society wish or be obliged to part with the lands of which they have possession'.[2] He was not alone in worrying about what would happen to the Trust's possessions in future.

Sir Robert Hunter drafted the 1907 Act of Parliament because it had become obvious that the National Trust had to find a way to make the property it owned (and the property it might acquire in future) entirely secure. Once it came into effect, the Trust was in the unique position of being able to declare anything it bought or was given – from a sand dune, to a sheep pen, a landscaped park or a stately home – inalienable.

What this means is that if the Trust chooses to accept (or buy) a property and then to declare it inalienable, that property cannot ever be mortgaged or sold, and no one else can take it from the charity. Only Parliament can nullify the declaration. This unique capability – no other organization had it then nor has it today – proved to be crucial to the National Trust's success. Not every property is made inalienable, it should be understood. Some are acquired – they might be cottages or farms or fields – with the thought that one day the Trust might find it useful to sell them. They remain alienable. But all the properties that the National Trust takes on in order to preserve them in perpetuity, whether landscape or coast or buildings, are made inalienable.

The Trust, with twelve years' experience of preserving beautiful and historically important properties for the enjoyment of the public, had found that other matters needed clarifying and codifying too. In the Act of 1907 the charity also sought and was given the right to set aside parts of its property for games, meetings and sporting events. By implication, of course, this gave it the right to keep other parts of its property off-limits to games, meetings and sporting events. And, after 1907, there would be no arguments if it wanted to make ornamental ponds, build tool-sheds – or charge admission fees, because all this was in the Act also. So was the prohibition on charging for access to common land and on fencing it off – except, temporarily, in order to help the regeneration of plants or trees.

Catering was catered for too. The National Trust now officially had the right to build cafés and sell refreshments.

But the overriding purpose for drafting the 1907 Act was to give the Trust the ability to declare its properties inalienable and that is its great achievement.

The 1907 Act of Parliament became the National Trust's Constitution. Once it came into effect, potential donors and contributors to appeals naturally felt more confident about the charity's ability to hold on to what it owned. And people at the Trust, of course, had less to fear from potential predators.

The National Trust began to grow. And it grew steadily but very slowly. By its tenth birthday, the Trust had 500 members. By its twentieth, in 1915, there were 700. In 1919 the National Trust owned sixty-three properties, most of them small, and amounting to about 6,000 acres. When it celebrated its Golden Jubilee, after the Second World War, it was still an organization with only about 8,000 subscribers. But by then the amount of property owned by the Trust was increasing fast. More than 112,000 acres had come into its possession; the charity was costing more than £100,000 a year to run. A half-million people visited those of its possessions where an admission fee was charged. Not coincidentally, the kind of property the Trust owned was also changing dramatically. As was the outlook of the people associated with the charity. The Country Houses Scheme was underway.

In 1930, Philip Kerr became the 11th Marquess of Lothian. Along with the title there were 30,000 acres in Norfolk and Scotland and four huge houses, three of them in Scotland, one a castle. A rather large inheritance tax bill came, too: death duties, as inheritance tax was then called, amounted to £300,000.[3]

Lord Lothian was a Liberal politician and diplomat. He spent most of his time in London or abroad. Middle-aged when he inherited, he had no family, nor did he have the intention of starting one. Obviously four vast establishments were more than he could use. They were also more than he could afford. The estates had not made a profit since before the First World War. To raise some of the money to pay death duties, which at the time were calculated at fifty per cent of the value of what had been inherited, he had to sell some of the rarest volumes in the exceptional library that had come to him with Blickling Hall, a Jacobean manor in Norfolk.

Lord Lothian was 'good looking, sensitive, intelligent and impressionable', according to one writer who knew him.[4] Devout and doubting by nature, he was given to worrying a good deal about the rightness or wrongness of things. He came to believe it would be wrong if houses like those he'd inherited were destroyed by developers and their contents sold off, as he himself had been forced to begin doing. As he saw it, the eventual result would be the destruction or, at the least, the dispersal of Britain's cultural capital. This, then, was the background to the speech he gave at the National Trust's 1934 Annual General Meeting.

Lord Lothian proposed that the government and the National Trust work together to save mansions, their contents and the estates of which they were the centre. In order for this goal to be achieved tax laws would have to be changed.

As things then were, a man with a mansion or an estate was able to give it tax free to whomever he pleased. But if instead he bequeathed his property, on his death the heir to it would also receive a tax bill. In the 1931 Budget the government had given people an alternative: houses or land could be offered *in lieu* of death duties. An heir could, in effect, barter his new mansion for his tax debt. But this hadn't attracted many people beause the government valued such property at a lower figure than did the marketplace. A person would do better by selling his inherited stately home for the full price and then using the money to pay the Inland Revenue. (It wasn't until the creation of the Land Fund in 1946 that this situation began to change. See Chapter 3.)

More than inequities in valuations of property would have to be altered if fine houses and great estates were to be saved, however. A means for paying for their upkeep would also have to be found.

The Inland Revenue didn't want to become the owner of country houses, of course, and made them over to other government departments or non-profit-making organizations like the National Trust. But the NT couldn't afford to accept many – either as direct gifts or via the government – unless the houses came with an income-producing endowment. Those donors who were prepared to create such endowments – say stocks and shares or farms – found that these were taxable even if the gift of the house was not. Part of Lord Lothian's proposal, therefore, was this: if a donor or an heir could produce such an endowment for his country house, that endowment should be tax-free.

There was one further important element to the scheme he was proposing: a donor who gave and endowed a house should be allowed to continue living in it after its transfer to the National Trust. This was bound to make the Country Houses Scheme more attractive to potential donors and thereby reduce the risk that they'd sell their estates to developers. While the nation might own his house, a man would be able to keep his home. He would pay for this by giving up some of his privacy; these houses would be opened to the public.

Lord Lothian said he was prepared to give the Country Houses Scheme a good start by leaving Blickling and its 4,600 acres to the National Trust. And the National Trust began to have discussions with the government to see how this might be arranged. While these were still going on people began offering their country houses to the National Trust.

Even before the 'country houses' speech in 1934, Sir Charles Trevelyan had been talking to his lawyer about leaving his Northumberland estate to the National Trust. Wallington consisted of 13,000 acres, eighteen farms, a house begun in the seventeenth century, two villages, and fine woodlands. It had been in the Trevelyan family for 150 years.

Because the proposed legacy was hugely generous, and because the character of Sir Charles Trevelyan who wished to provide it was so complicated and forceful, it came to have a pivotal role in the transformation of the National Trust. If the owner of such a large estate believed the charity was capable of preserving it in perpetuity, other men with similar properties would surely begin to take the Country Houses Scheme more seriously.

Sir Charles was far to the left of Lord Lothian who, like the rest of the Astor set to which he belonged, was antagonistic to Bolshevism. Indeed Sir Charles by this time was so mesmerized by socialism, Russian style, that he had the hammer and sickle painted on one of Wallington's ornate gates; the crown was painted on the other. After all Sir Charles Trevelyan was also serving as His Majesty's lord lieutenant for Northumberland. He was a man not only comfortable with his contradictions; he courted them.

Though aristocratic and rich, members of the Trevelyan family were also earnest and public-spirited; they had an aesthetic and ideological kinship with the founders of the National Trust. 'No Trevelyan ever sucks up either to the press or the chiefs or the right people,' George Macaulay Trevelyan had written to his big brother Charles in 1905, only a decade after the National Trust had been created. 'The world has given us money enough to enable us to do what we think right: we thank it for that, and ask no more of it but to be allowed to serve.'[5]

In time, one of the many ways Professor G.M. Trevelyan, Charles's brother, served was by joining and powerfully influencing the committees that ran the National Trust. (See especially Chapter 9.) Charles, in turn, was a member of Parliament for thirty years; twenty years as a Liberal and ten as Labour. And of course, there was the enormous gift of Wallington.

The Northumberland estate had passed to this branch of the family from Sir Walter Trevelyan, a cousin, on his death in 1879. His wife, the artistic Pauline, was a friend of Ruskin's and a patron of Pre-Raphaelite painters, some of whom decorated piers in Wallington's central hall. Ruskin, in fact, got to work on one of them; Lady Trevelyan, on others. And it was from this house in Northumberland that Mr and Mrs Ruskin and the painter J.E. Millais set off on the holiday from which the couple who returned was Effie Ruskin and Mr Millais.

Sir Charles inherited Wallington in 1928, when his father died at the age of ninety. He, his wife Mary and their horde of robust children who were living nearby in Cambo, moved into the mansion. Always before when any of the six boys and girls had rushed down the hill into the big house for Sunday lunch,

they'd felt as though they'd suddenly come into the British
Library. In the old people's house everything was hushed;
everyone seemed to be whispering. Now, they all gathered
in that central hall decorated by Ruskin and cousin Pauline.
They formed a circle, held hands and shouting at the top of
their voices, let out with 'One, two, three, Aye!!!' The young
had taken over; nobody whispered any more.

Sir Charles used a great deal of the money he'd also inherited
to improve the living conditions of his tenants and farmers. His
miserly father had allowed the estate to run down badly. And
he called in an architect to study the state of the house he and
his family were now inhabiting.

'The dome in the hall is barely held aloft,' the architect told
him. 'One loud noise and the whole thing will come crashing
down!'[6]

Only six years after inheriting, Sir Charles Trevelyan began
to talk about leaving Wallington to the National Trust. The
prospect surely must have pleased his brother George.

In a 1929 tract, George Macaulay Trevelyan (known familiarly
as GMT) had asked: 'Must Britain's Beauty Perish?' His answer
had been that it need not – *if* people supported the National
Trust. He had remained attached to the house where he'd
grown up. Indeed, according to GMT's biographer, 'all his life,
Wallington meant more to Trevelyan than any other home'.[7]
Now it began to look as if it would be made safe for ever, and
very soon.

Lord Lothian was going to bequeath Blickling to the National
Trust and at first Sir Charles Trevelyan planned to do the
same. In his speeches lauding the wonders of Russian life
under communist rule – no unemployment and the like –
he sometimes referred to his bequest to the nation as a move
towards the creation of such a marvellously egalitarian society at home. But after a couple of years Sir Charles had
a better idea. Why leave Wallington to the nation? Why
not give it straight away? It was to be a gift with strings
attached, however. Sir Charles had no intention of moving
out nor of abandoning the estate's management. His wife, if
she should outlive him, would have the right to continue living

in the house, and he would go on enjoying the income from his land.

Much as the National Trust wanted Wallington, their response to Sir Charles Trevelyan's suggestion was guarded. Could it manage such an enormous estate? And with these particular conditions attached to it, would the Treasury allow this enormous gift to be tax free? The matter would have to be studied closely.

While the National Trust deliberated about the implications of Sir Charles's plan, it was offered yet another house through the Country Houses Scheme. As Sir Charles Trevelyan had been inspired by Lord Lothian, he in turn had quickly influenced yet another rich, Socialist MP: Sir Geoffrey Mander. In 1936, after a visit to Wallington, Sir Geoffrey went home to the East Midlands thinking that he, too, would give his house to the National Trust.

The Trust, while delighted by the thought of eventually owning Wallington and its vast estate, even if initially there were certain difficulties, was not at all sure it wanted Wightwick Manor, just outside Wolverhampton. In fact it didn't – not at all.

The problem wasn't money. Like Wallington, Wightwick was unencumbered by a mortgage. Nor were there complex tax issues to work out. Unlike Wallington there was no vast estate of income-producing farms and woodlands. Sir Geoffrey, who was chairman of the family paint and ink manufacturers he'd inherited, was planning to give the Trust an endowment in the form of stocks and shares which would generate enough income to maintain the property. Yet the National Trust hung back.

The trouble was taste: there were those who thought Wightwick Manor was in the worst possible.

Taste had been an issue from the very beginning of the National Trust, and even before. When Fanny Talbot lectured Hardwicke Rawnsley on the proper sort of benches for her Welsh cliff, she'd been preaching to the converted. Things plain and 'honest', natural materials native to the district, this was all part of their aesthetic. At the National Trust noses have been going into the air ever since.

In 1950, Harold Nicolson who was then deputy chairman

went to look over George Bernard Shaw's house at Ayot St Lawrence. Shaw had given it in 1944 and now, following his death, the Trust was to take over. Nicolson found it 'dreadful'. Nor did he believe that in fifty years anyone would remember who Shaw was. 'I am not happy about it,' he wrote in his diary. In fact he was against the Trust taking on such a nondescript early twentieth-century house embellished with likenesses of GBS wherever you looked. But Nicolson didn't prevail. 'We decide that morally we must accept.' Later in that decade there was James de Rothschild's offer of Waddesdon Manor. A nineteenth-century version of a French Renaissance château, in Buckinghamshire, stuffed to the turrets with Sèvres porcelain and Savonnerie carpets? There was, however, also an endowment of three-quarters of a million pounds. The Treasury found this sum so enormous it wondered if the donor was involved in a sophisticated tax-evasion scheme. (At this same time Theodora, the Marchioness of Bristol, heiress to a railway fortune, was providing Ickworth House in Suffolk with what was thought to be a large endowment: the sum was £156,000.) Waddesdon became the property of the National Trust in 1956, as did Ickworth.

Wightwick Manor was to the Trust what cast-iron serpent park benches had been to Fanny Talbot: Victorian, abhorrent. It was big and brick with gingerbread decorations and, built in 1887, it was practically brand-new. As for its interior: the best that might be said for it was that while outside the house had a raw quality, its decoration already seemed passé.

Wightwick looked like what it was: the home built for a successful Victorian business man. It was comfortable rather than stately. The rooms were dark, some might think oppressively so. Others, certainly in the minority, might have called it a gem. The rooms were embellished with William Morris & Co. wallpapers, de Morgan tiles, Edwardian stained glass and Pre-Raphaelite paintings. Sir Geoffrey's much younger second wife Rosalie, a blue stocking, had become an expert in the latter and they were still adding to their collection.

Lady Mander's enthusiasm was shared by Sir Charles

Trevelyan's wife Mary who also lived in a house with Pre-Raphaelite decorations. Lady Trevelyan was a member of the Trust's Northumberland Regional Committee and she went to work trying to convince the charity to accept Wightwick Manor. It did. A cynic's equally plausible explanation is that the Trust took Wightwick because they didn't want to offend a rich politician if they could avoid it. And, after all, Wightwick wasn't going to cost them anything.

Many of the thousands who visit Wightwick Manor today would be puzzled if they were told that the National Trust once wanted to turn it down. Wightwick Manor has become the Santiago de Compostella of the Pre-Raphaelite pilgrim's trail; its contents are in vogue all over again. (As for its fate as a family house, see Chapter 10.)

No property could come to the National Trust through the Country Houses Scheme until the government first altered its position on tax and tenancies. By 1937, it did sufficiently for the new Act of Parliament, drafted by the Trust, to be passed. The Trust now was able to accept endowments with properties it was given, provided these properties were declared inalienable. And the Act also states that any member of the Trust can become a tenant in one of its properties if the Trust chose to let it, at a rent set by the charity – *or at no rent at all if it chose not to charge one.*

Building on Sir Robert Hunter's Act of 1907, the Act of 1937 now became the National Trust's Constitution.

(Two years later a new Act of Parliament was passed which fine-tuned the Act of 1937. Knole had been offered to the Trust but it was a settled estate and therefore wasn't any one person's to give. Settled estates are bound to be passed down from one owner to the next, often following the laws of primogeniture. The person inhabiting the house, therefore, is called a limited owner; he can only make major decisions affecting the property with his trustees' approval. With the Act of 1939 the Trust was able to accept settled estates as well as those which were owned outright by their donors. After years of exhausting negotiation, Knole came to the National Trust in 1946. More fine tuning came with the Budget of 1951 which allowed donors to give or leave the contents of their houses *in lieu* of death duties.)

From 1937 onwards the donor of a country-house estate was able to create an endowment fund made up of stocks, shares, farms, houses or cash and the Trust could use the income to look after the property when it became the owner. And the donor would be able to continue living in his house after it became the property of the National Trust just as he had before.

Though the Trust's fundamental structure wasn't altered by its new constitution there were other changes to the 1907 Act besides the critical ones already discussed. Especially worth noting is this modification to the charity's description of its aims. The National Trust which had been created to protect property of outstanding natural beauty and historic interest was now a charity engaged in the preservation of: 'buildings and chattels of national interest or of architectural historic or artistic interest and places of natural interest or beauty'. Furniture, pictures, china, carriages and dog carts, door stoppers, tapestries – any and all of a property's contents – had become as much a part of the National Trust's patch as the landscape.[8]

The Red Baron

As soon as the Act of 1937 was passed by Parliament, Wightwick Manor went to the National Trust. Lord Lothian kept his word and bequeathed Blickling to the charity. He became Britain's ambassador to the United States in 1939 and when he died in Washington DC in December of the following year, the process of transferring Blickling to the Trust began. It was completed in 1942. Lord Lothian had imaginatively proposed that the mansion be let to a family who would make it a centre of intellectual or artistic or political activity. In that way Blickling would not only be saved but would contribute to local and national life.

A member of the Cliveden set, Lord Lothian had been born a Roman Catholic, but was 'converted' to Christian Science by Nancy Astor. In turn, he seems to have converted her to the National Trust. Her husband William Waldorf Astor gave Cliveden, which also became a possession of the charity in 1942. W.W. Astor had definite ideas about the future use of his house, too. And these also were public-spirited. He told the Trust that when his family no longer was living at Cliveden, he'd like the mansion to be used by the Trade Union movement or an American university.

But before either Blickling or Cliveden technically had become properties of the National Trust, Sir Charles Trevelyan was pressing the National Trust to agree on the final details of his offer.

'He was very able and very confident,' says a man who knew Sir Charles well. 'And when he decided to do something, he was going to do it if it was in his power.'

The National Trust conferred; Charles Trevelyan Bt acted.

The Act of 1937 became law in July. But four months earlier while it was still being considered by Parliament, Sir Charles attempted a pre-emptive strike. He went on the radio and announced his plan to make over Wallington to the National Trust. In spite of this, it was Wightwick Manor that became the first house to go to the Trust through the Country Houses Scheme once the Act of Parliament was passed. What could be holding things up now?

The National Trust continued to worry. Its new constitution gave donors the right to live on in their houses as tenants if the charity agreed. But wouldn't the Treasury challenge the agreement if Sir Charles Trevelyan were allowed to manage Wallington and take at least some of the profits from the estate? The problem the charity faced because of Sir Charles's demands was a particularly hard one to solve. But he went some way towards sorting things out.

When is a gift not a present? Nor a legacy a bequest? Sir Charles Trevelyan and his lawyer came up with an answer to this riddle in the form of a document that made the Wallington estate over to the National Trust, while its donor retained a life interest in it. That seemed to clear up the issue of how Sir Charles could give away his estate while keeping control of it. But he went on insisting that his family be given future tenancy rights as part of the agreement. If, however, a lease were drawn up to that effect, whoever inherited it would be taxed. Say it was a ninety-nine year lease, for example. And, say, that there were sixty years left when one of his children inherited it. The Treasury then would work out the money value of the time remaining and tax the heir accordingly. This is not what Charles Trevelyan had in mind when he talked about redistributing wealth. It seemed that he and the National Trust were at an impasse.

In 1931 when Sir Charles had served as president of the Board of Education, he and the Cabinet disagreed about school-leaving age. Ramsay MacDonald more or less told Sir Charles not to bother about it; that they'd take care of the matter. Without any further discussion, Sir Charles Trevelyan up and walked out of the job. If they weren't going to do things his way, he wasn't interested. Sir Charles hadn't mellowed. If the Treasury or the Trust were going to object to the terms of his gift, he'd withdraw the offer of Wallington.

There's no tax on yearning

George Macaulay Trevelyan was both a son of the house, the brother of the potential donor and an influential servant of the National Trust. He became the broker of the deal, and, in the end, masterminded an extraordinary feat of legalistic alchemy.

A formula was created which when applied correctly could turn would-be donors' brazen – taxable – demands into mere – non-taxable – yearnings. This clever recipe was given a name: the Memorandum of Wishes. It remains in use by the National Trust today.

A memorandum of wishes works like this: the owner of a house or an estate or a garden who wants to give or leave it to the National Trust lists all the pre-conditions for his gift. These may include hours of opening, use of buildings, colour of the drawing room, rights of occupancy, those he'd like barred from living there in future. Then, by the waving of a lawyer's magic wand, these are changed from being contractual demands into becoming mere wishes.

Assuming the National Trust wants the house or garden or land, the donor draws up his wish list. It goes to the Trust's Executive Committee which meets to discuss the memorandum and vote on whether or not to accept it. If it does, the Trust becomes bound to honour it – but only in compliance with its own Executive ruling, which in theory can be changed. It is not bound by law. Technically, once a property becomes the inalienable possession of the charity, it alone decides what to do with it (though it can never sell, give away or mortgage the property of course.) The donors' wishes, when granted, would not be taxed – the whole point of concocting the memorandum of wishes in the first place.

This wizardry was appealing. But could a donor depend on the National Trust to honour his wishes, which after all might refer to actions to be taken long after his death?

The gentlemen of the Trust gave their word as gentlemen that they would not renege. And furthermore, as they themselves pointed out, it was in their own interest to be upright.

The National Trust existed because people gave it contributions of money and property. It would not grow, it could not survive, without public support. It had to be honourable and that included doing its best to fulfil the wishes of its donors. They would otherwise scare off potential givers of everything from houses, land, coastline, furniture, pictures, tapestries – and cash.

Sir Charles Trevelyan the Stalinist baronet, in a rare example of consistent behaviour, acted exactly like a dictatorial patriarch at home.

High ideals were the official motive for Sir Charles's decision to give the Wallington estate to the nation. But he had a more personal motive that may have been equally strong.

In 1934 when Sir Charles began working out the language of his proposed bequest to the nation, he talked about it with his lawyer of course. And he wrote about it to the National Trust. But – 'He didn't really consult us at all,' Patricia Jennings, Sir Charles Trevelyan's surviving daughter, recalled when I talked with her more than fifty years later. 'He certainly didn't consult George, the eldest child,' she went on. 'And he would have done it whatever we said.'

By 1941 Sir Charles Trevelyan eventually worked out a memorandum of wishes that the charity accepted. Both Sir Charles and his wife Mary, who survived him for eight years, occupied the entire house at Wallington; following her mother's death in 1966, Patricia Jennings became the Trust's rent-free tenant in a airy flat on the first floor, which originally had been an interconnecting suite of bedrooms. Each room can also be entered separately from the balcony that rings the central hall of the house with its celebrated painted panels.

Mrs Jennings, a straightforward woman in her seventies, walked through every room as she showed me the flat.

'The bars on this window were put up when this was the nursery,' she said when we'd reached the most distant corner of the flat. In the middle of this room, a swing still hangs down from the high ceiling. But today a dressmaker's dummy and a table set up for cutting cloth are also part of its décor. From the window a green lawn leads on to a green meadow. Only in the far, far distance was the greenness truncated; cut off by a blue-grey wall of sky.

The light that filters into the flat from its many tall windows makes its already enormous rooms seem even bigger. The feeling of the place is at once both expansive and homely. William Morris wallpaper has hung on the walls since 1897. 'The curtains, too, are the same period,' Mrs Jennings pointed out. They were rescued by her when the National Trust embarked on downstairs renovations.

Mrs Jennings is tactful in her dealings with the National Trust and seems genuinely pleased with the domestic arrangements as they've developed. 'I never grumble – I'm very comfortable,' she volunteers.

There's no doubt that some of the improvements since the Trust became the owner have been entirely welcome. For instance, where before there were only two bathrooms in the entire house, she now enjoys the 'luxury' of having one in her own flat. Yet there is an implied criticism of the new owners when the subject of heating comes up. In this she remains steadfastly Trevelyan.

'I'm pleased I can control the heat in this flat,' Mrs Jennings says, 'because the Trust supplies the house with rather a lot. We were used to being cold,' she says. The implication is clear: cold would not only be familiar; it would be an improvement.

All in all, she feels very lucky: for herself and for the estate. 'This is far better than what it could possibly have been if the National Trust hadn't taken it,' she believes.

But does Sir George, who inherited his father's title and who would have inherited the house in which we are sitting as well as all the green that stretches as far as we can see when we look from its enormous windows – and all the thousands of acres beyond – does he share his sister's detached appreciation and gratitude?

'He realizes that he could not have done the things he has done if he'd had the house, too,' she replied. It was obvious to both of us that this was not the fullest possible answer and that this was all that she was going to say.

I mentioned that her brother George hadn't replied to my letter asking for a meeting. As I left Wallington Patricia Jennings suggested I go to see the youngest in the family, her brother Geoffrey. As a kind of parting gift she added, 'He's not as pro-Trust as I am.'

At his home in St Albans, Geoffrey Trevelyan and I talked about the National Trust in the Lake District where generations of Trevelyans have walked and climbed. And we talked about the family. 'In her relations with the Trust my mother remained studiously neutral. And I think Patricia has been studiously neutral. She has to. She lives on their doorstep, after all.'

Geoffrey Trevelyan does not. He lives in a tidy, modern house in a leafy cul-de-sac near the cathedral. 'We built it when I retired,' he told me as a pack of silky, long-haired chihuahuas rushed about the floor like so many agitated, hirsute mice. Yet

Geoffrey Trevelyan practised as much neutrality as had his sister during our talk.

Mr Trevelyan led me through the house out into the back garden. There I was offered shelter from the hot sun of the Indian summer afternoon under the awning of an upholstered swing chair – an item that in a Trevelyan household seemed positively hedonistic. We sat, drank tea and, while his dogs yapped to get out of the house to join us, we talked.

'How did you and the other children feel as a result of your father failing to ask your views about his plan to give Wallington away?' I asked.

'It's not quite fair to say that he didn't discuss it,' Geoffrey Trevelyan replied. He added that during 1935 and 1936 Sir Charles wrote to his oldest son George about what he intended doing. 'But there was no question of discussing in the sense of whether it ought to be done.'

Later an old family friend of the Trevelyans said Sir Charles's decision to give Wallington to the National Trust had been a tragedy for George who had very much wanted to make his future home there. Several people had told me that Sir George Trevelyan, as he became when his father died in 1958, was now a crank living in a remote corner of the West Country. 'A faith healer of some kind,' said one old boy, contemptuously.

When he'd inherited, Sir George had quickly sold the gardener's cottage at Wallington which he'd been bequeathed by his father. More than forty years passed before he was able to enjoy spending even one night in the mansion, I'd been told. And there'd been rows or tiffs, anyway, with the National Trust. When he did visit Wallington for the day, Sir George would insist that, National Trust conservation practices be damned, the curtains must be opened and the blinds raised so he and his friends could actually see the inside of the house.

Between Sir George Trevelyan not answering my letter and all the gossip I'd been hearing, I assumed that, even after half a century, he was too heartbroken to talk about what his father had done. Then, apropos of nothing at all, seven months after I'd written to him, a note came apologizing for the delay and asking me to get in touch.

Sir George and Lady Trevelyan live in a converted hay barn in a tiny Gloucestershire village, thus far unspoilt, in spite of being not National Trust. Their daughter and only child Catriona lives in a larger house across the drive.

Each of the hay barn's two floors – a large room with a smaller bedroom at the back – is filled with books and pictures. It's the higgledy-piggledy accumulation of a lifetime rather than a collection of family heirlooms, say, or the product of hours spent in auction salesrooms. An electric chairlift allows Sir George, who has rheumatoid arthritis, to use his upstairs study.

Sir George has long straight grey hair and cloudy blue eyes. His bony features show a strong resemblance to his uncle the Professor GMT. He is a handsome man. When young he was a beauty.

Lady Trevelyan insisted on fetching the photographs to prove it. 'Everybody was always after him,' she told me: twice.

'You must have had your hands full,' I replied.

'Oh I did,' she said, both rueful and proud.

The troubles she'd had were caused by more than George's good looks. To judge from the intensity with which Sir George beamed in on me as we began our conversation, he happily has not lost his intention to captivate. Nor has his wife stopped finding this both maddening and winning.

George and Helen are quite a double act: he dreaming and drifting, one detail recalling another which he can't resist mentioning; she sharp, precise, down to earth, interrupting with 'Get on with it George. Don't take so long.' They've been practising this routine for more than fifty years; they married in 1940.

While Lady Trevelyan is five years older than her husband and quick to announce 'I'm ninety-three you know,' and had only just given up driving a car, Sir George at eighty-seven is suffering from a lack of oxygen to the brain as well as rheumatoid arthritis. He's also rather deaf. None of this appears to agitate him in spite of the fact that he suspects he may be embarking on an anecdote he has told only ten minutes before.

Through our long morning's talk Sir George disagreed with

his wife only once or twice and then only faintly. He is, however, a skilful employer of silences.

Sometimes there is no reply to what has been said because Sir George hasn't heard it. But more often he's silent precisely because he has heard every word clearly. It's not that Sir George is trying to communicate disapproval. The atmosphere his lack of response creates isn't heavy or claustrophobic. Rather it's as if he's trying to make a pocket of emptiness into which the sentiment he doesn't care for will disappear, as if by keeping quiet he will succeed in prettifying his world.

About many things George and Helen absolutely agree of course. Among them are these: Sir Charles gave Wallington to the National Trust because of his political beliefs *and* because he didn't want George to inherit it.

'He thought you were going to bring some cranky Alexander method or something into Wallington,' Lady Trevelyan piped out in her high clear voice, directing this and almost everything else she said during my visit to her husband on whom she dotes – however exasperating she appears to find him sometimes.

'I *was* unorthodox,' Sir George agrees. But then, as always on guard lest he's giving the impression that he's critical of his father, he adds, 'So was he. In a different way.' There followed an analysis of the contribution Sir Charles had made when the Labour government, in which he served, came into power after the First World War. (Unorthodox both may have been, but in one respect decidedly not: like Sir Charles the Communist, Sir George the crank has never, even briefly, considered giving up his title. 'It's come in handy,' Sir George observed.)

After reading history at Cambridge, he spent several years learning to make Cotswold-style walnut furniture. Then he moved on to be one of the first people in Britain to become a disciple of F.M. Alexander. From 1932 to 1936 he trained to teach the Alexander Technique. (Alexander proposed that both physical and mental well being would result from learning how to stand, sit, move 'correctly'.) Not coincidentally, as Helen Trevelyan made clear, it was at this point that Sir Charles found Lord Lothian's plan so tempting. The thought that after his death, George would turn the estate into some kind of centre

[57]

for this Alexander enterprise was not merely alarming; it was unacceptable.

George acknowledges that he did have ideas about Wallington's future use that were, what he calls, non-traditional. And he doesn't bridle at being called cranky – though the word he prefers is 'progressive'. There's lots of evidence around of what this means.

A mobile of Pegasus dangles from a beam in the roof of the hay loft; a stained-glass unicorn rests against one wall. Some of his lectures are available on video-cassette; among them: 'Poetry and the expanding of consciousness' and 'Looking into nature: God's grandeur'.

In his way of talking – the words he chooses to emphasize, for instance – and the style in which he makes his enthusiasms known, Sir George Trevelyan sounds like a large child telling a somewhat younger one a nursery tale (maybe not surprising in a man who was the eldest of six). The nursery tale isn't one with a subplot; there is no suggestion of complexity, sophistication and surely no cynicism in Sir George's manner.

It is only his silences and a stuttering cough that sometimes rises up which deliver the message that things have not always been either wonderful or simple. His optimism seems an acquired characteristic really. He employs it the way Transylvanians might carry garlic to ward off vampires. It appears to be more like a defence than a quality of temperament.

For many, many years Sir George was bitter because Wallington had been given away by his father. I told him that I'd expected to find him a man broken by the high-handed actions of his father; that it was a pleasure to discover that I'd been wrong.

'Yes,' the octogenarian Sir George Trevelyan replied. 'I'm realizing increasingly now, that I found my way through.'

Because Sir Charles had been the first to, as it were, put his wishes on the line, he had to have more faith in the National Trust than those who followed him. But because he retained a life interest in Wallington, he continued to control its management. Most people didn't grasp this fact.

How could they? In *The Times* of 1 November 1941, beneath a large photograph of the mansion house attractively framed by leafy trees was the announcement: 'The beautiful and historic estate of Wallington in the Middle Marshes of Northumberland has been given to the National Trust by Sir Charles Trevelyan. The gift includes the valuable contents of the house and overall 13,000 acres of farms and moorland.' But it was seventeen years before the National Trust took charge of Wallington.

While the public believed that he had given Wallington to the nation in 1941, Sir Charles felt himself to be the sole owner of Wallington for the rest of his life. As for the National Trust, it occupied a somewhat muddled middle ground and still does. Wallington is always cited as one of the first houses to come to the charity through the Country Houses Scheme following the passage of the Act of 1937. At the same time, the Trust does not dispute the Trevelyan family claim that Sir Charles was the owner of Wallington until he died in 1958.

However the legal technicalities are interpreted, the fact is that from the time he inherited until the day of his death, Sir Charles Trevelyan ran Wallington much as he pleased – farms, villages, house, woodlands. In the 1950s, for example, he gave the Forestry Commission a long lease on 3,000 acres of the estate – without a word to the National Trust. The idea that it might be courteous to keep the landlord informed probably never occurred to him. Landlord? He was Wallington's landlord. And though he had abhorred the way his father had let the estate run down and as a young man spent so much to improve it in old age, he too was prepared to watch cottages decay.

Undoubtedly Sir Charles Trevelyan appears to have been overbearing. But perhaps he was also wise to arrange things so that he could keep control of Wallington and try to guide its future direction.

Today Blickling is not a centre of intellectual, artistic or political life though Lord Lothian wanted it to be one. It is the East Anglia Regional Office of the National Trust. As for W.W. Astor's Cliveden: it is not being used by the Trade Union movement nor by an American university (though Stanford did lease it for a time). Cliveden is a luxurious, expensive country-house hotel. To some degree, at least, Wallington remains a family's house.

Enlightened and selfish; high-handed as well as high-minded, Sir Charles Trevelyan seems to eptomize the contradictory character of the National Trust as it went through its first great period of change. It seems likely that if selfishness hadn't been welded to Sir Charles's idealism, the future direction of the National Trust might have been entirely different. The memorandum of wishes might not have been created. Other donors of properties of comparable scale might not have been tempted to make comparable gifts. Wallington after all was three times the size of Blickling which started off the Country Houses Scheme and became the property of the charity in 1942.

Because of the magnitude of Sir Charles Trevelyan's generosity, the stubbornness of his will and the grip he insisted on keeping on what he had given away, he made the idea of giving one's estates to the National Trust much more attractive to others than it might otherwise have been. Within a year there was talk of another very large gift from another socialist baronet.

Sir Francis Acland and Sir Charles Trevelyan were Liberal MPs at the same time. Sir Francis, too, liked the idea of the National Trust but unlike Sir Charles he talked this over with Richard, his son and heir. On Sir Francis's death, at the outbreak of the Second World War, Sir Richard Acland became owner of what remained of the family's vast estates after death duties were paid. A lot had gone but there was considerably more than a handkerchief-sized plot left.

Sir Richard Acland's holdings amounted to 20,000 acres of West Country land. There was the Holnicote (it rhymes with honey pot) estate in Somerset with almost 13,000 acres of moorland, steep wooded valleys, coastline, farms and villages and the Killerton estate in south Devon with its large house, seventeen-acre garden, villages and farms.

In 1944 Sir Richard chose to give it all and give it outright. And he chose to give Killerton as well. He felt, his wife Anne later wrote, that this was 'the best way to continue his family's traditions and ensure that the estates remained intact in a world of increasing pressures.'[9] (Taxes and more taxes.)

Sir Richard, like Sir Charles Trevelyan, came from a long line of public-spirited men. And he, too, was a man who acted for the Public Good as he construed it without perhaps always showing respect for the feelings, never mind the views, of those who were going to be most immediately affected by his decisions. It wasn't the children, in Sir Richard's case. His were very young at the time. Sir Richard's high hand waved over the heads of his many tenants. He didn't give them any advance notice of what he was planning. When they heard that they suddenly had a new landlord, they were outraged and took to the newspapers to object.

Other large landowners criticized Sir Richard too. Wasn't it a scandal that on his way to making a very generous gift to the nation he'd behaved so thoughtlessly. And some found it ironic that the old guard, though mad keen to hang on to every acre, talked about stewardship and, however paternalistically, about their responsibilities to their tenants.

All or nothing at all

From the very first everyone connected with the National Trust seems to have been taken by the beauty of Holnicote – starting with Hardwicke Rawnsley who visited the estate in 1917. 'It was clear', he wrote, 'that the Lord of the Manor cared not only for the lives of his tenants, but for the beauty of their surroundings.' The canon enthused about the rose-covered cottages; their gardens 'gay with stocks and snap dragons', forests filled with Wellingtonia, chestnut, Douglas Pine 'not touched by the woodman's axe' since the grandfather of Sir Thomas Acland, to whom it all then belonged, had planted them.[10] Killerton did not attract a similar fan club. The trouble was taste again.

It wasn't absolutely lacking in admirers. Earlier in the century, for instance, when Sir Richard's great-uncle 'Charlie' owned

Killerton, 19,000 people congregated in the park to hear a speech by Lloyd George. 'The Castle Beautiful of Liberalism!' one member of the party shouted out. But the reaction of James Lees-Milne, Vita Sackville-West and Harold Nicolson in the 1940s exemplified the National Trust's assessment of the place – and the change in values that was taking place.

Harold Nicolson had just been made vice-chairman of the Trust and along with his wife and their friend, Lees-Milne, the charity's historic buildings secretary, off he tootled for a look at its properties in the West Country, rather as Canon Rawnsley had done thirty or so years earlier. At Killerton the trio stopped for tea with the Aclands. Lees-Milne later wrote in his diary: 'We all disliked this property, the garden, the ugly shrubs, the house, the menage . . .'

The fact that no less a figure than William Robinson who almost single-handedly had slain Victorian carpet-bedding and influenced Gertrude Jekyll (and through her generations of England's most admired gardeners) had designed its herbaceous borders was not good enough. Killerton simply would not do.

Why then did the National Trust not refuse Killerton and say 'yes' only to Holnicote?

The answer is Sir Richard Acland Bt. Unlike Sir Charles, he did not ask to retain management of his estates or to receive income from them. But he did have one very, very big wish: a 6,000 acre one. It was all of Killerton. Sir Richard evidently had little interest in his majestic Somerset estate apart from the shooting. But Killerton delighted him – and Anne, his wife – and they wanted to insure that it would be protected for ever. He was firm about the terms of his offer: there would be no gift of Holnicote if the Trust refused his estate in Devon. The charity capitulated. The 20,000 acres of Holnicote and Killerton came to the National Trust.

By the end of 1944, the Trust possessed still other great estates and a dozen more grand houses. Among the riches added to Blickling, Killerton, Wallington and Cliveden were Sir John Dashwood's West Wycombe Park – a lovely but then shabby Palladian villa in Buckinghamshire – and Lacock Abbey in Wiltshire where in the early nineteenth century Fox Talbot had taken the first photographs.

Lord Lothian, Sir Charles Trevelyan and Sir Richard Acland – everyone of them left of centre – had not only saved extraordinary properties for the nation but had also unwittingly altered the nature of the National Trust. There was a change in the sort of people who worked for and with it too. These big country houses often filled with exquisite objects created a magnetic field into which were drawn chaps who would have been repelled by talk of footpaths, common land, public rights of way.

Lord Esher became a member of the National Trust's Council in 1931 and soon after Lord Lothian's speech at the 1934 AGM he began trying to find a way of making the Country House Scheme workable. Rich, charming, witty – sometimes cruelly so, it's said – and a strong chairman, Viscount Esher was involved with other conservation organizations, too. For example, he became the president of the Society for the Preservation of Ancient Buildings in 1931, starting an association that lasted more than thirty years.

In spite of this Morris connection, Lord Esher did not otherwise follow the lead of the man who'd founded the SPAB. The Viscount was neither narrowly focused on the Gothic period nor hoping that a Marxist revolution would come swiftly. 'He got into things because somebody asked him to,' says someone who knew him well. 'The last thing he was interested in was consistency.' So while, for instance, he hated Victorian architecture, Lord Esher became chairman of the Victorian Society just the same. Along with being a member of the aristocracy, inconsistency is probably all he had in common with Sir Charles Trevelyan. The 3rd Viscount Esher, 'an easy going landowner', was part of the establishment, not one of its critics.

Lord Esher seems to have been a particularly influential man behind the scenes; one of those aristocrats who are said to mix comfortably with everybody. Another definition of 'everybody' in this case meant people who travelled first class, as Lady Brunner was doing on the day during the war when the following events took place.

She had left Greys Court, her Oxfordshire home, and was on the London train. 'Somebody came into the carriage, very delightful, and we started talking,' says Lady Brunner. 'We didn't then know him. This was Lord Esher. When he realized where I was living, he immediately set upon me because a Knollys family had lived here. There is the most wonderful tomb in our church. 1620. He said that at all costs this must be preserved; that it was being neglected. As a result of that we all got to know each other.'

And, after the war, when the time came that the Brunners began to wonder where tax increases were going to end – and what future tax bills might mean to their ability to look after their Tudor house properly along with its 300 acres, and with many medieval ruins to restore and preserve – there was Lord Esher to help and give advice. Greys Court became the property of the National Trust in 1969.

'As aristocrats ceased to be the governing class, they sought to carve out a new role for themselves as the self-appointed guardians of the national heritage,' asserts the author of *The Decline and Fall of the British Aristocracy*.[12] This seems something of a distortion. Being a guardian of the heritage was not a new role which evolved during the 1930s, nor were aristocrats the originators of the enterprise. Consider, for example, the following remarks: 'In destroying or injuring one of these buildings, we are destroying the pleasure, the culture, in a word, the humanity of unborn generations.'[13] These words were written not by a lord, but by William Morris. And even earlier it was Wordsworth who left no doubt that England's heritage meant the landscape, too. It was the poet who started warning people that the Lake District was in peril. While it is true that it was aristocrats who launched the National Trust's Country Houses Scheme and got it moving, neither Lord Lothian nor Sir Charles Trevelyan and Sir Richard Acland had the time or the inclination to involve themselves actively in saving the heritage. Nevertheless Cannadine's observation does at least match up with the behaviour of the men who came to the Trust to put the Country Houses Scheme into action. They were leisured aesthetes and, in addition to their passion for art and architecture, they not only wanted to save these often ornate houses, the pictures and the furniture, too, but also the way of life of the people living in them.

In 1932, Lord Zetland was asked to serve as chairman of the Executive Committee. This was not because Zetland, who'd been governor of Bengal, had shown any interest in the charity. You could say he had an interest once removed, I suppose, because he'd been Lord Curzon's secretary (and biographer) and George Nathaniel Curzon had shown a great deal of interest in the Trust. Not least in his ways of showing this was that, having bought and restored both Tattershall and Bodiam Castles, he left them both to the charity in his will.

It was R.E. Norman, head of the Trust's Finance and General Purposes Committee, who suggested that Lord Zetland be offered the job. Norman shrewdly reckoned that country house owners would have more confidence in the National Trust if it were run by one of them. (It was for this reason, he said, that he shouldn't take the job himself.) The selection of Lord Zetland as chairman both reflected and influenced the new direction in which the National Trust was heading. And just as one donation of a country house begot another, so did the presence of titled folk or those with titles somewhere in the family.

When the Earl of Antrim became chairman of the National Trust in 1965 he described it as a self-perpetuating oligarchy. It had been one for decades as he undoubtedly knew. In fact the Trust had been a self-perpetuating oligarchy from the day of its first meeting at 1 Great College Street in January 1895.

What had changed was the preoccupations and goals, the tone and the style of the small élite who ran the charity. And the change was radical, though that is perhaps an ill-chosen word, since by the end of the Second World War – donors apart – there was scarcely a radical in sight. Begun by a clutch of middle-class, high-minded activists, the NT was becoming a cosy club of aesthetically minded aristocrats. It would be wrong to say that snobbishness was now introduced to the National Trust for the first time. William Morris, after all, disliked Wren's churches, thought St Peter's in Rome hideous and found England's Georgian architecture revolting. His followers in the Trust's early days had shared such prejudices. What changed was the object of snobbery – now eighteenth-century houses were very much all right – and its magnitude.

In one of James Lees-Milne's diaries (the four volumes record the years from 1936 to 1949 when he was immersed in the Trust's acquisition of country houses), he writes of a visit to Lord and Lady Shuttleworth at Gawthorpe Hall in Yorkshire in November of 1949: 'Young Lord S. speaks of the inhabitants of Burnley and the neighbouring towns as one would of Hottentots. I notice that this view is commonly held by England's aristocracy and I think they, the aristocracy, are right on the whole, although I must admit it is the unwise who reveal these sentiments in public.'[14]

James Lees-Milne liked to make a modest amount of mischief. His use of the word 'Hottentots' is probably a fair example of that. But if the way he expressed himself here is inflammatory it also reflects genuine feeling. Whether 'they' are called savages, the great unwashed, the needy, the underprivileged or, for the moment, the underclass, these euphemisms refer to the very people whose lot in life the National Trust had been created to try to improve. Though the point must be stressed that such an attitude about the poor reflected a change of degree rather than of kind.

In 1903 Octavia Hill wrote to her lawyer about her purchase of Mariner's Hill which would go to the National Trust. The charity 'by no means plan to give access to the tramp, the London rough, the noisy beanfeaster . . .,' she declared. Its object was to 'preserve land in its natural beauty for the artist, the professional man, *and such of the public as appreciate and respect natural beauty.*'[15] The italic is my own.

It was the estimated size of this last-mentioned group that now drastically changed. Instead of seeing itself as a charity preserving the landscape for the benefit of the large number of people who could in effect be expected to behave themselves when they visited, the National Trust was becoming an organization attempting to protect the heritage *from* them. Even into the 1950s, the moments when someone penetrated this rather secluded, aesthetically preoccupied world with the news that there was something called the public outside who might want to share it, were not joyous ones. There was, for instance the day Lord De la Warr brought up the subject of signposts.

Might it not be a good idea to help people find their way to the National Trust's properties? You know, put up a few indicators of where they actually were. They might like to *visit*.

'People thought Lord De la Warr was mad when he first proposed this,' says Sir John Smith who became a member of the Historic Buildings Committee in 1952.

In many ways the public must have seemed like a terrible nuisance, getting in the way and preventing the old boys from enjoying looking after the houses, their contents and parks as they – and the donors – chose.

All along the people of the National Trust had felt themselves superior to the poor. But the founders and their supporters had been making an effort to try to raise the poor up to their level so that one day they might become equals. Maybe if enough time and attention were given to them, those London roughs could be turned into NT members. Starting in the 1930s, however, and for decades thereafter, the men at the National Trust began to try to keep as much distance as possible between themselves and the others.

After the death of Sir Geoffrey Mander in 1962 his widow lived on at Wightwick Manor and administered it for the National Trust. She had more than a quarter of a century of experience of the charity by this time and had been keeping an eye on its shifts in personnel and attitude.

'Because it was given by a Marquess, the Trust being the Trust,' she wrote in one of her letters to the landlord, the charity had given Blickling pride of place as the first house to come to it through the Country Houses Scheme. But obviously the first had been her own! She was right but in this case the Trust was being snobbish less about titles than about buildings. No one in London considered Wightwick a proper country house.

Possibly only its donor would. It wasn't large, it wasn't grand, it was surrounded by only sixteen acres and those in a suburb of Wolverhampton.

Like a Republican spying out Royalists, Lady Mander remained vigilant. And she found plenty to disapprove of. (See Chapter 10.)

Were the founders and early supporters of the National Trust and people like the Trevelyans, Aclands and Manders, their ideological heirs, superior to the aristocrats for whom Lees-Milne – and others at the National Trust – had so much empathy? This is a question that only veteran class warriors may find easy to answer. The whole lot of them, after all, whether middle class or members of the aristocracy, were aesthetic snobs and knew themselves to be superior to the poor.

It's already obvious that Sir Charles and Sir Richard for all their generosity to the public were not candidates for canonization. Lady Mander wouldn't have much of a chance either. And from a present-day perspective, Hill, Hunter and Rawnsley might not look much saintlier. It is, after all, the giver and not the receiver of 'aid' who makes all the decisions about what is provided, how much and how often. In this sense, therefore, not only is the dispenser of charity more powerful than its recipients to begin with, but actually perpetuates the power he or she has got.

Leaving aside motives and merits for the moment at least, the issue is not who was better – the founders, the upper-class (aspirant or actual) volunteers who orchestrated the acquisition of great estates and country houses, or the donors of them; the issue is this: as a result of the Country Houses Scheme the National Trust changed from being a charity focused on 'the people' to one that was focused on its properties instead; initially that meant it paid attention almost exclusively to grand houses and the treasures in them.

Was this a good thing? The answer to the people concerned was an unqualified yes. There were so many extraordinary places that might at any moment be stripped of all their wonderful decoration or might actually be pulled down and lost to the nation for ever.

Montacute, the noble Elizabethan mansion in Somerset, had been on the market for its scrap value in 1931 when it was bought by Ernest Cook, heir to the Thomas Cook fortune, and transferred to the National Trust. Hundreds of similarly fine houses were disappearing – literally – and at a rate that picked up momentum as the thirties went on. In the half century ending in 1919, about eighty stately homes had been demolished in Scotland, England and Wales. In the twenty years which led up to the outbreak of the Second World War, more than 200 others followed.

'Fortunate in her domestic history,' the Hon. Vita Sackville-West could write, and accurately, even during the Second World War, 'it seems likely that England . . . will witness the gradual destruction of her lovely inheritance by economic rather than violent means.'[16]

Off he goes

By the middle of the 1930s, Lord Zetland was the chairman and Donald MacLeod Matheson had taken over as secretary of the National Trust from S.H. Hamer who been secretary from 1911, when Octavia Hill was still writing its appeals, until 1933. The following year, Lord Lothian had made his speech and it was clear that the Trust could do with a committee to investigate the subject.

In 1936, a Country Houses Committee was formed in an effort to advance Lord Lothian's scheme. Lord Esher became its chairman.

How many houses were there? Which owners were most likely to have to give them up? Were their mansions places the National Trust wanted?

MacLeod Matheson mentioned to his sister Hilda that the Trust was looking for someone who could find the answers to such questions. Hilda, who was head of Talks for the BBC, repeated this to her adored friend Vita Sackville-West. Vita, rightly, imagined that this was a job that might interest James Lees-Milne.

Lees-Milne was not employed at the time. His predicament can be called voluntary only on a technicality. He'd quit his previous position as a secretary to Sir Roderick Jones, head of Reuters, just as Sir Roderick had begun pointing to the door.

By his own account, James Lees-Milne was temperamentally unsuited to journalism, being 'far too slow and totally lacking push'. Worse still, he had no interest in whether Reuters or someone else got there first with the news. But what had turned the job from being merely ill-fitting to being ghastly was the character of his boss.

'He was', Lees-Milne wrote of Sir Roderick, 'the very incarnation of Martinet, without the grisly charm of that French drill-master.'[17] The pages of description in his autobiography that support this are some of the most entertainingly bitchy he ever published. (Needless to say Sir Roderick was dead when he did.)

The position as secretary to its Country Houses Committee which the National Trust was creating must have seemed like something James Lees-Milne had wished into existence. It was exactly the sort of work he'd been yearning to do ever since an event six years before that he's called 'a turning point in my life'.

While still a student at Oxford, Lees-Milne had been taken to a dinner party at Rousham, a Jacobean house – its grounds and interior redesigned late in the eighteenth century by William Kent.

The host, to whom the house had been let, was a man who was 'rich, clever and slightly mad'. He was also an alcoholic. When the fine meal was over, everyone staggered from the dining room. This man 'got hold of a hunting crop and cracked it against the portraits. With the thong he flecked off chunks of paint.' Then, their host having collected a gun, they all went outside so that the fellow could take pot shots at the statues in the garden.

The other boys cheered him on. James Lees-Milne did not. But neither did he speak out in protest. He did, however, make a vow:

'It brought home to me how passionately I cared for architecture and the continuity of history of which it is the mouthpiece,' he later wrote. '. . . I would devote my energies and abilities, such as they were, to preserving the country houses of England.' Complete with their furniture and pictures, he added, which to him seemed as vulnerable as children.[18]

Ignore the fantastical self-dramatization, at least for the moment. Both the revulsion Lees-Milne felt that evening at Rousham and the mission it revealed to him were surely genuine.

If that party at Rousham had never taken place or if Lees-Milne had not been a guest at it, if in the years afterwards he'd found work that suited him (or received an unexpected inheritance), not only his future but that of the National Trust might have been different. For, while the post as secretary of the Country Houses Committee of the National Trust seemed an answer to his prayers, he must have seemed heaven-sent to the people running the charity. Socialist peers may have got the Country Houses Scheme rolling; James Lees-Milne got it snowballing.

Surely in 1936 James Lees-Milne was not the only man in England who needed a job. George Macaulay Trevelyan, alone, would have known a number of bright young academics who could have done the work. But it was this particular not quite young man they chose – sensitive, good-looking, charming and witty, devoted without appearing to be too serious, a fellow who did not make a scene, an amateur who advertised himself, accurately, as not being intellectual – 'I was middle brow,' he says categorically. With very, very few exceptions, a somewhat watered-down version has been the archetypal National Trust member of senior staff ever since, on the aesthetic side especially.

Not only did the position seem designed just for Lees-Milne; he helped tailor the pattern of the organization it was becoming. Lees-Milne describes working for the National Trust in the

1930s as a 'vocation'. Actually he needed the £400 a year they offered as salary. Though an upper-middle-class Old Etonian, he was also a man who had to earn a living. This was probably the only real difference between him and the men he met in the spring of 1936 when he went to work for the National Trust.

James Lees-Milne may have been slow and all too relaxed at Reuters, but in the diary of his years on the Country Houses Committee of the National Trust he appears to have become a man with an enormous amount of energy and ambition. Either on his bicycle or in the National Trust's rattle-trap car he was constantly on the road; the enterprise seems to have been a love affair.

The following synopsis of one of his diary entries can be taken as reasonably representative of 'a day's work'. Leaves London for Norfolk by car. On the way has a look at Wimpole outside Cambridge then on to Ely. From there to seventeenth-century Ryston Hall and an examination of its exterior. A stop at Stoke Ferry Hall, just vacated by soldiers. A look through a window at its interior.

'Not by any means a remarkable house. High, plain, red-brick façade to the street, dated 1788 – the category of doctor's or solicitor's house. Spacious and well proportioned within. Spacious, many-walled garden. Everything I like yet this pleasant old house is not worthy of the Trust, I fear. The conditions attached to the offer are not attractive; and besides who would wish to live here?'

A quick look at Oxburgh Hall and then to Swanton Morley where supposedly the ancestors of Abraham Lincoln had a cottage. 'No one of the four inhabitants could tell.' He made it to Blickling Hall not far from the coast in a downpour just before dark.

Adding to the adventure and exhaustion of it all, the Austin was forever breaking down. Lees-Milne sometimes lost his patience and his bounce but never his faith.

'During those starry-eyed years,' he writes, 'my work was a dedication to building up an organization in which I passionately believed.'[19]

With his help, it was no longer the organization it had been in 1895. Quite possibly those people who had a kinship with the Trust's founders found him trying. Though in this Lady Mander was an exception and he, exceptionally – since socialists weren't his natural habitat – enjoyed her company. As for other left-wing donors of houses:

After a visit to Killerton (not with Harold and Vita this time but on National Trust business), Lees-Milne recorded that he found Sir Richard and Lady Acland 'dogmatic'. What is more, they had populated their house with 'the Worker's Transport Company, people smelling of disinfectant, a working woman singing out of tune'.[20] An overnight stay at Wallington was only marginally better.

Sir Charles and Lady Trevelyan he found 'overwhelming' if also welcoming. Their two married daughters Patricia (who was pregnant at the time) and Pauline he found 'rather terrifying'. After dinner his hostess invited her guests to play a game. Lees-Milne found it more like a school examination.

Mary Trevelyan acted as quiz-master; everyone scored according to the percentage of her questions they got right. Each of the Trevelyans scored 100 per cent; Lees-Milne's score was 0. In an attempt to comfort the National Trust's Country House's secretary he was promised that in future he'd improve. Not if he could help it. 'I made an inward vow,' he wrote, 'that there never will be a next time.'[21] Lees-Milne was far more comfortable at his club, Brooks's, and at the dinner parties given by Emerald Cunard and Sibyl Colefax. Not only did he find the company more sympathetic, surely he was also better fed.

'The food at Wallington was disgusting, even when it wasn't wartime,' Lady Brunner told me later as she served me a delicious strawberry tart in her huge, warm kitchen at Greys Court. 'And the house was terribly cold.'

'What I would say about all the Trevelyans, you know,' Lees-Milne told me, 'is they're so high-minded that they're not quite human beings.'

As I travelled around Britain in my own rattle-trap car, which happily only once broke down, or as it sometimes happened in London, arrived for interviews with Lords on my own push-bike (my methods of locomotion predate my work on this book; I haven't been imitating James Lees-Milne), I met other people who had known Lady Trevelyan and everyone, except Lees-Milne, had warm feelings towards her. Peter Orde, the first chairman of the North-East Regional Committee which oversaw the management of Wallington after Sir Charles died, was among them. He told me the following curious story that puts the National Trust in the position of having been rather more high-minded – in its way – than she was:

'I don't want to be disloyal to the Trevelyans, many of whom are good friends of mine,' the now elderly Major Orde began, 'but it was a house occupied by an intellectual family who counted much more sentimental connections rather than historic values.

'I remember Lady Trevelyan, a wonderful woman, saying "Now I want to show you the library." And what she wanted to show me was not what books there were there, but a specific book which was Shakespeare, I forget which play, in the special part of the books which came from Lord Macaulay's particular selection. It showed blood stains on the page – he was reading it while shaving.'

To Lady Trevelyan that was the point, of course. What a wonderful and economic way to give Major Orde – and members of the public visiting Wallington – some understanding of her husband's illustrious great-uncle who read, read, read; no time to waste.

'That's charming,' Peter Orde acknowledged. 'I endorse that. But if you're going to open a house to the public, there must always be some fairly drastic rearrangement.' If only people like Peter Orde and all those who have followed him would worry more about what really is being rearranged when the National Trust takes on stately homes and what is drastically altered when it sets about presenting its properties to the public. (See 'Fashions in Fantasy', Chapter 10.)

Death and taxes

Taxation, like ideals and character, also plays a part in the story
of the National Trust. At first glance it appears that the size
of aristocratic land holdings and the size of the National Trust
are inversely proportional; as the former dwindled, the latter
grew large.

Death duties were introduced for the first time in 1894. They
were set at four per cent of the value of what was inherited. That
same year Hill, Hunter and Rawnsley got down to setting out
the structure and aims of the Trust. Like railways, tourism and
land developers, inheritance tax also was a threat to the British
landscape which for so many centuries had been kept intact
with the help of an aristocracy who never abandoned the law
of primogeniture.

The top rate for death duties became fifty per cent in 1930
and the bill for £300,000 that resulted when Philip Kerr became
Lord Lothian made him think about how to keep land and other
possessions from being sold in order to pay such sums. In 1940
death duties were raised to sixty-five per cent and, when the
war ended, the tax went to seventy-five per cent for those in
the highest bracket (estates valued at £1 million or more). And
the cost of looking after old houses was increasing all the time.
Government grants to help repair historically important houses
didn't begin until 1953.

Once death duties were introduced, when a man of property
died, his heir who wanted to keep his country house(s) might
sell a whacking great chunk of the land he'd owned to pay
the taxes. Then when he died the same thing would happen
all over again, reducing further an already shrunken estate.
Its boundaries came closer and closer in towards the house it
existed to support. If the person inheriting an estate happened
to be elderly, the likelihood was that it wouldn't be very long
after he'd settled his tax bill before his heir would have to find

the resources to pay death duties all over again. And on it went. By the time Labour's great scythe of taxation swept across the estates owned by England's aristocracy after the war ended in 1945, it threatened to mince anything the landowners still had left. Without farms or woodlands to provide income, how could the country houses be maintained? Without land left to sell in order to pay for the upkeep of the houses, how could people hold on to their houses any longer? In the decade following the end of the Second World War another 400 country houses were lost.

It might seem that the National Trust was feeding off the sorrows of the aristocracy. But the people who were running it absolutely did not wish to profit from the misery of the class to which they belonged or with whom they identified. The Trust would have preferred the government to help owners keep their estates by adjustments to the tax law. Today people at the Trust say much the same thing and see themselves as allies of the Historic Buildings Association – it would prefer houses to stay in private hands.

But then comes the question: whose?

Those who cherish the national heritage and want to preserve it, who revere fine architecture and the works of art which that have been accumulated over hundreds of years to furnish enormous houses, find themselves easily swept up in the effort to preserve one or another grand house that might otherwise fall into 'unsympathetic' or inept hands. Gold-plated dolphin taps in the bath; carriage lamps every five feet along the drive? To turn a stately home into a tawdry suburbanized villa: well, it would be a kind of rape. Wouldn't it?

James Lees-Milne and I talked about some of these matters when I went to see him at the flat in one of Bath's sweeping curved terraces which he uses as his studio. He lives on the Badminton estate nearby.

In his mid-eighties, nearly six foot tall, with perfect posture and handsome in a wistful sort of way – evidence of the tendency towards melancholy which he records in his books – there is a flickering wickedness that lights up his eyes.

Lees-Milne has written a biography of the rich, imaginative

libertine William Beckford whose house this was early in the nineteenth century. The brown and yellow 'Greek' Library with its marble columns and portrait busts designed for Beckford is sumptuous, stunning. There are grander rooms, this isn't a palace after all. But it's hard to imagine an atmosphere that would be better suited to an aesthete who discovered in himself a passion for architecture 'and the continuity of history that is its mouthpiece,' when still a young man. Now more than sixty years later, James Lees-Milne remains loyal to it and to the way of life that produced the great country houses – some of the finest expression of that continuity in Britain.

James Lees-Milne's mind hasn't gone fuzzy. Nor has his wit. If anything he may be braver now than when he was young. Fully aware that his views are no longer in fashion and that some people will despise him for them while others would guffaw, he is undaunted. This isn't blustering. It's as if he just can't see the point of not being himself. (This ease and the forthrightness it evokes may be one of the certifiable blessings of age – at least for the elderly.)

With neither blush nor apology, James Lees-Milne softly but clearly informed me that 'the squirarchy was probably the most successful form of local government that's ever been devised'.

And James Lees-Milne, along with the other gallants at the National Trust, rode into battle to try to save it. But were they knights or fools? Was the National Trust gravely wounded in the process, or were we, the people on whose behalf the properties are held in trust in perpetuity?

Squires in Wonderland

When the 1st Earl of Londesborough was in residence at the Lodge, his Scarborough house, the servants of this Victorian aristocrat were expected to roll out a red carpet before he or any of his guests set off for the Spa. This was a *mile-long* red carpet; it went over a bridge and on to the sands. The wonder is that he didn't have them blowing trumpets as his party strolled.

Osbert Sitwell, born in 1892, was Lord Londesborough's grandson and visited the Lodge as a child. 'It was pleasant, welcoming, luxurious,' Sitwell writes, 'and the thought never occurred to any of those living in it that it might not be deserved.'[1] From Northumberland to Cornwall, this thought was a stranger in many other grand houses too.

'Power houses' is what the social historian Mark Girouard called these mansions. They were built, frequently at literally ruinous expense, in order to help the men who lived in them feel superior to almost everyone else. All the pictures, the plate, the marquetry furniture, the pictures made for an English show-off's heaven, a place where a man could throw his weight around without necessarily seeming to. It went without saying that the chap to whom it all belonged was more important than his servants, of course. But why stop there? Add to this list many of his guests, neighbours and friends. After all how many of them had a house like his?

A cottage-owner has sleepless nights when he can't meet his

mortgage payments; imagine how despairing and alarmed the owners of great country houses felt, *en masse* practically, during the 1930s and after the Second World War when taxation began to boil things down to nothing. Their spirits sank with their bank balances and the way they lived in their houses began to reflect this.

Whole wings were shut off, the furniture and chandeliers were covered by dust cloths. The roof – well, bring out the buckets when it rains. And like their fellow men who lived in tenements, though without this producing much sense of kinship in either direction, struggling owners of country houses began making the kitchen their domestic headquarters.

In the late 1960s Philip Yorke III, the bachelor-owner of Erddig – a decaying, romantic seventeenth-century mansion in Clwyd – began thinking he might like to leave the property to the National Trust. Patrick Gibson who was then on its Executive Committee went with his wife on a visit to look it over. Yorke, who'd inherited from his older bachelor brother Simon, was last in the line of a family who had owned Erddig since 1733. 'It was the most fabulous place with the most wonderful furniture and the sheep wandering into the drawing room from the lawn,' recalls Lord Gibson. (Made a life peer in 1975, he was chairman of the National Trust from 1977 to 1986.)

When Erddig became the property of the National Trust and opened to visitors in 1978, the well-documented history of its downstairs life was made a feature of its presentation to the public, but at the time of the Gibsons' visit there were far too few servants to look after this vast, sagging house. (And sagging it was; coal having been excavated beneath it.) Philip Yorke did his best, in his own unique fashion. At night, for instance, he roamed the mansion, rotating the rooms in which he slept in an attempt to put potential burglars from nearby Wrexham off the scent. And just in case that didn't work, he kept a gun by his side.

During their visit, Yorke invited the Gibsons to stay the night. There was Mother's bedroom . . . or perhaps they would prefer Father's? The beds, Lord Gibson noted, had not been made since Philip's parents had died – possibly in them – many years before. The Gibsons did not accept the invitation but they did stay to tea.

Though there were many opulent, if neglected, rooms at Erddig, Philip Yorke did not lead his guests to an elegant tea in one of them. Quite the reverse: into the kitchen they went. Lord Gibson still remembers it vividly though decades have passed: the three of them had sipped their tea 'with his washing, his personal washing – *pants* – strung on a line from one corner of the kitchen to another, dripping down on to this table where we sat.'

Undoubtedly Philip Yorke was eccentric, but the way he lived at Erddig departed from the more conventional practice of besieged country house owners more in degree than kind. Like starving beasts, these great dwellings were beginning to feed on their masters for want of enough nourishment to stay alive.

James Lees-Milne might be enthralled by the squirarchy; servants were less so. When given alternatives, they'd bolted. About the time the National Trust was founded, no other occupation had more people in it than domestic service: these servants made up sixteen per cent of the United Kingdom's work force. But numbers were not a measure of the work's popularity.[2] The hours were far too long; the respect far too little. The children of servants did not want to follow in their parents' footsteps. The number of people in service, most of them female, kept dwindling.

There were about a million servants at the outbreak of the Second World War; by its end, 'downstairs' was merely a skeleton staff, if that. In the glass houses and the stables there was often nobody at all. There were, perhaps, a quarter of a million servants at the start of the 1950s; a decade later there were fewer than 100,000.

It's hard to be believe now in a world where dishwashers, vacuum cleaners and microwave ovens are commonplace, and a large country house like West Wycombe Park can be run with the help of a woman from the village who comes in during the day, but one reason some owners of grand houses decided to make them over to the National Trust was that they didn't believe it was possible to go on living in them without large numbers of staff to serve them. And considering how some of them had been brought up, it probably wasn't.

Lady Sitwell, though she had three children, 'could not even fasten her shoe-laces', according to her eldest son. (She did however prove to be exceedingly capable when it came to spending money.) And indeed Sir Francis Dashwood, talking about the early days of the National Trust's ownership of West Wycombe Park just after the Second World War, says the upstairs rooms were littered with his mother's clothes. Having always had a lady's maid before, Helen Dashwood couldn't change her ways. She simply left her clothes wherever she dropped them. Socialism didn't make for greater practicality: Mary, Lady Trevelyan 'didn't know how to dust a table', says one of her children. Nor could she boil the proverbial egg.

In retrospect it seems bizarre that people were so incapable of looking after themselves in the most rudimentary ways. And it wasn't only the women. When Sir Francis talks about his father selling off most of the 200 houses in West Wycombe village (for about £6,000 in 1934) or giving 999-year leases on one swathe of land after another in order to scrape together a few shillings a year in rent, he doesn't appear to be criticizing. To him his father had no choice. 'There was no cash capital anywhere,' Sir Francis explains. Well then, why didn't his father go out and earn some money? A completely natural question in another context, but in this one it has so little connection with what was thought possible as to sound scatterbrained.

Sir John Dashwood was relieved when he unloaded West Wycombe Park on the National Trust. The house had been in his family since 1698 but he'd been raised to think it hideous and, as if that weren't enough, it was so expensive to run.

There were many other owners of impressive houses as worried about the cost of keeping them as Sir John Dashwood but some had stronger attachments to their ancestral homes and greater admiration for their beauty. Such men, therefore, could not feel cheerful about the thought that they might have no other choice but to give their houses and estates to the National Trust.

The loss of power, of stature, of being able to lord it over the neighbours, the anxiety about how one was going to cope on one's own, as well as the sense of having failed the family – forebears and heirs – all this must have made the men who began talking about transferring their country houses to the National Trust a shaky, dispirited, unnerved lot. What a sad and sorry parade shuffled towards the negotiating table.

But not at all.

Donors-to-be often proved to be a buoyant group, full of hidden strengths. It was the men of the National Trust who evidently turned up damp with nerves and trembling with eagerness. But surely it was donors who had everything to lose and the National Trust, nothing really.

Yet Lord Esher and James Lees-Milne behaved like a couple of insecure girls eager for love when it came to the advances made by donors-to-be. They were neither confident nor detached. Instead they were keen to be found desirable; jittery lest they be rebuffed. In fact they appear to have been so anxious to save Britain's grand country houses – and the life lived in them – that it never occurred to them that theirs was a strong position from which to bargain.

Very few donors were so distracted by their misery or so high-minded in their purpose that they failed to see the advantage this gave them, or to take it.

What a splendid arrangement the Country Houses Scheme must have appeared to some of them: you give away (or sell) your grand house, yet you stay on living in it while the new landlord pays almost every bill. Let the skies open. There will no longer be a regiment of pails and pans set out across the Persian carpets to catch the drops as they descend from the library ceiling. (At Erddig, basins and a chamber-pot caught the rainwater as it passed from the ceiling through the canopy of the State Bed.) A new roof will be provided by the new owner – no matter if the cost is a quarter of a million. As for an endowment, if Esher and Lees-Milne really fell for a place and its donor seemed unable to give one, that could be left to worry about later. And even when endowments were given, the Trust didn't work out the sums that it would need to run these houses with a hard head or much foresight.

(In 1988, twelve years after the Marquess of Anglesey arranged for the National Trust to become owners of Plas Newydd, his family home with its wonderful views on to the Menai Straits and over to Snowdownia, a quarter of a million pounds is precisely what its new roof cost. Lord Anglesey had provided an endowment for Plas Newydd but the income from it wasn't nearly enough to cover such an expense. And in any event, the OPEC oil crisis which contributed to the inflation of the 1970s had intervened.

David Hancock, administrator of Shugborough in Staffordshire which is owned by the Trust but leased to the County Council, points out that when the lease was signed in 1966 'you could have probably maintained this estate and most of the buildings on it for about £120,000 a year.' Whereas in the mid-1990s 'the running costs of this estate are £1.3 million and rising'.

Plas Newydd in fact was the last property to be handed over to the Trust before it adopted the endowment formula worked out by Roger Chorley in 1978. A member of its Finance Committee at the time, Lord Chorley became chairman of the Trust in 1991. The complex formula establishes the sum that the charity needs to look after a property without running up debts in the process. Among the things it attempts to take into account are repairs that will have to be done, running costs and potential changes in the value of money as a result of inflation. According to Lord Anglesey, had the Chorley Formula existed when he gave Plas Newydd in 1976, he would have been asked to endow it with about £400,000, whereas in fact he supplied less than a quarter of that. By 1978, of course, a large number of under-endowed country houses were already in the possession of the charity, about which more will be said.)

The full burden for preservation – decoration and landscaping too – fell to the National Trust almost every time it took on a country house. It was the freeholder after all. The donor-tenants were not generally assessed for such repairs.

It was all like a nursery tale: a gifted sprinkler of magic

dust would appear, stretch out an arm, and Whoosh! Like a filmed explosion in reverse, a damp and collapsing, cobweb-covered pile of stones would suddenly become a sturdy palace filled with glowing ormolu and shimmering damask. Every diamond-shaped pane of glass would be back in the windows. And nothing would be done on the cheap; the National Trust does not use gold paint where gold leaf is the proper material to apply instead.

Not every donor has in fact lived happily ever after as will be seen. But in some cases it wasn't for lack of trying. Many donors of country houses made astonishingly good deals with the National Trust.

Sir Charles Trevelyan was merely the first potential giver of an imposing house who expressed the wish to stay on in it. (Granted.) And the wish that his wife should live there after him. (Granted.) Rent free. (Ditto.) And one of the children should follow Mary if he or she should choose, and that child was found suitable. Yes, of course, to that wish too. And after that; discussions about who will follow Patricia Jennings at Wallington and on what terms are in the preliminary stages.

As Sir Charles's donation encouraged others to believe that the National Trust, tiny, amateur and – it must be said – rather beneath them one way and another, was nevertheless capable enough to look after important properties, his wishes inspired them to do some fancy wishing, too. These were very often granted.

'There were some terrible terms accepted by the National Trust,' says Major Peter Orde, who in the late 1950s volunteered to look after its properties in the north-east of England. Houses surrounded by immense parks and huge estates were given with only an apron of land – the donor kept the rest for himself; agreements gave families the right 'to live on for ever, practically, in the house'. And, at that, 'open it one day a week'.

Knole, Wightwick Manor, Little Moreton Hall, Antony, Sizergh Castle, Mount Stewart House, Charlecote Park are only a few of the major properties that went to the National Trust with generous rights of residency agreed. Sissinghurst Castle, where Vita Sackville-West and Harold Nicolson created one of the most famous – and surely now one of the most visited – gardens in England, is another.

Sissinghurst belonged to Vita Sackville-West. She told her son Nigel that she was going to leave it to him. Nigel Nicolson could not imagine that he'd ever be able to afford its upkeep, and asked his father (who was vice-chairman of the National Trust, after all) to find out how Vita would feel if he later made it over to the charity.

A grand jamais! was Vita Sackville-West's reply. She felt that the inheritance of Knole, where she'd been raised, had been 'lost' to her because she was female; her bitterness about that was transferred to the National Trust when it became Knole's owner in 1946. In spite of this, on inheriting Sissinghurst in 1962 Nigel judged that he had no choice and negotiations with the Treasury for its transfer to the NT began. They went on for four years.

'I lived in terror,' he says. If during that time a crack had appeared in the sixteenth-century tower, the cost of repairing it would have ruined him. Nevertheless, when it came to his discussions with the National Trust, these terrors did not make him quaver. He had a *grand jamais* himself. 'I never would have given it to the Trust,' he says firmly, 'if I couldn't have gone on living here rent free.' (His son Adam will also be the beneficiary of this 'wish'.)

When the third generation appears, the Trust seems to feel enough time has passed to review tenancy arrangements. It says its policy is that a donor's granddaughter or great nephew will be asked to pay 'a fair market-value rent'. What can they possibly mean?

How is any rent officer going to calculate the fair market value of, say, the family apartments at Knole – a 300-room house that covers almost four acres? It is set in an enormous deer park which they own. And there are twenty-six acres of a private garden which, by the way, is open for a total of sixteen days during the National Trust season. The Sackvilles, therefore, can swim in their pool undisturbed almost any time they choose, weather permitting.

How would the 'market' for such a place be defined? Interested relations? The homeless rich? Directors of multinational companies? Anglophile multimillionaire Americans or Arabs with strings of oil wells and racehorses? And even if a 'fair market rent' could be set, what senior official of the National Trust would try to collect it from such families?

'Certainly Lord Sackville should not be asked to pay the fair market price for living at Knole,' says Martin Drury, the deputy director general. Taken aback by the suggestion, he adds, 'That would be quite wrong.'

At some of the houses the National Trust owns, its gentlemanly approach extends not only to the minimal amount of rent its donors, or their heirs, should have to pay, but it seems to feel that it must serve as the protector of the (ex-) owner's privacy too.

'Preservation comes before access' has become the National Trust motto. This was the almost inevitable outgrowth of the change that took place in the 1930s when its properties became more interesting to the people working with the charity than did the public. But of course the conflict between the goal of preserving its possessions and letting people use them has been a problem for the people running the Trust from the very beginning. There was Octavia's Hill's struggle with Ashbee and his boys, described in Chapter 1, for instance. And even before the Trust was set up, its founders were struggling to find ways to open land to ramblers. But finding a resolution for such problems has never been easy even among like-minded people. In 1886, for example, when Hardwicke Rawnsley tried to gather support for a commission to investigate the issue of public rights-of-way, William Morris refused. 'My firm opinion', he wrote back, 'is that we shall be quite helpless against the landowners as long as there is any private ownership of land.'[3] To Morris only a Marxist revolution would solve the problem. Hill, Hunter and Rawnsley, however, opted for the National Trust.

Had the Trust so changed as a result of the Country Houses Scheme, that those people who had given it property were now going to demand that the public be kept off – and be allowed to get away with it?

The Trust has a reasonably persuasive argument when it

asserts that if access to its farm land isn't controlled, productivity will suffer and its farm tenants may go bust. But how can it possibly rationalize restricted access to its country houses? The only thing they produce is income from people who pay to visit and that is non-existent when the houses are closed. Yet restricted access there is.

During the NT season, the public is welcomed to Greys Court outside Henley-on-Thames, less than a hour from London, for four hours on Monday, Wednesday and Friday afternoons. None of these twelve hours falls on a weekend – precisely the time when most people who live in a large city are likely to want to go out into the countryside and explore. Yet there is nothing mean-spirited or overtly selfish about Lady Brunner, widow of its donor Sir Felix.

Lady Brunner is an intelligent, handsome and amusing woman in her early nineties. She enjoys getting the house ready on the days when the public does come. 'It's like being a stage manager,' says the granddaughter of the celebrated actor Henry Irving. Apparently it simply never occurred to Lady Brunner that the opening at Greys Court may be a little on the mean side.

'I hadn't thought of that before,' she replies when the point is put to her. 'But it *is* like having your cake and eating it too.' She is not dining alone.

Helen, Lady Dashwood, who could not hang up her own clothes, nevertheless knew how to make a deal. When the National Trust presented her husband Sir John with the opening hours they proposed for West Wycombe's first season in 1945, Lady Dashwood baulked. The house to be opened two week-days all year long? The park open every Saturday and Sunday – the shooting season included? Oh no, this was not on.

Lady Dashwood reminded James Lees-Milne and Lord Esher that in their 1936 pamphlet inviting owners to join the Trust's country house scheme, fifty opening days a year was the figure suggested. Now here they were – merely nine years and a world war later – doubling that for West Wycombe.

This was the National Trust's idea of a compromise: the lush landscaped park with its lake, islands, bridges and temples, would be open for a total of twenty-eight days between 1

May and 30 August. Since 1945 when it opened as a National Trust property, the grounds at West Wycombe have never welcomed members of the National Trust – or the public – after 1 September. The right to disturb the pheasants has been reserved for the Dashwoods and their invited guests – seemingly in perpetuity.

Flamboyant Sir Francis Dashwood, who inherited his father's title as premier baronet in 1966, along with the contents of the Palladian villa and its surrounding estate, lives at West Wycombe Park as if it belonged to him still. He has both the temperament and the money to pull this off.

By his own reckoning Sir Francis has contributed 'massive' amounts to the upkeep of the property. This includes about £25,000 a year which is income from West Wycombe caves across the road, property of Sir Francis Dashwood. The house is never open to the public on Saturdays and the park, of course, is closed from the beginning of September until April. 'It makes little sense to go to all this effort,' Sir Francis explains, 'unless our friends, too, can enjoy it.' But members of the National Trust, contributors to its appeals and people leaving bequests to the charity could say the same, surely.

There are other National Trust houses that recoil from having visitors also. (Though there used to be many more. For a report on the typhoon that swept in this change, see Chapter 4.) Among the visitor-shy are Horton Court on the edge of the Cotswolds (open two days a week from two till six p.m.); Ascott, where Sir Evelyn de Rothschild makes his home in Buckinghamshire (closed all of June, July and August); Gunby Hall in Lincolnshire which opens its doors to the public one day a week for four hours; and Dudmaston in Lincolnshire which manages two afternoon openings.

There are explanations, and a different one, in every case. Sometimes, as at West Wycombe Park, a sense of ownership continues decades after legal ownership came to an end. Often the arrangement seems to be an echo of the tone established during the original negotiations. Take, for example, Antony, which *The National Trust Handbook* describes as 'one of Cornwall's finest early 18th century houses'. In a very pretty spot above the Tamar estuary across from Plymouth, it was made over to the Trust by Sir John Carew Pole in 1961. It is open three, midweek, afternoons, though at the height of the season access to it 'leaps up' by almost thirty per cent when Antony, in one of England's most popular places for people on holiday, opens on Sunday afternoons.

Sir John Carew Pole was a military man (Coldstream Guards), a courtier (a gentleman-at-arms for twenty-two years), and a shrewd horse trader. Antony went to the Trust with less than thirty acres of gardens while the family held on to the eighteenth-century woodlands at the foot of the garden and a great deal more beyond that. They kept the contents of the house, too.

Michael Trinick, since retired, was in charge of the Devon and Cornwall regions of the National Trust at the time. At the Trust he is still called 'Mr Cornwall' because he acquired so much for his patch. But when it came to Antony: 'I remember the negotiations about the endowment,' he recalls with a twinkle in his eyes and a rueful sigh. 'Sir John pretended he'd got nothing at all.'

Trinick was no pushover but he found himself in the position of an Italian tax collector trying to ferret out sources of wealth that might not be altogether visible.

Sir John, after much apparent struggle, managed to piece together an endowment. 'He got in the Pilgrim Trust,' recalls Trinick. 'They produced some money. And the Historic Buildings Council. Then,' Trinick continues, smiling, 'a man named Lascelles, being in the same regiment as Sir John, produced some money too.'

Included in the endowment package were a couple of tenanted farms. These were not to be declared inalienable; if ever there were the need, the Trust could sell them to raise capital. Meanwhile they would produce rent.

Sir John wondered . . . when the leases on those farms expired, would the Trust give him a chance to buy the farms back?

To the Trust this request didn't seem worth objecting to. After all, Sir John had no money. So the charity agreed. Later, when the tenancies came up, Sir John was there and ready to pounce.

'Of course he'd got lots of money!' Trinick chuckles. The Trust thereby lost control of the land and the income – or cash if they'd been sold – those farms would have produced.

Sir John Carew Pole died in 1993. He left an estate of more than £3 million. His land at Jupiter Point on the far side of Antony's woodland was bequeathed to the Carew Pole Garden Trust (and therefore is administered by the family, not the NT). Visitors to Antony who want to take the extensive woodland walk beyond the Trust's garden and stroll down to the water are invited to do so. There is an extra charge of £1, payable to the family's Trust.

Upstairs in the house, Sir Richard Carew Pole's boots are on the bedroom floor; one of his shirts on the chair. This isn't artful contrivance: Antony is a family home, though they frequently are elsewhere. Sir Richard in London, the boys at school, Lady Pole is lady-in-waiting to the Princess Royal.

Why, then, is Antony a house in such a favoured spot, open only twelve hours a week?

'But the Carew Poles *live* there,' is the Trust's anguished response. 'Their bedrooms are on view. Would you want people walking through your house all the time?'

But the house isn't theirs; Antony belongs to the nation, a fact you'd suppose the National Trust would find easier to remember.

Men like Sir Richard Carew Pole and Sir Francis Dashwood can, of course, help the National Trust in any number of useful ways in their respective corners of government, court and/or high finance. Then, too, they contribute to the cost of operating the houses in which they live. In fact the Trust doesn't have to spend anything on West Wycombe Park. Nevertheless, the balance seems all wrong. The people running the National Trust today appear to identify as much with the inhabitants of these grand houses as did James Lees-Milne and Lord Esher: which is to say, that they don't seem sufficiently inclined to line themselves up with the rest of us. Grand houses that belong to the National Trust ought to be open throughout its visiting season.

Those at the top of the Trust believe that donors should be

treated gently. For example, Julian Prideaux, the chief agent whose job it is to oversee all the people who work on the land and in the historic houses, and who is therefore one of the most influential members of the headquarter's staff, has great sensitivity to the predicament of donors.

'Sometimes they're misunderstood,' Prideaux explains, 'especially by newcomers to the Trust who think, "well you know they've given their property away; it's now the Trust's and we can do whatever we like with it." I don't take that view at all.

'I've got tremendous time for donors and their families,' he continues. 'They've given so much to us because they want to ensure that it exists in perpetuity. They've got so much knowledge; so much enthusiasm. O.K., they'll be a bit prickly occasionally, but so what?'

These men who were making the best of their misfortune, might some of them be people to sympathize with rather than to scorn? After all, the NT seems to have indulged donors excessively. As a result we may feel more contempt for them than they deserve and less for the Trust than is its due. The National Trust's deference to people with titles which Lady Mander found so objectionable surely hasn't gone away. Not every donor was self-indulgent, grasping or high-handed. Unacceptable as it is that there should be any, it's only a relatively few National Trust houses which close their doors and turn their backs to the public. And do we want these houses empty? If we're candid about our own feelings or kind to those of our friends, a lot of people like to visit country houses which have their family still in residence. In this regard we like having our cake and eating it too. While we feel we own the properties, we also like to rub up against the 'owners' when we visit. Or at least get a good look.

'Oooh,' a grey-haired matron whispers loudly to her friend as they come out of the National Trust shop into the courtyard at Knole. 'There's Lord Sackville.' And indeed there stands a rather pale fellow wearing a quilted jacket and gum boots with a black labrador at his feet. His social position and connection with the house make him seem more prepossessing – and it warmer – than either might appear on its own.

Whether it's Sir Francis Dashwood, Lady Brunner, Nigel Nicolson – we do seem to like having fancy families on the premises. Looking around other people's houses, which can be boring or even macabre if they are uninhabited, has some of the appeal of reading biography when the houses are lived in. And even the most innocuous revelation – seeing the circular stain on a table cloth made by a recently removed cup of coffee – can make a whole room come alive. One of the deadly things about the not-lived-in National Trust mansion is that no music comes down a distant hall; the refrigerator door never slams, no children have left their toys to worry about tripping over.

Not only do houses often have a more vital, attractive quality when they are inhabited; not only do people enjoy the potential for 'celebrity' watching or snooping in a genteel way, there's also the matter of money. Houses with people living in them attract visitors; visitors mean money from public admissions, sales at shops and tea rooms. The more money brought in this way, the more goes to the country house where it is raised and the less money the National Trust has to take from what it might otherwise spend on the countryside or coast.

The National Trust spends a whopping £33 million a year looking after the houses it charges people to visit, while it spends £25 million on its 600,000 acres of countryside and 533 miles of coast. This, we're told, is not because the people running the Trust think houses are more important; it simply cannot help itself. Big, old buildings are frightfully expensive to keep up. But should anyone fail to accept this explanation as a complete one and continue to criticize the Trust for spending such a disproportionate sum on its houses, an argument is presented that presumably is meant to silence objections once and for all. This is its gist: the National Trust recruits eighty-seven per cent of its members at properties and of these, seventy per cent join at houses and gardens. A mere eight per cent sign on at shops and information centres and only a fraction more (nine per cent) at the coast and in the countryside. Since more than a third of the Trust's annual income comes from subscriptions, it's obvious that houses – through visits and recruitment – are providing a lot of the money the Trust has to spend each year, even if they greedily consume more than their fair share of what is taken in. When Wightwick was accepted in 1937, 6,500 people were subscribers to the NT; in 1947 after the arrival of the first group of impressive country houses, the number of members had more than doubled and a half a million people were paying to visit these properties.

The trust now has 10 million people a year coming to its properties, taking into account only those places where a charge is made for visiting. Of these, 6 million are members. Which means there are 4 million who pay at the gate and, allowing for a percentage of repeaters, a good couple of million at least therefore of potential recruits. Then, too, there are the ten per cent or so of old members who have not renewed. They might think about changing their minds, and there are millions more who visit the coast and countryside. Maybe houses are not only a huge drain but a great money maker, too, just as the Trust claims. However–

Of the 500 or so recruiters hired by the Trust to work during the visiting season, only a handful can be found at its open space properties. It's awfully hard to sign up when there's no one around to hand you a form. (Where open space recruitment has been tried, it has not failed, see Chapter 9. For years the Trust's most successful recruiter worked from a Land-Rover in the Lakes.)

Obviously the charity could make a good deal more if it used recruiters at its countryside properties. That money could go towards looking after the landscape and the coast. Its recruiting policy hasn't been dazzlingly astute. The fact remains that as a result of the agreements made between donors and the National Trust since the Country Houses Scheme began, a lot of money has been needed to keep them going. But though no one could have imagined it at the time, not least of all because they weren't interested in the subject, the country houses attracted both new members and the public.

The deals made with donors of country houses, beginning with those overseen by Lord Esher and James Lees-Milne, were often so favourable to the tenants-to-be that it's almost impossible not to feel resentment, even anger towards the fat cats who took advantage of the charity. Yet often they were encouraged to ask for as much as they fancied and a number were given all they asked for because no one who objected found it possible to stand his ground. But while some are still purring and licking the cream from their whiskers, others have taken to hissing, and a number have fled. And it may be that, with important exceptions, we really haven't done as badly as a result of the Country Houses Scheme, as it's easy to suppose. There are donors, or their heirs, who on balance have been very generous to the nation. To start with the last category first.

A family keepsake

As Easter weekend approached and the 1994 National Trust visiting season began, Waddesdon Manor re-opened to the public after a four-year closure. The first phase of the restoration of the spectacular home Ferdinand de Rothschild had created for himself in 1889 was complete. Though the second phase, which includes rooms never before open to the public, would take another year to get ready, the gain to everyone concerned was obvious at once; the Buckinghamshire château glowed.

Lord Rothschild assumed control of running the turreted nineteenth-century extravaganza soon after the death of his cousin Dorothy in 1988. As widow of James de Rothschild who had bequeathed the mansion to the National Trust in 1957, she had led the management committee which oversaw the running of the château. Obituaries reported that the childless Dorothy de Rothschild left more than £90 million – perhaps the largest estate ever registered in England. Lord Rothschild was one of her principal heirs. He inherited the large estate surrounding Waddesdon Manor as well as the Eythrope estate four miles away, originally bought by Alice de Rothschild, Ferdinand's devoted sister, and later the home of Mrs James, as Dorothy de Rothschild is familiarly known.

'Without going into details about my cousin's financial affairs, which she would not have liked,' Lord Rothschild began when I stuck my nose in, 'there were and are Trusts whose resources can go to support Waddesdon Manor. Although they don't have to.' He then added that, 'I am delighted to have been able to contribute from my own resources.' Lord Rothschild was not prepared to say anything more on the subject of that money, the National Trust and himself. As for how many millions he has spent to date restoring Waddesdon from top to bottom, inside and out; aviary, car parks gardens, fountains, rebuilding the dairy: 'It is surely more interesting to talk about all the changes at Waddesdon,' Lord Rothschild replied, 'than to satisfy people's curiosity about money.'

Numbers in the region of £13.5 million have been quietly mentioned when the subject of the final cost of restoring Waddesdon comes up. There are the now almost routine matters of paying attention to rewiring, heat and humidity, preservation of textiles, security. Even smoke alarms have been installed in between carving on the ceilings. Fibre optic lighting has been used to illuminate the glass cases which display the fanciful work of jewellers who improvised on the shapes of large baroque pearls, turning them into a menagerie of animals with snouts or tails or fins of gold. The display of its many other collections, which have been added to, has been redesigned, a new family museum created.

'In the nineteenth century I think my family built altogether sixty major houses. Now there is only one great house that's left to show what my family did then; to show their collections. My main interest is that it should remain in its full glory.'

In pursuing his goal, Lord Rothschild has taken charge completely. The words National Trust do not appear on the business card of Col. Anthony Crawford, Waddesdon's administrator, which is instead headed 'The Alice Trust'. Everyone from the marketing staff to the caterers and gardeners is employed by Lord Rothschild directly. Rosamund Griffin, the curator of its collections, orginally employed by Mrs James, is in her knowledge, devotion and commitment both an exceptional asset for Waddesdon and at the same time a reminder of what the National Trust, at the treasure houses it manages, lacks. It simply has no one of her calibre on its paid staff at any of its properties.

Jacob Rothschild has remodelled the wine cellars and installed a wine shop selling only wines in which the family has an interest. While he doesn't foresee Waddesdon Manor making a profit, Lord Rothschild certainly aims to narrow the gap between what's gone out and what's incoming.

It is Lord Rothschild's intention that visitor numbers should go up. He intends to achieve this largely by making the grounds more engaging and attractive. The admission charge for the public visitors to house and grounds is £7.00, and £7.50 buys a family ticket to the grounds alone. A family season ticket for the grounds however is only £15. The National Trust has actually agreed to rebate to Waddesdon Manor a sum equal to two thirds of the public admission fee for every Trust member who visits. (A rebate of one third is standard almost everywhere else.)

Obviously Lord Rothschild has taken charge of the presentation of Waddesdon Manor. But what are the rest of us losing by it? The property costs the National Trust nothing. There are not the sort of public opening restrictions found at Antony or Ascott and the shops and tea room are one of a kind rather than one in a series. If Lord Rothschild is prepared to do all this to make Waddesdon Manor into a grand monument to his family, the public doesn't seem to be the loser in the exchange.

Nor is the public the loser at Croft Castle in Hereford, though the undertakings of Lord Croft and his sister Mrs Uhlman are on a more modest scale; virtually anything would be if compared with Waddesdon.

Reclaiming the past

'The Trust like you better if you are rich,' says Lord Croft, nearing eighty, who has been its tenant since 1957 when he arranged for the charity to have Croft Castle. It's safe to say that despite his losses at Lloyd's, Michael Croft is on the rich side still.

The Castle has been in Lord Croft's family since it was built in the sixteenth century, but there was a break in this tradition in the eighteenth century when it was sold to pay debts. It became Croft property again in 1923.

Though he speaks rather slowly, Lord Croft's conversation ranges from the paintings of Oscar Kokoschka to the writings of C.G. Jung. When talking about the education of the women among whom he was raised, he explained that they were not sent to university. 'That was for doctors' daughters,' he revealed.

'Did you think so too?' I asked Lord Croft when I had recovered from culture shock.

'Oh no,' he answered. 'I'm not narrow.'

Lord Croft was being candid not vain. As he was when, in talking about relations with the landlord, he said, 'They'll always stretch a point for someone who's rich enough to make it worthwhile.' He was speaking not only about himself, but also of his widowed sister Mrs Uhlman. (As a family member who contributed towards Croft's endowment, she also has a flat in the castle.)

Diana Uhlman, slightly older than her brother – 'the sort of woman who bosses everyone around,' as one observer described her, is likeable just the same. (Or maybe for that very reason.) She is an enthusiastic, dedicated student of Croft's history, a subject on which she's certain she's far more accurate than her brother. And – having enough money to be high-handed in the cause of improving Croft when she chooses to be – she gets away with it.

[97]

When the National Trust thought Croft needed a larger car park, it decided that the right place for it was in the derelict walled garden. Mrs Uhlman didn't approve and, without consulting them, she had herbaceous borders and even a vineyard planted. 'One year in three, Croft, gets a decent vintage,' her brother says crisply.

Diana Uhlman gives the National Trust £10,000 a year. It goes a long way towards paying for the upkeep of the garden she went ahead and had planted without their permission; because it is a substantial contribution, it therefore goes quite a distance towards keeping relations with the landlord cordial.

Lord Croft, even more than his sister, works to improve the castle. He buys furniture, china, pictures. Clearly he's devoted to the place. Yet he very nearly didn't take it when it came to him.

In 1947, ownership of the castle on the edge of Wales, along with fifty-four acres, made its zigzagging way to him. But, in an uncanny echo of the question James Lees-Milne and Co. were asking about other grand houses at the very same time, Lord Croft wondered, 'Should I accept it?'

'Don't do it,' his mother advised him. 'It's seductive but not worth it. The time and effort . . . it will take you away from other things.'

Lord Croft, who was just back from the war, had two young children and was attempting to establish himself professionally, could see her point. But such a compelling distraction would have advantages for him, too, because tragically, his wife had gone mad.

Lord Croft not only took on the castle, he managed to buy back the rest of the estate; more than 1,000 acres. Nevertheless after four years he sold it to a cousin. He felt that to do right by Croft was more than he could manage financially. 'I was never really wealthy enough to do it justice,' he declares. However, when the cousin died and his widow started selling off its contents, Lord Croft stepped in again and negotiated the agreement that brought the castle to the National Trust. 'For somebody like myself who is very fond of conservation it seemed the best way to get the place looked after for a long period of time.'

Lord Croft doesn't hide the fact that 'it isn't the same as being your own master or running your own estate'. But on the whole he readily accepts that. Despite the lavish terms they were given, quite a few donors found out that they could not.

In the early 1990s James Lees-Milne went around England preparing a book about fourteen of the houses he'd helped acquire for the National Trust decades before – Stourhead, Knole, Wallington, West Wycombe Park among them. He discovered that despite all that was done and all that was wished for, 'in only two do the families live as in days of yore . . .'[4]

What sent so many families packing?

Some couldn't cope with the change. 'I think it's an absolute shock to the family when it happens,' observes one of the Trust's volunteers. 'A lot of hostility has to be worked out before they can see why things are done in a way that they never were before.'

Not every donor or heir is a showman, of course; some don't like being ogled. But in many cases donors, or their heirs, who became tenants of the National Trust and leave or begin plotting their departures have got fed up with being bossed around. Though sometimes the complaints of tenants can seem pretty petty.

'Imagine being told, "You can't swim in the moat!"' one outraged tenant explodes. Imagine having one. Not many who work for the landlord do. Certainly most of the holders of NT membership cards don't.

Other things which seem equally small aren't necessarily petty at all. When, for example, during the months when the castle is open, Lord Croft and Mrs Uhlman invite guests to have a glass of sherry in the drawing room before going off to Sunday lunch, the NT insists that the tray with the bottles on it must be removed and hidden away before the public come in at two o'clock. But a tray of bottles on the sideboard, like the whiff of alcohol in the air, would remind people that this castle is still a home as it has been for many hundreds of years. Presumably it's all right to have boots in the bedroom, but in the 'important' rooms all evidence of occupation by men and women must be removed. When the landlord is interfering in this way, both the harassed occupants and the visiting public are the losers.

Landlord tenant relations are more than usually volatile when the tenant is the former owner and the landlord is the National Trust. Some tenants enjoy the contests of will that result; others find it disheartening. And even Lord Belmore, for example, who clearly relishes having the occasional skirmish with the Trust, does so by keeping a bit of distance.

Living in, at one remove

'Only the English would think it's possible to go on living in a house after you've given it away,' says Lord Belmore who makes the point that, having been born in Belfast, he is not. The strategy he's worked out as a tenant of the National Trust fits his notion of his nationality. John Belmore both lives at Castle Coole, his ancestral home in County Fermanagh, and he does not.

Though the National Trust has made a flat for him in one of the two wings that extend from colonnades on either side of this vast eighteen-century mansion, Lord Belmore uses it as his office. He lives with his family in a house in the walled garden. And as far as he's concerned, he wouldn't even live that close to the big house – much as he is attached to it – if he didn't possess almost everything in it.

'If you don't own the contents you might as well get on a Kon-Tiki raft and make for the Sargasso Sea,' Lord Belmore says. For a shy, middle-aged man who speaks with a slight stutter, he likes putting a bit of spin on his words.

'The Trust will listen to me occasionally,' he explains, 'because they know I have an interest in the contents here – in both senses of the word.' Much of the lavish furniture was designed and made for Castle Coole when it was built. The thought of not having it must give the National Trust a good deal of worry, as Lord Belmore is aware.

'It must be like driving a car without a hand brake,' he says. 'I mean if I lost £4 million at Monte Carlo one night,' the National Trust might wake up the next morning to learn that Sotheby's or Christie's was planning an extraordinary auction.

Happily for John, his father Galbraith Belmore, the 7th Earl, was one of the many owners who kept the chattels when their houses went to the National Trust. Sometimes donors did so because they didn't seem valuable enough to bother about, sometimes to provide a future heir, a grandson or great grandson perhaps, with the means of meeting an inheritance tax bill. The assumption was that the government would accept these heirlooms in lieu of all or part of a later bill for death duties because they were integral to the aesthetic and historical importance of a mansion which was already in the possession of the nation. And of course there were the donors who didn't see why they should part with one table or chair more than they absolutely had to. Whatever their motives, their decisions proved to be a boon to their families and an anxiety for the National Trust. Whereas, during the 1970s, inflation reduced the value of securities which had been given earlier as endowments, the market value of chattels has soared. And to make matters even worse, from the point of view of the charity, it is the National Trust that often has to pay the insurance on these now colossally valuable decorations and furnishings.

(Sir Francis Dashwood owns the contents of West Wycombe Park and like Lord Belmore believes it would be impossible to stay on if he didn't. Not only has Sir Francis bought back things for the house that his father earlier sold but he's added fine furniture and pictures too. To make his position still stronger, he owns the architects' drawings and so on which document the history of West Wycombe's contents.

'It's cost me a fortune,' he says. 'I've spent my life doing it really. They're jolly lucky we do all this.'

The National Trust doesn't always seem to feel blessed. There was, for instance, the time Sir Francis put a couple of large paintings he didn't much like up for sale at Christie's. In the Trust's opinion they belonged with the house and so it bought them at the sale. Sir Francis then got a letter from Dame Jennifer Jenkins, the chairman at the time.

'She said, well, we've got these paintings of yours, wouldn't you like them back? And we thought, perhaps it would be a good time to do some serious research into the contents of West Wycombe.' Sir Francis was furious. He wrote back saying 'I sold those paintings because I think they are hideous and I don't want them.' As for their trying to push in – 'And I'm not having any of this other stuff, either,' he told her. Keeping the National Trust away from his archive makes Sir Francis the authoritative intermediary. Along with owning the chattels, this helps keep his life as a tenant bearable. 'You might as well get out if you don't have the contents or money,' he says plainly. 'There's no point staying.'

Since it's always easier to sympathize with a tenant against a landlord, Sir Francis's position seems entirely plausible and if he didn't also use it to keep the house closed to the public as much as he does, it would be entirely sympathetic as well.)

Housed in the walled garden or not, Lord Belmore has been making himself at home at Castle Coole since he returned to live there in 1974. Like Sir Francis and Lord Croft, John Belmore buys art works and objects to add to the mansion. Sometimes he uses the grand rooms for special events; his guests occasionally sleep in the bedrooms. And he amuses himself in a half-serious, half-joking game of jousting with the landlord. When we met at Castle Coole, it was open to the public, and he led me in a game of musical rooms.

We'd be sitting on a sofa talking when, in the middle of a thought he would stop. 'I hear footsteps,' he'd say. 'Let's move.' Into another room we'd go. We'd begin talking again. And then, he'd hear footsteps again. And so it went as we stayed one room ahead of the guide and his tour group. In Northern Ireland, none of the Trust's houses allow free-range scurrying about.

The National Trust began major restoration of the façade of Castle Coole in 1980. The metal cramps holding the blocks of Portland stone in place were falling to bits; every block had to be removed, new cramps put in and the mansion refaced. The job took seven years; the bill was an astonishing £3 million. The National Heritage Memorial Fund gave £1.19 million towards the cost.

(Because it has played a crucial role in some of the major acquisitions made by the Trust through the Country Houses Scheme – 'it is the most important organization we deal with,' says Ian Bollom, the Trust's director of finance – and also because it illustrates one of the many ways in which the Trust though an independent charity often finds itself tightly intertwined with the government, it is worth going into some detail about what the National Heritage Memorial Fund is and how the NHMF works.

The NHMF started out as the National Land Fund, created in 1946 by Hugh Dalton, the new Labour government's chancellor of the exchequer. Set up with £50 million from the sale of surplus military supplies, with its dispersal to be handled by the Treasury, the Land Fund was charged with buying exceptional properties – landscape, coastline and houses – as memorials to the country's war dead. Once the government acquired these properties they were transferred to some agency or institution to look after; frequently the choice was the National Trust.

Though the Land Fund could buy property outright, it was hoped that the money would be used to encourage more transfers of property to the government *in lieu* of death duties. In a process that looks very like the government taking money out of one pocket only to put it in another, the Land Fund would pay the Inland Revenue a sum of money equal to the inheritance tax it 'lost' when a house was taken *in lieu* of death duties. And since they would now benefit along with the donor, this might encourage the Inland Revenue to raise their valuations of the property it was offered to something nearer the market price. In 1947 Cotehele in Cornwall became the first house to go to the National Trust with the Land Fund's aid.

The Treasury, alas, did not prove itself an enthusiastic dispenser of the Land Fund. On the contrary. By 1957, the Fund had been used so little that its value had grown to £60 million. Its income that year was £1,400,000. But instead of the Treasury applying itself to making memorial acquisitions with this money, Peter Thornycroft, the Conservative chancellor, chose to remove £50 million of the Land Fund's capital. Despite this shocking act the Land Fund made contributions to the purchase of exceptional properties. In the country house line alone these included Powis Castle, Hardwick Hall and Erddig – all NT. Then in 1977, Lord Rosebery offered Mentmore and its extraordinary contents, in lieu of £2 million of his bill for death duties. Art dealers, museums, connoisseurs of fine furniture – everyone it seemed wanted Mentmore saved for the nation: everyone except the Treasury, which had the audacity to argue that it couldn't afford it. The Land Fund was worth £18 million at the time. The auction of Mentmore's contents alone brought Lord Rosebery £6 million. Public outrage was followed by uproar. As a result, in 1980 the Land Fund was replaced by the National Heritage Memorial Fund. And while the NHMF gets all its money from the government, it is run by Trustees appointed by the prime minister, and they – not the Treasury – decide how the money is spent.[5]

As the Land Fund did before, the NHMF plays a key role in the National Trust's acquisition of country houses. The first of its big contributions came in 1984 when it gave the Trust £8 million to buy Belton House and its contents in Lincolnshire. In 1991 the NHMF gave the Trust £4 million to buy and help endow Chastleton House in Oxfordshire. And it also contributes towards such expensive repairs as those to the façade of Castle Coole, for example.

While the National Trust is independent of the government because it is a private charity and most of its money comes from other sources, without grants from the government-funded NHMF – and English Heritage too, which for example in 1992 alone gave it £2.5 million towards repairs to the fabric of its historic buildings – the Trust's acquisitions might come to a complete standstill and its properties might begin to decline rapidly. (The connections between the National Trust and the NHMF are not only monetary. For instance, Lord Rothschild who has charge of running Waddesdon is the current chairman of the NHMF; Sir Richard Carew Pole, the heir-in-residence at Antony, and Mrs John Nutting, the

Trust's regional chairman for Thames & Chilterns, are among the NHMF's eleven trustees.)

Changes to Castle Coole's interior were made while the building work was being carried on outside. Eventually all the rooms open to the public were redecorated. 'It cost £40,000 a room,' Lord Belmore reports. In fact the National Trust says it cost £143,469 to do all eleven rooms, many of which are on the small side for a stately home. It seems likely that the cost of redecoration of at least one of Castle Coole's grand rooms might have reached £40,000.

There were bound to be raised eyebrows and the question 'Is this money well spent?' Castle Coole is by far the largest, most impressive house the National Trust owns in Ulster. But County Fermanagh doesn't get many tourists; the overall number of visitors to National Trust properties in the six counties is very low. Castle Ward, for example, in County Down which gets the most people has about 50,000 a year whereas Polesden Lacey, one of the most visited of its houses in England, gets more than 200,000.

By the time all the work at Castle Coole was completed the Trust naturally wanted to attract publicity. Lord Belmore inadvertently gave them quite a lot of help, though not entirely of the kind they were after. He took one look at what the Trust had done to Castle Coole's elegant hall and squawked: 'They've painted it Germolene pink!' As remarks go, this one was all too quotable. He's been wary of talking for publication ever since. But once started on the subject of life as a tenant of the National Trust, he's practically unstoppable.

John Belmore sometimes feels that if only his father had been able to hold on to Castle Coole, he would now be able to afford to maintain it. He'd certainly like to have the kind of control that, say, Lord Rothschild has at Waddesdon. But John Belmore is quick to add, 'it's a very expensive arrangement. Rather like buying your passport from the Soviet authorities in the 1950s.' Opting out as he calls it would mean assuming the cost for all repairs, conservation work and maintenance of Castle Coole, employee salaries, upkeep of the grounds, the heating and insurance bills and so on. A reasonably well-off person might have the illusion that he could afford to take this on as long as someone else is paying for it, only to feel he was going broke as soon as he started writing out the cheques himself. John Belmore is aware of this, but it doesn't stop him from hoping that somehow he'll be able to take over managing Castle Coole from the National Trust. He feels he could do a good job, maybe a better one.

Country life as it's lived around Castle Coole is not 'frightfully efficient or professional', he observes. 'You get things done largely by getting people to do things for you because they actually like doing the job and because they also like you. So you have to build up a rapport. There's something extremely frigid about anything the Trust seems to want to get done,' he continues. 'It's very clinical.'

Castle Coole has been restored by the National Trust to a very high standard. The result, alas, is a mansion that is vast, and majestic in such a clinical way that everything seems sterilized. There isn't even a tea room to warm body and soul. National Trust Enterprises has done its sums; Castle Coole which gets fewer than 20,000 visitors a year can't have one because it wouldn't make a profit.

Lord Belmore carries on amusing himself and hoping that one day he'll have more influence. But he's seen enough to make him feel this is unlikely. 'If the National Trust could', he concludes, 'it would send all the donors and their heirs to Bosnia. Then they could run things their way.'

Lord Scarsdale the donor of Kedleston Hall sometimes feels this has already happened to him. Although he remains on the premises, he has the sense that the National Trust has sent him into exile.

Through a pier glass darkly

Curzons have been living at Kedleston in Derbyshire for 850 years but it is the work the 1st Baron Scarsdale, Nathaniel Curzon, had done to the house in the eighteenth century that makes it of such importance. Kedleston is one of Robert Adam's masterpieces, though he was just starting out on his career and was not the first principal designer to work on it.

Words like treasure house and stately home actually seem to fit Kedleston Hall. Its domed central portion is fronted by columns; classical statues decorate the façade; there is a double curved stair leading to the entrance on the first floor. Two smaller but also substantial wings flare out; they are fronted with columns as well. One of these wings is principally a service area – kitchens, servants rooms etc; the other, the nucleus of the family home. Doors in each connect to the centrepiece: the extravagant rooms for entertaining and impressing guests. And imposing they surely are, especially the sixty-seven by forty-two foot marble hall around which other elaborate chambers – music room, library and so forth – cluster.

Twenty green alabaster columns ring the Hall. Each is twenty-five feet high. Recessed niches hold classically inspired statues; painted panels portray scenes of war. There are no windows; light streaks down from the dome forty feet above. On a cold wet day the effect is chilling in spirit as well as in the flesh. (I've never been colder inside any place.) But when the sun shines, the classical coolness of the Marble Hall becomes transporting and takes the visitor back in time to an earlier more noble age. Nathaniel Curzon must have felt very pleased with himself as he strolled around his majestic new home; confident that visitors would be overwhelmed.

The 1st Viscount Scarsdale, George Nathaniel Curzon, viceroy of India, grew up at Kedleston but lived away from it most of his life. After inheriting it in 1916, this great-great-grandson of Nathaniel Curzon made plans for its modernization and restoration. These were put into action but he died before his intended return.

'We were thinking of putting together a book of their mistakes,' the current Lady Scarsdale said laughing as we had coffee in the pretty first-floor drawing room in the family's wing.

Lord Scarsdale, the 3rd Viscount, was late. Lady Scarsdale, his second wife, chatted. Then a fit man of seventy strode into the room beaming. 'I've been down at Littlewoods,' Francis Scarsdale announced. Two of his horses had raced the day before, ridden by Lester Piggott. He'd been to Derby to have a look at the replay. But however avid he is about his horses, he's more passionate still about his family's great house.

Francis Scarsdale clearly cherishes Kedleston; he loves talking about it and showing it off. He and Helene came to live there in 1969, the year after their marriage. He was invited by his cousin whose home it was. The idea was that he'd learn about the estate, become its manager and be prepared therefore when he inherited. (His cousin's children were all girls.) 'This was a wonderfully happy time,' he says.

Following his cousin Richard's death in 1977, Francis Curzon became Viscount Scarsdale and owner of Kedleston and the wonderfully happy time came to its end. The tax bill was so enormous that decades later he can't recall it exactly. 'Two or three million pounds,' he says vaguely. 'With interest beginning to run at £400 a day.' The memory of that still makes him tremble.

'All our wealth, if you like, was in the house, the contents and the land. There was no money in the kitty,' he confesses. At least nowhere near the amount of stocks and shares or cash to pay millions of pounds in tax and have enough left to live on and look after such a mansion. 'So what the hell do you do?'

Kedleston was a family trust and while Lord Scarsdale was its principal beneficiary he was not sole owner of the property. Some members of the family considered selling it all and dividing up what was left after taxes. But to him that would have been a kind of vandalism.

'Because it was all of a piece,' he says of Kedleston, 'all contemporary at that time, it was terribly important to save it all. I felt that. I was absolutely adamant in trying to find a solution where we could save everything.' And he did.

Kedleston Hall, its most important contents and the park in which it sits was to go to the nation. But it took seven years of negotiating with members of the family and with the government before the arrangement was worked out, which no doubt seemed even longer to him because of that £400 a day.

'The debt was running the whole time, with interest of course. In the end I don't know what the figure was but it was colossal.'

In addition to whatever compensation other parties to the family trust may have required for giving up their share of Kedleston when it was transferred to the nation, and the bill for inheritance tax – plus interest – there was the £6.5 million endowment which the National Trust, applying the newly worked out Chorley Formula, calculated it would need to run the property without going into the red. Altogether this added up to almost £20 million.

As a result of a special grant made to it by the government, the National Heritage Memorial Fund was able to contribute about £13.5 million. Lord Scarsdale, who retained ownership of 4,000 acres of the surrounding estate, gave the contents Robert Adam had designed for Kedleston Hall and he made over the house, the garden and park (800 acres of countryside). He also donated three-quarters of a million pounds' worth of chattels – furniture, silver and the like – and quarter of a million pounds in cash to the National Trust. The Trust put in £1 million from legacies it had received and decided to go ahead and accept Kedleston even though it was still £2 million short of what it needed for an endowment. It would launch an appeal, at that point the largest one in its history, to raise the remaining money.

'I had this great sense of achievement,' he recalls. 'I had saved this lovely place for ever. It's a nice feeling that, if you're proud and love your home as I do.' And, he adds, 'My pride and love of Kedleston is doubly strong, I feel. It's not just family property but property I know something about because I've been involved in running it.'

But it was just this combination of pride, love and experience that have made for some of the problems Lord Scarsdale has had as tenant.

'If I'd lived all my life in London or the north of Scotland and just visited Kedleston occasionally, I'd probably be a happier person because I'd come here for a week or a month and say, "Gosh what a lovely place. Don't they keep it well." Hah, hah, hah!'

Instead the Scarsdales live in what he calls 'the grandest semidetached in the country', and notice: 'Oh my God! Look what they've gone and done now! Why the hell do they do this?' For example:

One autumn evening Lord Scarsdale was out walking in the garden with his labrador. As he approached the orangery he froze. 'God in heaven,' he burst out, 'where's the fountain gone?'

The fountain in question had been at Hackwood where George Nathaniel Curzon had lived for many years in the early part of the twentieth century. When he inherited Kedleston in 1916 and began having improvements made to it, he had the fountain brought over and placed in the garden. It was a Victorian construction; circular, with four columns supporting a stone ring, the whole thing was topped with a domelike affair made of wrought-iron. Obviously the Trust had decided it wasn't 'in keeping'.

'It had been a feature of the garden for sixty or seventy years. Gone. Totally gone.' And wrecked in the process, Lord Scarsdale asserts. 'The stone mason and his mates used sledge hammers, if you please, because some of the columns wouldn't come away from their base.'

Lord Scarsdale was outraged.

'It was awful really. This was put up by not any member of the family but the greatest Curzon who ever lived – Viceroy of India and everything else. He was immensely proud of his home. He loved the idea of bringing this fountain here. Why shouldn't it stay?'

The regional director insisted that months earlier Lord Scarsdale had been informed of the Trust's intention to remove the Hackwood fountain and that he'd agreed. Francis Scarsdale claims that though they had mentioned the idea, he had been against it and, hearing no more about it, assumed that the plan had been dropped. Instead they went ahead with no warning. 'I think we don't exist to them. I find it very insulting and extremely unkind.'

For all his involvement in horse-racing, Lord Scarsdale doesn't seem to have the horse trader's turn of mind. Unlike Sir John Carew Pole, for instance, he kept little back.

'I must say it sounds naïve,' Lord Scarsdale replies when I bring this up, 'but you can't anticipate *everything*. It never really occurred to me or certainly not to my advisers to clear these questions. What about the future? How are we going to stand when you do open the house? Are we going to be consulted? Am I going to be able to have a say in it? You're not going to make it too museum-like, are you?'

Looking back, Lord Scarsdale reflects that the National Trust, with all its great experience in these matters, didn't volunteer any help.

'I went into the thing rather blindly,' he admits, 'thinking, "Oh the great National Trust, they're the boys to have it. It will be lovely. What fun." Huh, as they say. It didn't turn out that way.'

There is no doubting that the public have benefited from Francis Scarsdale's struggle to keep Kedleston Hall – its gardens, park and its furnishings – intact. And though he and his family have kept a splendid place to live, it seems wrong that his reward should also include an ever-replenished list of complaints. 'I feel so ashamed,' he says, about endlessly chasing after the Trust with criticism of what it does. Yet he feels he can't stop because so much seems wrong, especially in its management of the garden and park. Lord Scarsdale is not the only donor whose generous motives when combined with a lack of cunning made for unhappy complications later on.

Breathing fire from the ramparts

In 1951 Compton Mackenzie produced a book for the National Trust based on a tour he made of its properties. 'Showing round the public was still a new toy for Hornyold-Strickland,' he writes about the man who with his parents had given Sizergh Castle to the Trust the year before. Lieutenant-Commander Thomas Hornyold-Strickland, 'seemed to be enjoying it', Mackenzie adds. 'He certainly has plenty to show. I expect Sizergh will be a star draw to visitors in the future.'6

Instead, it sometimes seems as if Sizergh Castle has been a star nuisance to the National Trust. And, in a way, visitors were one of the reasons why. The original agreement was for the castle to be open one day a week.

'It needed the most assiduous arguing and bribery, practically, to get subsequent owners to renege on their predecessor's bargains,' says Peter Orde who, as the volunteer overseeing the Trust's properties in the north-east at the time, kept on eye on things at Wallington after Sir Charles had died. 'Eventually we got things right with the Trevelyans,' he reports. 'But it took years.' At Sizergh the arguing goes on.

Sizergh Castle on the southern edge of the Lake District a few miles outside Kendal is one of the very few country houses the National Trust owns in the environs of the Lake District.

A history of bankruptcies in the family and the selling off of some of the castle's contents had made Henry Hornyold-Strickland who had inherited Sizergh in 1931 determined that the family's home should never be in jeopardy again. The National Trust seemed to him a good way to provide that security. The house, gardens, and surrounding land all went to the National Trust in 1950; a joint gift from him, his wife and his son and heir Thomas. He gave the contents, too, because, in effect, they were the history of the family who'd inhabited the castle for 750 years.

An endowment of £40,000 was provided by him. According to his eldest grandson and namesake, the Trust had asked for a smaller sum, but Henry Hornyold-Strickland felt it was inadequate and gave more. His attitude couldn't have been more different from the chaps making clever deals for themselves and their heirs at country houses elsewhere at much the same time.

There was, of course, the matter of the memorandum of wishes. In addition to setting the open day, it was Henry Hornyold-Strickland's wish that, following the laws of primogeniture, a Strickland should go on living at the castle after him. 'The Donor wishes', he wrote, 'that the Trust should allow the selected occupier to reside free of rent in the Castle and to have the use of the chattels and of the gardens and grounds.'

Of all the words above, 'use of the chattels' proved to be the only ones that are not commonplace. Translated, they have meant that wherever the Strickland furniture, carpets, silver and china abides, the family-in-residence has the right to be also.

Lt Commander Thomas Hornyold-Strickland and his parents ran Sizergh for the National Trust after they gave it. This not only suited the donors, it also suited the Trust, which with only 20,000 subscribers had little money and a minute staff: altogether there were twelve people on salary in London and fifteen scattered around its domain; thirteen of them land agents and two regional representatives.

'Until Tom's death, he was the administrator,' Laurence Harwood (once regional director of the north-west) confirmed, 'and in a strange kind of way it was an easier life for the Trust when he was around. He and his father had done the deed of giving it to the Trust. They knew we were carrying a lot of the burden of the finances. So although he could be mighty pernickity and fussy to a fault, really, and would never spend money if he could avoid it – and never even allow the Trust to spend any – he was very conscientious about his administration of the castle. He appointed the guides, he trained them in the way he wanted – which meant they told all sorts of stories about the family rather more than about the furniture. In the end he was honourable and straight.'

Lieutenant-Commander Thomas Hornyold-Strickland, the last surviving donor, died in 1983. His widow Angela, whom he'd married the year after Sizergh was given to the Trust, has her base in the north wing of the castle, but 'it's all one house,' she makes plain. 'I come and go as I wish.' This is one of the rare Trust houses that doesn't get 'put to bed' for the winter.[7] At Christmas her six children, their spouses and children come to spend a fortnight there.

In the early 1950s, perhaps eight people showed up on Sizergh's open day. (It was a Thursday. And while this looks as if it were calculated to keep visitors out, the intention had been the reverse. Saturday as a day off, like car ownership, was still not commonplace. Thursday was the local half-closing and therefore the afternoon when most people in the area would be able to come.) Today the Castle is open five afternoons a week and is visited by more than 50,000 people during the National Trust season.

'In all fairness,' says Angela Hornyold-Strickland, 'they do ask me about extra opening days. One sees their point of view,' she continues, 'people want to come. There's not much one can do about it.' And, as it happens, her father-in-law noted in his agreement with the Trust that in time more open days might be desirable.

Mrs Hornyold-Strickland, in her late sixties, has an incisive manner and even when stationary it's obvious that she's a dynamo. It was easy to believe that in the days when she stocked and ran the shop at the castle, it operated at a healthy profit. But it was also easy to believe Laurence Harwood when he later said, 'You can never know which way the cat is going to jump with Angela. She can be charming, really charming, generous and warm and then she can be dreadfully spiteful and cutting you dead.'

She has in the past been reprimanded by the Trust for telling its gardeners to pick fruit and vegetables from the garden for her table. Henry, her father-in-law, had paid the gardeners; a tradition that died with him, though the attitude that its bounty belonged to the house had not. And negotiating a greater number of opening hours was a slower, more charged process than her words above suggest. Yet she was engaging and generous with her time when I visited Sizergh. And there was nothing the slightest bit dragonlike about her, though even she is aware that 'the Dragon' is what she's sometimes called.

Though she can be haughty, she can also be down-to-earth. 'I keep saying to the Trust: "Don't make it too grand, Sizergh. Because we were never grand. In that way,"' she can't stop herself from appending. 'People here were always slightly impoverished,' she explains. 'Being Catholics and suffering for your religion since the 1500s, you are poorer than most of your contemporaries. No bad thing,' she adds firmly. 'But it does mean that you didn't live as lavishly . . . You have to be careful not to make it too smart.' (Not spending a pound more than necessary may be a tradition as well as a quirk.)

She sees that there are family photographs on display. When some of the chairs were recently recovered, she chose the fabric. 'We have fresh flowers in the house,' she continues. 'I do them myself. Personally, I think people like this house because it looks very much as if the family do still live here. They want to relate the houses they see to themselves. If it's too much a palace it has nothing to do with them.'

She feels that 'the Trust changed about 1970. Or just before.' (This as it happens followed a great row that was, in part, about access. See Chapter 4.) 'They started coming to us with all sorts of revolutionary ideas. We were obviously in their way.'

With the new 'ideas' of the late 1960s, there came new conformity and an end to the individualism that had characterized the people working for the Trust before. 'Mediocrity is creeping right through,' she believes. 'And', she adds, 'when people aren't allowed to use their initiative . . .' The word 'morons' is just audible.

'I used to think it was better not to discuss these things in public,' said Henry Hornyold-Strickland, whom his mother had put in touch with me. 'But now I know it's always better to stand up to a bully.'

[115]

Within a month of the Lt Commander's death, the National Trust's Regional Committee had organized a panel of three of its members to investigate what it called 'the whole situation at Sizergh' and report its findings and recommendations. 'The whole situation' meant everything from visiting hours (it was open two days a week at this time), to where in the castle the tenants could set foot.

'They tried to get real tough,' Henry's mother had told me. 'They thought, "Now's our moment. The last donor has died. We'll push them into the north wing, lock the door between."'

Was this the National Trust's intention? Was Mrs Hornyold-Strickland being over-suspicious, not to say paranoid?

'The report was like a bombshell,' said H H-S, as he referred to himself in the family's annotated copy of the panel's findings. The family felt offended and insulted by its tone. But most of all they were furious about its conclusions. How could they not be?

The panel had recommended that the clause in the original memorandum of wishes which gives automatic rights of residency to future members of the Hornyold-Strickland family should be revoked. And, in future, if a Strickland were to live at Sizergh, he or she would not be permitted to live in the entire castle. The occupier would be 'required' to accept a lease, the terms of which were to be set by the National Trust. And one of those terms was that the occupant – and family – were to be confined to the north wing. In the meantime if any of them wanted to use the rooms in the castle apart from the north wing, they were to first ask the Trust's permission to do so.

The very last words of the long report prepared by the Trust's panel of enquiry reads 'We recommend that the Trust should at all times use its best endeavours to ensure that Sizergh continues to be occupied by a Strickland.' When the family came to those words they must have laughed bitterly. Best endeavours? What had preceded this paragraph gave them little reason to credit the Trust's sincerity.

'They had their thing really worked out,' Angela Hornyold-Strickland believes. 'Henry and I decided we would fight to the bitter end. If we had to go, then we'd go. That's how it was.'

'In the end,' she reported, 'they had to climb down.'

The Trust did, but it also fought on.

Four years of negotiation between the Trust and the family followed the panel's report. This was suspended in 1987 because it wasn't getting anywhere. As things have been left, the Trust's position is that once Angela Hornyold-Strickland no longer lives at Sizergh, the question of its occupation will have to be reconsidered.

She is secure as a tenant for life and she can use all of the castle, which she does – without asking permission first. Though there is clearly a good deal of friction between landlord and tenant about this; the Trust acts as if she is being naughty.

Henry, the eldest son, is next in line to inhabit Sizergh Castle following the law of primogeniture. He feels he's being threatened by the Trust, bullied as he says. Like Lord Belmore, he is an heir who yearns to be in charge of running his ancestral home and he can't quite believe it won't happen. He is sure that were he to do it, instead of Sizergh running at a loss (as it has been ever since the inflation of the 1970s shrank the value of his grandfather's endowment), he could make it profitable.

As a successful management consultant, he is full of plans and ideas and strategies for Sizergh to which he is devoted. He wants it to continue as the Strickland home it's been for nearly 800 years. He seems entirely reasonable but under his nicely cut jacket a chip on his shoulder seems to be growing.

'Looked at from the family's point of view,' says Henry, 'they have paid for their rent-free existence in perpetuity. They paid for it with an endowment and the loss of virtually all their assets.' And afterwards, they agreed to open the castle to the public five days a week. 'We've given a lot,' he says. 'What have we got in return?'

'I've heard that only five houses are in credit,' I said to Julian Prideaux, the National Trust's chief agent.

'Oh no, that's wrong,' he retorted. 'I don't know where you got that figure. There are many more than that.' A short speech followed about how it rather depended on how you did the accounting. I agreed that indeed it did.

'How does the Trust do it?' I asked. 'And what figure does it come up with since mine is wrong?'

We arranged to meet in ten days' time when I would have my answer.

In his office at the top of Queen Anne's Gate with windows overlooking St James's Park, Julian Prideaux sat with papers in hand. A small man, he wears well-cut suits; his double cuffed shirts are secured with knots of stiff silk. He is perfectly groomed; his grey hair combed straight back from his bony face. There's something about him that's like an eighteenth-century miniature of a courtier albeit in modern dress; it's easy to imagine Julian Prideaux in breeches and powdered wig.

The papers he held were a list; some items had been streaked with a yellow marking pen, others with a pale blue one.

Mr Prideaux began to read off the names of the houses owned by the National Trust which are not in debt. Kedleston was among them, and Kingston Lacy, given by Ralph Bankes in 1982, with its vast estates (including Corfe Castle on the Dorset coast) and a princely endowment.

'You see there are lots,' Mr Prideaux announced with satisfaction.

'Well, actually, how many?' I asked.

He looked as if I were neurotically numerate, you know, one of those people who keeps tabs on the number of lampposts in the street.

'Do you mean you want me to count?' he asked.

'Yes,' I replied. 'But if you don't want to bother, I'll happily count them up myself.'

Julian Prideaux did not hand over the list. I never found out what the blue ink indicated nor the yellow. Instead he sat there counting. It didn't take long.

'There are thirteen,' he told me. 'You see that's a lot more than five.'

Yes. But as its chief agent didn't need to be told, the National Trust owns more than 200 historic houses which can be entered by first buying an admission ticket. If thirteen of them are in credit, that leaves 187 houses where there's a shortfall. It can reach six figures. Being so eager, being so enthralled by the properties and the people in them, has brought the National Trust a lot of trouble. Signs of is were beginning to show even before the Country Houses Scheme was thirty years old.

[4]

A Poisoned Trident

On 4 November 1962, J.F.W. Rathbone, the secretary of the National Trust, had the curious experience of receiving a letter from someone he didn't know, asking for information about a post that hadn't been advertised.

The correspondent explained that he'd seen an item in the *Daily Telegraph* reporting that the Trust was planning to hire a director for appeals. Would the secretary please let him know more about it, 'if', the writer added, 'you think I might be a candidate worth considering'.[1] By the time Mr Rathbone reached the bottom of this closely written page, he may well have suspected that, while the writer's interest was obviously genuine, his humility might not be.

The man who wrote the letter had good reason to think that his enquiry would be welcomed and that full details about the job which was about to open would follow at once. This wasn't because he was a 'Naval officer with 20 years' service' nor because he had 'built up two successful businesses since retirement'. (One in educational publishing and the other a toy company that produced a doll with many changes of costume called Amber Jane.) In the fifth, and last paragraph of a communiqué which he disarmingly – but accurately – calls a 'brazen catalogue of virtues', the writer brought out his trump card: 'It might be thought,' he writes, 'that being the grandson of Canon Rawnsley, your founder, would be an interesting and acceptable credential for the job.'

[120]

As it happened the National Trust's advertisement for an appeals director was scheduled to be published the following day and appeared as planned in both *The Times* and the *Telegraph*. But while Commander Conrad Rawnsley, RN (ret'd) had got there first, neither that nor his pedigree gave him the advantage. Maybe the kind of pedigree he had didn't count for much at the National Trust any more; or maybe there was something in the correspondent's tone and details that put Rathbone off.

Jack Rathbone, who'd been secretary of the National Trust since shortly after the war, didn't ask Hardwicke Rawnsley's grandson to come for a chat, never mind a glass of claret. Instead he sent a note in which he thanked Rawnsley for his enquiry but added, 'I am afraid that your work in connection with publishing and manufacture, though varied and important, does not perhaps provide the experience that we seek.'

For some people, very likely most, this would have been the end of the correspondence. Plainly Rathbone was giving Rawnsley the brush-off. But to the canon's grandson this merely meant that the preamble was over and the plot could now move into its next phase. Or as he put it himself in another letter to the Trust two weeks later: '. . . The harder this job seems to get the more it attracts me, such is the cussedness of the Rawnsley streak.'

What followed grew into an extraordinary saga full of promise, achievement and misery which the commander, with his gift for heightening a phrase, would and did call a tragedy.

The way the canon's grandson saw it, Rawnsley cussedness had been responsible for the founding of the National Trust. But nearly seventy years later there came times when it looked as if it might be the Trust's undoing too. Hardwicke Rawnsley's tendency to behave like an active volcano had proved to be inherited by his grandson. Conrad also sent out bright sparks which occasionally were followed by a major eruption. Still, the Rawnsely genius for promotion had come down to him too.

'Lay not that flattering unction to your souls that the National Trust is solving the problem of rural amenity,' George Macaulay Trevelyan had written in 1937.[2] The Trust then owned 60,000 acres. 'What are these among so many?' the professor enquired. 'The coastline of England is being desecrated and its majestic lovely beauty is being destroyed for ever. Nothing but action by the State . . . can save the coastline on a large scale.' But the State did not act. And, in the 1960s, the National Trust began to.

The magnitude of the problem and, therefore, the cost of solving it, made it an audacious undertaking for a still relatively small organization. Though the Trust only had about 150,000 members when it started to look for an appeals director, its plan was to try to attract enough money and support to save what hadn't yet been spoiled of the English, Welsh and Ulster coast.

Enterprise Neptune was not seen as a new departure or a worrying example of the Trust struck down by a mania to expand but as an extension of the charity's role as preserver of the countryside. And a laudable one. It's been universally popular with everyone ever since, except perhaps the developers who wanted to build thousands of houses, hotels and businesses with a sea view. The only thing controversial about it turned out be Conrad Rawnsley.

The gardener at the church at Crosthwaite near Keswick, where Hardwicke Rawnsley became vicar in 1883, was known to call him 'a peppery old swine'.[3] Some veterans of the Trust who remember the commander might say that this applied equally to his grandson. 'A beast', a retired employee of the National Trust burst out, on hearing Conrad Rawnsley's name.

Righting the record

The Norfolk village of Burnham Market is a few miles from the north coast where colonies of seals bob around in the waters off Blakeney Point, one of the National Trust's coastal properties acquired even before Enterprise Neptune's launch.

Burnham Market is pretty in a self-conscious way. Good taste and plenty of money have managed to make it appear neither spoilt by development nor a museum of dear olde England. Though small, a wide triangular green gives the village an open feeling; there's an expansive interval before the through-road narrows again. Woven willow baskets are hung from the doorway to one emporium; the fishmonger sells dressed crab and salmon pâté as well as cod and plaice; farmhouse cheeses fill the glass cases at Humble Pie, the delicatessen. Altogether a cosy spot for an old salt to settle after 'swallowing the anchor', which I was to learn is what a Navy man does when other men are retiring.

Conrad Rawnsley, with his wife Elsin whom he met in Shanghai more than half a century ago and married three weeks later, lives in a brick house in a cul-de-sac that runs along one side of the green. Down among the shops, in what might be called the village centre, Jane, one of their two daughters, lives in a still larger brick house above her 'by appointment only' antiques shop. (Their other daughter, Rosalind, lives in the Midlands and was researcher for a 1987 book by Graham Murphy called *Founders of the National Trust*. Her name doesn't appear on its title page because it was thought the book might be discredited if it were widely known that Conrad Rawnsley's daughter had had a hand in it.)

Expecting to meet a nasty-looking chap, I was disarmed by the elderly man wearing a blue blazer and sharply creased trousers who opened the back door to me when I called. He had such a sweet smile and an openness that was almost childlike. He proved to be generous, too. Later that afternoon, Conrad Rawnsley sent me home with all the hundreds of letters, speeches, memos and newspaper clippings that made up his archive. I hadn't asked.

There is, however, a great deal more to Conrad Rawnsley's character than can be read in his face or deduced on first meeting. In the months that followed, in phone conversations and letters, Rawnsley sometimes acted in a way he clearly thought was cagey, even manipulative. This was so transparent, it seemed farcical. But there wasn't anything light-hearted about it when, accurately or not, he felt I'd failed to be stirred by something he told me or given me to read. Anything I said other than 'Yes', 'of course, Commander', 'how right you are', got the sparks flying. But all this about sparks and volcanic eruptions suggests a high temperature, which is wrong. There was something icy cold about Conrad Rawnsley's reactions when he felt he'd been crossed – as if to him I was no longer human and therefore had no feelings to take into account. The change could be abrupt and it was disturbing.

Heading towards ninety, Rawnsley wears thick spectacles; they are not able to make his vision acute again. He has some difficulty hearing. But his mind is sharp; his way of speaking, lively and direct. (Except in his cagey mode when he starts sounding vague and mysterious, as if spies were listening in.) Though he says, 'My memory has gone right out of the window,' not all of it has flown and certainly his energy hasn't gone with it.

'The NT has tried to suppress the story, to brush it under the carpet,' he says. And it certainly did.

Every official account of Enterprise Neptune written between 1967 and 1988 – from magazine article to book and press release – tells of a project in which no one called Conrad Rawnsley had any part. Only in 1988 when an official history of the National Trust was published was Rawnsley's role discussed. Written by John Gaze, a long-serving land agent, and published after his death, the manuscript had been much edited, not to say expurgated, before it went to the printers. And Rawnsley doesn't feel it gives a fair view.

The commander's position is a perfect counterbalance to the one the National Trust took for so long. 'I'd like to be vindicated before I turn up my toes,' he says. What he actually seems to mean by that is that he should be given credit for every single bit of the National's Trust growth and success since 1963. He might have taken a tip from Hardwicke and set down the history himself. Something very like this proved to be on his mind.

'I always hoped somebody would come along to set the record straight,' the commander was saying as we set about going through the piles of papers on the highly polished table facing the garden where he and I sat. On the floor were boxes and dusty suitcases full of still more neatly tied papers.

After talking nonstop for more than an hour, Rawnsley left me alone to study the papers for a while. When he came back he said, 'I have an impertinent suggestion to make. Instead of doing a book about the National Trust, which in any case would take more than ten years to do properly, why don't you do a history of Enterprise Neptune?'

It was brazen of him but also touching. The first comical moment of our meeting. I agreed that ten years would be about right considering the amount there was to do; though I didn't have that much time. Nevertheless, I didn't think I was the person to write the book he wanted instead. The commander appeared to accept this. When I came to know his story better, I realized I might not have got off so easily if he still had the prodigious drive and energy he'd possessed in 1962.

During the hours I spent with the Rawnsleys, I sometimes felt sorry for this intelligent old man with his warm smile. He'd been treated so high-handedly by that ingrown, snoozy bunch of aristocracy groupies who ran the National Trust in the 1960s. I felt grateful to him for his candour and his gift of documents to do with as I liked. One researcher compared the Trust's attitude towards its archive to the KGB's, but the Russians were probably better organized. Probably the only reason I was later given access to the Neptune papers may have been that I already had his. When I left Burnham Market I was on the commander's side, with a few amorphous reservations.

As I studied Rawnsley's Neptune papers and the Trust's, the story that emerged sometimes seemed like a weird operetta: as if instead of working with Sullivan, Gilbert had written his words to a score by Wagner. There was such silliness, dark drama and grandiosity; so many delusions and such real triumph. And all of it embellished by lots of nautical imagery which, be warned, proved to be contagious.

'In hindsight, I think the Rawnsley Row was a good thing for the National Trust,' says Sir Simon Hornby, former chairman of W.H. Smith, who was a member of the Trust's Executive Committee from 1963 to 1993, when he became president of the Royal Horticultural Society. Probably no one at the National

Trust would have agreed at the time but today most would say much the same thing.

It probably took a force nine gale to blow the National Trust out of the doldrums where it had been floating since long before the Second World War. And it had to get moving – the needs of its properties and the public required it.

Within a couple of years of the war's end, the problem of over-visiting had begun. The National Trust's Annual Report for 1947 warns that 'the mere presence of too great numbers may well spoil the peace and solitude which is the chief charm of open spaces'. In 1959 more than 100,000 people were visiting Clumber Park in Nottinghamshire on a Bank Holiday weekend. And by 1966, 2 million people went to those Trust properties – houses and gardens, mainly – where an entrance fee was charged; the charity had 112,000 members.

The men running the National Trust in the late 1950s and early 1960s, however fond of the charity they may have been, were no longer up to the job. If they ever had been. All those country houses, and the tens of thousands of acres that had come with them, and the size of the public that was making use of it all, demanded a bigger, more knowledgeable staff better suited to the task.

'It was absolutely clear to me, and to a great many other people who were concerned with management, that the National Trust was running on the same pattern as it had been before the war,' an elderly observer of the charity's affairs recalls. 'By the 1950s the whole thing had become an enormous business. . . . Rathbone, the secretary and Martineau, the lawyer, were not up to it.'

Throughout its long history, the National Trust had survived and grown because people gave it property and money. Yet in all its seventy-five years, the charity had never employed a person whose sole job was fund-raising. The advertisement that appeared in the *Daily Telegraph* and *The Times* on 5 November 1962 wasn't just for an appeals director, but for its first one.

Octavia Hill, though a Christian Socialist, wasn't at all

squeamish about asking for money. But by the early 1960s, the men running the Trust, who themselves didn't have to earn it, found the whole thing . . . well the pursuit was rather vulgar, wasn't it? Nevertheless, the fact that they decided to hire an appeals director must have meant that they were willing to have somebody get on with the dirty job. The same sort of attitude can be found among some at the National Trust today where the shops are concerned. The feeling is that the people who run these emporia are contaminated by wanting to handle as much of the filthy stuff as they, decorously, can. Yet in both cases the profit was all for the charity.

It wasn't only that the job of appeals director was new. So was the fact that it was going to pay a salary that a man might be able to live on. James Lees-Milne, for instance, calls working for the Trust 'a vocation'. The £400 a year he was paid in 1936 was considered by his employers as a supplement to a private income. And for a good fifteen years after the salaried post of appeals director was created, the assumption remained that any salary the Trust paid fell somewhere between pin money and a living wage – and on the pin money end of the spectrum. Even today its director of finance, Ian Bollom, observes, 'We don't pay the going rate to anybody. But we try to pay within ten or twenty per cent of the average – without noticeable success!' Nevertheless salaries at the National Trust are no longer meagre, particularly at the top end of the scale. Coming up to his retirement as director general in 1995, Sir Angus Stirling was earning about £85,000 a year. The advertisement for his replacement gave the job's starting salary as £90,000.

The application

On 7 November 1962, the day after receiving what was in effect a 'thank you very much but I don't think so' reply to his enquiry, Conrad Rawnsley was writing to the secretary of the National Trust once again. Though he begins with a softening up: 'I appreciate your point,' etc. he's soon on the offensive: 'Surely the race goes to the ingenious, the persuasive, the resourceful and the resolute,' he argues, 'rather than to those who, grown old in the strait-jacket of conventions, will be content to follow the precedent of their experience.' (Was he trying to shame these conventional old boys into giving him the job?)

Again he plays on the family connection though by now it can't be called a trump card. Just the same he points out – in case Rathbone hadn't thought of it – that its publicity value to the appeal should not be overlooked.

Conrad Rawnsley wasn't incapable of seeing reality. He recognized that his first letter had had 'cold water thrown over it'. But one of his gifts (and flaws) is the ability to proceed as if what he doesn't like simply doesn't matter or, if he really doesn't like it, that it doesn't exist.

The commander asked Rathbone for an interview with the selection committee. 'I would hope', he says in summing up, 'to persuade them in a very short time that I have the qualities . . . that would more than compensate for any lack of experience.'

The secretary was not convinced. Five days later he wrote saying that 'we feel that experience so far from being a handicap is a positive advantage'. Nevertheless Rawnsley had succeeded in wedging his foot in the door. Rathbone added that if he would send along his curriculum vitae, the secretary would pass it on to the selection committee.

Christopher Gibbs, a professional land agent at the Trust since 1935 and its chief agent since 1961, had pushed the Executive Committee to take up the project of saving the coastline. But he was opposed to the hiring of Conrad Rawnsley. So was Jack Rathbone, of course, who had also been against the idea of a coastal appeal from the beginning. But Rawnsley, rightly, suspected that Rathbone's objection to him had more to do with personalities than with policies.

'Rathbone had the perspicacity to see me as one who would not be a compliant and docile servant of committees,' Rawnsley said years later – yet another quality shared with his grand-father.

Undaunted, maybe even egged on by the rebuffs coming from Queen Anne's Gate, Conrad Rawnsley kept up the pressure. With his CV he sent a request for a meeting with the secretary.

In response to Rawnsley's letters, Rathbone was always cour-teous and always discouraging. 'Because of your relationship with our founder any application made by you for work with the Trust must of course receive very special consideration. But . . . I am very doubtful.' Rathbone didn't mention Rawnsley's temperament or style and certainly he didn't mention class. Instead the secretary highlighted such matters as Rawnsley's age. The Trust was looking for someone to make the charity his career. At fifty-five, near the end of his working life, the petitioner was too old.

Rawnsley inched ahead. He meet Jack Rathbone on 27 November, although the secretary did not want to 'raise any false hopes.'

Three days after that meeting, Rawnsley was writing again. He was bolder now, either because he was encouraged by having got as far as seeing Rathbone or because he reckoned that with the secretary so against him he had nothing to lose. He addressed what he called 'a broadside' at the secretary and the Executive of the Trust. It was an audacious move and a clever one. He was making the most of being not in the NT mould.

The job, as advertised, stipulated that the successful candi-date's first task would be to organize an appeal for money with which to buy up and look after coastline. Rawnsley, the humble tone which he'd adopted less than a month before now completely gone, wrote that their goal for this first appeal was much too low.

The Trust reckoned to aim for £500,000. Yet they were offering £3,000 to the appeals director. The Trust, he told Rathbone, were 'setting a mighty big sprat to catch your modest mackerel'. The proper target for their appeal ought to be £5 million instead.

To wrap his spiky message in a package the secretary might find easier to handle, Rawnsley asked Rathbone to remember the 'fiery evangelism' of the Trust's founders. (Presumably Rawnsley knew nothing about the character of either Octavia Hill or Sir Robert Hunter. But then, possibly Rathbone didn't either.) But whoever knew what about the Trust's early years, Rawnsley's point was plain enough: in time, his aggression would do the charity good.

Conrad Rawnsley, having raised the subject of evangelism, now took to some Bible-thumping himself. He assured Jack Rathbone that, 'He will lift the Trust from the rut of rank and file charities.' For the commander was 'as much at home with men of humble origin as with those of his own birth and upbringing, a man of invention, of initiative and resource . . . who will not only think out what to do but go and do it, too.' No question about it, he was exactly the fellow the National Trust needed.

J.F.W. Rathbone was right to believe that Conrad Rawnsley was not suited to rule by committee. And if he suspected that, were this live wire to be dropped into their sleepy lagoon,[4] people might not only be shocked but actually electrocuted, Rathbone was right about that too. Sadly for him, his prescience served neither as protection nor reward.

When Rawnsley later called the outcome tragic, he meant for himself. But the word seems more applicable to what happened to Jack Rathbone. In less than four years, Rawnsley was leading a rebellion against the way the National Trust was run and the people running it. One result of it was that Jack Rathbone, a bachelor in his late fifties who had served as secretary of the National Trust for almost twenty years, was forced to resign from the job which he'd referred to as 'his family; his life'.

Rathbone can't be faulted for lack of trying. He kept telling Rawnsley 'no'. Even as Santa was busy sliding down England's chimneys in 1962, the secretary of the National Trust was playing Scrooge. But others softened up, and the canon's grandson got his meeting with the selection committee.

Unlike the handful of other candidates for the job, Rawnsley decided he would not submit any of his ideas for the coastal appeal in advance of meeting the panel. They had no idea what to expect when he arrived. Conrad Rawnsley wowed them.

'I could hardly believe my ears,' John Smith, chairman of the Trust's powerful General Purposes Committee and one of the interviewers, wrote to Rawnsley afterwards. 'And the notes you left behind are much the most imaginative I have seen.'[5]

Commander Rawnsley had made good use of family history. At the time of Queen Victoria's Golden Jubilee, Hardwicke Rawnsley had acted as coordinator of a scheme to light bonfires on cliffs and hilltops as part of the celebrations. His grandson gave it a lively new look: the ancient system of lighting bonfires, used in days before the Armada to warn of invasion from the sea, as Conrad Rawnsley saw it, could now be used to warn the British of the dangers to their coast coming from within their own land.

In spite of the reluctance, not to say disapproval, of both the Trust's secretary and its chief agent, Rawnsley's imagination and John Smith's enthusiasm for his ideas won out. Commander Rawnsley was chosen to be the National Trust's first director of appeals.

John Smith has been an MP and a director of Coutts, the Royal bankers. He founded the Landmark Trust: a miniature, more personal, version of the National Trust. (It saves and restores small buildings of character – Classical pig sties, Gothic follies, Derbyshire weavers' cottages – and turns them into well-appointed, short-term holiday lets.) Since the days when Rawnsley was petitioning the National Trust for a job, John Smith has also been knighted and made a Companion of Honour. Yet he says, 'I am anti-establishment.' Politics, banking, heritage charities, honours. Brooks's, Pratt's, the Beefsteak . . . he certainly looks like a fully paid-up member.

What Sir John must mean is that he has a weakness for mavericks. Take for instance Rodney Legg. Legg represents the Open Spaces Society on the National Trust's ruling Council. He appears to be a cross between a feral man of the wild and an advertising whiz kid (the former image, perhaps, being an example of the latter gift). When Legg wants to criticize the Trust for failing to keep some footpath open, or otherwise exercise proper vigilance about public access to its countryside properties, he manages to get thousands of words of press coverage. Noticing this, the Trust asked Legg to serve as a member of its countryside access review committee, which he did. 'They'd rather me inside the tent pissing out; than outside pissing in.' Legg wrote his own account of the Trust's history as a countryside preservation body, which he published for its centenary. It is dedicated to Sir John Smith 'who brought me back into the fold'.

In the early 1960s when the old boys at the National Trust were amusing in the most sedate and decorous way, John Smith's eyes lit up at the sight of the commander. He was just the person to make things more lively. On 3 February 1963 Smith wrote to Rawnsley congratulating him on getting the job.

'I enjoy working for the Trust,' he told Rawnsley, 'because it throws up such extraordinary problems: because there is always great scope for improvement; and because none of the staff or committees are rigid – they all always listen to anything (and usually agree).'

On 18 February 1963 Jack Rathbone sent Conrad Rawnsley a formal letter of appointment as appeals director for the National Trust. Even before he'd been given the job officially, Rawnsley had met the secretary and laid out new terms and conditions for his employment.

Rathbone responded to some of these demands in the letter of appointment. No, he tells Rawnsley, the Trust will not promise him the fixed annual salary increases. Nor, given the commander's age, would the Trust provide him with a pension. But yes, in spite of space being so scarce at 42 Queen Anne's Gate, which was then the charity's headquarters, they would agree to his requirement that he have an office to himself 'even if it means renting something outside'. The Neptune Appeal was carried out from offices at no. 44.

On 6 May 1963 the new appeals director reported for work at the National Trust. He had a vision of what could be done and he was ready for action.

'I thought', he says, 'here's an island race and 60 million of them go to the coast every year for their holidays. This is something that will really appeal to the people of this island. It will put the National Trust on the map.'

Commander Rawnsley, RN (ret'd) didn't dawdle. He immediately got to work trying to make improvements and expecting the men of the National Trust to listen – and to agree – to what he proposed.

Rathbone's repeated reaction to the new appeals director was: 'Don't try to reform the National Trust.'

Conrad Rawnsley was not a reformer by nature. But he was no shirker. And he had seemingly limitless energy. As he saw it, if an organization had to be changed from top to bottom in order to do things the way things ought to be done, there wasn't much choice but to reform it. His grandfather had created the organization, he would make something of it.

Rathbone, the Trust's secretary, Robin Fedden its historic buildings secretary, Christopher Gibbs its chief agent, Lord Antrim its chairman – not one of these men could be called a go-getter. By the time Rawnsley appeared there were Empire Builders at the National Trust but they were far away: Michael Trinick down in Cornwall, Cubby Acland up in the Lakes, Nicholas Corbin in East Anglia and 'the Border Raider' as they called Sheila Pettit, in Northumberland. But these people were serving parts of the country to which they were devoted and, if they were in competition with one another for money, they all saw themselves as serving the National Trust.

Conrad Rawnsley was an entrepreneur. He had an unashamed love for the labour of turning not very much into something big and flourishing. He saw Enterprise Neptune as a project which though still only an idea could grow and flourish. He might have to drag the boys at the National Trust along with him in order to achieve it, but no doubt about it, Enterprise Neptune had tremendous potential for success.

Map making

As chief agent, Christopher Gibbs's job was to oversee the running of the National Trust's entire estate – houses, farms, castles, ruins, even the Farne Islands which the public had stumped up the money to buy in 1925. In 1937 G.M. Trevelyan had tried to get people to see that the British coast was being swallowed up by developers (or turned into an industrial rubbish tip); by the time he became chief agent, Gibbs was convinced that the danger had reached a critical stage.

A 1958 government survey had found that forty-seven per cent of the Sussex coast had already been built over; as well as twenty-three per cent of Lancashire's shoreline and twenty-three per cent of Essex. Gibbs went before the Executive Committee in March 1962 recommending that the charity embark on a campaign 'for money to buy land or covenants for the protection of the English and Welsh coasts'.[6] The committee agreed and Northern Ireland was included too. But just how much actually needed protecting? And where?

The land agents of the National Trust pretty much walked the entire coast of Britain (Scotland with its own Trust since 1931 was not included). The agents were asked to judge not only how much was unspoiled, but which parts of the coast were worth preserving if the Trust obtained the money to go ahead. Though they weren't given any sort of detailed checklist, there was a general principle to guide them: the land should be beautiful, undeveloped and not buried under layers of filth. (It was only in the 1980s that this last prohibition was lifted and the National Trust began acquiring and cleaning up coastal land in places like County Durham where the sands were black with coal debris.)

By the time Conrad Rawnsley was appointed, the agents had

made their report. They reckoned that, of the 3,083 miles of coast in England, Wales and Northern Ireland, nearly a third was already beyond saving, while another third was not worth saving – or put less crudely – that it had no special aesthetic or recreational value. But nearly 1,000 miles of Britain's coast was exactly the kind of land Enterprise Neptune must try to save.

Because there had been less development to blight its coves, steeply wooded glens and mythic, eerie sites like Giant's Causeway, a disproportionally high amount of this coast was in Northern Ireland: the agents judged that 275 miles, a third of the Ulster coast, should be acquired by the National Trust or protected by covenants.[7]

A map had been drawn. Now the Trust had to get moving. Every year, another four to six miles of Britain's coast was being ruined by industry or lost to people who wanted to build on it.

The National Trust had seventy years of experience in property acquisition and preservation; it knew that if the proposed coastal undertaking were to succeed, local governments and voluntary organizations would have to co-operate. By the time the appeal was launched, twenty-one ministries and government agencies as well as sixty-three voluntary societies had promised the Trust their support. The Duchy of Cornwall and Crown estates promised to give the Trust long leases on the relevant foreshore. And the Military assured the Trust that it would have first refusal on the coastal land it owned. (In 1993, after having kept a beady eye on it for decades, the National Trust acquired Orford Ness, more than 1,500 acres of Suffolk coast. Merlin Waterson, another empire builder with an aptitude for stretching definitions and resources for the benefit of his district, was at work as regional director for East Anglia. Neither conventionally beautiful nor unspoilt, Orford Ness had been the site of a top secret atomic energy research station. In addition to its shingle ridges and the salt marshes which were a home to plants, insects and wintering wildfowl, Orford Ness – it could be argued – had become a site of outstanding historic interest; its derelict buildings a menacing specimen of political-scientific archaeology. To buy it cost £3.5 million, of which Enterprise Neptune contributed £500,000.)

Neptune makes waves

In May 1963 when Conrad Rawnsley began to give all his attention to being its appeals director, the National Trust already owned 125 miles of coast in England, Wales and Northern Ireland. The Trust assumed that Rawnsley would spend his first year doing what they had hired him to do and set about raising the money to buy or protect more. It didn't work out that way.

Rawnsley had risen to the rank of commander just before retiring from the Navy. But whether they perceived it or not, the National Trust had hired themselves an admiral-in-the-making. And since you can't be an admiral without a fleet, he reckoned that his first task was to build one.

At the time of Conrad Rawnsley's arrival, the National Trust's entire salaried staff in England, Wales and Northern Ireland consisted of forty people; most of them land agents. Then, as now, its committees were served by volunteers. But then, because there was such a small paid staff, the volunteers had even more power than they have now in setting the Trust's policies. Fewer than 100 people made up its ten influential committees, which included Historic Buildings, Gardens, Estates, Publicity and Finance.[8] Elsewhere in its domain, committees of local worthies oversaw regional affairs.

Conrad Rawnsley reported for duty. He had already been given his own headquarters. Now he set to work building his Field Force, as it was called. It's hard to say whether or not the commander was touched by the fervour for social revolution then building up among the young. It seems unlikely. And it seems certain that while a new breed called the hippy-entrepreneur was visible on the distant horizon, the commander was entirely of the old school. 'Small is beautiful' was not one of his mottoes. His idea seemed to be, the bigger the fleet and the larger the crew that manned it, the more it could conquer when it set sail.

It would take time (and money) to deploy a Field Force of the size Rawnsley wanted. It would have to be done in stages. But, he contended, it would be foolish to begin the Enterprise Neptune appeal before the organization to run it was ready. It was *two years* before Enterprise Neptune was launched.

The developments between May 1963, when Conrad Rawnsley began work as the National Trust's appeals director, and the official launch of his first appeal in May 1965, can be summarized this way:

Prince Philip was asked to be Enterprise Neptune's royal patron. The campaign director (Conrad Rawnsley) and his staff would be based in London. Britain would be divided into districts run by four regional directors. One would be in London, one in Manchester, one in Birmingham and another in Cardiff. All of these men would be on genuine, not token, salaries. There would also be a gargantuan crew of volunteers who would have their expenses reimbursed.

Two years after he started the job, the Field Force was still growing in his mind. 'If all goes according to plan,' he wrote in 1965, 'and if the volunteers can be found, there should eventually be some 60 County Commissioners, 900 District Supervisors, and 3,000 Wardens.' The wardens' job was to recruit new members. (In 1895 a subscription to the National Trust cost ten shillings a year; a life membership, £20. And so it did seventy years later. Only in 1953 was the annual subscription raised to £1. In 1965, as part of the push to make money to pay for purchases of coastal land it was doubled. But lest this seem grasping, the increases applied only to new subscribers; a person who'd joined the National Trust in, say, 1951 would still be paying ten shillings a year to belong in 1968.)

These plans were not all. They merely covered the fund-raising operation. Still other people would be needed to organize local events and give talks. Say a crew of about 5,000 in all would be involved in implementing the Neptune Appeal.

By 1961, Rawnsley had his regional directors in place and

sixteen county commissioners. As for supervisors and wardens, by the time of the launch he simply stated that 'a large number' had been appointed to date. In 1967 there were in fact twenty county commissioners, seven district supervisors and about 300 recruiters.

The number of people on Conrad Rawnsley's field staff rivalled that of the National Trust's payroll. While Enterprise Neptune's voluntary staff would be bigger than the body it was created to serve. There was some anxiety at Queen Anne's Gate about how much this was going to cost. And not only in pounds, shillings and pence. Yet even decades later the commander could not understand why.

A former council member who'd come to live nearby told Conrad Rawnsley years later that Lord Antrim, when he succeeded Lord Crawford as chairman of the Trust in 1965, 'was afraid that the tail was beginning to wag the dog!' By 1965 the men running the National Trust must have been thinking that if the tail grew any bigger and fatter, the dog wouldn't be able to walk any longer. Nevertheless, Rawnsley derides Antrim for suspecting that he'd wanted to take over the National Trust. 'It never crossed my mind,' he insists. Mrs Rawnsley backs him up. 'I would have known. It never did.'

There was another, related aspect of Enterprise Neptune that caused a certain amount of fretfulness at 42 Queen Anne's Gate. The goal of the appeal was now £2 million. The date for achieving it was December 1966. Because of Rawnsley's ambitious plans, Enterprise Neptune wasn't even going to begin until the spring of 1965. All these people and all that money was for a project that was going to last for only eighteen months. Was Rawnsley suffering from *folie de grandeur*? Could he count?

On 23 April (St George's Day) in 1965 nearly 1,000 bonfires and beacons were set alight on high points near the coast of England, Wales and Northern Ireland by Boy Scouts, Girl Guides and other young volunteers. This was the public launch of Enterprise Neptune. The following month, on 22 May, at the Mansion House a more exclusive launch was hosted by the Lord Mayor of London.

Prince Philip was guest of honour and addressed 250 guests.

The National Trust now controlled 170 miles of coast; about 40,000 acres of coastal land; a tenth of all they land in their care. Even before the launch, the Treasury had given the appeal £250,000. Enterprise Neptune seemed to be on course for a wonderful voyage. But there had been trouble on the bridge for a long time, and it didn't go away.

In the winter of 1963 when John Smith had written congratulating Conrad Rawnsley on his appointment, he'd assured the new appeals director that the people at the Trust were good listeners, not rigid, and prepared to take suggestions. By the summer of 1964 his message had changed:

'I continue to worry abt. you and the N.T.,' Smith was writing to the commander. 'I think you ought to consider how much y. wd. mind if the Trust asked y. to give it up. I know the Trust well enough to assure you that that is a *real* risk run by all who stir things up.' Smith goes further still: 'If y. *wd.* mind being sacked, then I do most earnestly advise you to resign now.'

Conrad Rawnsley was not diplomatic by nature. To him attack often seemed the best method of defence. He didn't resign, of course. But in August 1964 he wrote to Lord Crawford, the chairman, and threatened to, 'unless . . .'

'I know very well', David Crawford began in reply, 'that, as you say, your heart is in this job and that this is the largest single enterprise so far undertaken by the Trust. But it must be understood that this is only part of the Trust's work – part of the whole.

'You say that you must fight for all you think is best for the appeal,' Lord Crawford continued, 'and this is right – provided you bear in mind what I have said above that you appreciate that some of your ideas will be accepted and others rejected, and that you accept the authority and decisions of the Committees and of the secretary.'[9]

On its side, the National Trust was taking a big risk. They had not only hired a man who was not 'one of us' as Lady Thatcher was later to put it, they kept him on when he refused to obey the party line. But they wanted him to know they wouldn't go on doing this for ever.

Either because they were daring, or because it was easier not to think much about it, the men running the National Trust allowed Conrad Rawnsley to build up a large, separate organization parallel to their own. The Field Force reported to the appeals director. But Rawnsley, as Lord Crawford reminded him, was an employee of the National Trust just the same. He must report to his superiors and abide by their judgments and subject himself to their policies.

Like a parent who spoils a child by letting it have everything it wants, and then when the child becomes a teenager suddenly gets worried about the dangerous mischief it might get up to and starts trying to control it, the National Trust left attempts at discipline too late.

An attempt at improving family relations was made. Instead of insisting that the commander continue reporting to Rathbone, when they clearly didn't get on, and instead of making him go to the Executive when he needed decisions about Neptune, which was a cumbersome process and therefore slow, the Neptune Committee – a decision-making body chaired by Lord Antrim – came into being. This would be a means of giving Rawnsley more of what he wanted while enabling the Trust to keep a closer watch on him. Both sides must have hoped that things would move ahead more smoothly now.

The setting up of the Field Force progressed but Rawnsley's relations with his employer did not. The commander's attitude and tone when communicating with the Trust's secretary seemed calculated to rile him. Rathbone had 'embarrassed' Rawnsley by questioning his expenses. Would he have done that to Lord Crawford or Lord Antrim? As for the Earl of Antrim: In a letter to him marked PERSONAL AND CONFIDENTIAL, Rawnsley opens with the words, 'I really must protest about your performance yesterday afternoon. Let's try to keep our balance.'

The Enterprise Neptune Committee headed by Ran Antrim began trying to reign in the appeals director with more than words of warning. The 1965 expenses for operating the Field

Force must be held to no more than five per cent of the appeal's income, with a ceiling of £75,000.

Rawnsley's annoyance took the form of further attacks: Lord Antrim was told that the commander had prepared background information for a meeting between the Earl and Lord Perth so that 'you would talk in a businesslike and informed way'. But, Rawnsley continued, 'as far as I can make out, you did not bother to read it. If you know it all, please don't ask for a brief! . . .'

Within a week of his dressing-down Lord Antrim, who by this time was chairman of the National Trust, discovered that Rawnsley had written a letter to Richard Dimbleby, then preparing a radio appeal for Enterprise Neptune. In his letter Rawnsley criticized the policies of the Executive Committee. Now the threat came: if the Commander didn't begin to accept its authority, he'd be 'terminated'.

If there is something about the way Conrad Rawnsley acted during his employment by the National Trust in the 1960s, that on occasion makes him appear trapped in the repetition of an adolescent's emotional dramas, he also showed an adolescent's outrage at the perversion of ideals.

'The whole thing was rotten from top to bottom,' he says looking back at the Trust as it then was. Rottenest of all, he felt, was its Country Houses Scheme.

He says now that he can't understand why the people running the National Trust in the mid-1960s minded so much when he criticized *that*. After all they weren't to blame for the Trust having made such a disastrous mistake in the 1930s.

Conrad Rawnsley may sometimes be led around by his temper, yet he's no less bright or perceptive for that; but he has his blind spots. In the 1960s the men running the National Trust were completely committed to preserving great country houses; not one of them – Rathbone, Crawford, Antrim, Fedden – felt that it had been a mistake to embark on the campaign.

Rawnsley wanted total control of his project. He wanted the men of the National Trust to work for him, in effect, rather than the other way round. And he wanted the Trust to concern itself only with goals he believed were the true ones. As if this wasn't enough, it wasn't just the policies of the National Trust that he thought were rotten, nor its management, it became personal.

'Rathbone, Antrim, Fedden ... they were all against me,' the commander reported. 'They early sensed my antipathy.' He might have been talking about class warfare, but he wasn't.

Policies and prejudices

Robin Fedden had taken over as secretary to the Historic Buildings Committee when James Lees-Milne gave up the position in 1951. (Lees-Milne remained as part-time adviser on historic buildings until 1966.) Fedden remained in the post for twenty years. A lot of people continue to talk about him with affection and respect – his taste, his flair, his charm and good manners. 'He wrote beautifully, too,' says St John Gore who, in turn, became historic buildings representative when Fedden left.

Conrad Rawnsley was not a member of the Fedden fan club.

'Fedden knew that I deplored the strong homosexual element which he had introduced. He recruited entirely homosexuals as representatives. He built up his own little organization of chaps to look after the upholstery and the curtains and the carpets and the interior decoration of the houses. They had no qualifications, apart from their artistic inclinations.'

Rawnsley then added, 'Fedden disparaged me and what I stood for.' Whichever felt antipathy to the other first, there must have been continual bickering between the Country Houses contingent led by Fedden and the Neptune lot, led by Conrad Rawnsley who is still at it:

'You tell me where there's any decent furniture or pictures?' the commander asks rhetorically. 'It's mostly rubbish in those houses.' (All this from a fellow who, when he left the Trust, opened a successful antiques shop, no less, across the road from

Petworth House in Sussex where the walls are hung with so many radiant paintings by Turner.)

It certainly wouldn't help to remind the commander that the world is full of gifted heterosexual aesthetes or that more than one outdoorsy chap had been hired by the men of the National Trust because he was thought ravishing. And, to a degree, Conrad Rawnsley's bombastic outpourings are the evangelist in him talking; the man who exaggerates to make a heartfelt judgment.

The Country Houses were wrong! The Trust should be the protector and preserver of countryside. And the coast, too, of course. But nothing more. Get rid of the lot who thinks otherwise . . . and so on.

'I'd determined I was going to put things right,' says Conrad Rawnsley. Enterprise Neptune was only the first step.

And, as it happens, though he didn't get to take a second step, life in that sleepy lagoon hasn't been the same since.

In May 1966 Rawnsley went to the Neptune Committee and proposed that the appeal be extended until at least 1968. To him this was only logical. An enormous fund-raising apparatus had been set up at great cost. Keeping it going would be less expensive than setting it up had been. The benefits would, therefore, become proportionately greater.

From another angle, the logic looked different. Keeping the Field Force in place had already been a bigger drain on the National Trust's resources than had been anticipated. It had taken much longer to set up than anyone had imagined. And a recession was beginning. On top of all that, the director was proving to be quite a lot to handle.

The committee listened to Conrad Rawnsley's proposal. They then told him that they would discuss it in a private session. This was an unusual move: the people responsible for overseeing Enterprise Neptune were telling its director to go home and wait.

Conrad Rawnsley did not tread water.

In advance of the October 1966 meeting of the Committee, the appeals director prepared and sent around a paper in which

[143]

he made the following argument: Enterprise Neptune had been a success. Neptune had raised £830,000 even with the recession that had begun after it had been launched; its administration had cost thirteen per cent of that figure; an added seventy-six miles of coastline had come under the Trust's protection since the launch. And not only had it acquired money and coastal properties, it was educating a largely uninformed public about the work of the Trust. To Rawnsley it was only logical that the appeal should not only be extended, it should be expanded.

'To keep the life and vigour of the organization going,' he wrote, 'it would be essential that the terms of reference should be wider and embrace *all aspects of the work of the Trust.*' (My italic.) He and his Field Force should have all of the Trust's domain as its theatre of operations and they 'should be vested with a suitable measure of authority, power of decision and representation in the government of the Trust'.

On 17 October 1966 Rawnsley received a written reply to this latest, perhaps most ambitious, and surely the most ill-judged of his proposals. Lord Antrim thanked him, and gave him six months' notice. Was he pushed or had he jumped?

Lord Antrim told Rawnsley that other changes were going to be made also. The administration of Enterprise Neptune would be integrated with that of the Trust. There would no longer be a need for a separate staff or quarters or regional officers. And with all that gone, a man 'of lesser calibre' would be appointed to serve as 'Assistant to the Secretary'.

One week later at Saltram, a National Trust estate three miles outside Plymouth, one of the regularly scheduled press conferences that were part of the Enterprise Neptune Campaign was held. Its director would make a speech, as previously planned, keeping the newspapers up to date on the progress of the appeal.

The men running the Trust had cottoned on to the commander's style by this time. They, therefore, asked Warren Davis, a newspaper reporter in Devon who'd done some freelance press relations work for them, to be at Saltram for the appeals director's talk. In today's jargon, Davis was there to take charge of damage limitation. But he couldn't possibly have controlled what followed from Conrad Rawnsley's oration.

A rousing account was given of what Enterprise Neptune had so far achieved. This was followed by a reminder of all that yet needed doing and all that the Trust might – and should in future – achieve. The commander's off-the-cuff remarks could now begin:

He, Conrad Rawnsley, the grandson of one of its founders had found the Trust 'inert and amorphous' and worse yet 'part of the establishment'. The committees were run 'on the old boy net'. At their meetings, the professional employees of the Trust were forced to sit around the wall 'like schoolboys, while those who hadn't given perhaps more than half an hour's time or thought to the Trust's affairs since the last meeting, and had often not even read the papers sent to them, gave decisions which would affect future generations perhaps for ever.

'Where is the democracy in this?' the commander cried. 'Where is the life and vigour? I determined to see if I could create it!'

Conrad Rawnsley had presented himself for the job with the Armada on his mind. He was leaving it with those ships still in his thoughts – though this time he was calling on them for a very different purpose.

'The Armada of mediocrity, of inertia, of incompetence, is sailing now upon the shore of England,' his words rang out. Who could save our country? Why, the reporters present, that's who. They could be the Drakes and Hawkins of their day. With their pens they could repel the enemy and save Enterprise Neptune.

Even without the flattery, journalists would have paid plenty of attention to this juicy story. The staid old institution was being labelled 'incompetent'. And from somebody high up in it.

The media went on loving it. The *Observer*, *The Times*, the *Sunday Telegraph* ... in the *Guardian*, John Grigg became Rawnsley's champion. Warren Davis, who eventually became the Trust's press relations officer in London, only half-jokes when he says he owes his career to the commander.

Davis was given a fulltime job almost immediately after Saltram.

'It must have been hard on all of you,' I said to Elsin Rawnsley. Her husband, at fifty-nine, lost the job he'd fought to get, planned to keep until retirement and on which they depended financially.

'Yes,' she said gravely. 'Yes, it was. I had no idea it would be like that. The press ringing up nonstop and so on.'

Yet what has upset Mrs Rawnsley most of all is that her husband has never got over what happened. 'Righting the record,' she says, has been on his mind ever since.

The appeals director's speech at Saltram got a quick reaction from the Trust's chairman as well as from the press. Or as the commander puts it, 'The balloon went up'.

He returned to London. 'I was summoned into the noble presence,' he recalls, 'and given the sack. The door of 42 Queen Anne's Gate shut behind me and as far as I was concerned that was the end.'

No one who has read this far will believe that.

What had ended was Conrad Rawnsley's employment by the National Trust. His six months' notice, plus holiday time on full salary, had been cancelled.

Rawnsley got busy. First there was a postal campaign. The commander sent letters insisting that it was *morally* wrong of the Trust to cut him off without any money. His former bosses did not agree. Was it penury that led Rawnsley then to write to Antrim asking for a 'testimonial' to help him in his job hunt? He says he had to 'swallow my pride', to request it.

A gentleman, Lord Antrim provided such a letter. He didn't perjure himself when he wrote: 'Rawnsley is a man of extreme energy and imagination ... who has brought to the Trust's work originality and intensity of purpose and', the chairman continued, 'it is an undoubted fact that the success of this campaign, which is considerable, must largely be attributed to him.' Rawnsley had not wanted a letter of reference as much as he wanted vindication. And for him this was a proof that he had been valued by the National Trust after all. The memory that it had been begged for fell away. Acrimony, alas, did not fall away with it.

The battle escalated. Its next skirmish took place at Cheltenham on 13 November 1966 where, less than a month after the press conference at Saltram, the Trust's Annual General Meeting was held.

For many years before 1966, and for years afterwards, National Trust AGMs were sleepy affairs. Lord Gibson recalls, 'There'd be a dozen people present and you had to have a speaker to keep the thing going for three-quarters of an hour.' But that year at Cheltenham between 500 and 700 members turned up. Loudspeakers were installed so that those unable to crowd into the hall could follow the proceedings outside.

This was not an occasion when the National Trust could get away with pretending that nothing had happened and wait for people to forget that something had. So Lord Antrim explained:

The Enterprise Neptune Campaign was costing the charity thirteen per cent of the contributions it received. Far too much money was being spent on the administration of the appeal. The set-up had to be changed; its running costs reduced. As for the former appeals director, Lord Antrim said: 'It is impossible to believe that his criticisms, however worthy some of them may be of discussion, are not motivated very largely by grievance and spite.'

Considering how betrayed everyone was feeling by this time – and how fed up – indeed considering some of the things Rawnsley had earlier said to Lord Antrim, the chairman's remarks aren't the character assassination they might have been. Nevertheless, Conrad Rawnsley felt he'd been slandered.

After the AGM, the commander looked into the possibility of suing Lord Antrim for slander. Lord Goodman, who offered to act for Antrim, took the view that the AGM was 'a privileged occasion'. The solicitor Rawnsley consulted advised him that given such a defence – and defender – he would not win.

Rawnsley dropped it. But to this day he believes he was slandered.

The chairman tried to prevent Conrad Rawnsley from having the floor, claiming that the former appeals director was not entitled to speak because he was no longer on the staff and was not a member. This foolish tactic was bound to madden many besides Rawnsley.

When the commander finally spoke, he let loose. Among his criticisms of the charity, well reported in the days and weeks that followed, were these:

The Trust showed a lack of respect for its members. 'They're treated as a captive source of money,' Rawnsley asserted. Members had no way of becoming part of the Trust's ruling council. Nor were there enough facilities for the public at Trust properties: there were too few camp sites and caravan parks not to mention lavatories. Houses were not opened to the public as often as they ought to be. 'The days when the National Trust could be run as a closed shop . . . were long passed,' he asserted. Its undemocratic nature, 'must be changed'.

The men in charge of Neptune's fleet – which was still in position around England, Northern Ireland and Wales – did not rally round their former leader. On the contrary, the regional directors of the Neptune Appeal, still salaried members of the National Trust staff, presented a declaration at the AGM denouncing Rawnsley's 'calculated attacks'.

In this instance, it was the crew who remained steadfast and their admiral, even though he'd been stripped of his fleet, who mutinied. Conrad Rawnsley called for an Extraordinary General Meeting. It would have two goals: to save Enterprise Neptune – as he'd conceived it – and to reform the National Trust.

A coup

The rules governing Extraordinary General Meetings of the National Trust were the same in 1966, when its membership was 163,000, as they had been three-quarters of a century earlier when there had been perhaps 200 subscribers. All that was needed to call an EGM was a written request from ten members.

What had changed, of course, was the size of the group that had to be notified of the EGM and the cost. The Rawnsley Row is reckoned by the Trust to have cost it over £6,000. (In today's terms that might be about £100,000.) It cost the would-be reformers, led by Rawnsley, a sum that ran in the very much lower four figures. The commander's eight-page 'Case for Reform', which he produced for the EGM, alone cost £650 to print and distribute.

Rawnsley's base of operations during the months before the EGM was the Naval & Military Club in Piccadilly. From there he began a letter-writing campaign soliciting contributions for a war chest he named The Rawnsley Fighting Fund. He even tried to get the establishment to help knock down one of its own pillars. He solicited the support of James Callaghan, then prime minister, and the leader of the Liberals, Jeremy Thorpe; the Conservative party's backing was asked for too. They were all terribly busy.

The National Trust was the only source for much of the information the commander planned to use as ammunition against it. A torrent of telephone calls and letters poured down on Queen Anne's Gate. Rawnsley wanted attendance figures, opening hours, income reports. In one two-day period, according to the secretary, Rawnsley made eight calls to people at the Trust. He was reminded by Jack Rathbone that he'd been asked to submit his demands for information in writing; further calls to him would be shunted directly to Latham, the National Trust's lawyer.

On neither side was the tone cordial. The Trust could be chilly, the commander overbearing. And occasionally Rawnsley resorted to something very like 'if you know what's good for you, you'll do as I say!'

In its preparations for the EGM the Trust was soliciting testimonials from members of its Regional and Local Committees. When it feels it's being attacked at meetings of the membership, the Trust still favours these awkward efforts at patting itself on the back in public. Rawnsley, occupied with his own Reform movement, nevertheless tried to run the Trust's defence of itself at the same time. If it went on getting these testimonials, he warned, 'the days of the National Trust as an independent institution will be numbered. Its lands and buildings may well be confiscated and handed over to the local authorities . . .'

The letter ends with a demonstration of sabre-rattling that is simultaneously an outcry from a man suffering from wounded vanity. If only, Rawnsley wrote, 'you and your committees had paid attention to my many warnings and made use of my abilities . . .'

It is entirely believable when Rawnsley says, 'those were the unhappiest years of my life'.

Rawnsley next published an article for the *Observer*.[10] It is a marvellous example of what he could produce when he was not being autocratic or in the grip of rage. Building on the remarks he'd made at the November meeting of the National Trust, it is measured, perceptive and crammed with proposals that even though they might not all need adoption – very badly needed careful consideration.

The commander questions whether the Trust should continue its policy of honouring earlier arrangements with donors – and especially their heirs – when the result is that the public has little chance to visit the properties. He worries about the direction of cash outflow in the countryside. Too much, he feels, goes to acquisition of property and not enough on developing its potential for recreation.

He goes on to attack the committee structure for its failure to select members democratically – and he attacks the members selected for failing to take their participation seriously enough.

In his *Observer* piece, Rawnsley goes on to point out that the Executive Committee, which actually runs the Trust, met fifteen times between May 1965 (when Neptune was launched) and October 1966 (when Rawnsley was told to go). At these meetings, he says, there were 188 attendances and 222 absences. When the committee gathered to rule on the 'fate of Neptune' less than half of its twenty-nine members were present. The so-called ruling Council of the National Trust was in fact 'supine'. It did whatever the Executive told it to. (See the next chapter for more on the Council's long career as a rubber stamp.)

Not only was the National Trust an 'old boy network', but it was lazy to the point of somnolence. So much of Britain's finest property went to the Trust in order that the public might benefit as a result. But the people connected with the charity seemed to have forgotten that. And they didn't care to be reminded.

In February 1967 when the EGM took place, any member who wanted to vote had to show up and cast one. 'A Case for the Reform of the National Trust' written by Commander Rawnsley was available to the more than 4,000 members who came to the meeting at the Methodist Central Hall in Westminster. A thousand or more subscribers had to follow the proceedings over loudspeakers set up outside the auditorium.

Almost four years exactly from the day Conrad Rawnsley had triumphed and won the job as the National Trust's first appeals director he was unemployed and leading a fight against the policies, structure – and if possible the administration – of the charity his grandfather had helped found. He would have it all replaced with policies, structure and administration that better suited his idea of what the National Trust ought to be.

Enterprise Neptune has been the Trust's biggest and most unqualified success. The National Trust, with more than 500 miles and 115,000 acres, has become the largest owner of coastal land in Britain. The Neptune Appeal has raised more than £18 million and is still going strong; there remain hundreds of miles of coast in England, Wales and Ulster to acquire. And its overall target has increased because land which in the 1960s was thought too spoiled to consider, for example beaches along the north-east coast ruined by coal waste, have now become candidates for cleaning and reclamation.

'Rawnsley routed!' the *Observer* announced after the EGM.

He wasn't a hero who had triumphed, though the project he'd launched has. The character of the Trust at the time was in part responsible for that; but so was his own.

'Why won't you give us something?' he'd ask a rich, potential donor to Enterprise Neptune. 'You have plenty of money! How much do you earn a year?' he'd demand. Those who were there at the time say the commander also tried to bully the Trust's staff. Summary firings – by him – were not unknown. Surely the charity's members, having heard the eruptions, must have felt a little nervous of what he might get up to. The membership did not vote to support Conrad Rawnsley's proposal that a group made up of subscribers and Council members investigate all aspects of the Trust's work.

But the membership of the National Trust did hear what Conrad Rawnsley had been saying. It spoke to hunches and experiences of their own. They paid attention and they were sympathetic in many ways, if not the one which was crucial to him. They, too, wanted an investigation. (And a commission was set up, see Chapter 5.)

The membership of the National Trust knew changes had to be made. They simply would not caste their votes for a volcano for fear of the tidal wave that might follow; it was not their way.

As Conrad Rawnsley sees it, he became the leader of a revolution from motives as broad as they were selfless. 'I had to choose,' he's said, 'between loyalty to the Trust as an institution and loyalty to its ideals. I settled for the ideals.'

It is clear that Conrad Rawnsley had ideas, goals, a vision, and a need to prevail during his tenure at the National Trust. But what were his ideals, in fact? Did he have a commitment to the work for which the National Trust had been founded?

During a moment alone with her I asked Elsin Rawnsley if her husband's years of bitterness about what had happened during the launch of Enterprise Neptune were the result of a feeling that he'd let down his grandfather by not making the National Trust into the organization he felt it should be.

'Oh no,' she answered at once. 'Before he took the job he had no interest in the Trust. He wasn't even a member.' Apart from his attempts to seek vindication, he's shown little interest in the National Trust since.

'We've recovered our finances,' the commander says about himself and his wife. 'We've had fifty-three very happy years together. We've been through many vicissitudes and now we're into port more or less. I'm in excellent health. We've got a nice little home in a very pretty village. So Bob's your uncle.'

That leaves the National Trust.

'Why are you writing about the Rawnsley Row?' several veterans of it who are still associated with the National Trust have asked. Or as Sir John Smith put it, 'It's all old hat; it's history by now. All that happened such a long time ago. It's like writing about the murder of Edward II, isn't it? I do assure you,' Sir John counselled me, 'the Trust is completely different now'.

But have all the reforms hoped for in the middle 1960s come about? Is it all over and done with now? It's true that because of the Rawnsley Row, as a result of what the commander stirred up, many of his criticisms have led to changes being made in the way the National Trust works. But then there are the others. And new ones too. (See, for example, Chapter 5.)

The National Trust is both defensive, that is to say quick to take offence and behave as if its feelings have been hurt when there's been the most trivial suggestion that something may not be altogether wonderful, and at the same time it is complacent. This is not a healthy combination. After all, with a membership of more than 2 million, a fulltime staff of 6,000 (half of them seasonal) and 26,000 volunteers, there are bound to be a number of mortals around with reason to comment on the way it does things – and doesn't, not to mention the public.

By pretending that nothing is really wrong, by refusing to

admit mistakes out loud, in front of outsiders – and that includes its members – it builds a wall. The longer the Trust follows this practice, the higher the wall becomes. In time people with grievances, suggestions, visions of change will look at it and feel it's impenetrable: the only way to get through to those running the National Trust is to storm this barricade. It does sometimes appear that the National Trust brings on rows by not having found a way to listen to what people are trying to say to it. Why not encourage people to speak up, rather than turn off the hearing-aid?

[5]

How to Build an Oak

'They'll never give you permission,' the conspiracy theorists assured me. I thought so too, and very nearly didn't bring up the subject with the chairman of the National Trust, Lord Chorley. But when I finally did ask him if I could attend a meeting of the National Trust Council his answer was, 'I see no reason why not. When would you like to come?'

It happened that the next quarterly meeting of the Council was being held the following afternoon. I reckoned I'd better go to that one, before he could change his mind. But Lord Chorley managed to find the time to think again, nevertheless.

'I'd better take it up with my Executive Committee,' he told me. (Was this evidence of the Trust's predilection for consulting everyone about everything or a sign of indecision?)

At 12.45 the next day, Lord Chorley's secretary rang. They all have lunch in the board room before the Council meets, she said, would I like to come? 'You'll have to get your skates on. It starts at one.'

I raced to Queen Anne's Gate and joined the queue for quiche.

'You'll be so bored,' some Council members said, apologetically, as they chose from the buffet.

No doubt they were. But I found this study in inertia utterly engrossing in its lugubrious way. Only, however, because it was all new to me.

Lunch had been lively enough: plenty of chatter in the queue, lots of seemingly friendly catching-up going on. There'd been a fair bit of hopping from seat to seat as people had coffee. Council members who aren't on any of the Executive's subcommittees were learning what had happened since the last Council lunch and so forth. Then, lunch over, everyone had trooped out of Queen Anne's Gate and down Birdcage Walk to the Institution of Civil Engineers. A meeting for a Council of fifty-two was just too big for comfort in any of the Trust's own meeting rooms, it was felt.

Two large U-shaped tables filled the huge, high-ceilinged, panelled room; one U nesting inside the other, though nesting suggests a cosiness the setting entirely lacked. A pad and pencil had been laid out at each place. In the front of the room, facing the Council members were the chairman, the director general and the National Trust's lawyer, Mr Pullen. Mavis Kentish, the Trust's long-serving assistant secretary, took notes. Over us all hung an enormous modern glass chandelier; we might have been in the conference room of a Texas hotel.

A shy Council member, or anyone without practice in speaking up in public, would find it very hard to say a word in such a formal, cavernous room. But as the afternoon passed it became clear that this hardly mattered because not participating seemed to be the done thing here.

At 2.15 the chairman, hunched forward and leaning on his elbow, called the meeting to order.

Everyone had previously been sent a copy of Lord Chorley's draft statement for the upcoming Annual Report. Rodney Legg (appointed by the Open Spaces Society, which is one of the groups given the privilege of nominating a Council member), came up with several suggested additions. 'Make more of Neptune's achievements,' he exhorted the chairman. 'Boast about it!' Legg then came out with a list of Neptune facts and figures. In response, he was told that a number of his facts were wrong.

'Can't we get a Doctor of Literature to rewrite the chairman's remarks?' Sir John Smith piped up. 'The grammar is shaky, the thought unclear. We don't really want this to go out to the members in this form.' Several heads nodded in agreement.

Lord Chorley didn't seem particularly offended. In fact, as he sat listlessly in his chair, he showed little emotion of any kind as the meeting went on. Was it possible that the chairman was the most bored person in the room?

Now on to the main business of this session of the ruling Council. Jenny Baker, the National Trust's volunteers manager, was to read a research and policy paper she'd prepared.

Ms Baker, a short, round-faced woman, her brown hair cut in a Dutch boy bob, looks like a university student. Only up close is it, just, believable that she's middle-aged.

The world of volunteering for the National Trust could hardly be sunnier, Council members learned. Numbers were way up. The policy, begun in 1985, of replacing paid room stewards with batteries of volunteers was well underway. (And batteries it is, though Ms Baker didn't mention this. Because of the rota system the Trust employs, it takes twenty volunteers to replace one paid guide; a property that had five salaried room stewards before would now have 100 volunteers to do the same job. The administrator, or his second in command, the chief steward, would have the added work of keeping track of them all.) In the Mercia region, all paid guides had now been replaced with a saving of £84,000 a year.

In 1994 alone, Ms Baker told us, more than 4,500 men and woman would be taking their working holidays at Trust properties and volunteering their labour and expertise on a wide range of projects. And it wasn't only Acorn camps for youngsters any more. There were Oaks, too, the over-thirty-fives. Pensioners were taking part also, and foreigners. A group from France would be working for the Trust during their holiday at Fountains Abbey.

When she finished, Ms Baker was thanked and praised for her admirable work. (Then and intermittently throughout the meeting, the Council seemed very like a classroom full of boys and girls with whom a few older 'men of the world' like Sir Simon Hornby and Sir John Smith had been told they must spend the afternoon.)

Questions or comments were requested.

A middle-aged woman with straight grey hair, pointed features and thick spectacles began to speak. Hermione Hobhouse, a member of Council nominated by a clutch of small groups, among them the Victorian Society, had a question. Didn't the Trust find that in phasing out paid room guardians and replacing them with volunteers, a change in social background had occurred? And she also wondered, was the Trust, in fact, taking jobs away from people who really needed them badly?

Jenny Baker replied that, as she travelled around Britain visiting National Trust properties, she had 'received no feedback of that kind from the regions'. Indeed, she went further. 'It was', Ms Baker told the Council, 'usually the same people who stayed on as volunteers who had been paid guardians before.'

Fancy that. The forbidding, ex-Colonial policemen who was administrator at Hardwick Hall in Derbyshire – an area of high unemployment – had said there'd been a good deal of local resentment when the Trust stopped paying its room stewards there. The new volunteers were all middle-class folk, retired doctors and the like, who commuted from as far away as Sheffield.

And had Jenny Baker never heard the views of David Hancock, the administrator at Shugborough? He doesn't use volunteers, he pays and, he says, 'and we train our guides to be knowledgeable and to have charisma'. Lord Faringdon who is the Trust's tenant at Buscot Park in Oxfordshire does the same as does Lord St Levan who runs St Michael's Mount in Cornwall given to the Trust by his father. Had Ms Baker ever talked to him? Not only does he prefer to hire, train and pay the guides, he bluntly states that: 'the Trust should be employing more local people'. In Lord St Levan's view this means as conservers and producers of publications too. Owners of great country houses had seen it as their duty to give work to as many people nearby as they could. Like a chain of hotels, the Trust House Trust seems to be taking a corporate rather than individualized approach. As for it saving money, that may be only for the short term. (See below.)

Jenny Baker didn't appear to be duplicitous; perhaps she actually hadn't heard such things herself. But if she hadn't, to whom had she been speaking and what questions had she been asking? Instead of a policy review, her paper seemed more like institutionalized self-congratulation. And that is how it was left to stand.

Hermione Hobhouse did not ask a follow-up question. Nor did anyone else. Yet the reception of the Trust's decision to increase the number of its volunteers at its properties is certainly important. If the Trust saves money but creates ill-will in so doing, the profit-and-loss statement looks rather different from the one Ms Baker described. Shouldn't the Council want to explore this? Evidently not.

A person who'd had a drop of wine at lunch would have found it very very hard to keep awake. Apart from the subject of the chairman's prose style, nothing elicited any spirited comment. At no point during the Council meeting was there anything approaching a snappy observation, never mind a dialogue. It was disheartening. Later when I mentioned this to a couple of Council members I was assured that there is always a rousing debate when the subject of the price of subscriptions comes up. Though it's nice to hear that some of them care so much about keeping the charge for young members low, as an illustration of the Council's involvement in the Trust's affairs, it was not especially comforting.

Sir Simon Hornby assured me I'd got it wrong when afterwards I told him my feelings about the Trust's Council. 'Nearly all the members have a common purpose,' he explained, 'and many of the issues discussed are not controvertible. People don't get up and say, "I agree." Do you understand that?'

I think so. But just the same I can't go along with it. For example, I had found it possible to dispute the content of Ms Baker's presentation. And there've been other matters, among them some that are quite serious, which deserved discussion and debate and didn't get either. Take for instance, Angus Stirling's efforts to expand his own empire.

In 1983, Angus Stirling was made director general of the National Trust. He was brought in by Pat Gibson, then chairman of the charity. Before that Gibson had served as chairman of the Arts Council where Stirling had been its deputy secretary. When Stirling was passed over for the secretary's job, Gibson, his mentor, brought him into the Trust.[1]

According to its Constitution, Angus Stirling ought to have stepped down as director general at the end of 1993 when he reached the retirement age of sixty. Had Stirling's tenure been only ten years, it would have been an unusually long one in the Trust's history. But, he says in explanation, 'They asked me to stay on through the centenary.' Who is 'they'?

The Council did not discuss this, nor the Executive. Yet a precedent was being set. And there were other implications, too. For example, there were the good people who might have been candidates to replace him who would be ruled out as a result of the extension. Martin Drury, for instance, the historic buildings secretary, whom a number of people thought would make a fine successor to Sir Angus, was fifty-five years old in 1993. Had he become director general then he would have had five years in the job before retirement. But to start in 1995, at fifty-seven there might not be time enough left to make it sensible.

During much the same period that Stirling's tenure as DG was extended (more or less by fiat it seems) he had another interesting proposal to put to his employer. He'd been offered the chairmanship of the Royal Opera House and if the Trust didn't mind, he'd like to accept – a great honour, crowning achievement of a long, distinguished career; goodbye present to the DG, etc.

It's difficult to think of one single thing the National Trust could gain if it agreed to Angus Stirling's request to be both chairman of the Royal Opera House and its own director general. The Trust, after all, was already the largest, richest charity in Britain; the biggest most successful independent conservation organization anywhere. Whereas at the time, Covent Garden, though world famous, was in a terrible financial and administrative mess. Mightn't the Trust be dragged down by association, as it were? But, above all, wouldn't it be losing the full attention of its chief administrative officer who already had a very demanding, geographically far-flung job with them? And since both positions are highly visible, would it not lead to confusion in the public eye?

During Easter week of 1993 the Trust made public the results of its working party on deer hunting – a highly charged announcement, since there was a very vocal group of members against. Angus Stirling announced that the Council was advised to allow deer hunting on Trust land. The very same week, Angus Stirling disclosed that the Royal Opera House would go ahead with its much argued about plan for redeveloping the Covent Garden Piazza. Deer and divas, property development and conservation – a very peculiar mixture. Similarly in 1994 and 1995 both organizations were launching monumental appeals and though in each case there was going to be a well-known public figure as the head, someone from each body had to be its representative leader. 'Angus Stirling had to decide which appeal to run,' Jeremy Isaacs, the ROH's director, told me from his Covent Garden office. 'He decided to do the Opera House; Lord Chorley will take charge of the Trust's.' It's immediately apparent that the Isaacs/Stirling pairing is a fine example of what a director/chairman partnership is meant to be. Isaacs is feisty and forthright; the style of the ever-tactful Stirling he aptly describes as 'emollient'.

The chairman of the ROH does not get a salary but the effort the job involves is terribly demanding. The National Trust's chairman Lord Chorley, also unpaid, finds his a three- or four-day-a-week occupation. Jeremy Isaacs asserts that even were being chairman of the ROH a one-day-a-week job, it would be too much for the director general of the National Trust to undertake simultaneously. But he insists that it's not. It is difficult to believe as he goes on to describe what's involved: a meeting a month; telephone calls; performances at the opera house; discussions with members of the government or the heritage industry. Then there are the faxes from the ROH to the NT and vice-versa, chugging away day and night.

None of this was discussed by the National Trust's Council, the body created by its Constitution to act as Trustees protecting its properties on behalf of the nation. Angus Stirling became chairman of the Royal Opera House. But from Hadrian's Wall to the Isle of Purbeck and the west of Cornwall, it's hard to find a person with experience of the National Trust who thinks this should have been allowed to happen. Some are extremely cross: 'hubris', one observer called it, while the silkiest diplomats stare down at their hands and say, 'You can't expect me to comment on that.' And even Lord Gibson, Stirling's mentor, even he only managed a dark look when I brought the subject up. No one disputes that it has taken Sir Angus away from giving his concentration fully to the National Trust – except Sir Angus himself who avers that there's been a synergistic effect: involvement in one has helped his thinking about the other.

The National Trust's Council rubber-stamped its chairman's assent to the director general's requests, just as they rubber-stamped the chairman's vote when he extended his own tenure for another three years to run until 1997. Indeed they hadn't discussed or debated his original appointment.

While there have been times that a struggle has existed among contestants for the chairman's job – Sir Simon Hornby is said to have very much wanted to be the replacement for Lord Gibson in 1986 but Dame Jennifer Jenkins's supporters won out. Yet Roger Chorley was the single name the appointments subcommittee of the Executive presented to the Trust's Council at the end of its search for a chairman to replace Dame Jennifer Jenkins on her retirement in 1991. Lord Chorley had served on its Finance Committee for twenty years. Maybe the members of the Council hadn't had a chance to observe his manner. But by end of 1993 when he was 're-elected' they surely had, since he chairs all the Council meetings. Quite a few of them, along with tens of others, had grumbled about how poor he was at the job.

Wags had their explanation for this unlikely choice, of course. There were those who said Dame Jennifer wanted Roger Chorley because she liked him politically. Those even cattier insisted that it was Angus Stirling's doing. Dame Jennifer had been such a dynamic chairman with such a strong public presence, that while she served the director general seemed to live in her shadow. Not surprisingly there had been friction as a result. 'She couldn't bear Angus,' one onlooker contends. As gossip often does this builds on a truth. For several years during their joint reign, at press conferences and other meetings I assumed that Angus Stirling was a kind of glorified clerk who worked for Dame Jennifer, the person running the National Trust. There was no doubting it: she was in charge. Now, the rumour went, he wanted his chance to shine. This is the sort of thing it's hard to refute. And who could possibly look as if he were existing in Lord Chorley's shadow? Roger Chorley has negative charisma.

Lord Chorley, who sits on the cross-benches, is down-to-earth and approachable. He is refreshingly unsnooty. When he wants a cup of coffee at Queen Anne's Gate he goes and makes one. 'Can you imagine any of the heads of department doing that?' a Trust staff member asked rhetorically. Roger Chorley is courageous as well as straightforward.

A keen mountaineer, he contracted polio when a young man training for a Himalayan expedition and has had a bad leg ever since. Lord Chorley told me – and not for effect – that he hadn't been at all sure about accepting when he was asked to become chairman of the National Trust. His doctors had warned him that his leg would get worse with age and he had thought he'd spend what good years he had left travelling the world when he retired from Coopers & Lybrand, where he'd been a partner. Instead, he has been spending three to four days a week at Queen Anne's Gate or in the Trust's regions.

Having seen him tremble terribly when about to speak – even to a group of four journalists – I asked the chairman if he was shy. He looked very surprised. Later I understood why. Lord Chorley is not at all shy. He is diffident and not comfortable. Whether in the Chair at the Annual General Meeting, the Council or at the opening of a property, he gives the impression that it is an unwelcome strain.

Roger Chorley, though he shakes when making a speech, can otherwise be relaxed to a degree that's disquieting. A bit in the mould of Prince Philip, when he talked about some of the small nations that have emulated the National Trust by creating their own versions, he referred to them as 'silly countries'. Trying

[163]

to recall the head of one of these Trusts, he began looking in a file for someone with a 'funny name'. As a person with a funny name myself I stared at him. I didn't feel insulted, but I did feel embarrassed for the National Trust.

These issues highlight weaknesses in the structure of the National Trust, which simply cannot afford to be indulging itself in this way. It has grown too large, become too powerful, has too much to contribute, to drift into a situation where it is being run by a team that appears to be writing its own job descriptions and is not answerable except to itself. The system of 'checks and balances' is not working.

What is the check on the Executive? Who balances the power of the chairman or the director general? On paper the answer should be the Council. In practice it certainly is not.

Lord Gibson, formerly head of Pearsons, became a member of the National Trust's Executive Committee in the early 1960s. He was the Trust's chairman from 1977 to 1986. 'When I first joined the Trust,' he says, 'the Council *was* a rubber stamp.' They had rubbery minds, too. Council members, he went on to say, often didn't know the names of committee members whose policies they were agreeing to just the same. 'Supine,' was Commander Rawnsley's overheated word for it at about the same time. And he did his damnedest to make people aware of the urgent need for change. That was in the 1960s. Yet in the 1990s Rawnsley's comment can still stand. The Council remains supine, and a rubber stamp.

First you plant an acorn

The National Trust's Constitution – the Act of Parliament of 1907 – like the cost of an annual subscription, remained virtually static for half a century and more. There had, of course, been alterations in the form of other Acts – those of 1937 and 1939, for instance – which brought the Country Houses Scheme into operation – but this amounted to tinkering with the Constitution rather than an overhaul of the basic structure set down in the 1895 Articles of Association.

Sir Robert Hunter had based the National Trust's construction on that of the American conservation group, The Trustees of the Public Reservations.

Set up in the state of Massachusetts in 1891, the Trustees were founded by the landscape architect Charles Eliot, a member of the republic's aristocracy. (Later he went into partnership with Frederick Law Olmsted, designer of Central Park.)

The Trustees were the first holding company in the world established to preserve exceptional landscape and buildings in order that people would have access to them all, in perpetuity. Or, as the Trustees put it in their 1891 Act, they existed: 'for the purpose of acquiring, holding, arranging, maintaining, and opening to the public under suitable regulations, beautiful and historical places and tracts of land . . .'

Many high-minded people on both sides of the Atlantic were aware of the threats to historical places and beautiful landscape and anxious to find a way of fighting them off. For that reason alone, the first society created to try to solve the problem in such a far-reaching way was given international publicity. Octavia Hill asked her American friend Ellen Chase to visit the Trustees outside Boston to see what they were up to. In 1899 when Hardwicke Rawnsley travelled the American lecture circuit trying to raise interest in – and money for – the National Trust he, too, stopped in Massachusetts to see what there was to learn from the Trustees.

'The child has far outstripped the father, to be perfectly frank with you,' Gordon Abbott, the child's former chairman says with good humour. Abbott reports that in 1991 when they celebrated their hundredth birthday, the Trustees owned seventy-six properties amounting to about 18,000 acres of land, by design, limited to Massachusetts. They had a membership of 9,000 people.

Obviously, no one could have foretold that either organization would be successful nor that one would grow so tremendously. Nevertheless, the Americans, and then Hunter who took their Constitution as his model, prepared themselves – just in case.

The ruling Council of the Trustees in Massachusetts, which was responsible for its properties on behalf of the public, was to consist half of people elected by its members, half of those appointed by nominating bodies. These would include the notable academic and scientific establishments and the major art galleries. The National Trust chose to do exactly the same. Hunter drew up a blueprint for a Council of fifty; twenty-five of whom would be appointed by great institutions; twenty-five of whom would be elected by the National Trust's subscribers.

But fifty English men and women to serve as the Council for a holding company that had eight members when the Articles of Association were registered? Such immoderateness wouldn't seem to have been the founders' style.

Canon Rawnsley liked to call the National Trust an outdoor National Gallery. Why then didn't he and Hill and Hunter model their structure on its? The Committee of Gentlemen who were the Trustees of London's National Gallery (founded in 1824) were six in number in the year the National Trust was founded. The Royal Horticultural Society had fifteen Trustees. William Morris's Society for the Preservation of Ancient Buildings (SPAB), established in 1877, had a main committee of twenty-five to oversee its affairs. The RIBA, set up in 1834, had a council of thirteen.

Surely amassing such a large Council was an attempt at

attracting social and cultural support. Among the fifty who made up the first Council of the National Trust were the Dukes of Devonshire and Westminster, T.H. Huxley, Mrs Humphry Ward, the Provost of Eton and Frederick Leighton, president of the Royal Academy. The influential people and societies who participated would naturally take an interest in the fledgling group and try to help it along. And by having on its Council twenty-five people nominated by established learned and artistic institutions, a large amount of expert advice was available to the National Trust whenever the need for it arose. (You couldn't necessarily depend on even the most like-minded of individuals in this regard. William Morris, for instance, though asked in 1896 to give the Trust aesthetic advice, declined. 'I find as a rule only one kind of opinion is expected,' he wrote, 'and that an adverse one is ill received ... People must do their best and take the consequences.'[2] But the SPAB which he founded has had a member on the National Trust's Council giving the charity its views from the beginning to the present day.)

Neither its Articles of Association nor the Act of 1907 were an attempt to create a democracy. The National Trust was conceived as a society of sympathetic people who shared a common purpose. Out of this pool, an Executive was appointed, not elected, to run the organization. The Council, though it had shunted virtually everything else on to the Executive, was the body which held all the National Trust's property in trust for the nation.

The Act of 1907, which provided the Trust with the critical ability to declare property inalienable, like the Acts of 1937 and 1939 which extended the charity's powers, all retained this element of its original structure: 'The entire business of the Trust shall be arranged and managed by the Council,' reads the 1907 Act of Parliament and all that have followed to date. But even before a permanent Council had been set up in 1895, the Trust's provisional Council had appointed an Executive Committee and given it power to make policies on its behalf. The Executive Committee, in turn, had the power to appoint subcommittees as it felt the need.

In 1897, two years after the National Trust was founded,

a Works & General Purposes Committee was created by the Executive. Finance came in 1899 and Estates a year later – by which time the charity had 200 members; Publicity came in 1928, Country Houses in 1936 and then in the late 1940s there was a burst of growth by committee when five more (including subcommittees for Nature Conservation and Forestry) were added. The staff was growing too and by the 1950s there was a legal adviser, a chief agent, the secretary to the Historic Buildings Committee and the chief accountant. There were also fourteen land agents in various parts of the Trust's domain and ninety-nine local committees of volunteers who ran many of the properties since there wasn't staff enough to do the job.

When Michael Trinick went to work for the Trust in 1950 about 20,000 people were members of the charity.

'The little office in London tried to run everything themselves,' he recalls. 'In fact they couldn't.' For him – and for Devon and Cornwall where he did so much acquiring of property – this was a blessing. 'It sounds silly and petty,' he admits, 'but the fact is this independence enabled a lot of good things to happen which wouldn't have happened if we'd been at all a bureaucratic business.'

Trinick, in time, became both regional director and historic buildings representative for Devon and Cornwall and got busy making the most of it pretty fast.

'I took the bull by the horns,' he says, 'very much encouraged by Cubby Acland.' Cubby Acland, younger brother of Sir Richard who gave Killerton to the charity, was the Trust's man in the Lake District from 1949 until he retired in 1973. Acland told Trinick, who was supposed to go to London every time he wanted to buy a pitchfork, 'Don't put up with them. Do it yourself.' Instantly, he took this advice.

'I got away with it,' Trinick says beaming. 'It was a long way from London. And', he adds, 'if I could have a row, I rather enjoyed it.'

When Trinick got word that a cliff farm might be for sale, he'd nip over to the farmer, make a deal, take a £5 note out of his pocket to seal it and then go back to his house, ring the office in London to tell them that the National Trust had just become the new owner of a beautiful stretch of the Cornish coast.

'Michael always knew somebody who would give the money to buy the thing,' says Peter Orde who clearly envied him this gift. 'It's a great flair to have.' Major Orde headed the committee of volunteers looking after the Trust's properties in the north-west during the same period. In later years when things weren't quite so free and easy, Trinick's talent for finding funds probably kept him his job.

But while the empire builders were hard at work, who was seeing to the rest of the Trust's domain?

'This was totally unofficial,' says Peter Orde about this period during the 1950s, 'but I always understood that what happened was that in one of the Executive Committees of the Trust, the then treasurer who was a man called Holland-Martin said, "Look here. There must be something wrong about this. We've been offered a number of properties and virtually nobody in this room has seen any of them. We're going entirely on photographs and what the staff say. I've got nothing against the staff, but we really are making very important decisions and we shouldn't do it without real knowledge. We're becoming frighteningly big. We ought to have a foot on the ground in every region, especially the distant ones."'

'Ruby' Holland-Martin wasn't the only person at the National Trust who had his eyes open. In 1956, Sir Philip Nichols, a diplomat serving on the Executive, wrote a memo saying that he thought the Trust needed to change its way of working. He duly became a member of the committee set up to look into its operation. His collaborators included James Lees-Milne, Lord De la Warr and John Smith.

The Trust had fourteen land agents and a handful of historic buildings representatives who looked after aesthetic and architectural matters. This was not enough to do the job properly while being more than enough to cause trouble, chiefly as a result of rivalry. Historic buildings representatives and land agents competed for influence at the various properties. The war between the lilies and hobnailed boots, it was sometimes called.

[169]

In 1958, two years after Sir Philip had written his memo, the Nichols Report was presented to the Executive. Among its recommendations were that a great many of the responsibilities involved in looking after its properties could be better fulfilled closer to them. It was suggested that a new position called the regional secretary should be created. These people would be employed as fulltime, salaried members of the National Trust's administrative staff. This was to solve the confusion about who was in charge. They would be.

Nichols considered that five regional secretaries would be a good beginning. Head Office in London should continue to set the Trust's nationwide policy and go on making decisions about such far-reaching issues as which properties to accept – and which to declare inalienable – what salaries were to be paid. But it was assumed that as the size of the staff around the country increased, the number of people in London – committee members as well as staff – would naturally shrink, as it should.

The Council was to be untouched. 'Some of its members may well be unfamiliar with the work of the Trust,' was the diplomatic language the Nichols Report used to describe the ignorance and lack of involvement of many who served on it.

The tortoise responded by nibbling lettuce, which is to say that after the Nichols Report not much changed. But since there already were a few honorary regional representatives scattered around Britain, the Executive decided to give these volunteers the title of regional chairmen and ask them to appoint members to committees with whom they would oversee the properties in their respective parts of the country.

Nicholas Ridley had been the honorary regional representative for the north-east. When he ran for Parliament, Major Orde, a childhood friend, took it on.

'I had practically nothing to decide or advise on for about three years,' Orde recalls. But as a result of the Nichols Report he was made the regional chairman for Northumberland and Durham. The Regional Committee for Devon and Cornwall, chaired and selected by General Julian Gascoigne, came next.

Orde and his committee of volunteers oversaw a Regional Office of Trust employees consisting of one land agent, a bookkeeper and a secretary. 'We had far fewer properties, of course,' he says, 'but we did have Wallington, the Farne Islands, Lindisfarne Castle, Washington Old Hall . . .' (Today Tiffany Hunt, the first woman regional director, oversees a staff of thirty-three.)

Peter Orde, who was working as a stockbroker in Newcastle, sometimes felt he'd taken on more than he could properly handle. But he clearly enjoyed himself. 'I do remember the tremendous feeling of loyalty and terrific camaraderie of it all. We all fitted in. And we didn't cost the Trust much at all.'

A few years after Orde became regional chairman for Northumberland, Sir Marcus Worsley was asked to create a committee of volunteers in Yorkshire. Unlike Orde, he made his a minuscule group. When Major Orde questioned him about the wisdom of this, the baronet answered 'I think a committee should be small enough to all travel in the same Land-Rover and have meetings in the back of it when we visit a property and decide what should be done.'

'In the 1950s and 1960s we were the National Trust up here,' says Peter Orde. And so they were. What local Trust staff existed in the area was, in effect, there to serve them.

But who was the National Trust far away in London?

'It's long ago,' says Sir John Smith thinking back on the days leading up to the Rawnsley Row in the mid-sixties, 'but I think had Lord Crawford been a more diligent chairman, I don't think these troubles would have occurred.' If the chairman of the National Trust had implemented the recommendations of the Nichols report or in any other way attended to the building of a stronger staff to look after the Trust's growing number of properties, a movement to reform the charity might not have got underway.

A club of their own

The Earl of Crawford and Balcarres, much admired and respected for among other things his knowledge of art, was chairman of the National Trust from 1945 to 1965. He found it possible to carry out his duties by coming down from Scotland and taking the chair of its Executive Committee one day a month.

People like Cubby Acland and Michael Trinick of course liked working under a leader who held the reins so loosely. But not everyone was a fan. In the estimation of Sir John Smith who began his connection with the Trust in 1952, 'he was an aesthetic aristocrat and a very remote figure. I overlapped with Lord Crawford, and you know he did very nearly nothing,' Sir John continued. 'The Trust was run by Lord Esher.'

Officially, Viscount Esher was chairman of both the Trust's General Purposes and Historic Houses Committees.

'Lord Esher was a wise man, very,' says Sir John. Oliver Esher was also a rich one. 'And an amusing man. For many years he not only ran it, but was responsible for setting the tone, entirely.'

What interested Oliver Esher were above all buildings, and their contents. He loved beautiful landscape, but he wasn't interested in what was involved in looking after it.

'The Trust in those years was his creation,' Sir John underscores. 'He was a very sophisticated man.' But in addition to finding the management of land rather boring, Lord Esher was also 'not frightfully interested in the public' either. As in so much else, Oliver Esher had set the tone in this too. (See Chapter 2.)

Lord Crawford might be in town on his monthly visit; Anthony Blunt might call to give his advice on pictures; Lord Esher was likely to be there and Jack Rathbone, of course. Rathbone, secretary of the Trust, was Lord Esher's acolyte. They might sometimes be joined by Ran Antrim, who served on the Executive and was head of the Northern Ireland Committee for fifteen years before becoming chairman of the Trust in 1965. They'd say a few words about the National Trust's business and then they'd totter across St James's Park to their other clubs. In Brooks's they might chat with an owner of a great country estate who was thinking that the National Trust might be just the thing to secure its future.

'If you take down Debrett and work out the relationship of the owners of the houses and the men on the Committees and the chairman of the Trust,' says Michael Trinick about those days in the 1950s and 1960s, 'they're all each other's relations.

'I used to roar with laughter,' Trinick goes on, 'the Trust was so small and I was being quite active in acquiring bits of land and I used to go to every monthly meeting. And they used to come in, all these old Lords, and say, "Good morning David, Good morning Herbert, How are you John, Morning Chorley." They would never call him by his Christian name. He thought it was rather funny too. But I mean they were either all relations or friends.' Professor Chorley on the other hand was a mountain-climbing Labour MP, who'd been created a baron in 1945; he had begun his service on Trust committees in the 1920s. (His son Roger became chairman in 1991.)

Lord Antrim, who headed the Trust from 1965 to 1977, was a more modern and practical man than David Crawford, in Sir John's view. And many people who served on committees he chaired talk about how charming he was and how much they enjoyed his company. 'Ran Antrim had the most marvellous touch,' said Major Peter Orde who as a regional chairman for Northumberland was an ex-officio member of the Executive Committee. 'He didn't let everyone ramble on, but he did make it all great fun. He was very witty himself and we had people like John Betjeman and John Julius Norwich who were themselves amusing to listen to. I really looked forward to it.'

Led by Lord Antrim there was reason to think that the National Trust might begin to have a less narrow approach to its work.

'Ran Antrim had a much better idea of the growing importance of the public,' says Sir John Smith. 'And he was worldly in a good sense. Both he and Lord Crawford knew how the world worked, but Ran was capable of doing something about it.' However, before the Earl of Antrim had a chance to do much at the Trust, the Rawnsley Rumpus exploded.

Or, as Sir John puts it, 'Conrad Rawnsley sorted out that log jam.'

One of the many results of the upheaval that followed the Rawnsley Row was that 1970 produced a bumper crop of new Executive subdivisions. A Properties Committee emerged, for example, and from it dangled six panels, among them one each for Architecture and Arts. But a growth in the Trust's administrative apparatus was only one of several major changes with far-reaching, if often unforeseen, implications for the future that began to take place. The Benson Committee had met and studied; it had made its report and this time, unlike its response to the Nichols Report a decade earlier, the men running the National Trust did not ignore what was said.

'You know,' says Sir Simon Hornby, 'in a big organization like that you need occasional issues that are going to generate change and stir things up. It's difficult to step back and ask: "should we be reorganizing ourselves; should we be organizing ourselves in a different way?"'

And with Conrad Rawnsley's help (though that's not the word some at the Trust would have used to describe it) change was being generated. The Executive Committee asked Sir Henry (now Lord) Benson, a distinguished chartered accountant, to chair a panel of enquiry.

Rawnsley and some of his supporters feared a whitewash, naturally – but also with reason. The members of Sir Henry's committee were Pat Gibson (then a member of the Trust's Executive and an elected member of the Council), and two men who were nominated Council members: Len Clark from the Youth Hostels Association and Sir William Hayter from the British Museum.

A reformer reading the opening of the report Sir Henry

eventually published might have confirmed his suspicions that the committee were apologists for the Trust. For background Sir Henry had relied almost exclusively on what Robin Fedden, the Trust's historic buildings secretary, had published in *The Continuing Purpose*, his 1968 book about the charity's history and aims. Not only did Sir Henry quote from Fedden, he alerted readers of the report that he had also frequently paraphrased 'without indicating in either case that this is the source'.

Yet with all this, the Benson Report, published in December 1968, proved to be a remarkably clear-eyed look at how the National Trust was operating. It is also a long, detailed manual setting out how the Trust should be changed.

Sir Henry insisted that his guide to improving the National Trust should be seen as 'a tribute to its success', and not a litany of shortcomings. Critics, of course, were more likely to see a half empty glass than a half full one. But either way, it was plain that a great many alterations were needed; so many in fact that a new Act of Parliament would be required if they were to be put into effect.

To Parliament, to Parliament

The Constitution of the National Trust was still based on the Act of 1907 and in sixty years this skeleton had developed brittle bones. In fact, as Benson saw it, all that had kept the Trust from collapsing was 'good will and mutual understanding'. The ill-will that blew into the Extraordinary General Meeting could so easily have caused crippling fractures. But even without the Rawnsley Row, the bonhomie of a handful of like-minded men was a poor substitute for the sort of structure the National Trust needed if it was to administer effectively its by now rather impressive holdings.

At the time of Sir Henry's investigation – when the Trust had been soliciting millions of pounds for Enterprise Neptune alone – the charity still did not have a fulltime financial officer on its payroll. And though it had finally raised the price of an annual subscription to £2, since this only applied to new members, some loyal men and women continued to pay ten shillings a year. Yet it was costing the National Trust eight shillings to service each and every member! Very soon the long-time supporters who were trying to help the charity achieve its goals by keeping up their subscriptions were going to end up costing the National Trust money.

Sir Henry Benson and his committee produced a report of 152 pages with an alphabet's worth of appendices. In its total of 187 pages the report addressed everything from money management to membership, structure to tea rooms.

Vast numbers of things that before had been left to whim or custom now were to be put into writing. Some were trivial – children had been entitled to the same voting rights as adults since 1907. Others only looked as if they were: in future all ordinary members of the Trust would pay the same annual subscription.

The responsibilities of the Trust's various committees and subcommittees was now put in writing for the first time. As was the retirement age for its chairman, regional directors and secretary (called the director general from 1968, when Jack Boles came in to replace Rathbone). These ages were seventy, sixty and sixty respectively. And while none of the chaps was chastized for arrangements past, the Benson Panel did recommend that in future the National Trust should be more careful when granting rights, in perpetuity, to families who donate properties.

When he was appointed to head the investigation, Sir Henry had asked the Trust's wardens to carry out a survey of its properties. They reported that there was an enormous backlog of work that needed doing on the Trust's farms, cottages and great houses. In all about £5 million would be needed – and fast – to bring them up to the high standard they wished to set.

The Benson Report advised the Trust to shut down Enterprise Neptune and to launch instead one grand, general appeal. Rather than acquisition, its goal would be to raise the millions required to look after those properties the

National Trust already owned and were charged with preserving for ever.

The panel then had a look at the way the hip bone was connected to the thigh bone of this fragile skeleton. The changes that were found necessary after this examination make Commander Rawnsley's Field Force look modest by comparison.

Keeping Council

Members of the Council, the Executive and the subcommittees could scarcely manage to attend meetings.

Only about half the men on the Executive Committee, which after all was running the Trust, turned up when it met; the Gardens Committee was slightly better attended: six of the ten people were there when it gathered twice a year. As for the four men on the Finance Committee which met quarterly, two found the time to show up. Among the fifty members of the so-called ruling Council, one in three actually went to meetings.

Benson judged that the Council had given over too much of its power to the Executive Committee and ought to take some back. For instance, in future the Council should approve the National Trust budget and accounts and should make the final decision about which properties the Trust agreed to take on. Although, according to its Constitution, the Council chose the Executive, the Executive in fact appointed itself. In an attempt to open the Executive Committee to people who might not be Old Etonians or members of Brooks's (or both) – and, who knows, maybe to women, also – Benson advised that the majority of people on the Executive should be members of the Council. In that way, at least a few might have been elected by subscribers at the Annual General Meeting. To insure that the Council was better attended, it was suggested that those who failed to appear for twelve months be 'retired'.

Who's minding the properties?

In the 1950s, most of the Trust's properties were administered from London with volunteers in the regions overseeing their management. The Trust, following the Nichols report, had three salaried regional secretaries, the precursors of today's regional directors: one for Devon & Cornwall, one for Northern Ireland and one for a region that took in the northern Home Counties, East Anglia and the south Midlands. Aesthetic matters as well as land management were in their charge.

By 1968 while the number of regional secretaries had not grown, there were seven Regional Committees served by volunteers, five National Trust historic buildings representatives overseeing 'matters of taste' and 15 NT area agents looking after the landscape. Two new Regional Committees had already been proposed. Benson saw that this wasn't enough. He recommended that every region of the National Trust have its own which would bring the total to fourteen. Devon & Cornwall was a single region at the time, as was North and South Wales and their Regional Committees remain combined to this day. But each now has its own paid administrative staff which means that the National Trust has sixteen regions in all.

Benson noted that paid staff, from secretaries to land agents, accountants and public relations officers, would have to be hired for each region. Like Nichols, Benson reckoned that as the Trust's countrywide staff grew, the size of head office would shrink.

All this was going to cost still more money. But what was earned through the new appeal would go to improving its properties. Benson, therefore, came up with a plan that would generate enough income to pay the salaries of the employees he believed must be hired. The Trust must begin a mammoth membership drive. In 1968 there were about 160,000 subscribers; the target should be 500,000 by the early 1980s.

And since it couldn't be expected that so many people would be able to attend its Annual General Meeting, proxy voting was to be permitted; members could, of course, chose to give their proxies to whomever they wished.

The conclusion of the Benson Report was straightforward: the National Trust should have a bigger staff deployed around the country so that people would be close to the properties they looked after. As Benson conceived the 'Chain of Command', this staff would report to the Regional Committees made up of volunteers who in turn would work with the Trust's people in London. A small staff at its headquarters could look after national affairs and policies. Further recommendations were that the make-up of the Executive should be broader and its responsiveness to the Council greater. As for the Council, it should eat more spinach and use its muscles to become more vigilant about safeguarding the nation's interests.

The Act drafted by the National Trust and passed by Parliament in 1971 incorporated many of the suggestions made in Sir Henry Benson's Report. The Trust, however, did not adopt such suggestions as streamlining its head office operations by cutting the Executive committee to no more than twenty people, or dropping the Historic Buildings Committee, which both Benson and Nichols before him recommended. Nevertheless, where previously there had been only gentlemanly good will, the National Trust now had been given an elaborately worked out structure both for its central and its regional operations, with the responsibilities of each component set down. Rules and regulations had been introduced; such things as retirement age and minimum attendance required for Council members who, if they did not comply, could be asked to step down. Benson and his panel had diagnosed what was needed if the National Trust was to achieve a sturdy, healthy maturity. But in recommending that the Trust dramatically increase its membership, the report had also written a prescription for a long and recurrently uncomfortable period of growing pains. A half century later they are still being felt.

The boom

Staff were taken on; the drive to increase membership was wholeheartedly embraced. And once the door to what in the past must have looked like a rather exclusive club was opened, millions paid their money to walk through it.

In 1970 the National Trust had about 225,000 members. By 1981 that figure had *quadrupled*. And in the decade that followed it doubled again. The result of all this was that the National Trust had 2 million subscribers in 1990 and these men and women were contributing thirty-four per cent of its annual operating income. As has been mentioned, its fulltime, year-round salaried staff numbered more than 3,000; during its six-month season double that number were employed and there were 26,000 volunteers.

Sixteen Regional Offices were in operation, staffed by land agents, historic buildings representatives, press officers . . . More housekeepers were employed at properties; education officers were taken on, and conservation experts of all sorts. Shops and tea rooms and holiday lets all became part of National Trust Enterprises, a profit-making business which by the Centenary was contributing about £5 million to the charity annually. Eventually there were regional enterprise managers, too.

Students of the biology of bureaucracies will have guessed that though the National Trust expanded in every direction it shrank in none. The Council added two members, in fact; the Executive five. Including the chairman, the director general and the various chairmen of Regional Committees, the Executive weighs in at a hefty thirty-three. The staff at headquarters grew so big in the years after the 1971 Act of Parliament that it split into three. Besides the administrative offices at Queen Anne's Gate where the director general, chairman, historic buildings secretary and public affairs department, the lawyer, library and such can be found, a second head office was opened at Cirencester to advise on the running of the 'outside' aspect of the Trust's work – Forestry, Gardens, Nature Conservation. While National Trust Enterprises Ltd and the Finance Department have their offices in Westbury, Wiltshire.

Yet in spite of so much build-up at its centre, 'for fifteen years devolution really was working,' Michael Trinick asserts. Then, 'suddenly it began to go wrong'. The centre seemed to panic and it started grabbing back control.

Fifteen years after the publication of the Benson Report takes us to 1983. Two related events occurred which appear to be the explanation for the tightening up that Trinick observed. Another row had led to another EGM, this one known as Bradenham. And it, in turn, was followed by another report, this one called Arkell, published in 1983. That year also saw the recruitment of the National Trust's one millionth member. The gargantuan membership had begun to take on a life of its own.

Whose Trust is it anyway?

In 1928 when the National Trust had a membership of 1,550, Princess Louise, who had served as its president for more than a quarter of a century, spoke out against G.M. Trevelyan's idea of raising money through increasing membership. Missionary work might be effective, but the people drawn in would be strangers to the Trust's work and its aims. A small group of subscribers, staff and volunteers could both cope better and would be more harmonious because all would be of like mind. Princess Louise was perceptive, but her view hadn't prevailed then and it was certainly ignored now. After the Benson Report, growth became astronomic. Disharmony was probably inevitable. So many people joining the Trust, myself included, had so little idea of just about everything connected to it.

When I joined the National Trust and set out to visit one of its properties, I used to joke that I was going to see one of my houses. But like hundreds of thousands of other people, I also half believed it. A lot of us have felt that these houses, gardens, mountains, belong to us. Life members evidently feel this even more strongly and don't hold back from giving gardeners or wardens advice when they feel something's wrong. Donors are not the only people on National Trust properties who can be bossy.

Since we see ourselves as owners, we believe that the management ought to keep us informed about what it is doing or planning. It should listen to our reactions and, of course, take our opinions into account. That's what the AGM is for after all. 'You're working for us!' more than one indignant subscriber has said to the men on the podium in a moment of frustration during a heated AGM. But, as it turns out, we're not owners and they're not our employees.

A membership heading towards a million was bound to produce a fair number of people with such views. And they were bound to give one another courage and conviction. So they did and Bradenham erupted in 1981.

The RAF Strike Command at Bradenham in Berkshire had requested a lease on twelve acres of adjacent land. This was part of the more than 1,000-acre Bradenham estate, the inalienable property of the National Trust. The reason the Military wanted the land was to enlarge an existing underground command bunker. The Trust without consulting its members eventually agreed.

How could they!

With hindsight, people at the Trust acknowledged that it had been 'naive' in its handling of the whole affair. Others might say it was blundering and completely out of touch. The decision was bound to have been contentious and taken up as a political issue. This was a period when the Campaign for Nuclear Disarmament had many passionate supporters and they felt there was reason to suspect that the bunker at Bradenham might be used as a nuclear command post. Steadfast National Trust supporters who were members of the peace movement were offended; some felt betrayed.

An EGM was demanded. Unlike the Rawnsley Row, this one didn't aim to reform the National Trust. What members wanted was an administration more responsive to their views.

At the November 1982 EGM the majority of the National Trust's members who bothered to vote at all (with proxies this was about sixteen per cent of the overall total) supported the Trust. But as had happened after the Rawnsley *fracas*, it was clear that many more were unhappy with the way the Trust was being run, and so the Trust commissioned another examination of itself.

Led by John Arkell, a five-man team of Council members was to review the relationship between the National Trust's management, its Council and its membership.

Arkell (the Council for the Protection of Rural England's nominee to the Trust's Council) published his report in 1983. His tone is cooler and his language sharper than studies before – and since. Arkell actually uses works like 'weaknesses' when describing National Trust practices. And he notes that even among its supporters, many felt that the men in charge appeared to be closed, autocratic, patronizing and defensive.

Though there were many more Regional Committees since the Benson Report led to a new constitution for the Trust, all over Britain members who belonged to local supporters groups often didn't know who was on their Regional Committee nor what policies they considered. Subscribers to the National Trust wanted to be kept informed and they wanted to be heard. The Arkell Report advised the Trust to make more of an effort to attract a wider variety of people to its Regional Committees[3] and above all to become more open and to show 'a greater willingness to listen and to communicate'.

Angus Stirling who became director general in 1983, the year Arkell's findings were published, has adopted a policy of openness ever since.

'I remember when I came here,' Angus Stirling says, 'I tried to get Sotheby's to sponsor an exhibition that we were having. And I got a little note from somebody in the Historic Buildings department saying that they thought it was disgraceful that Sotheby's "ill-gotten gains" should be applied to the National

Trust's affairs. As if there was something wrong with the money! Well I mean that was just an indication. It was such a closed feeling. It needed changing, my goodness it did.'

But this was more than a decade after the Rawnsley Row and the Benson Report. Why hadn't it changed yet? And if the people running it were so dug in, what could get things moving at last?

There have been many signs of a shift in emphasis since. Sir Angus likes to recall, when he arrived at Queen Anne's Gate, *Country Life* and the *Daily Telegraph* were on the table as you entered and that was it. 'When I came into the office I deliberately sent to the Public Affairs Department and said, "I'd like to see the *Guardian* please".' He smiled. 'I think,' continued Sir Angus, an Old Etonian and grandson of an earl, 'the feeling was, "Who is this radical left-wing chap, who's come into the building?"'

But 'openness' still seems far from the word an out-side onlooker would chose to describe the attitude of the National Trust. Consider, briefly, the AGM of 1992 held in Birmingham.

Lord Chorley opened the meeting with the message that 'We are of good heart, thought we have to tighten our belts,' the long recession having finally made itself felt at the National Trust too. But whatever chirpiness the chairman was hoping to project would not have created a buoyant mood even if he were a lively public speaker. The senior officials of the National Trust sitting on the stage of the Conference Centre along with him soon began to look tight-lipped and restless.

A good deal of that day in Birmingham was given over to the discussion of a Member's Resolution having to do with the Trust's management of one particular property – a waterway – called the Wey & Godalming Navigation in Surrey. There was, it transpired, some rather expensive, private property on this twenty-mile stretch of water and, since the Navigation has two sides, that meant, for those so inclined, forty miles of property boundaries could be in dispute. There were more than a couple; something like twenty-five people were lined up to testify: dog walkers with good words for the Trust, property owners with complaints – a few of the latter in a stage of rage that produces burst blood vessels and strokes. There was talk of 'a climate of fear', the result of the Trust's attempts to intimidate those who disagreed with the way it was doing things.

Besides boundary disagreements, money also appeared to be an issue. And then there was a most troubling allegation about conflict of interest. It was asserted that the Trust had allowed the man it employed as foreman of the Navigation to have a second source of income: he actually owned and operated a business that tendered with the Trust for contracts to do maintenance work *on the Wey Navigation*. So it was said. This sounded over the top.

'I must say,' Angus Stirling recalls, 'it was the most dispiriting AGM that I've been to and it was my fourteenth. It was dominated by people who had a grouse against the National Trust. These were not great national issues of the Trust. The whole grand design and purpose of the National Trust and what it was doing was of apparently no interest.'

There certainly had been a feeling in that hall in Birmingham that these people were being awfully tiresome, going on and on about the Trust's policy at this one single property. Why hadn't a local problem been handled locally?

But there'd also been a feeling in the auditorium that the men running the Trust were being touchy, dismissive and even antagonistic towards the members from Surrey who were so cross when it could so easily have been generous instead. Were the people complaining about how the Trust did things really being pigheaded and exhibitionistic? Or were they, instead, bringing their troubles to the AGM because everything else had been tried and had failed, and they felt they had no other choice?

'We want an independent investigation!' they demanded.

A good many members in the room seemed to feel that would be only fair. But the wall of men in dark suits up on the stage – the management board of the National Trust – did not open a gate. Instead they said they were willing to undertake a review made up entirely of Council members. (Sound familiar?)

Those who had called for an investigation naturally objected that this isn't what they meant by 'independent'. (This too has an echo.)

Angus Stirling, looking irritated and impatient – rather like an older brother whose authority is being challenged – insisted the National Trust Council was totally independent of the Trust's Executive.

One could not accuse those in the hall, who did not entirely believe this, of being paranoid. And, in time, outsiders were in fact added to the panel.

For months afterwards people who work for the National Trust referred to how depressed they felt about that AGM. And it had been a dreary affair, the mood not helped by a feature of these meetings: the Trust's presentation of its work in the preceding year. Sometimes this is given by the director general, sometimes by one of the regional directors as it was at Birmingham. Peter Nixon who heads the Mercia region gave a slide show talk about what they'd been doing in his part of the Trust's domain. It would not have been over the heads of a class of sheltered eight-year-olds. (Nixon shouldn't be singled out for criticism, perhaps, because this is the level at which most National Trust presentations are pitched.) Several hundred people left Birmingham feeling more melancholy than when they'd arrived.

Council member Ron Rowland's report about Navigation was sent to the Executive of the National Trust in advance of the 1993 AGM, which was to be held at the Wembley Conference Centre that November. Its findings would be presented to the membership at that time.

A larger, more expensive auditorium had been hired for 1993 because hunting was on the agenda. The anti-hunting members were well organized and expected to attend in force. Packs of members keen on field sports were expected to also crowd in.

At Wembley, Angus Stirling presented a summary of what Rowland had written to the director general. Yes, he told the subscribers, there had been problems in the Southern Region. And there had been a conflict of interest on the Navigation. As for the attitude of people working for the Trust, he stressed that

'It is a matter of policy of the Trust's that there be a friendly, helpful attitude on the part of the staff.' Problems were being dealt with. Negotiations were progressing with the parties who had complaints the year before.

As far as it went, the director general's summary was accurate. The faces of the principals who again were present in the hall were proof that conditions must be getting better. Where the year before there had been throbbing temples and black scowls, now there were modest smiles. Only a person who had actually read the report could know how very bad things had been and how much the director general had skated over. For example:

Rowland found that the Southern Region, though it had known about the conflict of interest, had been prepared to let their foreman's company go on bidding for work on the Navigation for a further three years. Only in 1996 would it have to 'disengage totally'. The Rowland panel insisted that this must not be allowed.

Evidently there had been many complaints to the committee about National Trust staff who were 'unhelpful and at times provocative'. Rowland judged that it would take years before the damage that had been done could be repaired. Changes in personnel might be required. (No one at the Trust likes to use the word 'fired'.)

At the 1992 AGM, and during the year after it, many on the Trust's committees shared the director general's view that the people who had called for an investigation into the Wey had been wrong to do this at its national meeting, since it was a local issue. A few were downright contemptuous. So it was particularly interesting to read: 'That the proposers and signatories of the resolution were justified in presenting their problem as a resolution for discussion at the Annual General Meeting.'

It is not necessary to believe that the proposers were a hundred per cent in the right to conclude that they had been ill-served and harshly judged. It hadn't been their fault they'd had to bring their problems to Birmingham: it had been the fault of the National Trust which had failed to solve the difficulties locally. Why, then, didn't Angus Stirling as director general acknowledge this at the AGM? The Trust never should have allowed such a messy and, indeed sometimes highly questionable, situation to continue for so long. The director general could have taken the opportunity offered by the AGM to apologize publicly for what had happened.

It would have been nice. It would have been just. By showing respect for members in this way, the Trust could have lost nothing and actually gained good will. Instead it appeared shifty, somehow, and uppish. Did the Trust think that its members couldn't be trusted with hearing that the National Trust had any shortcomings? Did they believe the subscribers really are overprotected eight-year-olds?

'They haven't been altogether too clever about communicating to the public or to the membership what they are doing,' said the Rt Hon. Lord Oliver of Aylmerton, PC, formerly Lord of Appeal in Ordinary when we met to discuss this in his office in Lincolns Inn Fields. He was referring to the Trust's senior staff, generally. 'Also they have not perhaps been altogether forthcoming to enquiries or complaints by members.' (Lord Oliver was not singling out the Navigation; examples are plentiful.) Yes, he agreed, they are defensive. 'Not only among the volunteer element, but among the permanent staff as well, who don't take kindly to criticism of the way they're running affairs.' And, he added, a great many of its members feel the people running the Trust are all members of the aristocracy.

Lord Oliver had formed these opinions in the course of a review of the Trust's operations which Lord Chorley had asked him to undertake in 1992. The chairman's question to the Law Lord had been a simple one: can the National Trust's Constitution see it into the twenty-first century? But there was a crucial complication underneath: the Constitutional rights of members needed clarification, urgently.

Tally ho!

In 1990 at the AGM held in Llandudno, the majority of the Trust's members voted in support of a resolution to ban stag hunting on all National Trust land. This created quite a problem for the charity's administration. Some donors had given estates with the wish that hunting continue: Sir Richard Acland, for example, when he gave Holnicote in Somerset. If the Trust were to ban deer hunting on Exmoor it would be going back on its word. Potential donors of property might baulk. And in the case of Holnicote particularly, hunting appeared to be very much a part of the social and economic life of the people living there.

The National Trust had set up a working party to study the implications for the charity and their properties, were the ban to be put into effect. Simultaneously it evolved a policy of its own: banning hunting was the business of Parliament, not a private charity. All this angered those members who had already made their contrary view perfectly clear.

At the 1992 AGM, the anti-hunting members expressed more anger. Why had the National Trust still not banned stag hunting?

The Trust explained that the working party hadn't yet finished its investigation. To members this only looked like foot-dragging, cheating, obfuscation. The AGM in 1993, by which time the working party was bound to have reported back, promised to be a real rafter-rocker. That is why the National Trust hired Wembley.

'Why', I asked Angus Stirling after the 1992 AGM, 'why didn't you tell the members the truth; that they don't have the right to make policy?' By this time I had read the Trust's Constitution and it was plain fact. Subscribers are supporters of the charity. They are given a season ticket to the properties; they are not shareholders. Nor are they voters in a democracy.

The Constitution of the National Trust simply does not give members the right to vote policy, whether the issue is hunting or anything else.

'That's what we're hoping Lord Oliver will do,' Angus Stirling, the director general said in answer to my question.

Oh, the timidity and lack of forthrightness of it all! What causes the people at the top of the Trust to have so little confidence in the membership? This is the very opposite of the policy of openness that is averred. Do they fear that members, if they knew the truth, would stampede and crush all that the National Trust has achieved? If so, who are the conspiracy theorists here?

Lord Oliver explained that the impressions on which he based his report were 'derived entirely from submissions made by people in writing and a few who came and actually gave evidence. I've had myself no personal experience of the Trust except for the occasional visit to a Trust property.'

What Lord Oliver produced from these impressions and his reading of the various Acts of Parliament which have served as the National Trust's Constitution is a document that is a great pleasure to read, although, admittedly, given the number of technical issues considered at length, only a person with a substantial interest in understanding the workings of the National Trust – or hoping to change them – would probably read it from beginning to end. There are, for example, twenty-six long, closely argued paragraphs on the subject of proxy voting at AGMs.

The Oliver Report was duly presented to the Executive, adopted by the Council, highlights presented in the NT members' magazine and reported in the press, before the AGM at Wembley in November 1993. As it happened a last-minute objection to the way their resolution was worded on the voting papers meant that the proposal calling on the Trust to set up a new Working Party to address 'the issue of cruelty and animal welfare' arising from the hunting of deer with hounds on the Trust's Exmoor and Quantocks property was not discussed at Wembley, which proved to be a particularly sleepy AGM. Large numbers of the Trust's pro- and anti-hunting activists had managed to hear about the postponement even though it occured late in the day and they did not attend. The resolution supporting the National Trust's view that hunting is an issue for Parliament to decide, was voted on, however, and passed. Subsequently, the proposers of the animal cruelty resolution gathered more than 1,000 signatures and called for their resolution to be taken up at an EGM. The Council scheduled it for 16 July. In both its statements supporting its 'let Parliament decide' policy and its objections to the resolutions proposed by those wishing to ban deer hunting, the National Trust made extensive, if selective, use of Lord Oliver's Report.

Having followed the progress of investigations by Nichols, Benson and Arkell and seen the pace at which the National Trust typically reacted to suggestions for change, it is not a surprise to find a number of by now predictable observations in Lord Oliver's 1994 Report, through no fault of his own. For instance: the centre had still not devolved sufficient power to the regions. On the contrary, headquarters' control seems to have increased. The Trust's bureaucracy is swollen and has begun reproducing itself. When Lord Oliver asked the finance director to tell him how many man-hours were spent by staff servicing the Trust's committees, 'I was startled,' he says by the high altitude results.

But to get to members and their rights, the issue that had led the Trust to Lord Oliver in the first place: the Report acknowledges the important part played by subscribers to the Trust; the income they provide which is essential if the Trust is to go on preserving properties at the standard to which it has become accustomed, the time and labour they volunteer. This does not cause him to pander to members nor to attempt to appease the more ambitious subscribers to the charity when he adds:

'In the governance of the organization, however, the membership plays, and was from the inception envisaged as playing, only a peripheral role.'

The Constitution of the National Trust gives adult subscribers the right to elect half the members of the Council. And it gives them the right to vote on proposals put before them at the AGM. That is all.

After considering various arguments that were put before him, Lord Oliver concludes that those who have the idea that the National Trust's Council is bound by the resolutions of members is 'not one which I have found myself able to accept'. He could find no evidence to support that in its Constitution.

'But hasn't the Trust allowed its members to assume that they have a policy-making function?' I asked Lord Oliver.

'It shouldn't have done,' he replied. 'It was a point that was made perfectly clear, a good many years ago now.' (By Arkell, for instance.)

Lord Oliver suggests that the National Trust embarked on its massive drive to recruit new members starting in the 1970s, 'without any pre-education, if I may put it that way, of what it was they were joining.' As a result hundreds of thousands of people joined who had no knowledge of its Constitution. This of course is just what Princess Louise had worried about in the 1920s. Many may even think it's a part of the government rather than a private charity which benefits from government grants; then there's the old 'Isn't it a building society?' joke.

People who support Save the Children or the Royal Life Boats, for example, don't expect to dictate the way its policy-makers should spend their money. Why do members of the National Trust believe that because they choose to subscribe to it, they have the right to decide how it should be run?

'If you say, as I think you are saying,' Lord Oliver answered my queries, 'that the Trust didn't do sufficient to disabuse their members of this view, I think I'd agree with you. I think it could have been more carefully handled, and better handled than it was.' And it could have been done so simply, 'by some form of notification or note on the application form,' he suggested.

Weak nerves might be an explanation. The men running the Trust feared no one would join if the role of members was made clear. But most people don't become subscribers because they're seeking power. In the same way that aesthetics set the tone in the 1950s, anxiety seems to be the tone of today's National Trust.

The Oliver Report sets out the various recommendations for changing the membership set-up that had been put before him. These included a suggestion that members should be given the power to elect every one of the Council's fifty-two members instead of the current twenty-six. 'I find it beyond doubt', he writes, 'that the system of selection by appointment results in securing the services of those willing volunteers best qualified to oversee the great work which the Trust carries on.' This will not please romantics or Athenian democrats but his logic is persuasive.

'The acid test', writes Lord Oliver, 'is how it works in practice.'

And when it comes to the Council, the question has to be: Does it?

Lord Oliver acknowledges that, despite all the reviews, reports and working parties over the years, the Council is not what it should be.

Several proposals that might make the Council more effective are discussed. For example, the Trust should try to attract more highly motivated people to serve on the Council. It should make better use of them when they get there. Despite a 1984 recommendation by the Working Party headed by Sir Simon Hornby that the Trust must do more to educate new Council members about the charity and their role in it, Oliver feels there's need for more along those lines to be done. Those Council members who don't serve on Executive committees feel under-utilized, frustrated and bored – with good reason. But to do much more than this to alter the Council would mean going back to Parliament for a new Act. And this Lord Oliver is against.

The debate about a new Act would be the occasion for turning the National Trust into a political football, he believes and the anti-hunting forces and other special interest groups would try to force their way in. 'That's the biggest block to reform,' he says. 'In a sense it's almost an insoluble one.'

Nevertheless Lord Oliver observes that 'no business man,

if he were starting from scratch to devise a constitution designed for the most efficient running and management of an organization of this size and complexity,' would come up with a constitution that looked like the National Trust's.

In a new, ideal constitution of the sort that might be constructed by his imagined business man, Lord Oliver writes 'the ultimate policy-making body would be a small body of professionally qualified trustees with the executive management confined to a board of directors and with support for the charity derived from a voluntary organization of "friends".

That's it exactly! This is just what the National Trust needs.

A new Constitution 'would be feasible,' Lord Oliver allows, 'if the Trust were prepared for it'. But, he adds, 'I don't believe anybody is.'

In fact probably everyone from its members to the volunteers in the regions would object. Understandably. Nobody chooses to give up whatever power they've got – even when it's only imaginary.

A new Constitution could make the Trust far more responsive to the membership. The pity is people assume it would do the opposite.

Subscribers, no doubt, would be outraged if a new Act of Parliament took away their ability to elect Council members. Or if the Council were suddenly limited to a dozen men and women. But while members now have the right to elect half the Council of fifty-two – what are their twenty-six Council members doing for them?

The greatest number of votes ever given to anyone running for the National Trust's Council – more than 75,000 – went in the early 1990s to a housewife who, people report, has never once spoken at a meeting. While it's both understandable and sympathetic that the Trust's subscribers would want to counterbalance the élitism they perceive, what use is it if the people they choose don't take advantage of their position? Whether an aristocrat or a brickie, it hardly matters what a person's experience or outlook is if they arrive at Queen Anne's Gate and turn into a rubber stamp.

Many may believe that a smaller Council would make the National Trust less democratic. But the Trust is not a democratic institution and never was. If there were fewer Council members, say fourteen, and they were gifted, responsible, genuinely engaged men and women, there would be a better chance that these Trustees would do the checking and balancing of the Executive that the existing constitution assumes they will. The members would be better served; so would the properties.

And, after all, most subscribers join the Trust not because they want to help administer it, but because they support its aims to save outstandingly beautiful and important properties and because their membership card is an inexpensive season ticket giving free entry to all the Trust's houses, castles and gardens where they would otherwise have to pay.

As for the Council and the Executive – staff as well as committees – who is going to vote himself out of a job, even out of those positions that are voluntary?[4] Indeed volunteers may be the least inclined to step down of all the people connected with the Trust. Those same Council members, who drone on about how bored they are, nevertheless seem pleased to stand again for election.

But the biggest deterrent to a new NT Act of Parliament to create this new constitution appears to be the fear that the anti-hunting lobby would somehow hijack the National Trust. The temptation is to see this as still another example of the charity's overreaction to any perceived threat. After all it chose to go to Parliament for a new Act after the row about Bradenham. But perhaps any group that has a violent fringe can be said to be legitimately worrying however laudable the goals of those who pursue them peaceably. And with a weak government in power, trying to shepherd a new constitution through Parliament might seem more like attempting a dare-devil fairground stunt.

Let's say, for the moment, that a new Act of Parliament which would bring into being a smaller Council and a leaner, more effective administrative structure is too radical a solution to the Trust's current lack of checks and balances, the failure of the

Council to show independence of the Executive, the inability of the centre to relinquish sufficient power to the regions – and too unpredictable in its outcome. The fact is the idea is pretty academic at the moment because it doesn't seem to have a constituency to support or promote it. Another approach, more realizable, at least in theory, could accomplish some of the same ends without the need of a new constitution.

'The rot starts at the top,' an irate observer of the way the Trust sometimes handles its affairs said to me. But if that's so, at least there is hope for change by starting there.

Lord Rothschild was for seven years the chairman of the Board of Trustees at the National Gallery in London. He followed this with the chairmanship of the National Heritage Memorial Fund. He considers that a smaller Council and Executive along the lines of the National Gallery might benefit the Trust. When asked about the qualities of its chief executive he didn't want to be drawn. But he did speak in general terms about the attributes one would want in its director general.

'The person has to be judicial and fair minded,' says Lord Rothschild. In addition, he or she should be 'somebody with a strong aesthetic sense and judgement, who cares passionately about the subject. Ideally,' Lord Rothschild continues, 'the individual should also be a good administrator and delegator given the size and complexity of the National Trust today.'

Lord Rothschild's words were spoken before the announcement in June, 1994 that a Director-General designate had been appointed. But they fit the man chosen as if they'd been crafted with Martin Drury in mind. On January 1, 1996 Drury will assume the Trust's top job. Admirable as he is in many ways, Drury will reach the mandatory retirement age two years later. His appointment can only be considered a holding action. Or, more optimistically, a bridge to future change. He has the flair.

As for the chairman, it has to be said that with all his many personal qualities, Lord Chorley was a mistake. And not because of a few foibles – an awful lot of people in a position to judge but unwilling to say so in print, agree. 'He was the best available,' was one popular remark around the Trust *circa* 1990. But even they admit they didn't begin their search early enough in Dame Jennifer's tenure nor look with the thoroughness that they might have. Though perhaps it was just a failure of imagination or an error in judgment. However it came about, it wouldn't be wise of the National Trust to repeat the process of selection it used in 1990. In 1993, a firm of headhunters was hired to help with the search for a new director general. Might not that be sensible when a new chairman has to be found?

Sir Simon Hornby considers that the Trust has in fact become such a big enterprise and makes such demands on those at the top that in future it should begin paying its chairman a decent wage rather than an honorarium. Lord Rothschild, too, sees the logic in such an idea. Sir Roy Strong, former director of the Victoria and Albert Museum, is certainly in favour. 'The difficult thing about the chairmanship of all the great institutions that really need to move on, is that they are unpaid.'

But not everyone who knows the National Trust and its needs agrees. Martin Drury, for instance, finds the talk about a salaried chairman at the National Trust far from sympathetic. And he doesn't care for the idea that the chairmen of the various Regional and Head Office Committees ought to be replaced by salaried staff, either.

'I hope very much,' says Drury, 'that we shall never think of paying them in the foreseeable future.' He reasons that 'it would at a stroke remove the thing that distinguishes the Trust from so many organizations. It's a charity which manages a business. I think that charitable element is very precious.'

But surely so are the properties and the interests of people who visit them. For all that it's invested in professionalism since 1971, how much longer can the National Trust afford to enjoy treating itself as a society of amateurs?

[6]

Pretty as a Picture

The National Trust had no business acquiring gardens. It was yet another major detour from the original idea. Though the contrary might be argued, I suppose. Octavia Hill wished to provide open-air sitting rooms for the poor, didn't she? And Ruskin's gardener landscaped the plots adjacent to her London tenements in an effort to do so, didn't he? Yes. But just the same, the Trust's setting out to acquire gardens had more in common with the aesthete's pursuit of treasure houses than with the attempt by do-gooders to lift the spirits and improve the health of the poor.

The masses weren't much on the minds of the men running the National Trust when the idea to start acquiring gardens came up in the late 1940s. And if Lord De la Warr was later thought mad for bringing up the subject of signposts, imagine the reaction to talk of the public tramping through fine gardens. Think of the grass, the paths, the mood.

Though it was both a departure for the Trust and an horticultural extension of posh people's self-interest (see below), the National Trust's attempt to save gardens seems so much easier simply to celebrate than its collecting of stately homes.

There certainly were plenty of titled folk involved when the plan for the Trust to become garden-owning was being incubated yet the overriding appeal of garden-visiting is not to see how fancy folk lived; it is fundamentally democratic. However out of reach a garden may be owing to its size or scope, a person with even a tiny urban patch can steal an idea or two from a visit to Hidcote or Bodnant. Whereas only the most tortured article in a decorating magazine could suggest ways to adapt the panelling at Waddesdon, say, or the use of silver furniture in the King's Bedroom at Knole.

And the gardens, at least, don't seem to have become museumified. A dusting of NT Good Taste may have been flung over most of them but they are full of plants and trees and fruit and flowers – living and dying, budding and blooming, wilting and multiplying. There's change all the time. And head gardeners – most of them appear to have more imagination, talent and strength of character than most historic buildings representatives or administrators. (About which, more in the next chapter.)

'We're stubborn,' Peter Borlase proudly announced soon after retiring as head gardener at Lanhydrock in Cornwall. He'd been gardening for the National Trust for more than thirty-eight years. And they're outspoken, too. Borlase, lecturing as part of the Trust's 1994 Glorious Gardens series, showed tens of slides of plants and shrubs and trees. Then he came to two slides showing an area of lawn in the garden at Lanhydrock: in one a pair of elephantine marquees could be seen. In the slide that followed the marquees were gone and so was the grass. 'I know the Trust has to diversify,' he told the packed audience at the Purcell Rooms on London's South Bank, 'but. . . .'

The mostly grey-haired, subduedly dressed crowd was right there behind him. We all stared at the wounded grass. 'I was promised it would not happen again,' he said severely. Future fund-raising events would be held in the park but not the garden at Lanhydrock. Peter Borlase hasn't left the area; he'll keep a watch on those to whom he refers somewhat unconvincingly as 'the higher-ups'.

Hatching the plot

Like the Country Houses Scheme, acquisition of gardens only started after the Second World War. And for many of the same reasons: money worries, the Labour government's tax plans, the lack of servants, the cost.

'In 1935,' Sir Simon Hornby says, 'twenty gardeners could be hired for £2,000 per year.' That was for the lot of them. Today a head gardener at a private estate might get £15,000 a year. But, in addition, and as a reflection of the personal nature of the garden-making enterprise, there were also a variety of idiosyncratic reasons why owners of important gardens began wondering about the future fate of the private Edens they'd attempted to create.

Major Lawrence Johnstone made his garden, Hidcote, from what had been Gloucestershire fields at the time the National Trust was founded. The results were admired, often passionately, by many who were keen and ambitious gardeners themselves. Among them Vita Sackville-West. But after the war the major decided to spend his remaining days at Menton, in France, where he'd established yet another exceptional garden. The friends and neighbours to whom he offered his beautiful spot in the Cotswolds turned it down. Was it going to be abandoned or sold to someone who wouldn't possibly be able to keep it up aesthetically even if they managed the money? These were the two likely possibilities. And then, in 1947, the problem of gardens in peril was brought to the attention of the National Trust.

The Trust wasn't new to garden-owning. Its very first mansion, Barrington Court in Somerset given in 1907, came with nine acres, for which Gertrude Jekyll had drawn up planting schemes, border layouts, even designs for paths. There were gardens at Wightwick, Blickling and even a small one at Beatrix Potter's farmhouse, Hill Top, in Westmorland. But these had been thrown in with the houses; much as stable blocks were and laundries, say.

Now the Trust began to think about the gardens which were at risk of destruction, or rather, Lord Aberconway began considering the problem. And he came up with a solution.

Lord Aberconway, head of English China Clays, was president of the Royal Horticultural Society as well as a captain of industry. His gifts, interests and assets all found an outlet at Bodnant, his estate in North Wales. Begun by his grandfather, its eighty-acre garden was one of the most admired in Britain. Its hundred-year-old laburnum tunnel alone – a curving passage 180 feet long that hangs heavy with honeycombs of blossom in May – was already the emblem of one of Britain's most spectacular gardens: dramatic, elaborate, in parts romantic and a plantsman's showcase. (Though as with paintings, say, whether the spectacle is also thought beautiful depends on who's doing the looking. Graham Stuart Thomas who became the National Trust's gardens adviser in 1955 saw Bodnant for the first time as a member of the public on one of its open days in 1930. A horticulturally sophisticated friend encouraged the visit, telling him that it was 'a pleasure and a duty'. Graham Thomas went back again and again and writes about it at great length and with enthusiastic appreciation in his book, *Gardens of the National Trust*. James Lees-Milne, however, after staying the night as a guest of the Aberconways wrote in his diary on 20 May 1949: 'I find this famous garden frankly ugly and lacking taste. I don't like conifers and rhododendrons . . . I am not interested in rare shrubs. . . . The house the most graceless I have ever beheld.'[1] He was suffering badly from sciatica that day.)

Because of his position, his own experience as a gardener and his involvement with the RHS, Lord Aberconway knew many other keen and wealthy gardeners. He was bound to hear about those owners of great gardens who for one reason or another worried they wouldn't be able to go on looking after them much longer. He had heard enough to alarm him.

It was in his capacity as president of the RHS that Lord

[201]

Aberconway approached the National Trust. Something had to be done and the RHS couldn't do it alone.

In spite of their very different ways of life and extremely different politics, Lord Aberconway and Sir Charles Trevelyan seem to have had quite a lot in common. Both had the ferocious drive and a craftiness and vision which enabled them to tie selfishness to the wider good. As a result, both the baron and the baronet played critical roles in getting two fledgling National Trust strategies into a position where they could become great successes. Both were owners of such exceptional properties, that the gift of them to the National Trust was bound to encourage their peers to think more seriously about doing likewise.

For a very long time Bodnant had been considered one of Britain's outstanding gardens and Lord Aberconway naturally took great pride in what he and his family had achieved on the steep banks of the river Conway. And he was delighted that visitors found it a marvel. The money brought in from admissions was modest, of course, compared to his overall expenses – and his overall income – but welcome just the same. What Lord Aberconway did not welcome, indeed what he abhorred, was the tax he had to pay on every single admission ticket.

And that was one very big reason why the baron was so interested in establishing a charitable body which, when the need arose, could take on the ownership of Britain's most important gardens. He would make it a gift of Bodnant. And having done so, he would never again have to pay tax on admissions to it. (It may seem that he was throwing lovely baby Flora out with the scarcely dirty bath water, but wait.)

Gardening in tandem

This was Lord Aberconway's proposal: the Royal Horticultural Society and the National Trust would become partners. They would establish a jointly run Gardens Committee and it would decide which of Britain's choicest properties to accept. Once it owned them, the Committee would go on to manage the gardens too.

At first the National Trust agreed. But very quickly – and with unprecedented fiscal caution – it reconsidered.

Who was going to pay the bills? If the RHS didn't deliver half the money needed, the difference would have to be paid by the other partner – the National Trust. Where was it going to get the money? And, for that matter, where was the money to acquire the gardens going to come from in the first place?

Lord Aberconway was a determined man. He persisted. The Trust considered: slowly. Then, very like Sir Charles Trevelyan when he lost his patience over the transfer to the Trust of Wallington, Lord Aberconway went before the RHS and announced the existence of the joint Gardens Committee as a *fait accompli*. There was still a fair amount of negotiating afterwards, but he had achieved his goal. A deal acceptable to both organizations was worked out.

The National Trust would become the owner of the gardens. These would then be managed by a committee made up of three members from each institution. Once the Gardens Committee was set up, its fund-raising campaign could begin. The Gardens Fund that resulted would then provide the money for both purchases and upkeep.

Lord Aberconway was one of the RHS delegates to the committee and its chairman, of course. Also representing the RHS were Dr H.V. Taylor and the Hon. David Bowes-Lyon. (Bowes-Lyon became president of the RHS on Lord Aberconway's death in 1953.)

[203]

Lord Rosse, a member of its Executive, was one of the Trust's appointments to the Gardens Committee. So was Sir Edward Salisbury, director of Kew. The Trust's final appointment to the committee was the Hon. Vita Sackville-West, who besides being a great gardener wrote regularly on the subject for the *Observer*. The note announcing the Committee's first meeting reached her in Casablanca; she got back to England just in time to attend it on 23 March 1948.

It was understood that Hidcote would become the Committee's first acquisition. Bodnant came second.

Relative values

The Committee members were expected to have a hand in deciding which gardens to accept and how they should be looked after. They were also expected to help raise the money to get the scheme going. Everybody on the Committee was somebody, which meant their friends were somebody too, and then there were the relations.

The Earl of Rosse's father-in-law, Lt Col. L.C.R. Messel, for instance, owned Nymans, a thirty-acre horde of old roses in West Sussex. It was bequeathed to the National Trust in 1954 and managed for the charity by Messel's daughter Anne, Countess Rosse until her death more than thirty-five years later. But long before this happened, other garden-owning in-laws of Committee members made their contribution to advancing its aims.

Vita Sackville-West, who gave a talk on the BBC to tell listeners about the scheme, arranged for Lord St Levan to open the five acres of terraced gardens dug out of the face of St Michael's Mount in Cornwall for the benefit of its Fund. (The 3rd Lord St Levan was married to the sister of her husband, Harold Nicolson.) Major Bowes-Lyon's brother-in-law agreed to do much the same; though for two days rather than one.

Lord St Levan was a mercurial fellow and kept changing

his mind. First he would open St Michael's Mount in aid of the Gardens Fund, then he would not. Another yes; then a final no. He rescinded his pledge, remained adamant about it and went off on holiday. At the very last minute, with just enough time to send out announcements, he said yes again.

Vita Sackville-West, who had been raised at Knole, was not shy about letting it be understood that there was no drawer in all of England which topped her own. But when it came to status via marriage, David Bowes-Lyon handily won. And this was reflected in the amount of money raised when each of their brothers-in-law opened his gardens in aid of the Fund. While Lord St Levan's sent less than £27 to the appeal following the opening of St Michael's Mount, so many people visited Sandringham after its two-day opening for the benefit of the fund, that the king sent more than ten times as much.

A firm hand

Lord Aberconway was not a man to be daunted by the social position or connections of his fellow committee members. He was a strong chairman, indeed a bit of a bully.

Everyone on the Gardens Committee had a large number of other commitments, interests, obligations. Yet Lord Aberconway set the time and date for the meetings to suit himself. Then, once a sufficient number of the other members agreed to fit themselves in, he might capriciously change the date. His imperiousness was not confined to his dealings with his fellow volunteers.

Jack Rathbone, the National Trust's secretary, was informed by the chairman of the Gardens Committee that their appeal would be launched in July.

Rathbone, who was an employee of the National Trust, replied that from the Trust's point of view, this wasn't very good timing. July was when their annual membership drive usually reached its peak and, therefore, his small staff would be awfully busy. He worried that if the appeal coincided with

the projected crest of the Trust's membership drive, money
from potential subscribers might be channelled to the Gardens
appeal instead.

Lord Aberconway wrote back assuring Rathbone that the
Fund was bound to collect so little money there'd be nothing
lost to the Trust when the Gardens Appeal went ahead as
he'd planned – in July. This was transparently disingenuous;
if it wasn't going to make much money, why bother about
the date when it would start? Having signed the letter, Lord
Aberconway added as a postscript: 'Crawford who is staying
here agrees.' Some afterthought: Lord Crawford, chairman of
the National Trust, was Rathbone's boss. The Gardens Fund
Appeal, announced on 15 June in a letter to *The Times* was
duly launched in July.

The letter announcing the appeal explained that the Fund
needed to raise money so that it could acquire and look after
gardens of outstanding historic or aesthetic importance. As soon
as it appeared, envelopes started to arrive at the National Trust.
But they were not filled with bank notes.

A woman who had bought land in a village near her home in
order to make a garden for the villagers to enjoy was getting too
old to look after it and was worrying about its fate. Would the
National Trust take it on, please? A vicar in Peterborough had
a three-acre garden he'd made for the pleasure of the working
class. For fifteen years he'd been 'puzzled over the fate of this
oasis'. Could the Fund help him out? One letter came from a
head gardener looking for a job.[2]

Rathbone replied to all of them politely. His letter to a Mr H.
Ford at Lilleshall Hall in Shropshire is typical. After carefully
refusing the offer of the Lilleshall garden, the secretary adds: 'I
think it extremely probable that we shall never find ourselves
in a position to manage more than 3 or 4 gardens.' This was
not just a way of letting a petitioner down gently. He meant
it. A very few, very choice gardens were the goal.

Unwelcome offers were not the only response to the
Gardens Committee's announcement of their needs and inten-
tions, however. There were enquiries from Mr de Rothschild
who was thinking about all his rhododendron and azaleas at

Exbury on the coast below Southampton. The Marchioness of Londonderry was speculating about the future of her seventy-eight acres of fantastical gardens at Mount Stewart in County Down, complete with a Dodo Terrace and an Irish harp in topiary. The Earl of Morley got in touch from Saltram in Devon.

In his reply to Lord Morley, the chairman of the Gardens Committee wrote that, 'The owner would have practically the same control over the garden as he has at present because it is a very strong desire of the Committee of the Trust that previous owners should, as far as possible, continue to manage the garden; for, after all, who would do it better?'[3] Lord Aberconway used virtually the same words when he wrote to other potential donors who had gardens the Committee fancied too. Does this have a familiar ring? Almost exactly the same pitch had been used by Lord Esher and James Lees-Milne a decade earlier when they were trying to interest donors in their Country Houses Scheme.

As with country houses, the National Trust would have the responsibility and perhaps the entire financial burden. Nevertheless, the garden's about-to-be-ex-owner was promised that he or she could continue to be horticulturally and aesthetically in charge. This, evidently, suited everybody. Fortunately, it didn't prove the financial disaster in the making that the same arrangement with houses has been. There really isn't the equivalent of reroofing a palace when it comes to gardening. Each year, out of all the money the National Trust spends on its properties, seven per cent goes to capital projects in gardens; fifty-two per cent to capital improvements at mansion houses. Yet, *'more people pay to visit gardens than any other part of the Trust's estate'*, according to the Annual Report. Its gardens cost the Trust about £10 million a year. But because of how it does its accounts, this includes the cost of gardens and landscaped parks that came with houses as well as those accepted in their own right. Were the cost of looking after gardens and landscaped parks belonging to mansions calculated with those houses, the sum quoted for keeping up its mansions would be higher still, of course, and that for gardens still less.

Drought

In assuring the secretary of the National Trust that the Gardens Fund Appeal wouldn't bring in much money, Lord Aberconway may not have been sincere but he was accurate. It was a flop. During its first few months all it managed to scrape together was about £6,000. But the same wind that had brought the taxes which made the owners of elaborate gardens shiver, now began to blow warmly over the National Trust's plans for garden preservation.

One of the major projects of the Welfare State was to create a National Health Service. Before it was established, district nurses had been trained and supported by charitable contributions. And from the late 1920s, one of the sources of income for the Queens Institute of District Nursing came from hundreds of owners of private gardens who opened them to raise money on its behalf. Once the NHS was set up, the district nurses obviously no longer needed the same degree of support and the Gardens Scheme was able to extend the number of charities it could help.

In 1949 the National Gardens Scheme (as the Queens District Nurses came to be called in 1980) decided that a portion of its annual income from garden openings would go to the National Trust's Gardens Fund. No percentage was fixed; and none ever has been. There is no contractual obligation on the part of the NGS to give the Trust a penny. It was and remains a gentleman's agreement. (Each year, after the garden visiting season is over and its receipts have been tallied, the NGS decides what it will contribute. This depends on its earnings and on which National Trust projects it wants to support. Its gifts always have a specific target.)

The National Trust, in turn, agreed to help the NGS set up its regional organization and to encourage people to visit NGS gardens by publicizing the Gardens Scheme at the Trust's growing number of properties open to the public.

In 1949 the NGS raised £12,282 of which £856 10s. 5d. was given to the Trust. The following year it gave twice that amount. The money was instrumental in helping the Gardens Committee of the Trust to acquire its first properties; there were eleven gardens by the end of 1950. In 1980 the NGS's contribution to the National Trust was much what it had been fifteen years earlier, but then interest in gardens and gardening seemed to explode. (Membership in the RHS, for instance, went from 17,000 in 1980 to 170,000 ten years later.)

By 1987 more than 400,000 people were visiting gardens open for the NGS and it was contributing £120,000 to the National Trust. By the mid-1990s, the NGS yellow gardens directory, had full-colour illustrations and was rivalling the telephone directory in bulk. More than 1.5 million people were peering around other people's gardens for the benefit of NGS charities, and more than a quarter of a million pounds was going from it to the National Trust every year. It is one of six charities supported by the NGS.[4]

Less cheerful effects of the burgeoning enthusiasm for things floral and arboreal was the increase in thefts. This might be anything from the stealing of marvellous eighteenth-century lead ornaments as has happened at Powis Castle in Wales, for instance, or the practice of taking such samples home from garden visits as seed heads and cuttings. The National Trust had to tell people this was not included in the price of admission. It also had to move the rarer crocosmias that form the National Collection at Lanhydrock into a walled garden because so many had been stolen. And of course the erosion caused to garden paths by millions of feet carrying horticulturally interested men and women across planted Britain led the Trust to issue timed tickets for some of its most popular gardens, starting with Sissinghurst. But all this takes us far beyond 1949 and the lifeline thrown to the Trust by the NGS.

With the help of the Gardens Scheme, the worst of immediately pressing money worries seemed to be over for the Trust Gardens Fund. But there was no staff, not even one individual, to manage these new acquisitions. And there was no guidance about what should – and shouldn't – be done.

'In future,' Rathbone wrote to all the Trust's area agents at the beginning of 1950, 'no major alterations or departures from long established practice are carried out in important Trust gardens without reference first being made to the Gardens Committee, or if in any doubt, to me.'

The personal touch

Of all the different sorts of property held by the National Trust gardens may be the trickiest to look after. For one thing, Britain is filled with gardening experts; and foreigners are not lacking strong opinions either. In fact just about everyone except the most diehard urbanist has an opinion about what a garden ought to look like. But the Trust has had worse headaches than this since it set up its Gardens Committee.

A grand house may turn into a museum (or a stylish mausoleum) if, in the name of preservation, nothing about it is altered, but at least it stands there as a record of what existed at a particular time in the past. Not gardens. 'They are so transitory,' says Angela Aziz, chairman of the National Gardens Scheme, her shoulders sagging. Even within the lifetime of the person who has developed it, gales, severe frosts, inundations may destroy what has developed over decades.

'Gardens *are* incredibly difficult,' says Sir Simon Hornby, the gardening tycoon who is president of the Royal Horticultural Society. And it's not just nature or the army of critics that puts the Trust as a gardens-owner in such a difficult position. 'They are personal things,' Sir Simon notes. Made by individuals who were stubborn, passionate, fickle, knowing, inept. But each with his own vision. Personal, Sir Simon very well knows, having been on its Executive for thirty years, is just what the National Trust is not. In part, at least, it gardens by committee and by the book.

Archives are studied. Nursery lists scrutinized. All must be true to the period – once the various people making decisions about the garden have chosen which period in the sometimes very long history of a property they want the garden to reflect.

People who work for the Trust put a lot of effort into trying to be stand-ins for the once-upon-a-time owner (as will be soon seen). They try to look at the garden through his or her own eyes. What would the donor have wanted here? Why did she move the glass houses there? They put up the rickety shelter when they were elderly, should it now be taken down? But if the owner happens to still be around, well, no need to play such guessing games is there? For that matter, why garden by committee, or by the book, at all?

Lord Aberconway knew the answer to that question. Undoubtedly the best person to maintain the garden at Bodnant was himself – Henry, the 2nd Lord Aberconway.

The Gardens Committee's attempt to acquire important gardens had been given a huge boost by the announcement of Lord Aberconway's extravagant gift in 1948. As had happened with Wallington, many potential donors of important gardens surely now felt that if such a discerning and wealthy man believed that the National Trust was a suitable owner for his place, the charity might be just the solution for their own.

What most people didn't quite take in, however, was that while Lord Aberconway had given the National Trust his garden at Bodnant, and amply endowed it, he – just like Sir Charles Trevelyan – had kept control of its management. Lord Aberconway, however, also continued as owner of the surrounding estate of 2,500 acres and the house.

Donors of gardens, too, were permitted, even encouraged, to draw up a memorandum of wishes. And as was the case with houses, some of these documents gave owners and their offspring a rather sweet deal.

Lawrence Johnstone kept the right to come back to Hidcote from Menton any time he pleased and to have his garden opened to the public only three days a week. After all when in England he would want his privacy. Then the major had an even better idea. Why not wait until he'd arrived from France each year before deciding just which three days in the week Hidcote would open? Lord Crawford graciously agreed.

This time Rathbone stood up to him. The secretary argued that the Trust couldn't list the opening days for Hidcote, have the public turn up and then announce that the garden was closed because Lawrence Johnstone who'd just returned from France preferred to have visitors on Tuesday, Wednesdays and Thursdays instead of Mondays, Tuesdays and Fridays as was printed. The chairman of the National Trust conceded and the creator of Hidcote had to put up with having its opening days chosen by somebody else – who also happened to be its owner. But did the Trust think: 'Could someone please walk my dog while I'm away . . .?'[5]

Among sweet deals made by garden donors, it will not be startling to learn that Lord Aberconway's was sweeter than most. And, in his case, Lord Aberconway very much wanted his wishes to apply to his son Charles as well.

A grandee's gift

'We don't work in the same way as most National Trust properties – gardens or houses,' Charles the 3rd Lord Aberconway informed me. He and I were in his vast, Victorian mansion on the edge of the garden at Bodnant. As an explanation he added, 'The National Trust are wise and broad-minded enough to leave everything to us.'

I divined that I was not meant to smile.

'The Trust', Lord Aberconway continued, 'knows that we never do anything stupid. We know the garden far better than anyone else.'

The 'we' Lord Aberconway uses is not royal even if his attitude is on the imperious side. It refers to Martin Puddle his head gardener and Bodnant's manager, as well as himself. Nor is he being altogether arrogant. Lord Aberconway is the third generation of his family to garden at Bodnant; Martin Puddle is the third generation of his to serve as head gardener there. The pair of them clearly have a better grasp of the garden than anyone else.

'The Trust knows no one could do it better,' Lord Aberconway declared. This, almost word for word, is what his father had written to potential garden donors half a century before. Henry may have been trying to flatter other owners of important gardens but he knew without a doubt that the words were applicable to him. This confidence clearly was passed on to his son. Charles is secure in the belief that being in charge of Bodnant is part of his destiny. But it's part of what he was trained for, too.

Like his father, the 3rd Lord Aberconway was president of the Royal Horticultural Society. (He served for twenty years and, as the Bodnant guidebook puts it, since 1804 when it was founded, he is the only RHS president 'of note' to have retired before death removed him from the post.) Charles Aberconway was chairman of English China Clays even longer and remains president of its parent company with which he's been associated for sixty years.

Vita Sackville-West wrote after visiting Henry and Christabel Aberconway at Bodnant that they didn't even know how to turn on the wireless.[6] Lees-Milne describes Henry as having an 'old fashioned keep-your-distance manner'. The 3rd Lord Aberconway is on the archaic side also. His manner was downright Edwardian when we met and so, for that matter, was his appearance.

A tall, large man, approaching eighty, Lord Aberconway was wearing plus fours. His long stockings were held up by garters decorated with cockades. The cloth of his suit was a rough tweed, possibly thornproof; its pattern a greenish plaid. He wore brogues. The one contemporary item of his costume could hardly have been more conservative. Lord Aberconway had on a National Trust tie.

Later, looking through the guidebook to Bodnant, there he was all over again, albeit rather younger and in a painted version.

Seated outside the house with the garden in the background his costume was identical to the one he wore for our meeting – cockaded garters and all. The portrait reproduced had been commissioned by the RHS in 1973; it hangs there in its Council Room now. But perhaps the suit was the very same one; it certainly looked as if one brush past a thistle and it would be in shreds. Having seen him at the RHS in London wearing a finely tailored suit, I judged that this attire for our meeting at Bodnant did not reflect economy but rather the establishing of an atmosphere.

As we sat down in the dark, lofty drawing room, Lord Aberconway asked: 'Have you told the people at the National Trust you were coming to see me?'

'No,' I replied.

Lord Aberconway stiffly informed me that he would have felt less guarded if I had.

'It was Sir Jack Boles who suggested I talk to you,' I quickly said. I thought he'd find this reassuring. After all Sir Jack is a former director general of the National Trust.

'Why?' Lord Aberconway asked warily, not looking in my direction then or in the exchange that followed.

'He told me that you might not wholly approve of the way the National Trust does things,' I candidly replied. Since Sir Jack had said this lightheartedly, I assumed Lord Aberconway would find it benign, maybe even amusing.

'That is totally wrong!' Lord Aberconway barked from across the room.

There were now such long pauses between his words that each one seemed to rise very slowly in the high-ceilinged room, propelled upwards by invisible but nevertheless perceptible puffs of anger. Just as one reached the picture-rail another word would begin its unpleasant ascent.

'I – can't – imagine – how – Jack – Boles – had – such – an – idea! What – were – his – exact – words?'

The atmosphere of the Victorian house had been gloomy enough before. It was downright oppressive now. I felt like an employee of English China Clays about to be given the sack.

The circumstances didn't encourage ease of recall. Had I got it wrong? What had Sir Jack's said actually?

When later I looked at the transcript of my meeting with the former director general in Devon, I found that in fact I had been quoting him correctly after all. But probably it was just as well that I hadn't had the evidence in Wales, and that when challenged I hadn't felt more confident of my memory. My being so muddled may have been what saved my meeting with Lord Aberconway.

Lord Aberconway thundered and paused and then thundered again. What to do? I tried grovelling. Head bowed, I made repeated stumbling apologies. Eventually this worked.

'It's a very dangerous thing to misquote someone like that, isn't it?' Lord Aberconway asked rhetorically, looking, as he had throughout, not across to where I was sitting but straight ahead into the air.

But his tone was changing. This reprimand signalled the end of the uproar.

'I know there are many people who are donors of houses, who go on to live in the houses, whose relationships with the Trust officials are not as good as they might be,' Lord Aberconway now began, almost conversationally. 'My relations with the Trust officials,' he continued, 'are perfect.' By the end of the afternoon Lord Aberconway, though no pussycat, had become courtly. Despite a problem with one of his legs that caused him a great deal of pain, he offered to show me around the garden and did so at length.

The baron gave me a rundown of all the heads of the National Trust – Council and Executive – he had known, beginning with Jack Rathbone. And to prove how good his relations had always been with the Trust's higher-ups he added, 'Freddie Bishop when he ceased to be a director general joined my English China Clays Board in Cornwall.' As for the man who was director general as we talked, 'I get on splendidly with Angus Stirling . . .'

I was about to learn what getting on with the Trust splendidly means, if you are Lord Aberconway.

'We decide whom we employ,' he said, 'in what capacity, for

what pay, when we open the garden, when we close the garden, the beginning and end of the season, the hours of opening.' There was more he and Martin Puddle saw to, also.

'The guidebook which we have, we do entirely in-house,' Lord Aberconway continued. 'The text is largely mine.' (It celebrates his family as well as the garden they produced.) 'The photographs are chosen by the Puddle family. Martin Puddle does all the accounts. With the approval of the Head Office.' (Ah mention of the National Trust, at last.) 'He sends them direct to Warminster,' Lord Aberconway continued. 'We do our own marketing. Martin Puddle has charge of that, again quite apart from the National Trust.' And Mr Puddle directs the running of the expansive Garden Centre at Bodnant which opened in 1992; the handsome airy building modelled on a giant conservatory. That business, too, is independent of the National Trust.

What goes around, comes around

Lord Aberconway did allow that he had one complaint about arrangements with the National Trust. Ironically, but on reflection perhaps predictably, the issue was the same one which had led his father to give Bodnant to the National Trust in the first place – a tax on admission tickets. This time it wasn't the government who was taking a cut from every ticket sold. It was the National Trust.

The National Trust's policy on admissions works like this: all the money from a ticket sold to an ordinary visitor goes to that property. But when the person is a member of the National Trust (or comes along as the guest of a subscriber) the property is later credited with a sum equal to one third of the price of the public admission ticket. So, in the case of Bodnant, if admission for a non NT member costs £3 all of it goes to the garden. But when a member of the Trust comes to have a look around, he or she pays nothing at the gate of

Sir Robert Hunter

Canon Hardwicke Rawnsley

Octavia Hill

The Trevelyans at Wallington, Christmas 1938: Sir Charles (second from right);
George (seated on step)

Below left: James Lees-Milne *c.*1950; *Below centre:* Alan Clutton-Brock;
Below right: Sir Francis Dashwood at West Wycombe Park

Lord and Lady Scarsdale at Kedleston Hall

Mrs James de Rothschild and
Lord Rothschild in the garden at
Waddesdon Manor

Left: Long Crendon
Courthouse: acquired
1900

Below: Castle Coole:
acquired 1951

Above: Cdr Conrad Rawnsley RN (ret'd) aboard the 'Hurrah'

Right: Enterprise Neptune Appeals brochure mid-1960s

Below: George Elliott, head warden at the Golden Cap

Above; Lady Emma Tennant and Graham Stuart Thomas at Mottisfont Abbey

Left: The Pin Mill, Bodnant

Below left: Nigel Nicolson at Sissinghurst
Below centre: Jimmy Hancock, head gardener at Powis Castle
Below right: Dave Mason, head gardener at Coleton Fishacre

Brandelhow Park, first acquisition in the Lake District

Beatrix Potter, Rupert Potter, Hardwicke Rawnsley *c.* 1900

Hill Top Farmhouse, near Sawrey

Left: Beatrix Potter with sheepdog

Below: Stan Edmondson of Seathwaite Farm, Borrowdale

NT
Mistakes

Top: Mr Straw's House, Worksop

Centre: A la Ronde, Exmouth

Bottom: Calke Abbey, Ticknall, Derby: an 18th Century painting

course, and Bodnant is given a 'rebate' of £1 from the charity. As the proportion of its visitors who are NT members increases, its income from visitors goes down. (Lord Rothschild may be the only family member in charge of managing a National Trust property who has negotiated a more generous rebate. When Trust members visit, two-thirds of the admission fee is returned to Waddesdon. I would not volunteer to be in the room with Lord Aberconway when he finds out.)

Returning to his main theme again, Lord Aberconway announced, 'It works very well. Martin Puddle has a very good job, responsible to me and not to any other employer or amorphous body. We never receive the gardens adviser John Sales,' Lord Aberconway added. 'He may come here to walk around. He never makes a suggestion.' As far as the baron is concerned, John Sales is just another member of the National Trust, a £1 pound admission you might say, instead of the full £3.

Sales who has been chief gardens adviser since 1974 could refuse to accept such treatment. The garden after all hasn't been the property of an Aberconway since 1950. But if John Sales did go about Bodnant making suggestions, the fate of his schemes would probably be very similar to what happened when Graham Stuart Thomas, his predecessor, unwittingly set his fancies against the caprices of a Lady with a Trust garden in Suffolk.

According to Nicolas Corbin who was regional secretary for East Anglia when the National Trust acquired Melford Hall from the Hyde Parker family in 1960: 'Finances were dodgy. We had to be very careful about what we spent.' Part of the arrangement was that the Hyde Parkers had to pay for and keep up its garden. The results were disappointing. It was felt their head gardener wasn't really doing a good enough job.

'I got the famous Graham Thomas,' Corbin told me, 'and I said, "You go there, Graham, and set up what we ought to plant."

'He spent a long time,' Corbin remembers, 'and stuck canes in the lawn with the names of plants on them, showing where they ought to go.'

Several months later the Trust's gardens adviser and its area agent went back to see how the garden at Melford Hall had progressed.

'Oh Mr Thomas,' Lady Hyde Parker chirped in her delightful Danish accent. 'It's such a funny thing. By mistake I've picked up all your little sticks and labels and burnt them. I didn't know what they were!'

Lord Aberconway, taking the words out of my mouth (not that I would have dared to speak them), said, 'So, we are really a law unto ourselves.' And he congratulated the National Trust for being so astute.

'The Welsh Committee for the National Trust was here with the new regional director, Peter Broomhead,' he reported. They asked, "Are you satisfied with everything ... With your relations with the National Trust. Or could we do any better?"

'No. You do absolutely everything I want, namely you leave me severely alone.'

As for the regional director's reaction: 'He took it very well. I think he was warned that would be my answer to the inevitable question.'

To Lord Aberconway the only sensible approach to dealing with the National Trust is plainly the one he has taken. And there's no doubt in his mind that it is completely justified. 'They will admit', he says of the Trust, 'that horticulturally Bodnant is the jewel in their crown.'

Lord Aberconway is unique, not only because he seems straight out of the Edwardian age. Or because he's property proud. There doesn't seem to be a donor who doesn't believe his National Trust house or garden or castle is Best of Breed, or even Best of Show. What sets Lord Aberconway apart, in this context at least, is that no other Trust garden is now managed as independently as Bodnant.

Head gardeners elsewhere may mutter – three generations of Puddles; three of Aberconways – Bodnant could use a fresh eye. And of course there are people besides James Lees-Milne who fancy a different garden style. But Bodnant which doesn't cost the Trust a penny, is big, vigorous, horticulturally interesting, packed with marvellous trees and thriving. It is very much the product of a powerful vision. And that is what visitors who peer around other people's gardens want: variety, stimulus, inspiration. It's possible to find all that at Bodnant even if you don't adore rhododendrons.

Lord Aberconway is one of a kind. What is the National Trust to do about its other gardens, then?

In the absence of a rich plantsman with long experience and fine people to help him work out and implement his schemes, what can the Trust do at the many ambitious gardens it acquired?

It can do what a rich, horticulturally aspiring, non-plantsman does when he wants to improvement his patch. He can call in an expert.

Back to Bucks

'What was really the biggest damn nuisance was the landscape,' says Sir Francis Dashwood, thinking back to the days after his father's departure to Majorca and his move into West Wycombe Park.

'Being the best Palladian villa, I've always taken the view that everything had to be done in a prima donna way. So everything had to be the very best.'

Though the house was already their property, he did not rush to his landlord for advice. 'When it came to the interior, I didn't consult the National Trust at all,' says plucky Sir Francis. He called in John Fowler. And for the park . . .

'I had Lanning Roper in,' Sir Francis reports. And after him, he had Russell Page. 'He'd been doing Longleat and he was absolutely wonderful. I carried out all the things he wanted.' Then, after a pause, Sir Francis became willing to try the man at the Trust.

'John Sales has been absolutely brilliant,' he says. 'He comes once a year and walks around with me and the local National Trust agent. He produces a three- or four-page letter of the things we're going to do, and we've done them all. He's got a marvellous eye; he's a charming man. Extremely knowledgeable. In many ways he's better than Russell Page who was so grand and so difficult to handle.'

Yes, Sir Francis reflects, 'that's been a great plus. We even went off to Kew to find out which species of tree were here then. He's been absolutely marvellous and the landscape is back as it was in 1770 I suppose.'

At the centre of the world

When he first went to work for the Trust as Graham Stuart Thomas's assistant, John Sales's office was the dining-room table at his house in Essex. Once it became clear that he would succeed Thomas as gardens adviser, Sales decided to move house to somewhere more convenient for all the garden scrutinizing he now had to do. There had been eleven gardens for Graham Thomas to oversee when he began his work with the Trust, there were now more than a hundred. 'The biggest horticultural collection', in Britain or perhaps the world. Sales looked for an area that would be a pleasant place to live and put as many gardens as possible within easy striking distance. He chose Cirencester.

John Workman who'd been advising the Trust on Forestry from an office at the round table in his Sheepscombe sitting room, heard that Sales was moving to Cirencester or round-about, and suggested they open up an office there. Both of them needed more space and more help. Mrs Sales was having trouble keeping up with her husband's workload.

Workman, an eminent forester who says, no doubt accurately, 'You could parachute me blindfold into any forest in England and I'd know exactly where I was,' was a bachelor with no one to do his typing. The Trust's first Cirencester office opened in 1976.

He remains a man for whom trees are not only plant matter and his field of expertise but also a creative medium. When he talks about what he cut down, what he planted, how to manage woods or parkland, his long fingers separate – his forearms move. For all his seventy-odd years and painful arthritis, he suddenly gives the impression of being a lively conductor, for whom trees, somehow, are the notes of the score he's playing.

'I settled here because I was born here,' admits Workman who joined the Trust in 1945. But Gloucestershire had other virtues, too, he was quick to add. 'The Trust always accepted that this was the centre of the universe. Within 200 miles you cover England and Wales right into Cornwall and right up beyond Manchester.'

(Poor Yorkshire, Northumbria and the Lake District as well as Northern Ireland, for the moment they'd all had fallen off the map.)

As soon as the new office existed, people came to fill it. Archaeologists, nature conservation experts, countryside managers, volunteers managers, gardens advisers – and their secretaries – appeared at Cirencester which has become the headquarters for the National Trust staff who look after their countryside properties.

'The roads are good, and rail,' said Workman, continuing his catalogue of the virtues of this new hub.

'You see they all travel a lot,' he explained. 'I mean the travelling almost killed me. It really did. One year I did over 50,000 miles.'

As the Trust's bureaucracy grew, so did its operation in Cirencester. When I went to see John Sales, fifty people were employed at the large office building purpose-built for the National Trust in 1991 – tastefully faced with local stone, to be sure, but charmless just the same. Inside are none of the eighteenth-century bits and pieces – the odd Baroque mirror or gilded clock that turn up in the offices at Queen Anne's Gate. All is stripped down and utilitarian. If a Savile Row suit passes through this front door, the wearer is probably calling in from London. The most splendid article of apparel I saw at Cirencester is the red, man-of-the-mountain beard worn by David Russell, the Trust's current forestry adviser.

The number of people looking after gardens, like the number of gardens in the Trust's care, has grown since the 2nd Lord Aberconway introduced his plan. From his office, John Sales oversees the work of more than 300 gardeners at more than 150 gardens in England, Wales and Northern Ireland and about fifty landscaped parks. He and a staff of three other gardens advisers divide up this territory.

The Trust's structure is no less confusing in gardening than elsewhere. Besides the salaried gardens staff there is a Gardens Panel – a committee of horticulturally interested and/or knowledgeable volunteers. They advise the adviser about major alterations, improvements and new undertakings. In turn, they may be advised by the historic buildings representative for the region in which the garden sits, or even the architectural adviser if he gets interested.

Socrates in the potting shed

For about a quarter of a century John Sales has been in charge of the National Trust's gardens. He hasn't become jaded. The huge historical projects the Trust undertakes like the one at Stowe don't phase him. 'Reconstruction, that's easy,' he says somewhat surprisingly. 'It's keeping the garden going that's difficult. Anything you do affects the garden in the long term – even how high or low you cut the grass.'

Sales talks about the relation of plants to earth and climate and how not a bit of it stays fixed. 'We're not just assembling objects in spaces; we're continuing something that's been going on for a hundred years,' he points out. 'One has to have an overall plan for a garden, but you also have to have a degree of flexibility because you've got to respond – technically and critically – the whole time. You take a border for example,' he continues burrowing deeper into his subject. 'It may be designed at the outset . . . Herbaceous plants, bulbs, whatever . . . But it never quite works out the way you expect.'

It's Sales's job and his gift to design the border, keeping in mind how it will look in five, ten, twenty years. 'You will constantly go back and alter that border over time,' he says. 'You won't do it with a plan, because the best way of doing it, is looking at it. You'll say, take that out, move that over there. And that's what makes gardens good or bad. That's what has to be done with the eye.'

The chief gardens adviser, Sales trains his eye on all of its gardens and parks of course. But he also takes on his portion of the share-out of properties that are given particular attention by the individual advisers. In that role, Sales may visit these two or three times a year but up to six times if there is a special project underway.

'The main thrust of our advice is routine,' he says. No item is too small to talk about with a head gardener. 'It's the cumulative effect of a lot of very small decisions in gardens that counts. This may seem boring but it isn't. Gardens get better or worse in small stages. Even if you put a lot of things in at once, they grow at different rates, so that one has to keep going back.'

Sales is on the road all year round. He'll spend a day at a property seeing the gardeners, the managing agent of the property, maybe the historic buildings representative. 'Generally speaking,' he says, 'the decisions are made there and then and priorities worked out.'

Probably the first thing that has to be established is a kind of overview. 'It's got to begin with an objective approach,' he says. There has to be the understanding 'that we're all trying to make that place as perfect as possible. As soon as they get the message that we're all looking for what's right for that place, that you are not trying to score points, then you may have differences of opinion – everybody does – but you can usually resolve it eventually.'

He describes the process this way: 'Almost always it's a matter of asking the right questions,' he says. 'If you ask the questions to yourself out loud, other people will give you the answers, very often.'

For example, some trees could not work in a given spot because of the climate, the soil conditions, the amount of light. What would?

'We know we must decide whether we want a plant which is going to be evergreen or deciduous; how big it is going to be; what period it should relate to historically,' he explains. 'Then we refine it down to what colour the flowers ought to be. Should they be quiet? Should they strident? If you ask enough questions you finish up with the right plan for that case.'

Everyone has contributed to the plan by the time Sales has finished asking his questions. The report he then writes up is sent to the managing agent. Technically, it is only advice and not a set of instructions but 'ninety per cent of the time it's taken,' he says, 'because we've agreed on the spot'.

John Sales knows all about the criticism that the National Trust's gardens look the same. 'It's so obvious that one doesn't need to say it,' he volleys when this is brought up. 'We regard it as a professional problem to prevent it happening.'

One way of averting this is to establish a fruitful dialogue between the gardens adviser and the head gardener at each property. Sales absolutely rejects the assertion that the most sensational gardens have always been the product of an individual vision.

'It's a wonderful fallacy. There aren't any gardens I know, any great gardens, that were made by one person, it was always two or three people together,' he believes. 'You know Sissinghurst was Sackville-West and Nicolson; Hidcote was Johnstone and Norah Lindsay. And Jekyll and Lutyens worked together. It really needs a combination of talents, not forgetting the head gardener who nearly always has an important input to every aspect.'

Let's say that the combination of gardens adviser and head gardener can replicate these famous, successful partnerships. But doesn't it also mimic the friction and competition that partnerships have been known to propagate?

'One of the snares in the Trust is to become too proprietorial,' Sales concedes. 'There are some properties in the Trust I feel quite protective towards. I won't tell you which they are,' he says smiling. But then like a parent with a large brood, he adds, 'I feel the same about them all really. One gets to love them all. They're marvellous places.'

Head gardeners, of course, have only one such place to love and might therefore feel more easily pinched in the heart when someone else is possessive of it.

'We encourage head gardeners to have the feeling that the gardens are theirs,' says Sales. 'When the gardens are good, it's because of that pride.'

Yes, but don't they see him as a rival and resent him when he comes along with his 'advice'?

'Well a certain amount of tact has to be employed you know,' he laughs. More soberly he adds, 'Of course they do. And quite right that they should. It *is* their garden.'

Sales clearly admires as well as respects the head gardeners. 'They're terrific fellows,' he says. As for the head gardeners, who are not deferential by nature, they all have good things to say of the chief gardens adviser. Their one criticism of Sales is that sometimes they feel he doesn't fight hard enough on their behalf with those higher up.

But to Sales the suggestion that there is such a thing as 'higher-ups' at the National Trust is offensive as I learned when, in passing, I said, 'I saw your boss Julian Prideaux the other day.'

Charm and cool skittered out of sight.

'He's *not* my boss,' Sales said sternly, his expression hardening. 'The National Trust is a horizontal organization, not pyramidal.'

This was another occasion when I could be glad my notes were elsewhere and my memory sometimes ragged. I had talked with Julian Prideaux, the Trust's chief agent, the week before at Queen Anne's Gate.

'The Trust is all about property,' Prideaux had said. 'I am the Trust's head professional property manager.' Its seventy land agents and many chartered surveyors all answer to him.

But that's not all by any means. 'I have a wonderful role,' he confessed, 'because I can actually, I think legitimately, put my nose into almost anything that the Trust is doing, should be doing. I have a large and rather expert department in Cirencester.'

John Sales now sitting across from me had regained his composure. We returned to talk of his collaboration with head gardeners.

'If you ignore people,' he says, 'the decisions they make become less important in their minds. And they're not. Everything is important.'

Sales believes the head gardeners look forward to his visits. This is not an example of personal vanity but an acknowledgment that a fine craftsman knows what can be gained from high-level shop talk.

'I think what they do appreciate is another professional coming and talking on their subject at their level, on their terms. And really talking it out. They see relatively few people at that level.'

Very few, I would say, judging from what I've heard.

'We work to the Gardens Panel,' Sales went on to explain. 'Our activities are monitored by them. We don't so much need technical expertise. We ought to have that. The most important thing we want from them is good judgment about our proposals.'

A day in the country

Six panels, of which Gardens is one, advise the influential, which is to say powerful, Properties Committee of the National Trust.

Back into structural Byzantium we go: the Properties Committee has nineteen members in addition to the chief agent and the historic building secretary. Of those nineteen, six are the chairman of the various panels: Architecture, Gardens, and so on. These people are not only busy multiplying the number of meetings they have to attend, but when they get there, they seem to be advising themselves.

Just as with the accounts, so with management: gardens are no longer separated into two categories; those that came to the Trust through the Gardens Committee and those that were included when a house or estate was transferred to the Trust. In fact, as Sir Henry Benson recommended in his report, the original Gardens Committee was phased out in 1969. 'We have received a good deal of evidence', Benson had written, 'to support the view that it is difficult to run gardens, each of which is a continuing act of creation, by a committee.' Lord Rosse on his own kept an eye on the gardens. But then six years later the Gardens Panel was set up.

Lord Gibson, one of its nine members, tried to explain the reason for its existence.

'A national body has to have national standards and somebody has to see that they are actually maintained,' the Trust's former chairman argues.

But how does the Gardens Panel actually accomplish this?

'Four or five times a year we visit a site. We wander around the garden in the morning. We have a sandwich lunch. And then we have a meeting in the afternoon in which we discuss what we've seen,' Lord Gibson answers not altogether revealingly. 'We have a gardener there who tells us about the problems. We have an exchange. Emma sums up at the end of the day and John writes it down.'

John is Mr Sales, the chief gardens adviser; Emma is Lady Emma Tennant, the Panel's chairman.

The Lady in the chair

One of the members of the Gardens Panel is Ted Fawcett who now is a dowser but decades ago he was the Trust's public relations officer. ('Public relations, oh Gawd!' groaned the chaps at the time. Along with talking about money and thinking about visitors this was not at all to their taste.) Richard Bisgrove is an horticultural historian; Tom Wright whose field is garden management and Paul Edwards whose specialty is garden buildings are panel members, too. There is, of course, also Lord Gibson as well as George Clive, a landowner, Lady Mary Keen who writes about gardening and works as a garden designer and Robin Compton whose garden at Newby Hall in Yorkshire is well known. Above all there is Lady Emma Tennant, the Committee's chairman.

Those who are feudally inclined would immediately warm to the idea that the daughter of the Duke and Duchess of Devonshire who grew up at Chatsworth, their enormous Derbyshire estate, is chairing the National Trust's Gardens Panel. And indeed Lady Emma Tennant is among those who believe that having countrymen (and women, obviously) on its committees is invaluable for the Trust. These people know from experience what's involved in running large estates whereas others need to have everything explained. Although the announcement of a planned visit by the panel is not always welcomed by gardens staff, the head gardeners I've met had a good word for its chairman.

'I'm an absolutely born, trowel in hand, hands-on gardener,' says Emma Tennant. We were in the workroom at her sheep farm in Northumberland. Through the window I could see her own garden. This apparent wilderness was no Giverny; but just the same many of the plants in it are grown to serve as models for her watercolour paintings.

'I can see if my life had been different,' she continues, 'I could be quite a happy head gardener. I'd never learn to run the machinery,' she admits, 'but I could do the propagating in the potting shed.'

Her life would have had to have been very different indeed for that to have been its outcome. Tall, thin and only initially nervous in her manner, Lady Emma Tennant has the bone deep self-confidence that comes with being a rich Duke's daughter. Still, there was something obviously sincere in what she was trying to put across. Gardens do mean a lot to her and her interest in them is emotional as well as aesthetic. When she says, 'to throw yourself into a place is a very rewarding thing,' there's no doubting she's speaking from experience.

Lady Emma Tennant is a quick thinker and talker; her mind is sharply focused and she knows a lot about gardening. What's more she's always learning. 'I try and visit privately run gardens, too,' she says. (A sketch pad is often on the car seat next to her.) 'In this game of looking after gardens and houses and estates, too, we learn from each other. None of us is in isolation.'

Though the panel meets four time a year, 'Obviously that's only the tip of the iceberg,' she notes. 'The more time you put into it, the better it will work.'

Individual members of the Gardens Panel keep an eye on properties where major restorations are underway. They look in on gardens which may come to the Trust. But once a garden does come, the Panel don't rush in.

'We try to time our meetings not at the very start,' says the chairman. 'Research is not yet done.' But as soon as they feel they've got enough to go on, a site visit is scheduled.

'We arrive from all different directions, rather exhausted, lots of people having driven for a very long time,' she says. After several cups of coffee to wake themselves up, they start.

Usually either the historic buildings representative or the gardens adviser fills them in. 'We have maps,' she says, 'and they've boiled down the research to the key issues. At Dunham Massey there's a wonderful set of paintings in the house showing the park as originally laid out. That's gold dust to us,' she adds.

But as important as she feels this research is, she tries to

[229]

keep it in its place. 'Anything to do with nature, whether it's landscape or a top of a cliff or a wood or a garden, which is obviously manmade, nothing stands still,' she says. 'They're all moving forward and changing all the time.'

The panel and staff walk around the garden and talk as they go. 'You stand at the head of the steps looking at the view and see what the original thing would have been. Very often it's been very overgrown through years of neglect or inadequate maintenance.'

Rarely is a garden in tip-top condition when the NT gets it. Few people or institutions with money enough to keep such places up feel the need to give them away. Some like the High Victorian extravaganza Biddulph Grange in Staffordshire with its Chinese Pavilion and an Egyptian vault, which has turned into a Cheshire cottage when you come out the other side, are derelict. In 1988, the National Gardens Scheme contributed £100,000 to the £800,000 restoration appeal launched by the Trust.

'Prune that tree!' is not the sort of statement the Gardens Panel utters. 'I see our role as very much supporting and backing up the staff,' says Lady Emma. But', she adds, 'not just rubber-stamping. Often new ideas emerge, or new approaches. Or, if there's a clear choice between two ways of doing something, we try to decide.'

Though this suggests there might be sometimes be disagreement, there's not a bit of it, evidently.

'I can't imagine ever coming to the point where you'd actually take a vote at a Gardens Panel meeting. In fact, I've hardly ever seen it at the Head Office meetings in London. We all know each other very well,' Lady Emma adds.

It does sounds very cosy. But the fact that friction produces pearls seems a foreign idea.

'John Sales and his team and me and the other members of the Gardens Panel, we've all been working alongside for . . . well I don't know, twenty years,' she explains. 'We have millions of lines of communication really. Obviously new people join the staff,' she concedes, 'but they soon get into our way of thinking and doing things.'

'Our way of thinking and doing things . . .' No wonder there are staff members – Sarah-Jane Forder who edits the magazine comes to mind, as does Janette Harley the archivist; people who come with high standards and new ideas for how things can be better done – who become anxious about holding on to their independent judgments. Seeking consensus can sometimes look like a process of grinding everyone down.

Talk turned to conservation because just as exacting standards are being applied to houses and their contents, they are being adopted in the management of the landscape too. And sometimes its seems with an equal tendency towards excesses of zeal. This, too, the panel has to consider.

'There's been vast growth in interest in nature conservation,' Lady Emma agrees. 'Gone are the days when you just looked after an avenue. Now you've got to think about all the creepy-crawlies that live in the bark.'

Should the dead trees be removed or should they be left so the beetles continue to have a home?

'It's a constant balancing act,' she says. 'It's got more complicated as more has been found out.'

And sometimes it's become preposterous. People want to be able to walk in the woods, not run an obstacle course through a housing estate for beetles. There are moments when a person gets the feeling that the Trust has quietly converted to Buddhism.

During a visit to the loft above the tea room in the Cromwellian Stables at Grey's Court for instance, which was to be used as an NT bookshop when the visiting season opened, Lady Brunner led the way up the stairs. The place turned out to be filled with bat droppings. 'We would have gone in and been done with them,' Lady Brunner told me. Now the bats have to be coaxed to go live somewhere else. This would be fine except they don't seem interested in budging.

In her rapid-fire way, Lady Emma was on to another topic.

'An idea I must do something about,' she reminds herself,

'is opening gardens in the evening. People can come along after they've come home from work. The scent is always so much better,' Lady Emma Tennant adds, already absorbed by the smells and the vision of it all, 'the shadows are long and the light's very beautiful'.

There are other, less attractive, long shadows cast over the National Trust's gardens. Its system of committees and consultation does not invariably achieve the desired result. For example, the estimable *Good Gardens Guide* announced that the Gertrude Jekyll garden at Lindisfarne Castle had been removed from its 1994 edition. It is one of the only complete Lutyens/Jekyll collaborations in the NT's care. The *Guide* noted that in spite of the efforts of Professor Michael Tooley who had worked for decades restoring Miss Jekyll's scheme, 'if inadequate provision is made for maintenance, no design, however historic can survive'.

In May 1994, Professor Tooley (a Durham University geologist and Jekyll authority) resigned from the Trust. He had been honorary gardens advisor at Lindisfarne for twenty-three years. He feels that while in the early days people at the Trust were responsive and appreciative its management structure now is 'hopeless'. Prof. Tooley met Lady Emma Tennant only once, in 1993, and John Sales never. His repeated admonitions that staffing at the garden should be increased were effectively ignored.

'It *was* being somewhat neglected,' John Sales allowed when questioned about the situation. 'Now somebody's got to do something about it smartish.'

Once again the NT has 'found' money. This tiny, poetic garden near the water's edge on Holy Island is going to be the recipient of a 'planting blitz'. Some will be placated by this; others, like Professor Tooley, find the prospect appalling.

[7]

A Mixed Bouquet

The two most applauded and least criticized of the National Trust's success stories since the war have been its accumulation of fine gardens and its acquisition of coast. Both are embraced, yet they represent extremes of the landscape. While it was Nature more or less on her own who shaped the rocks, sand dunes, cliffs, marshes and coves, that make up the more than 500 miles of coast, much of it amassed as a result of Enterprise Neptune; the Trust's 130 gardens were all contrived by the hand, eye and imagination of women and men. But whether the terrain is artful or natural, the people who preserve and restore it all for our pleasure and solace are among the most hard-working and gifted employees of the National Trust.

'They really are fantastic people,' Sir Angus Stirling agrees. 'Exceedingly dedicated; often very knowledgeable and willing to put in twenty-four hours a day practically. They are good to be with those people: great ambassadors.'

There's nothing to argue with here. Nevertheless the question has to be asked: Just what is one to make of the Trust's words, really?

Looking at its practices rather than its preachings, an inverted logic seems in operation at the National Trust. The head gardeners and coastal wardens who do some of the finest and most admired work – and just about everyone does say so – are amongst the lowest men on its totem pole. On several totem poles in fact, among them – wages; budgets; staffing. And yet –

If I had all the money in the world and wanted to make a garden, I'd try to poach a head gardener from the NT. And were I, with my riches, to buy lands alongside the shore; I'd hope to interest an NT coastal warden to come to work for me. Certainly some people with the money to be choosy do. Richard Broyd, for instance, who has invested millions in recreating seventeenth-century Hartwell House in Oxfordshire and turning it into a lavish country house hotel, employs as his head gardener Brian Saunders, who once worked at nearby Waddesdon where for many years his father was head gardener. But the National Trust would not be the first place I should go to look for a lawyer, nor help with pictures nor the hiring of a land agent. Indeed few people outside the National Trust who have had experience of its land agents have anything positive to say about them except that they are 'nice'. Among the other adjectives I've heard used to describe some of them are 'amateurish' and 'second rate'.

Coastal wardens and head gardeners all feel connected to the land they tend, and they're proud of what they've been able to achieve in looking after their gardens or cliffs or dunes – and with very good reason, almost always. But frosts, gales, and drought have educated them out of any uppishness that might have been theirs earlier on. Sometimes there is bitterness, but not because years of their work is suddenly undone as happened in the great storms of 1987 and 1990, when hundreds of thousands of trees on landscape owned by the National Trust alone came crashing down.

Botanical Bravery

' "What a wonderful life you must have looking after this beautiful garden," say the visitors'; Graham Stuart Thomas records in *Gardens of the National Trust*. 'Of course they have,' he continues, 'if not they would not stay.' But, he adds, 'life is never unadulterated bliss, and they, garden philosophers, know it.' They know it and they don't keep it to themselves.

Volunteers and indoor staff call them 'the salt of the earth', but when the head gardeners talk about the way the National Trust is run and how they are treated, peppery seems a more apt description. And, as already suggested, they have reason. They are the unsung heroes of the National Trust.

Take for example, *The National Trust Gardens Handbook*, a paperback, special interest guide meant to provide more detailed information than what's given in the annual *Guide to NT Properties* that goes to all members.

The reader is told about the soil conditions of each of the gardens listed, even its altitude. From the *Handbook* the horticulturally inquisitive will also learn, for instance, that Osterley Park is home to many fine specimen trees, oaks particularly; that there's a fernery at Tatton Park; at Polesden Lacey a walled rose garden will be found (and the grave of its donor Mrs Greville just outside it). But – in all its almost 200 pages – the guide does not mention the name of a single National Trust gardener. The excuse for this cannot be that the book would have to be too often updated. Head gardeners are not a nomadic tribe.

At the Chelsea Flower Show in 1994 the charity finally did something which seemed to suggest it had changed. That was the launch of *Garden Tips from the National Trust*, a paperback collection of forty-four contributions from its gardeners and designers. But this wasn't even the Trust's own idea!

According to Jackie Gurney who is responsible for its

gardening publicity, 'Someone in marketing who had no connection with the Trust pointed out how popular gardens and gardening has become and that there would be a market for advice from National Trust gardeners.' So it decided to do the book as a way of making money; not in order to give recognition to the gardeners, help them share their knowledge with the public and, through that, promote the gardens they've done so much to create. Yet even as a money-making venture, the Trust seems to have been incredibly slow to catch on to the potential income its gardeners could bring to the charity. The book is welcome and better than nothing, if long overdue. Let's hope some other outside whiz comes along and points out to the Trust that its best head gardeners are each of them a walking encyclopedia.

For love, not money

'Self-opinionated. That's what I am!' Jimmy Hancock announced with a wide smile. He is head gardener at Powis Castle in Wales, not far over the border.

Powis with its lyrical lead statues and venerable yews is a garden with sweep and sumptuousness. 'Outstanding' is how John Sales describes it. All over Britain and in America, too, people who know it – from daydreamers to gardening amateurs and pros – agree. Powis has an elegant eighteenth-century terrace, a nineteenth-century woodland and ambitiously Edwardian borders. Since his arrival in 1972, the twenty-five-acre garden has been reworked through and through by Jimmy Hancock. He now heads a team of eight – a large number of staff for a National Trust garden.

From almost any spot at Powis, the twelfth-century castle, mightily Victorianized, looms above. And looms is the word. Though built from red stone, Hancock refers to the hulking monster as 'The White Elephant'. It's as hungry as one, too. The castle's preservation and maintenance consumes vast amounts of the money that comes from admissions to Powis. Even more galling, some of the income from the sale of the very desirable plants Jimmy Hancock propagates and sells to visitors is spent on the castle too. (The garden shop, with its plants arranged according to their degree of hardiness, is one of the Trust's best.) And though the Earl of Powis is not impoverished, the Trust – as it does elsewhere in similar circumstances – has to come up with the money to pay for insuring the furniture on view, although he continues to own it.

Jimmy Hancock was eager to take me on a tour of his ambitious and delightful garden but first he had a few things to get off his chest.

'We've dedicated the whole of our lives, in a way, to this job,' he says about himself and the other head gardeners. 'It isn't just an ordinary job. All right,' Hancock allows, 'they don't necessarily ask us to. And we might be silly for doing it. But at the same time that's what gardening has been about in the private sector.'

Jimmy Hancock calculates that he works between sixty and eighty hours a week.

'A lot of people say I do it because I like it. And I do like it. But mainly I do it because I've got the alternative of letting it go.' With staff numbers fixed, when more needs doing in the garden, Jimmy Hancock is the one to do it. If he kept to the working day of, say, many of the people employed at the Regional Office, or Queen Anne's Gate, for that matter, the gardens at Powis Castle would deteriorate fairly fast.

'The Trust is shortening the hours,' Hancock says, sounding neither enthusiastic nor impressed. The idea is to make a uniform work week for all employees. 'They're not afraid to give people extra holidays and all that, which is all right,' he believes. But with the same number of staff now taking more time off, he feels he has to work harder just to keep things as they were before. 'The plants grow whether you have three Bank Holidays or none,' as he tersely puts it.

I mention that in conversation the men running the Trust praise what its head gardeners have achieved.

'Mr Kennaway did know how much I put into the garden

and did appreciate it,' Jimmy Hancock acknowledges. (Ian Kennaway, head of the regions, was previously regional director for North Wales.) 'I used to get nice letters from him. But', Hancock continues, 'I think it's what you do, not what you write.'

And in case I hadn't got the message he told me that in the early 1980s when the garden shop was established, Ian Kennaway had given him to believe that most of its profit would go to the garden. Instead much of it – £40,000 in a good year – has become elephant fodder, which hardly seems fair.

There are a few other areas in which the deeds of the National Trust towards its employees who work on the ground have not been a match of its appreciative words. Among them: housing; retirement; employee benefits. But probably the overriding issue for him was the attitude of the men running the charity which is Britain's largest private landowner and landlord.

'They've tried to pay people a more realistic wage,' Jimmy Hancock agrees. 'But at the same time they've obviously looked for methods of keeping their profitability way up. They've put that as a priority above their duty to their staff, really.'

The Trust has gone commercial. Enter the villain in the guise of National Trust Enterprises PLC. Everybody who works for the National Trust is certainly aware that it is a charity that spends more preserving its properties than it takes in from the people visiting them. The decision to make such things as tea rooms, shops and holiday lets part of a separate money-making, professionally operated business – the profit from which would go to the Trust – was taken in 1973. The hope was that this would increase income. It was also done to satisfy certain tax regulations since charities themselves are not allowed to be profit-making businesses.

To judge from its critics within the Trust, the money motive and the predatory behaviour seem to have married one another. Tea rooms may be the only one of the offspring that is generally thought benign or even attractive, though certainly not to the architecture purists. They believe that shops and tea rooms if they have to exist at all should be so far away from a house that a person will not be aware of their existence when inside the mansion or studying its façade. An argument can be made, however, that if more of the tea rooms baked their own goods and were located in the kitchens of houses where cooking as well as eating belongs, the houses would be humanized as a result.

'Don't dare tell Enterprises about this,' one staff member of the Trust alerted another during the restoration at Chastleton House in Oxfordshire, when some rooms in an outbuilding were discovered for which no plan had been made yet. The fear was that greedy Enterprises would barge in and take them for a shop.

What Jimmy Hancock holds against Enterprises is their stalking of houses and cottages for use as holiday lets. And many people at the Trust feel that this has become a growth industry that is growing out of hand. In fact, it's advancing slowly, if also unrelentingly. In 1985, Enterprises had about 160 holiday cottages; in 1994 there were 207 which were bringing a profit to the Trust of £611,000.

The head gardener at Powis Castle waved his arm towards the ornate gate between us and the road. A lovely house stood beyond it, at the roadside. The Countess had lived there after the death of her husband, the 5th Earl. She died at the age of ninety-seven – and in marched Enterprises. It is now a holiday cottage.

'It could have been used for the head gardener instead,' Hancock said meaningfully.

But surely the National Trust had given him a house to live in?

'Yes,' Hancock answered, motioning to a building across the lawn, covered with yellow roses.

In the old days, these dwellings were called tied cottages. Now, the National Trust, which likes jargon (as, for instance, using the word 'manager' as often as possible), calls these houses 'representative accommodation'. Some, though not all, of its head gardeners, wardens and foresters whose jobs require them to live very near their work, live in representative accommodation. But what does it represent? Less than you – and the staff – might have thought.

[239]

'All the Bodnant staff, for the estate, the garden, everywhere go on living in their own houses,' Lord Aberconway assured me. 'I'd never turn a past employee out of his house.' Nor would the Duke of Devonshire at Chatsworth, nor would quite a few other landowners of the old school make their staff move on their retirement.

The Trust has stated that its goals include not only the perpetuation of the landscape but also of 'the best of the traditions' that created it.

The 'countrymen' who serve on the Trust's various committees are there in part to provide this kind of continuity. Jonathan Peel, for example, was on the East Anglia's Regional Committee for eleven years before becoming chairman of the Trust's Property Committee, an even more influential job. He owns an estate in Norfolk.

Peel, in his forties, has the unhurried manner and ruddy complexion of a man who spends a great deal of time in the country. Though he undoubtedly lives in the grandest house in the village of Barton Turf and a number of farms are part of his domain, Jonathan Peel says that the local perception of himself as a rich landowner 'isn't very true'. But he admits, 'it's still a perception'. And he believes that he has the duty 'to look after the people who have served you for the whole of their lives'. He helps them by making sure they have rented housing at a very low cost, for life.

Peel is aware that 'some people might see that as being excessively patronizing in today's society'. Nevertheless he believes it is right. And not only for himself. 'Against all the urban views that are being thrown at them from outside, that sort of paternalism should still be part of the National Trust.'

And so it is part of the National Trust, but seemingly in all the wrong places. 'The men of the soil' continue to be treated as loyal family retainers, but when it comes to housing them, the Trust suddenly leaps into the modern age and rather crudely begins to calculate its bottom line.

The argument from Queen Anne's Gate and the various

regional offices of the National Trust is that they – unlike Lord Aberconway or the Devonshires, say, or Jonathan Peel for that matter – haven't enough houses on their estates to provide for retired employees. Since it has a year-round staff of more than 3,000, the explanation seems plausible. But houses for all is not what is needed, asked for nor suggested. It's those people who have worked long hours over many years at low wages and who have been asked, or required, to live in places owned by the Trust while they did so, who should have houses available to them when they retire.

No wonder Jimmy Hancock and others are maddened when they see the Trust transforming houses it owns into holiday cottages or, as on the Ickworth estate in Suffolk where it owned alienable houses, selling them off. How can men in his position have accumulated enough savings to buy a home of their own on retiring?

Merlin Waterson, regional director for East Anglia, says, 'it shouldn't be a situation that they're coming up to retirement and no thought has been given to that. I would hope that in this region either I myself or my staff would talk to them well in advance, well before the thing becomes an issue. We're trying to get help to people in various ways,' he continues. 'Sometimes we have used contacts on district councils to try and make council housing a possibility.'

For a person who has spent twenty years living in a charming cottage at Blickling or Powis or Cotehele, surrounded by acres of magnificent gardens which he or she knows and helped create, being offloaded to a housing estate may seem a harsh reward for the seven-day weeks many have put in all those years. And despite it being the avowed policy of every regional director with whom I talked, very few staff in any region of the NT that I met had had the subject of plans for future housing mentioned to them.

Some people are inclined by temperament or training to think ahead and try to make plans for retirement. Others fail to understand that the National Trust, though it provides them with housing during their working life and is patronizing in the old familiar paternalistic way, is not going to look after them later. But even in cases where people are helped to prepare for the future, the results are sometimes disturbing.

Late frost

At the Lanhydrock Estate, which was given to the National Trust in 1953 by Lord Clifden, the Victorian grey stone house now serves as the Regional Office for Cornwall. I walked around the thirty-acre garden with Peter Borlase who had come there in 1966 and retired twenty-seven years later. Before that, for eleven years, he'd been at Trelissick, another of the Trust's Cornish gardens. For thirty-eight years he'd gardened splendidly for the National Trust. In 1988 Borlase was made an Associate of Honour, the highest award given to a working gardener by the Royal Horticultural Society and in 1991 he was given a BEM.

When he first went to Lanhydrock, Borlase noticed how well magnolias seemed to be doing on its lime-free soil. Trees that had been planted in the 1930s were already sixty-five feet tall and more. He began to make these waxy-flowered trees a speciality of the garden; raising many from seed. 'Magnolia Peter Borlase' has magenta petals streaked with cream.

From the time he went to work at Lanhydrock, Peter Borlase and his wife lived in a tied cottage. Then, after a tenure of a quarter of a century, a staff member at the Trust suggested that it would sensible for them to start paying rent. If they did, by the time he retired they would have acquired rights of tenancy and would be legally entitled to carry on living there. It seemed a good idea and they agreed.

The local rent agent came and set his figure. He told Borlase that the sum he'd quoted was the maximum the Trust could charge for the property. If it chose, his landlord was at liberty to charge less. And since the Trust's head gardeners had not been paid anything like the maximum salary for men in their field, Borlase was confident that he would be asked to pay something lower. He was wrong. His rent which was twelve pounds a week in 1980 rose and rose until in less than a decade it reached fifty-three pounds per week. When he thought about his retirement he reckoned, he says, 'that my entire pension would have been taken up with the rent'.

Borlase went to Dick Meyric, the regional director, asking that his rent at Lanhydrock be lowered. Their exchange, he says, went like this:

Meyric to Borlase: 'No. It wouldn't be fair to the other staff.'

Borlase, to Meyric: 'Doesn't it matter that I've worked for the Trust for thirty-six years?'

'No, it does not,' Dick Meyric replied.

While Peter Borlase sat there nonplussed, Meyric asked him, 'Don't you wish you'd bought a place years ago?'

The head gardener explained that he would have liked to buy a house but the National Trust's wages had never been high enough.

Peter Borlase left Dick Meyric's office an irate man. 'I loved my work,' he says. 'I can never remember not wanting to go to work unless I wasn't well. The money side – as long as you had enough to get by, it never worried us.'

That was because it never occurred to the head gardener or his wife, who has long worked at Lanhydrock's shop, that when they became older, they would have money worries brought on by the actions of the National Trust.

Borlase didn't keep his feelings to himself. And when Michael Trinick, the previous regional director who lived at Lanhydrock, heard the story he stood up for the head gardener and argued his case; but the rent stayed as set – the maximum allowable.

For a long time Peter Borlase felt the sting. Other head gardeners heard about what had happened, of course, and it only confirmed the view many already had that the National Trust was better at exploiting its gardeners than showing appreciation for their devotion and achievements.

While the deputy director general says, 'It would be quite wrong to charge Lord Sackville the fair market rent at Knole,' (see Chapter 3), it was perfectly all right for the National Trust to charge Peter Borlase at Lanhydrock the most they could get out of him. It certainly looked as if fairness had been turned on its head. Go easy on the rich and/or titled and squeeze the people who can least afford it.

In May 1992 when I heard this story I was outraged; in early July interviewing Lady Emma Tennant, the chairman of the Gardens Panel, I told her what I'd learned and how appalling the Trust's behaviour looked to an outsider. Perhaps coincidentally, within two weeks Peter Borlase was called in to see Dick Meyric. Borlase then learned that Julian Prideaux, the Trust's chief agent, had instructed Meyric to have a chat with him and make the following suggestion: 'He said that if we would move they would give us suitable accommodation,' Borlase reports. 'I said, let me get this right. Are you saying this would be *rent free?*' The regional director said yes, it would be. Peter Borlase talked it over with his wife and accepted. It was November before the Head Office 'found' the money for the modest cottage two and a half miles from Lanhydrock into which Mr and Mrs Borlase moved in April 1993.

'They've come up trumps,' says Peter Borlase who lived through years of anxiety about his financial future before they did. They were years during which he, rightly, felt that instead of being rewarded for a lifetime of fine work he was being penalized. Perhaps it wasn't the fear that their harsh behaviour would come out in print which motivated people high up in the Trust to do something to help Peter Borlase. Perhaps, despite Michael Trinick's involvement and all the head gardeners who knew about it, those in a position to help simply hadn't been aware that there was a problem at Lanhydrock. If the latter is the case, then its policy of decentralization may be creating as many problems as it is intended to solve; as is the spread of an accountant's mentality.

'I think almost every head gardener who's been here over twenty years is a very dedicated man,' says Jimmy Hancock. 'And', he goes on, 'in nearly all the cases of the ones I know anyway, they are bitter in that they think the Trust have changed and that now it doesn't care.'

A not so charmed circle

'How can I put it so it doesn't sound too awful?' Jan Michalak, head gardener at Ickworth in Suffolk, asks rhetorically. 'I really like what the Trust does. The gardens are lovely. The people I've met in gardens are wonderful. But the system stinks!'

Michalak, in his forties, has been at Ickworth for two decades. It's not the existence of the Gardens Panel that irks him. 'They've only been here once since I've been here,' he explains. 'By the time we invite somebody here to give an opinion on what's going to be done, we need a yes or a no, we don't need planning. By the time we put it forward, we're ready to take the step of doing something.'

He does his preparation thoroughly and the bureaucracy doesn't hold him back. But Michalak feels that Ickworth with its continual deficits, when compared with Blickling, say, which is also in East Anglia, is not thought to be a star attraction by the National Trust. And while he's pleased enough to be left alone to get on with his development of the gardens, no one likes to feel that their passion is somebody else's back-burner. And it isn't only pride that is involved but also money. More publicity means more people coming to Ickworth and, therefore, through members rebates or the sale of admission tickets, there is more to spend on the garden.

'For what it's worth,' he confesses, as we walk through the gardens he's done so much to improve, 'it was once put on my report that I was the most loyal and devoted person that the agent had ever come across. But for the first time in all these years I actually said the other day, "If somebody thinks I'm doing that for no extra money, they've got another think coming."'

One explanation, and a crucial one, for Michalak's attitude is that he's come to believe that the people running the Trust identify too much with the upper class and look down on people like him.

'The Trust is a very elitist group, that's my biggest criticism of it,' says Michalak. Aristocrats seem to be permitted anything and forgiven all. This is something which the National Trust denies but candid aristocrats like Lord Croft do not. (See Chapter 3.)

Yet Michalak recalls a time when he felt all this was going to change.

'When I came we were called by our surnames and we called our bosses "Sir". I came very fresh and enthusiastic and young. I just refused to have anything to do with that.'

Some old-timers may complain when they overhear members of the Trust's staff calling one another by their first names – and there are donors who find this rather shocking, too – much of the current staff clearly likes it better this way. And the fact that the kind of people considered by the Trust for jobs has widened out a bit is welcomed also. Retired army officers, for instance, are no longer the inevitable first choice for the administrators who look after its stately homes. In Northern Ireland, for example, where individualism may be given freest reign, Chris Correy-Thomas, an ex-African farmer is at Florence Court; Terence Mack, a retired teacher, is at Castle Ward; Harry Hutchman, a former mineral explorer, is at Mount Stewart and Emma MacNeice, a twenty-six-year-old whose only previous job had been at a regional museum, is administrator of that stateliest – and most costly – of the mansions in the six counties, Castle Coole.

Salaries have risen, with the result that it isn't necessary for a person to have an army pension or the equivalent, to be able to afford to work as an administrator for the National Trust. Although they haven't risen sufficiently for it not to be a considerable help.

'It was very low pay when I arrived,' Michalak remembers. 'And being a gardener was low status.' But, he continues, 'when all the changes began, suddenly I got a lot of recognition from the Trust. And better wages.'

But changes that appeared fundamental in the way the Trust

was run did not stick. Michalak says that the new people were absorbed by the Trust and began to adopt the old ways of looking at things. 'They soon get into our way of thinking and doing things,' as Lady Emma Tennant had put it, though in a different context and in praise of the harmony this produces. The Trust's new generosity towards its head gardeners was also short-lived.

'They keep chiselling away,' says Michalak. 'All the time bits are peeling off. Little things. They don't pay expenses any more for some things, so I'm paying for those. We just lost a warden. They can't afford him any more. No talk of extra staff. The forester does his job plus half the warden's. I do my job, plus half the warden's. In time, that means sixty hours a week instead of forty. In wages, it's the same as before.'

Michalak lives with his family on the estate in representative accommodation not far from Ickworth House. His mood and outlook over the years no doubt suffered because, as a result of the memorandum of wishes drawn up by the Marchioness of Bristol, he acquired a rather troubling neighbour.

Lady Bristol, who endowed Ickworth when it became a possession of the National Trust in 1956, wished that the heir to the title should live in a wing of the mansion. Her nephew Victor was given a ninety-nine year lease in 1960. His son John Hervey became the 7th Marquess of Bristol in 1985 but in fact the lease on Ickworth's east wing had been made over to his trustees in 1979 because his father went abroad. Lord Bristol, by his own admission, has had more than a fling with heroin and cocaine. In 1994 it brought him first-hand knowledge of life as an inmate at Her Majesty's prison in Brixton.

Ickworth is not one of the dwellings you enter and think, 'How did the National Trust ever get saddled with this dreary place?' Begun in the late eighteenth century, the house is over 600 feet long. From a rotunda more than a hundred feet high, two curving wings fan out each ending in a rectangular pavilion. The classically inspired decoration inside manages to be inviting rather than imposing. It is a lovely stately house, both enveloping and impressive.

The National Trust is obliged by its constitution to preserve and protect Ickworth and its wonderful grounds. And if its tenant had been a reclusive chap for whom drugs were his only company, it might not be an issue worth discussing. The question is not one of morals in this case but of practicalities.

For years there were reports of raucous parties, attended by the like-minded, in Lord Bristol's wing at Ickworth. Mention has been made of his helicopter buzzing the property, of cars careering through the grounds and aggressive Irish wolfhounds let loose in the park. Michalak might as well have been raising his children in one of the more lawless housing estates, for all the feeling of physical safety he sometimes must have felt he could provide for them at Ickworth.

Even the landlord of a shed might feel alarmed about the potential threat to his property with such a tenant in residence, never mind the trustees of a treasure house.

The National Trust was slow to act. In fact for more than a dozen years, until 1994 when the marquess was behind bars in Brixton, the National Trust did almost nothing except issue the occasional warning. By then the sometimes hair-raising details of Lord Bristol's antics at Ickworth had been well reported in English newspapers. (For a rather different attitude towards its non-aristocratic tenants and their leases see Chapter 9.)

The Trust excused its inaction by saying it had to honour Lady Bristol's memorandum of wishes because, if it failed to, potential donors might be put off. But even before Lord Bristol went to prison, this seemed a feeble argument. For one thing, it's been years since the Arkell Report recommended that in future the Trust should not give such far-reaching assurances. For another, the risk to properties from occupants with Lord Bristol's recreations has become obvious to most of the grandees by now. After all, the Duke of Marlborough's trustees have moved to bar Jamie Blandford, his son and heir, from having the right to inherit Blenheim Palace. What if, having snorted away millions, a loan were taken against the property and Blenheim Palace were seized to pay the drugs bill?

Then too, from the beginning of the 1990s, the Trust has entered a phase where it doesn't yearn for country houses as it did in the 1940s. Largely this must be the result of the terrible deals that were made in the early years of the Country Houses Scheme and the enormous financial drain that has resulted. According to the Chorley Formula, which calculates the endowment needed if the properties can be expected to stay in credit, the amounts required by the Trust are now so vast that very very few owners could hope to meet them, even with grants from the National Heritage Memorial Fund. For example, sixteenth-century, half-timbered Pitchford Hall in Shropshire, with original contents and a wonderful Tudor tree house, was offered to the Trust in 1992. The Chorley Formula was applied and it was calculated that the Trust could accept the house, grounds and contents if an endowment of between £10 and £11 million were given with it. The Trust had discovered by this time that, even when the Chorley Formula is applied, it was still possible for unforeseen preservation work to put them in the red. The unanticipated £7.5 million cost of restoring fourteenth-century Ightham Mote in Kent, left to the Trust in 1985, had taught them that looking after old half-timbered houses can be exorbitantly expensive. Since there was no hope of a £10 million endowment being produced, the Trust said it could not take on Pitchford Hall and its owners, devastated by Lloyd's losses, sold the house; many of its original contents were auctioned off. (The Chorley Formula is always used to work out what endowment the Trust would need to look after a potential acquisition and remain in credit. This doesn't mean that the Trust always insists that it is given the sum before it will accept a house. Sometimes it decides to go ahead with less and to launch an appeal to make up the shortfall.[1])

Jan Michalak has three children. He's tried to plan ahead. But when he and his wife went house-hunting in East Anglia, where house prices are relatively high, the building society took one look at his annual income of £14,000 and, politely, laughed them out of the office.

'I'm in a poverty trap,' he says.

Yet there are signs of a more optimistic mood. His old neighbour has gone, for one thing. And Michalak, whose Polish father flew for the RAF during the war, managed to obtain a Churchill travel grant which took him on a two-month trip to Poland to study the practical training they give to gardeners, which is something he does a lot of at Ickworth. Administrative changes, too, have made him feel more buoyant. Since May 1993, Ickworth has had a property manager, Caroline Sier, rather than an administrator. Not only does she look after the house but she co-ordinates all the activity on the estate. The heads of each department – this includes Michalak – report to her. Sier, in turn, deals with the Regional Office.

Many more decisions about how the estate is run are now made at Ickworth, the head gardener says. And it seems to have had a good effect on attracting people to the park, with visitor numbers increasing by about 5,000 a year. Ickworth House still gets about a third of Blickling's 112,000 visitors but, for the moment at least, Jan Michalak feels he's not on the back-burner any more.

A sound investment

'I'm one of those people who've fallen into a manure heap and come up smelling of roses,' says Dave Mason. In his middle forties, after years of wandering the world, he's been head gardener at Coleton Fishacre on the south Devon coast for six years. That's the longest he'd been anywhere since leaving home.

Mason is proof that the National Trust hasn't become so hidebound that original characters have no way in. Before he was given this job, he'd never even been employed as a gardener – unless you count the weekends one summer in his teens when he did garden chores in Surrey for half a crown an hour.

With thinning blond hair combed back from a bony, intelligent face, Dave Mason speaks with just a trace of a South London accent. (He was born in Lambeth but grew up in Surrey.) And there's a trace of hippy vocabulary too. 'A real buzz' is a phrase that comes up every once in a while as we chat in the exuberant eighteen-acre garden that winds down to the sea.

The head gardener at Coleton Fishacre has lived in Australia, India, and northern California where he spent several years helping run an estate in the wine country. It was only when he reached his late thirties that the novelty of always being on the move lost its appeal. 'I wanted to feel located,' he says. 'To get my teeth into something.'

In 1986, while staying with his parents in Devon, he went to a careers adviser. Social work was suggested as a future path. But through the job centre, Mason learned about a government-sponsored National Trust adult retraining programme, and since he'd always had an interest, he decided to chose plants instead of people.

'What am I doing raking leaves at this age?' he asked himself during his training at Killerton. He already knew about organizing a staff and budgeting, he says. What he didn't know nearly as much about was plants. Yet by the time the programme was ending three jobs were offered including this post as head gardener at Coleton Fishacre, the garden created by Lady D'Oyly Carte in the 1920s as a setting for the family's new house. When the Trust acquired it in 1982, the garden was badly neglected. Mason says that because of that, Coleton Fishacre 'had a terrible reputation' when he accepted the job there.

'Lady D'Oyly Carte was a keen amateur; the development of the garden was due very much to her enthusiasm,' he said. As she went along, she developed a knowledge of its possibilities and of the plants that could strikingly embellish it. He, another enthusiastic keen amateur to begin with, has done very much the same thing.

'I'm not over-trained horticulturally,' he says candidly. 'I work out of instinct, intuition, feel. It was a great challenge.'

There have been no visits from the Gardens Panel in his six years at Coleton Fishacre. He does not feel neglected. 'I'm a bit dubious about committees and committee decisions,' he admits. 'You end up with diluted compromises.'

Coleton Fishacre has an individualistic stamp. Clearly Mason is a quick learner. 'Since I've been here I've grown,' he says. 'You get an empathy with the place. It's not a textbook thing.' And John Sales, who was gardens adviser at Coleton for the first four years Mason had the job was, he says, a great help to him.

'I developed a very good working relationship with John,' he reports. 'It was over a period of time,' he continues. Sometimes they disagreed about what should be done. 'I've got him to change his mind,' says Mason, 'and he's convinced me about one or two things.'

But Mason is cautious, too. 'I don't want this garden to become Trustified,' he says. 'A garden is not a museum. It's a dynamic, evolving and changing place. It's important to get an historical perspective, you want to know why the place was set up; what the people were like who were doing it. But', he goes on, 'you want to work within the spirit and feel of the place. I'd certainly hate us to keep looking over our shoulder all the time.'

Coleton Fishacre with its mixture of familiar plants and many exotic varieties – specimens from India, Latin America, Australia that flourish in this sheltered micro-climate – seems a specially favoured spot. The drop from the gazebo with is views down on to the sea is dramatic; the plantings are often flamboyant, yet because there are smaller gardens within the larger space, there is intimacy too.

The walled water garden in which we talked is particularly successful. Mason has created four beds inventively stuffed with hardy perennials and such exotic specimens as giant red-headed cannas from Central Mexico. He seems to be in sympathy with its spirit and is on his way to becoming quite a plantsman too. It was, therefore, startling to learn that Jim Marshall, who took over as gardens adviser at Coleton from John Sales in 1992, had suggested ripping out these beds and replacing them with a formal rose garden. It would be 'true to the period' and it would also replace splendour and surprise with a cliché.

This doesn't make Dave Mason wish for less contact with his gardens adviser. He'd like more. 'I think it's important to have a gardens adviser,' he says. 'A new set of eyes to come in and point things out.' Then, too, he adds, 'part of it is encouragement'.

He's aware that the advisers are so busy that they haven't the time to come more often. They arrive in a region and allocate one day to each of the gardens they oversee within it. Often they follow a pattern that applies to many National Trust site visits; it is the antithesis of high-pressured.

Dave Mason describes the event this way: there's coffee on arrival, a pub lunch in the middle of the day, and departure perhaps at four o'clock. The time spent actually studying the garden may be less than four hours overall. 'I'd like to see them come here at eight o'clock in the morning,' he says, 'have a sandwich lunch and coffee up in my office and finish here at five. To get stuck into the place. What worries me,' he continues, 'is that I wonder if they have enough time and a sense of the place to make decisions about it?'

Aspects of the feudal system have been noticed at Colcton Fishacre too. Neither the head gardener nor the coastal warden for the estate were given offices. 'The only reason I've got one,' Dave Mason says, 'is because I took an old storeroom over, stripped it out and redid it. We're treated as if we were serfs,' he says bluntly. 'Our status should be recognized for what it actually is.'

Like many gardeners, wardens and foresters, Dave Mason has observed that in the course of its great expansion, the National Trust has developed an ungainly, lopsided look. 'Over a period of ten to fifteen years,' he notes, 'the office staff grew by more than 300 per cent but the estate staff by less than forty. It's a huge imbalance.' Paying for its office staff, like looking after the mansions, has become a huge drain on the charity's finances.

'I don't want this to get into a griping session,' he says, 'but recently I went into the Regional Office and I said, "This place smells of paint and money." They've spent all this money refurbishing and I'm struggling to get a glass house for £2,000 which we've absolutely got to have here in order to overwinter plants.'

When he looks at the Trust's indoor staff, Dave Mason, like many who work outside, does so with a critical eye. 'I think they could improve their management – a lot. People generally get very frustrated if you've got a weak middle management and it escalates into all kinds of problems.'

He's optimistic, if wary. 'Change will only come about,' Dave Mason believes, 'if those who've got the power now are prepared to delegate it. If the Head Office puts out a working practices review report and doesn't do anything about decentralizing, it's just an exercise in internal and external PR.' It is too early to know yet whether the changes seen at Ickworth, for example, will be far-reaching and equally successful. Imagine, for instance, what would happen if the Trust replaced the administrator at Powis Castle with a property manager to whom Jimmy Hancock then had to report!

No longer married and with no children to support, Dave Mason has more money to spare than many National Trust gardeners. And maybe because he was out and about in the world so much before settling down, he's looking after his future too. He contributes more than the minimum to the Trust's pension plan and has investments. 'I don't want to end up living in a council house, to be quite honest.' Then he adds laughing, 'If the worst comes to the worst, I've got a really good tent.'

He reckons that one day he might like to become a gardens adviser himself. It would be an inspired appointment. For now, Mason's obviously enjoying the work that he has and he's at it about fifty hours a week. 'I don't look upon this as a job,' he says, 'it's a way of life.'

Although he may criticize aspects of the National Trust, David Mason is not sour about it; on the contrary: 'The Trust has great potential as an organization to work in. It has tremendous resources, a lot of very experienced people.' But, he adds, 'The future of the gardens is in the staff. Unless you are prepared to invest in it – and be supportive of us – you're going to have problems.'

On the one hand . . .

Of all its head gardeners, Mike Snowdon may be the most philosophical. And he certainly looks the part with his long white hair and a very long white beard, although he could also pass for an elfin version of Father Time.

For twelve of his twenty-five years with the National Trust, Mike Snowdon's been head gardener at Rowallane, a fifty-acre garden in County Down. Before that, he spent years restoring the derelict park at Erddig, recreating an august eighteenth century formal garden that is a beautiful companion for the romantic house. (Philip Yorke, Erddig's donor – last met in Chapter 3 – was no less eccentric in his care of its gardens than he was as a host. His only gardeners were sheep.)

Looking back on his time at Erddig, Snowdon recalls that, 'Someone asked me after we'd worked for many years behind closed gates, "You're open to the public now, won't you resent having people coming round?" "Quite honestly, no,"' he'd answered. 'The whole driving force behind what we'd been doing all those years was to produce a situation where the public could come round.'

More than many gardeners, Mike Snowdon actively wants more visitors. He works at encouraging people to make use of the garden at Rowallane, where there are so many unusual plants and fine trees – cedars and wellingtonia among them. A local art club regularly paints in the grounds; many school children visit, as do various Irish horticultural societies, from both north and south.

'Ever since I joined the Trust, I've been very conscious of the fact that one of the reasons we are here is so that people can visit and enjoy what we are producing,' he says. 'If you aren't, it's a wee bit like doing a painting or a sculpture or woodcarving and then putting it away in a dark cupboard.'

Mike Snowdon's approach is an outgrowth of his character

but putting it into practice is made much easier for him because the Trust's properties in Northern Ireland get so few visitors. Rowallane, for instance, sees fewer than 20,000 people a year. On the afternoon during which we were enjoying a sunny corner of flower-filled garden 'room' there was hardly anyone around. 'If you were to be sitting on this seat in the middle of Sissinghurst,' he says, 'you wouldn't be able to see across the lawn for the other people.' When the Trust introduced timed ticket entry there in 1992, Sissinghurst was heading for 200,000 visitors a year.

Not far from us is the house that serves as the charity's Regional Office. But the staff at Rowallane has grown so much that they can't all fit into it any more. 'Any cutting back,' he says, 'is at the root.' Gardeners, wardens, foresters. While the number of people producing memos and reports grows. As does the number of memos and reports he has to write in response.

'Twelve years ago I kept the paper work that was required in a wire basket beside the phone on the worktop in the kitchen,' Snowdon said. 'I now have an office with a filing cabinet that's falling over when you pull the drawer out! There's the demands for everything from Health & Safety,' he explains, 'fire regs, our own internal method of management.' But he's given to turning an idea, and trying to see it from at least one other angle.

'It's something I've not been trained in so I feel my way along it, if you like.' It's a challenge, he adds. And his wife helps. She always has and now her contribution has become officially recognized. Mrs Snowdon has gone on the payroll as her husband's administrative assistant.

'Gardening . . . You throw yourself into it a hundred per cent,' he confesses. 'It does in many cases lead to marital problems. I've been very lucky, touch wood. But I've been through that. My wife has said, "Hey hold on. Don't forget us." Still, today, I consciously have to be aware of that.'

The Snowdons live in part of what had been Rowallane's stables. 'It takes quite a bit of heating,' he admits, 'but it's rather a charming place to live.' He knows it's not theirs for ever.

'It's quite difficult having lived and worked for many many years in this type of situation suddenly to find that you have got to live in the middle of a housing estate or something like that,' he admits. And having once worked at Bodnant, he knows that Lord Aberconway's staff continues to live on there after retirement. But instantly looking at the issue from the Trust's point of view, too, Mike Snowdon points out that, 'it's a mighty big headache for them actually to undertake that'.

The Snowdons have not yet planned what they will do. 'Maybe I'll purchase a big mobile home and travel around visiting gardens,' he says with a chuckle.

But there is one subject about which Mike Snowdon doesn't feel he has to try to see the other side of the story. 'People who work a long time for the Trust develop an incredible loyalty,' he says. And are 'very often taken advantage of'.

Financial exploitation wasn't what Snowdon is hinting at. 'It's recognition of what we do,' he says. 'I think that many of the people who are now in managerial positions have come from situations where there is a very cold, calculated look at a business. And they've applied that here. They don't see, or don't appreciate, the dedication.'

Mike Snowdon asserts that 'within this management that is evolving, you are a pool of labour and if there's something that wants doing, then that pool is drawn on.' There are exceptions to this, happily. He mentions Martin Drury, historic buildings secretary and deputy director general; Lady Emma Tennant, chairman of the Gardens Panel. But he makes it plain that there are others, and a growing number, who are far less sympathetic. Right there at the Regional Office too.

'If you employed a surgeon you would not expect him to work as a hospital porter,' Snowdon explains. 'If you employ a gardener, particularly one in the modern day who is now involved in very complicated machinery, complex sprays, a complex system of propagation ... To be regarded as a general hand is very diminishing. Very demeaning. I don't know whether I've made my point clear.'

We both sat staring at Rowallane House.

Mike Snowdon has been ordered to do the equivalent of

picking up litter by the Trust's office staff. These managerially minded people don't seem to have grasped that their approach is not cost-effective, to use their own lingo.

'I honestly don't think the Trust could survive in the form it's in if there wasn't a large number of people who felt that dedication and loyalty to it,' says Snowdon who feels that the dedication is perhaps not being appreciated and the loyalty severely tried. 'It certainly would not.'

Other Worlds, and Other Seas

The Giant's Causeway is the exception to the rule that few people visit National Trust properties in Northern Ireland. In fact it rivals the Trust's most popular attraction, Fountains Abbey in Yorkshire. 'At the moment, something between 300,000 and 350,000 visit every year,' says Philip Watson, head warden for the north coast. No country house comes close. A great many people drive up from the south or come via the ferry from Scotland, land at Larne, see the Causeway and then drive on out of Ulster, often without spending even one night.

Philip Watson oversees the care of 2,000 acres, making up ten properties that leapfrog from Down Hill right around the north-east corner of Ireland, along the wild Glens of Antrim, only stopping south of Larne. His office is in a nondescript small building beyond the Causeway's visitors' centre and car park, both of which are owned and operated by the Moyle District Council – though there is an NT tea room and shop. Far below at the end of a winding track stand some 40,000 huge blocks of basalt: the dark rock looks as if it was hand carved and then piled along the water's edge and far out into the sea. There is a legend of course: Finn McCool, a very large fellow indeed, used these rocks as his stepping stones whenever he wanted to cross back and forth to Scotland. The Giant's Causeway has been a tourist attraction for more than a century.

Having the Causeway as a base would not suit a retiring soul. But the same thing seems to apply to National Trust wardens as to holidaymakers: people who like to pass their summers at the sea tend to be a convivial lot; while those who head for the hills, never seem to feel, no matter how high up they go, that they're ever quite far enough away from civilization.

'A large part of our work on the ground is dealing with-day-to day public relations,' says Philip Watson, 'which if you like doing it, is good fun.' He clearly does.

'We keep a record of our complaints and criticisms.' He believes that, 'quite a lot of them come through misunderstanding or plain ignorance; you can defuse them quite successfully. I've seen people who have arrived foaming at the mouth go away delighted.'

Watson, a ruddy-cheeked man in his forties, is married and lives in his own home. 'There's an advantage in being able to go to your own house at the end of the day, especially when you're a head warden,' he says, 'to switch off for a bit.' But he can't live far from his properties.

In addition to being phoned at all hours, the wardens have radios so they can be reached while they're travelling around. 'We get called out quite a lot,' he says. And because his wife works some distance away and often does overnight work, they don't see a lot of one another. 'If she was a housewife she'd probably be saying "Why are you working such long hours?" But, because she's equally to blame, you might say, I don't come up against that one.'

Like quite a few other coastal wardens, Philip Watson has not been a lifetime employee of the Trust. In fact he's only been with the National Trust for five years and within that there was a gap during which he had another job elsewhere. The Royal Society for the Protection of Birds, the Ulster Wildlife Trust, the World Wildlife Fund are all on his resumé. So is the government, where he used to work on fisheries.

'The great difference between the Trust and most of the other conservation bodies', he says, 'is the variety of its work. We've got buildings, landscape, and nature conservation.' When he interviews people who want to come to work with him,

Watson tells them, 'If you're a real specialist and you want to spend all your time watching birds, or looking at flowers, you're probably barking up the wrong tree.'

Like gardeners, coastal wardens love looking after their patch. 'It's a way of life, it is,' says Watson. 'I don't think we'd stick the hours, or the pace of the work, and the occasional frustrations if we didn't enjoy doing it and working for this amazing organization.' But in the recent past there had been periods of high turnover among the Trust's wardening staff, with mutterings about the Trust having a 'glass ceiling'. While its head gardeners almost always seem to be exactly where they wish to be, wardens feel more thwarted or just confused about whether or not they want to move. Would movement mean advancement? And even if it did, do they want that?

'At the head wardens conferences that happen about every nineteen months, you pick up the feeling that there isn't the scope for promotion,' Watson observes. It's extremely unlikely that a head warden would become a land agent. For one thing they haven't got enough spare time to take the courses they'd need just to apply for the job. And some people were attracted to wardening in the first place because they like being out of doors.

'It's a little bit like the police sergeant who loves his job and refuses promotion because he doesn't want to be stuck behind a desk doing paper work or move to the city,' says Philip Watson. 'But when you get up to head warden you have a lot of paper work. I have a lot of administration, a lot of public relations work.'

Having been on the scientific side of the civil service, Watson has seen this before. Personally he doesn't find it distressing and he seems to have worked out a system for handling his paperwork with reasonable efficiency.

'I've had a very chequered background,' he says, 'lots of job changes. I can see a countryside manager post on the horizon. But I am a very contented person with the Trust.' There is one thing, however.

'I'd certainly like to see the Trust be able to invest enough money in staffing to enable the property managers – that means the wardens – to live up to their responsibilities in the way the Trust wants us to. It's becoming quite a struggle.' Watson doesn't even have a fulltime year-round secretary.

'If you were to ask me what is the single improvement the Trust could do to make our job more enjoyable,' he continues, 'it is to give us a little more help in terms of permanent staff so that we're not so thinly stretched. As head warden I would be able to devote more time to thinking about strategies, policies and – most important – to have more time to be out on the properties.'

It costs the National Trust something like £200,000 a year to look after its properties on the north coast of Ireland – and that includes the six wardens who report to Watson as well as other staff.

'I don't want much,' he says. 'Too many staff are a headache. Then you have the burden of administration. But I could make a genuine case for one and a half wardens more on this coast.' The cost to the National Trust would be about £50,000 a year. (This is about the price of doing up a grand room at Castle Coole; a loaded comparison and therefore perhaps an unfair one. But as a charity with limited resources, one such activity may well be carried out at the expense of the other.)

'We're keeping our fingers crossed,' Philip Watson says, referring to a couple of beach defence projects then underway. 'Once you've the knowledge built up and you have the courage to go and tackle it, it's best done within a limited time-scale. You can predict tourism pressure but you can't predict what the weather's going to do. I would love to finish them within a year, because one strong easterly storm could wipe out everything we've done.'

Watson and his staff know very well how much money has been allocated to buildings. 'We say, "My god, if we had a tenth of that and could apply it in a very long-term conservation manner, we could do wonders with it."' And he adds, 'You would probably get better value for your money!'

A soft habitat

Cerise fuschias climb up the front of Mike Freeman's house, but the background to his conversation was not buzzing bees; it was sea gulls shrieking. Freeman, head warden, is based at Low Newton-by-the-Sea, a tiny village, half of it holiday cottages, on the Northumbrian coast. He is responsible for twelve miles of coast, 1,500 acres, heading both north and south from this stretch of rocks and sand where mute swans, teal and sedge warblers nest. Only a few miles away are the Farne Islands, that incredible nature reserve where the wild life has been so used to tourism that creatures go about their lives as if not a human were there: puffins and other sea birds by the thousands breed on minuscule natural terraces carved out of the rocks, and seals cavort in the waters.

In his thirties, Freeman lives with his wife and young son at the end of a track behind the dunes. Like the village square, this hidden-away house belongs to the National Trust. But the family have their own place in the Scottish borders.

No sooner had we settled down on a bench near the rabbit pen and across from the goose run, than a party of volunteers arrived. He went to fit them out with equipment, which in this case – a group of retarded young adults – meant handing out shovels.

'Groups like this are best doing estate maintenance, fairly large-scale jobs where a lot of hands can be useful,' Freeman explained when he came back. 'Bracken control. Racking hay. Pond work. Where there's a big area to work over and not too much sensitivity within the environment.' Rather than have volunteers turn up and ask for jobs to do, he sets up a list of what needs doing, has a roster of people who are willing, and matches them up.

Mike Freeman says he's a restless fellow and runs through a list of past enterprises every bit as chequered as Philip Watson's to prove it, but he's been with the Trust for fourteen years, and at Low Newton-by-the-Sea for all of them.

'The reason I've been here for so long is that the job has changed,' he says. 'Here we're not talking about estate wardens where there is a house and grounds and a forestry department and gardening department, but outposted individuals like myself, you are really site managers for the Trust. We're very remote.' As a result they have more responsibility and more freedom.

Freeman believes that all wardening has changed greatly since the 1960s when the people doing the job were often retired policemen or gamekeepers. 'They were just a presence on the ground,' he says. 'It's gone way beyond that. We're like general practitioners.'

The diverse sites he's responsible for include what he calls 'hard coastline', which means rocky headlands, outcrops of limestone, boulder shoreline, windsill plateaus. ('Windsill is a local volcanic rock,' he explains.) And there is soft coast too: sand, sand dunes, salt marshes, coastal pasture and the sea bed. 'My role and the Trust's role does extend into the marine environment,' he points out. To him this is an important new departure.

Part of Mike Freeman's job is to try to discover how man has had an impact on the coast – beginning in prehistoric times. 'Underneath these sand dunes were preglacial settlements,' Freeman says. Evidence of medieval settlements have been found too. 'They all tell stories,' he says. 'As site managers and as practitioners and as representatives of the Trust, we need to know as much as we can about these areas.' And what he knows he wants to share.

'I try to get the adults and the children to put themselves in the position of an animal living on the coast; or a plant,' he says. 'Maybe I get them to lie down and see if it's warmer or go into a sheltered part of the dunes and feel the difference in the temperature. We'll look at animals with shells and question why they've got shells – They've got to put up with being knocked around by the sea and being sand blasted. . . . I'd even like to involve people in how to go about making simple surveys like

[263]

counting birds.' Which means first teaching people how to tell what bird it is they're looking at.

At the same time Freeman wants people to know about the work he does too. 'There's a concept,' he says, 'I even had it in the past, that people like myself have a fairly laid-back job, driving around in a Land-Rover.' Besides all the habitats he looks after, the budgeting, the paper work, staff training and efforts at educating the public, he's also trying to educate himself formally. Since being with the Trust, Freeman's earned a certificate in environmental management at Durham University and is thinking about doing an MA. 'If', he says, 'I could sustain the mental pressure on top of my job.'

There isn't a fixed daily routine in this work, something his wife, Linda Carpenter, appreciates. It's given them flexibility. He sometimes looks after their son while she sees to her own work. For three years she was his assistant warden, now she's a community worker and a weaver. But as head warden he works six, sometimes seven days a week. 'It's like being married to a vicar,' Ms Carpenter laughs. Though she confesses that earlier on, when she didn't have engrossing work of her own, she didn't always find it amusing.

While Mike Freeman is aware of the value of someone coming in with fresh perceptions and new ideas, he sees advantages, too, in staying rooted in one spot as he has. 'You become intimate with your site,' he believes. 'You develop an intuition about how to manage it; a bit like an old, traditional farmer who doesn't need to go and do a survey to know when he's going to cut the hay or when he's going to put the grazing on or take it off. He has a feeling for it. And I think those of us who have been on our sites for a number of years now are developing that intuition.' But he allows that 'the difficult thing will be passing it on to somebody else. Maybe technology can help us there.'

At the point of origin

A person visiting Dinas Oleu, the National Trust's first four acres above Barmouth in Gwynedd, can – when it isn't too misty – see across to the Llyn Peninsula, some of the loveliest landscape in North Wales.

From a central ridge of high heathland, the Llyn falls to the sea, its coast ragged with coves protecting sandy beaches. This is solidly Welsh-speaking territory and Gareth Roberts, born and raised on a farm there, is the National Trust's bilingual warden for the Llyn Peninsula.

'I'm not a Nationalist,' Roberts says. And while he can see the advantages of having Welsh people running the Trust's North Wales Regional Office (which they now do not), he doesn't feel exercised about it. 'The Welsh and the English are different, no doubt about that at all,' he says. 'The Welsh are more happy to plod on; not so pushy.' In other words, Welsh people just might not be interested in having an administrative job at Llandudno. But when it comes to a position like his own – 'It's a definite must, I would say. I can't see anybody could do the job properly on the Llyn without speaking Welsh. You would miss out on far too much, you'd lose too much help. It's the little bits around the edge that make the difference.'

Gareth Roberts has ginger hair and even on a warm day he wears a brimmed tweed hat. There is something opaque in his expression which at first makes him appear phlegmatic, which is entirely misleading.

We met at Plas-yn-Rhiw, the former home of the three Keating sisters who not only left the house to the Trust but were the force behind its acquisition of the more than 400 acres – most of it coastal – which the Trust now owns on the Llyn. Plas-yn-Rhiw is one of National Trust's most beguiling properties. The tiny manor house is furnished as the sisters left it and because it's so remote and doesn't get many visitors,

[265]

there are no ropes to keep a visitor from having a good look around.

The house sits high above Hell's Mouth Bay. Gareth Roberts and I found a bench in the steeply terraced, informally planted garden where a streak of blue water could be seen through the tree tops.

'My patch is the Llyn Peninsula,' he began. Unlike Cornwall's Michael Trinick and Cubby Acland in the Lake District, Wales has never had a buccaneer gathering up properties and legacies for his region. Roberts is doing what he can to make his patch bigger. But he's more of a devotee than an empire builder.

'I thank them very much for it,' says Gareth Roberts. But he doesn't always welcome the result. Because the Trust may have money in the bank from legacies earmarked for Cornwall, 'it will then spend the money on a second- or third-rate property there,' he says, 'whereas they'll miss a first-rate property here.' So he keeps alert and makes the best case he can when something worth while comes on the market.

'There are two schools of thought about acquisition,' Roberts explains. First, there are the consolidators who say 'look after what you've already got to the highest possible standard'. While others believe that if you don't buy coastal properties they will only deteriorate. 'I tend to adhere to the second rule really,' he says. 'Where we have the properties, maybe they need work on them, but they're not going to spoil. Whereas if the Trust doesn't acquire the others, there's a definite danger.'

Gareth Roberts has his own ideas about volunteering too. Jenny Baker, manager for volunteers, would not approve.

'I'm not a believer in volunteers myself,' he says forthrightly. 'A lot of people, their heart is in the right place, but they want skilled work, putting up fences, hanging the gates.' When they are given it, the results are not always satisfactory. 'You get a row of poles with wire strung up between them, but you've got to go there and do it all again. It's specialist work really, and volunteers aren't what is required. I don't subscribe to that at all.'

Gareth Roberts clearly is attached to both the Llyn and to the men and women who live there. His attitude has a kinship with people like Lord St Levan at St Michael's Mount when he says, 'It's as important for the Trust, I think, to look after the people who live in the area as to look after the area itself.

'What is the point of a picture on the wall, if it doesn't have any life to it?' he asks. 'What's the point of keeping the Llyn like a museum, if nobody lives here? If nobody can afford to live here? I feel very strongly about that.'

Much more satisfactory, from Roberts point of view, is the Employment Training gang he has working with him. A group of between eight and fourteen men (and their supervisors) are paid ten pounds a week on top of whatever unemployment benefit they collect to work on various projects he sets up. They stay for about a year.

'A lot of them are long-term unemployed,' he reports. 'They've got into a rut. They don't get up in the morning until eleven; what's the point?' But now they come with their packed lunch and are busy all day.

'They become good ambassadors for the Trust,' he says. 'They see what we're doing. They've got relatives and the story goes out.' And evidently it's also a very good thing for the men. 'A very high percentage of them go into employment afterwards,' Roberts says. Some take jobs using skills they've learned while working for the Trust. But others may take jobs that are completely unrelated. For all of them it seems that the year with the Trust has 'brought them out of themselves; given them confidence'. That, Gareth Roberts believes, is what's made such a difference.

By his own account, the warden for the Llyn is no good at meetings, or courses. 'You could go on a course every day of the week, if you wanted to,' he says about the life of a Trust staff member. Nor does he take to paperwork.

'You can maybe see the value of it, if you've got stupid people there; but if you haven't, it's an awful waste of time, an awful waste of paper and it's a waste of effort, a lot of it you know. You've got to trust people,' he says with emphasis. 'You've got to put your trust in your staff. Keep an eye on them. If they don't do it, fire them and get somebody that you can trust. But this forever filling in forms for this, that and the other. I find it an awful bind, I must admit.'

Not 'career oriented', Gareth Roberts' first love was farming. But he wanted to marry and his parents' farm wouldn't support all of them. He saw an advertisement for this warden's job, applied and got it. That was seven years ago.

'I don't think I would get it today,' he declares, 'because they require more conservation skills and paper qualifications. It's the in thing now, countryside management courses in the colleges.' He is not impressed by the results. 'They haven't the slightest idea about what's going on. But they think they do because they've attended the course.' And, according to Roberts, what they're taught is completely unrealistic because the goal is to make the student an expert in everything.

'It's impossible,' he believes. 'It's the same as with a building. You can't be a plumber, a carpenter, an electrician and everything. I don't have to be a forester to manage a plantation,' he continues. 'As long as you've got a bit upstairs, the forester will tell you what needs doing.'

Nevertheless the Trust appears to be committed to this sort of training and paper credentials for all outdoor staff.

'It's a sad day, I think, if the Trust goes along that road in thinking of qualifications and nothing else,' says Gareth Roberts. And, he believes, if it goes down that road too much longer, it risks losing most of what sets it apart and makes it so valuable now.

'The Trust is all about character,' says the warden for the Llyn.

'What is a view? It is character. What's Plas-yn-Rhiw? It's just stones and mortar, but there's character about it. If you have every house with bees coming out of the roof, well what's different about Plas-yn-Rhiw? I think there's a danger in this professionalism; the Trust is too interested in it. You just become another big organization without any feeling and character about it at all.'

Are there any more at home like you?

'The best training for a gardener is under a head gardener,' says Jimmy Hancock. Agreed. But the National Trust says it's having trouble finding promising people to train. According to Dave Mason, when two positions came open in Devon not long ago, out of a hundred people applying, 'there were maybe only one or two who had any realistic chance of actually getting the job'.

'We're very worried,' Lady Emma Tennant admits. 'It's getting more and more difficult in all practical jobs,' she says, 'to find good people to fill them. Because there's so much emphasis on academic training now, they channel everyone on towards university. University. University.'

Mike Snowdon sees it from a slightly different perspective. 'Gardening has always suffered and still does from the attitude of many that you have straw sticking out from under your hat.' Or straw in your head. 'In the past if there was a young fellow born in the village who was a few slates short of roof, people said, "send him up to work on the gardens at the manor".'

Gardening was not for bright young people or those with many choices. And except for those children of the upper middle class who have now branched out from cookery and do garden design as well, it seems as if horticulture and wardening have as little attraction for students as, say, becoming a fishmonger. And even those people who would be interested often don't know there are such jobs available. For instance in 1970 when young John Walton went to his careers master and said he wanted to work with birds and animals, he was advised to become a gamekeeper. Since this isn't quite what he had in mind, he went to work in a bank instead and did volunteer work with the RSPB. It was only eight years later that he found his way to the National Trust,

[269]

and now he's the head warden for the Farne Islands. He isn't going to budge. 'It's the peak,' he says.

Because of the difficulty in finding suitable people, in 1989 the National Trust began planning a training programme of its own.

An experiment

Careership training is the name the National Trust has given the scheme it put into action in 1991. The aim of its course was to produce the gardeners and wardens of the future, or, in the language of its brochures, to prepare young people for a future in Countryside Management or Amenity Horticulture. You can bet they didn't call Gareth Roberts in as a consultant.

The three year course, open to sixteen- and seventeen-year old school-leavers, combined practical work at a variety of National Trust properties with classes at Cannington College in Somerset in such subjects as money management. Each applicant was required to have a Training and Enterprise Council Grant.

There were twenty-four openings each year, divided equally between trainee gardeners and wardens. All expenses are paid by the Trust and students are given a salary. The properties to which they have been assigned include Wallington, Anglesey Abbey and Kingston Lacy, Coniston, West Penrith, the Isle of Wight. Yet even during a time of record-breaking unemployment, the Trust had trouble finding enough people, particularly for the garden openings.

'Wardening has a greener image,' says John McKennall, the National Trust's coordinator for careership. 'It's got a higher profile too. Driving around in Land-Rovers, giving orders' – that sort of thing appealed to school-leavers.

'What a pity', McKennall says, 'that nobody sees a head gardener at the top of his career being on a par in status to a five-star chef in one of the finest kitchens in the world.' Does he know that Sir Terence Conran not only has a fine chef in Simon Hopkinson at Bibendum but also a partner in the enterprise?

It would probably be wrong to say that some of the head gardeners and wardens, who criticized the training scheme as it was set up, were gleeful when the Trust had trouble filling its openings. It's fair to say quite a few of them were not fans.

'The Trust is trying to talk about it as being "The Rolls-Royce" of gardening training,' Jimmy Hancock says disdainfully. Not that he's against the programme itself. 'I think an organization as big as the Trust does need a training scheme,' he comments. But he says the people they got 'were not high flyers' and the reason had to do with the narrowness of the age band the Trust was selecting from.

'Somebody in their forties who finds that life isn't going very well, who is not getting much satisfaction out of life and who turns to horticulture, becomes an absolutely amazing person to train,' Hancock has found. 'It becomes a way of life.'

He had one man working with him at Powis who was in his forties when he arrived and had never held a job for more than two years. 'The main reason for that was boredom,' Hancock believes. 'He wasn't intelligent educationally,' Hancock continued, 'but he had quite a snappy mind.' The work at Powis engaged him, and he stayed eight years, though the pay was less than he'd ever made before. And Hancock has a woman in the greenhouse who also began working with him when she was in her forties.

Yet when the Trust decided to choose only sixteen-year-olds right out of school, the head gardeners were told they couldn't have anybody else. 'I think they'll pay very dearly for that in the end.'

Jan Michalak says of his own trainees that 'the two bands we've had most success with are people who are very qualified at something entirely different and decide to become gardeners. And at the other end, a lot of success with people who had no idea what they wanted to do and no qualifications but enjoyed their time here enough to want to work and become gardeners. Those two bands are both excluded by the system the Trust set up.'

[271]

Dave Mason also believed the National Trust should change its programme. He speaks from experience when he says that older people are the ones 'who are actually able to make the commitment and to get something out of it'. Which means they will be in a better position to put something back in.

In 1994 the Careership Training programme was finally altered. But only because the Trust hadn't been able to fill all their openings. The net was cast wider – adults as well as teenagers can now apply. The upper limit of adulthood, however, has been set at 35! And only four places have been reserved for those in this rather narrow category. At the same time, the overall number of openings has shrunk to 16. The reason for this was money. Without the government grants given to school leavers, and because mature people would need higher salaries, this version of Careership Training was going to cost the NT more to run.

Everyone will gain from it if Careership Training is successful, and not only at National Trust properties. 'I think that the Trust realizes that they should be putting something back into horticulture,' Dave Mason says. 'They should be training people not just for the Trust but for horticulture in general. It's part of national heritage as much as the houses are. We are supposed to be the gardening nation of the world. Or at least we used to be.'

[8]

Strangers in Paradise

There's nothing new about people saying 'Not In my backyard you don't!' Preservation-minded men and women have been more inclined to fight to save a precious part of their own neighbourhood than someone else's for a very long time, and to crack open their piggy banks to do it if need be. This was certainly the case with the founders of the National Trust. Robin Fedden in his history of the charity notes that in its first years 'many of the new properties were either in Kent and Surrey or the Lake District, the areas where Octavia Hill, Robert Hunter and Canon Rawnsley lived'.[1] But in this regard, the Lake District was exceptional.

While the fate of Westmorland and Cumberland were Hardwicke Rawnsley's local issue, everyone everywhere wanted to try to help protect the Lake District too. In Britain – and abroad – this became a crusade that thousands of people felt inspired to join. Almost anyone who has spent time there will understand why.

Wet, cold and windswept, the Lake District is a very English Eden. No one who chooses to go there on holiday could be accused of being a languid sybarite. But the region has not only attracted those who feel their pleasures must be worked for. Sometimes pastoral, sometimes fierce, these fells, lakes and hidden valleys have such an impressive beauty that the landscape continues to seem fresh and marvellous in spite of all the promotional prose, those overwrought poems and centuries of awful painting. Today the National Trust owns nearly a third of it.

One quarter of all the countryside protected by the nation's largest private landowner is made up of those parts of Lancashire, Westmorland and Cumberland that are now called Cumbria. But it isn't only land it owns there. The Trust has more than 2,000 built structures, too, from the fifteenth-century Courthouse at Hawkshead to Lilliputian stone huts just visible through the desolate mists of the Kirkstone Pass above Patterdale. The charity even owns a wood-panelled, plush-seated Victorian steam yacht; the *Gondola* which chugs away from the pier at Coniston, dropping off passengers at Brantwood, the house where Ruskin spent his last years (not National Trust).

'Eventually they'll own the whole Lake District,' a canny Cumberland shepherd says as he talks about the changes he's seen in his seventy years. 'The time's on their side.' So it seems to be.

The National Trust feels it can afford to wait out any of us. We are just passing through, after all, while it will go on for ever. The Act of 1907 says so.

There is something seemingly inexorable about the steady expansion of the National Trust's holdings in the Lake District. The Trust's passionate attempt to save the squirarchy was probably a lost cause from the start; its efforts to protect the Lake landscape, which were no less heartfelt, have been formidably successful.

In 1937, when E.M. Forster's essay 'Havoc' was published, the Trust owned only a comparative sliver of the Lake District, about 17,000 of the 550,000 acres, which was less than three per cent of the whole. Yet even then Forster judged the Lakes to be its 'supreme triumph'. The Trust, he believed, had 'saved the most magical corner of England, where delicacy and strength have united as nowhere else in the world'.[2]

Obviously a very great deal has happened in the region since E.M. Forster wrote his appreciative words. It isn't only that the amount of land and buildings in the National Trust's ownership has grown, so has the number of people it employs

[274]

and the number who visit its properties every year. What can it mean now to say that the National Trust has 'saved' the Lake District? Is the region still magical, or is it on its way to becoming a stupendous outdoor museum? This is a question with a history.

There was no such thing as a 'Lake District' until the eighteenth century. That is when lovers of the picturesque discovered this corner of north-west England. Until then the 550,000 acres merely existed, 'an island of mountains set down in a plain', as one writer described it.[3] It's a crammed and compact island, too. But even so, topographically, the Lake District is remarkably varied and often dramatic.

The mountains are hump-backed and mossy in the south, precipitous dark, slatey walls in the north, with long, iridescent green valleys cut between and acres of woodland climbing the lower slopes. Within minutes a lake, whether it's cosy Rydal Water or the rather imperious Ullswater, can go from being placid to being whipped with white caps. Nor will it do to ignore all those daffodils, even if at the time of the Lake District's discovery, Wordsworth wasn't yet around to write about them bobbing their yellow heads in the fields near the sixty-five-foot Aira Force waterfall.

This was also the era of the picturesque country-house landscaped park, like the one created by Henry Hoare at Stourhead in Wiltshire. Such gardens were an attempt to transform nature into a work of art, using the atmospheric and often fantastical landscape paintings of the period as their model.

Very few were wealthy enough to follow this vogue, of course. And besides, why not leave out the middle man, so to speak.

'It is amusing to think of the pains and expense with which the environs of several seats have been ornamented, to produce pretty scenes,' wrote Arthur Young after a tour which took him to the vale of Keswick in the eighteenth century. 'But how very far short of the wonders that might here be held up to the eye in all the rich luxuriance of nature's painting.'[4]

Those hardy aesthetes among Young's contemporaries who had the time and money to spare packed Claude glasses in their baggage and set out for the lakes. It is they who put the Lake District on the map. Having trekked up the slope of one fell or another until they came upon a suitable vantage point, these men and women would look into their boxed lenses and *voilà*! the countryside was now a painting. Nature, suitably outlined in this way, became art without further effort. And the views were very like the bluey green vistas painted by Claude.

It was only a matter of decades before there was even more interest in visiting the lakes, though a drastic shift in motives had come about. The Romantics had arrived: Coleridge, Southey and Wordsworth – the men Byron waspishly called 'the Pond Poets'. In Lakeland they found their muse. Never mind trying to look through a glass at 'pictures', when a cow in the same spot saw only water to drink and grass to chew. Stop trying to put a frame around Nature and begin to give yourself up to Her wildness instead.

It was William Wordsworth who most famously told readers about this savage landscape. He did that in many poems of course, but he also got busy communicating his impressions and ideas in prose. In 1810, Wordsworth published his *Guide to the Lakes* and though this was not the first book on the subject nor possibly the best one, it surely was the most successful. Partly practical, it was also a rhapsodic testimonial.

More rain may pour down on the farm at Seathwaite in Borrowdale than on any other inhabited spot in England, but in Wordsworth's view there was nothing soggy about the outcome. 'Days of unsettled weather', he wrote, 'with partial showers, are very frequent; but the showers, darkening, or brightening, as they fly from hill to hill, are not less graceful to the eye than finely interwoven passages of gay and sad music are touching to the ear.'

Wordsworth was acting not only as a propagandist for the Lake District but for England's virtues. Those of his contemporaries whose incomes matched their aesthetic big ambitions were busy travelling as Grand Tourists and everyone had agreed that to see the most marvellous works of nature and man it was necessary to go abroad. But now Wordsworth and the other Lake Poets insisted that crossing the Channel was not required. The Lakes, though small, were surely more rewarding to explore than Switzerland or the north of Italy.

More or less, their reasoning went like this: because the region is compact and its fells don't reach a height much above twenty-five hundred feet, it wasn't necessary to be a mountaineer to imagine that all of them might be successfully scaled given time. And it wasn't only accessibility that was the attraction. There were the views. Scafell and Great Gable and the other fells were much lower than the Alps but from their summits a walker could look out and see not only lakes and valleys and the other mountains all round, but also right across to the sea. Even the 'cultivated beauties' of such spots as Bellagio on Lake Como could not compete with the 'wild graces' of the Lakes, Wordsworth insisted. His arguments appealed.

Alas, thanks to the poet who wrote 'I wander lonely as a cloud', it soon become impossible to do so. By the time the National Trust was founded in 1895, the countryside ringing Windermere, Ullswater, Coniston and the other by now well-known lakes was crowded with poets, painters, philosophers and muscular pilgrims with artistic inclinations.

And there was something if not religious then surely spiritual in the attachment to the Lake District that was growing up and which continues to his day. For many the physical demands of hiking over the countryside have been mixed with something else. The rough, chill and misty beauty – harsh and changeable on the howling fell tops but radiantly verdant and hushed in the valleys – has drawn people looking for peace, stability, inspiration and indeed communion.

There was even what might be called an intellectual side to all of this, though it's hard to separate it from something more social. The strenuous exercise that became part of a public school boy's education during the nineteenth century found its continuation in remote country 'reading holidays' for chaps at university. When they were not out climbing and getting drenched with sweat and rain, students sat by the fires of guest houses and read. George Moore took his Apostles to

Cornwall; the Trevelyans were among the many who headed for the Lakes.

Trevelyans took to play in the outdoors with the same intense competitiveness James Lees-Milne later found so ghastly when, after dining at Wallington House in Northumberland, they quizzed one another about current events. At Seatoller, a boarding house at the foot of the Honister Pass in Borrowdale where they often stayed, the Trevelyans' game was called 'The Man Hunt'. One person was the 'hound' and was chased over the fells by the rest. For many years George Macaulay Trevelyan was Master of the Hunt. His Cambridge friends Bertrand Russell and Ralph Vaughan Williams are among the names in the Seatoller visitors' book, which dates from the eighteenth century. Sir Charles was the very first of the family to go there in 1892. Following the break-up of the Leconfield estate in 1960, Seatoller was bought by the Trevelyans and remains a guest house for serious walkers, members of their family included.

By the middle of the nineteenth century, of course, the Lake District was no longer only a place visited by the privileged. The railway, feared and fought against by such lovers of the lakes as Ruskin and Wordsworth, came to Windermere in 1847. It brought even more people which meant even more change.

'In 1845 there cannot have been more than a dozen three-storey houses in the Lakes,' wrote Bruce Thompson, the Trust's deputy secretary, in 1930.[5] But to cater for the trainloads of workers from mills and manufacturing plants, hotels and boarding houses were built in the valleys and the towns. Windermere and Ambleside began a swelling that continued until they were transformed into what some call buzzing honey pots and others call noisy, overcrowded tourist traps.

And in 1901 G.M. Trevelyan was already mourning 'the sudden destruction of rural life'. Cities, he wrote, had grown not only large but vulgar and their denizens took this vulgarity with them 'into every corner of our island . . .' The ruin of 'all that was characteristic of Old England', was the lamentable result.[6]

Trevelyan, like Octavia Hill before him, wouldn't have believed that not everyone was equally besotted by the countryside nor equally appalled by city life. Yet the balconies of London's music halls were packed with bedazzled men and women who would not have swapped their seats for a return trip even if it were to Windermere.

Nevertheless, because of the aesthetic, literary and even sensual associations which attached themselves to the landscape, the Lake District became ever more idealized until, symbolically, it came to stand for England's green and pleasant heart and soul.

There grew up a half superstitious conviction that the Lakes must be kept as they always had been, or not only would they be lost but so would we.

Danger signals

The problem right from the beginning was people, that is to say, 'off-comers', which in Cumbria means anyone who lives south of Kendal or beyond Keswick in the north.

The fells fulfilled the demand made on them to be inspiring all too well. After centuries during which mountains seemed something terrible, they all at once had become alluring. Where before, only a few of the hardiest beasts and their shepherds, or traders leading strings of pack horses, or hermits who could not bear the company of their fellows, had sought out mountains, now they were seen as a challenge and the means of making an aesthetic as well as a metaphysical journey. And so they have been ever since – for an algebraically expanding number of people. By the end of the twentieth century expeditions wanting to climb Mount Everest had to go on a waiting list; so it was that the muse of the Lakes had been chased out of the fells by tens of thousands of trampling feet.

First the railways brought them. Then they came by charabancs which might seat, say, fourteen. Coaches came next carrying double that number. And then came people in their own motor cars. Nowadays in the summer months there are times when traffic is at a standstill for miles in all directions heading into the Lakes. And when, finally, they get there, drivers creep through the narrow roads of the valleys unable to find a single place to stop and park.

William Wordsworth was not only the first to alert great numbers of people to Lakeland's beauty, but in that influential 1810 guidebook he also alerted people to the ways in which the area was already being threatened.

There were mountain goats in the fells above Ullswater when the first edition of Wordsworth's *Guide* came out. They had all gone by the time the second was printed. Smallholdings were being sold; farms were being consolidated into large estates. Dorothy Wordsworth, the poet's sister, companion and inspiration, noted in her journal the comment of a friend that 'in a short time there would be only two ranks of people, the very rich and the very poor'.

'In truth,' he had written, 'no one can now travel through the more frequented tracts, without being offended, at almost every turn, by an introduction of discordant objects, disturbing that peaceful harmony of form and colour, which had been through a long lapse of ages most happily preserved'.[7]

The wholesale planting of conifers is not an idiocy dreamed up in the twentieth century, as it turns out. Both Dorothy and William Wordsworth were outspokenly against it. Larches particularly offended them and not only on grounds of their 'foreignness'. Just as recent critics have taken against the planting of chrome yellow fields full of oilseed rape, the Wordsworths carped about the strident green produced by all those larches. And then there was the skyline problem, of course. Conifers form such a deadly, straight outline. But trees were far from the only 'discordant objects'.

'The craving for prospect', as William Wordsworth called it, led rich people to want their new houses built on high ground. As a result these rose 'from the summits of naked hills in staring contrast to the snugness and privacy of the ancient houses'.[8] While sister Dorothy was even more irate:

'The walk', she wrote in her journal on 14 May 1800, 'was very green, many sweet views up to Rydal head – when I could juggle away the fine houses'.

It was William Wordsworth who pushed for the region as a whole to be protected. 'Persons of taste', the poet wrote in his 1810 book, 'who by their visits (often repeated) to the Lakes in the North of England, testify that they deem the district a sort of national property, in which every man has a right and interest who has an eye to perceive and a heart to enjoy'. A great deal more pushing in this direction was needed before the Lake District at last became a National Park in 1951.

In 1900, at Hardwicke Rawnsley's instigation, the National Trust undertook its first Lake District Appeal. Because the entire shore of Derwentwater was privately owned, the public's access to it depended on the whim of various landowners. For that reason the Trust set out to raise £6,500 so that it could buy Brandelhow, a 106-acre park abutting Derwentwater at the Keswick end.

In less than six months, £7,000 was raised and in 1902 Brandelhow Park became a possession of the National Trust. The Trust was five years old; this was its largest-ever land acquisition as well its first purchase in the Lakes. It has been acquiring land there, and trying to raise the money to buy yet more, ever since.

Passing the hat

More than one pound in every three that the National Trust has to spend each year comes from members. Its subscribers are so important to the charity that it is prepared to spend £7 million annually 'servicing' them. That includes producing the magazine, mailing out the season tickets and, to the tune of more than £1 million, recruiting.

About 500 men and women are hired each season to work as recruiters at National Trust properties. The very great majority of them earn a bit more than £3 per hour. Each region decides, with an eye on its budget and the previous year's tally of visitor numbers, how many recruiters to take on and where they should go. In all the National Trust's domain, only Cornwall and the Lake District have assigned recruiters the job of travelling its open-space properties trying to interest people in joining. Yet the Trust continuously asserts that a great many more people than the 10 million who visit its properties for which admission is charged explore its open spaces. And the National Trust has all the evidence one would think it needed to know that recruiting in the countryside is a good idea.

'She's massively successful,' says Siobhan Edwards, the Trust's membership administrator, referring to Myrtle Longcake who works in the northern Lakes. And surely, one measure of how strongly people feel that the Lake District must be preserved is that the recruiter who has more than once led the unofficial league table for signing up new members in a given year has been Mrs Longcake who can be found between Keswick and Buttermere. But of course her personal qualities also have something to do with it. She's attractive, clever and convinced.

'I've never seen an organization where style is so important as at the Trust,' says a former member of its senior staff. Recruiters, he explained, were a good example of this. 'The people who handle the signing up of new members are white-haired, unthreatening. This is a choice.' Whether or not he's right about this being a conscious marketing decision, you couldn't get anyone more stylish-in-the NT fashion than Myrtle Longcake, though she's not altogether the cosy grandparentish figure most of National Trust recruiters appear to be.

Myrtle Longcake ('it's a very old Cumbrian name,' she said on being introduced) has straight grey hair cut in a bob. From her Wellington boots to her Barbour and the black velvet band holding her hair off her face, she manages to seem at the same time chic and in keeping. On this cool autumn afternoon, not far outside the village of Buttermere, Myrtle Longcake had set up her shop at the edge of a wooded field. Though many arduous walks begin nearby, this was a gently pastoral spot. Beyond it was the lake and on its far shore the wall of stark fells.

'I was a member before I worked for them,' Myrtle Longcake said in a reassuring way. 'And as a result of working for the Trust,' she continued, for all the world as if she were softening me up for the sell, 'I've been even more impressed. The staff are wonderfully dedicated.'

In 1982, the Lake District became the first region of the National Trust to employ people who, like Mrs Longcake, are mobile rather than remaining fixed to a spot. These roving recruiters, as they're called, work a rotation of seven days on and then seven days off. None of the Trust's recruiters is paid a bonus for signing up a bumper crop of new members; there are no trips to Bermuda to reward the high scorers. But rovers do earn more than the £3.20 an hour paid to most property-tied recruiters. They have more work and more responsibility. And Mrs Longcake was at the top of the salary scale, in recognition of her skill at the job.

At a house all a recruiter needs to do is to show up, sit down at a table, line up the pens and brochures and start the day. But Myrtle Longcake describes her preparation and that of her fellow rovers this way: 'We do all our own ordering, accounting. We're responsible for the van. It's a self-contained unit. We are responsible totally for our own little ship.' The craft in question is a Land-Rover.

Mrs Longcake's self-contained unit was parked nearby. Its back door was open, revealing a stock of National Trust pamphlets inside. That's where the membership packs are kept, too, each with its dotted line awaiting its signature.

Professional experience has led her to calculate that she will recruit one person in every five she approaches. But she assures me that this is very a rough estimate based on her own approximate accounting. 'I'm not very good at maths,' she says, true to the unthreatening stereotype. 'If we make between 2,500 and 3,000 members a year, you've got some idea of how many people we approach.' And of Myrtle Longcake's enormous value to the National Trust – just to keep things simple (I'm not very good at maths either) – let's say it costs a couple

£35 pounds to join the National Trust when they sign up at Mrs Longcake's Land-Rover. And let's say they aren't in the 11 per cent who fail to renew. If they carry on belonging to the Trust for a decade – and staying simple let's assume there's no increase in the annual subscription, which is most improbable, they will have contributed £350 to the charity. Multiply this by the 3,000 who join in this way each year, and you've got over £1 million in a decade.

When Myrtle Longcake says 'we' she's referring to the other half of her recruiting team. There are twelve roving recruiters in the Lake District; they work in pairs. While one is having seven days off, the other uses the Land-Rover. It so happens that Myrtle's teammate is Mr Longcake.

The 15,000 people or so whom the Longcakes approach in a year are mainly walkers. 'They're not necessarily the backpacking, really hard walkers,' she says. 'They can be the saunterers around the lake.'

Sauntering here has become more appealing since 1990 when, using money from bequests and a Countryside Commission grant, the National Trust bought the 103-acre Wilkinsyke Farm, part of which runs from the leafy spot where Myrtle Longcake had parked her Land-Rover down to the water's edge. Almost 400 yards of the lake front belong to the farm, and before the Trust owned it, anyone wanting to circumnavigate Buttermere could go nine-tenths of the way and then, coming to the Wilkinsyke Farm, they'd have to stop and return the way they'd come. Now the Trust has opened a footpath around the whole of the lake – except during lambing time when Wilkinsyke is off limits again.

Though very successful, Myrtle Longcake is not a recruiter who's worked incredibly long hours to make sure she's explored every last possibility. 'There will be a number of people we will miss,' she acknowledges. 'I've been out on a beautiful sunny day and loath to leave. There are recruiters who have a very relaxed routine and will stay for as long as they feel.' But the Longcakes keep to a more conventional working day. She starts packing up to leave at about five o'clock. 'Although I would love to stay, there are other things that I have got to do. And', she adds, 'at the end of the day you find you're getting a bit rusty and your throat's going. At the end of the season,' she says with feeling, 'your throat starts to give.'

Myrtle Longcake drives out from Keswick through the Newlands valley to Buttermere and stops where she reckons the pickings will be richest. This corner of the lake outside the village of Buttermere is a favourite. With a wave of her hand, the arc described by her arm takes in a panoramic view of the work done by the National Trust in the Lake District that is so worth the public's support.

'You've got your maintenance of footpath,' Mrs Longcake begins, 'you've got your planting of trees; you've got your dry-stone walling and your re-establishment of hedges, and your lake shore erosion. People understand it,' she says. 'They look at it, and say, "of course. Yes. This is all part of the fabric of the countryside." '

Many people have no idea that so much work has to be done to look after the landscape in which they are walking, nor who is doing it. 'They are very quickly appreciative when you point it out to them,' she says.

Myrtle Longcake had been selling the National Trust to the men and women who come walking in the Lake District for more than ten years when we met. 'One of the bonuses of the job,' she says, is 'that people come back and say, "Oh hello! Are you still here?" It's quite touching that you're supposed to remember them.' She isn't being cynical. Nor are they. 'I think it's lovely that people bother to come back and remember, "we signed on this very spot x number of years ago." It's part of the ritual of the holiday.' She makes it sound practically like a romantic assignation.

In 1994 the National Trust finally noticed that it was not making enough – that is, practically anything – of the countryside and coast as recruiting territory. Perhaps years of severe recession made them too hungry to go on dozing. Myrtle Longcake was made a recruiting coordinator. Her job now is to help other people acquire some of her skill. She's been training the future roving recruiters of Northumbria, the

East Midlands and North Wales – which regions at last are all beginning to employ them.

In Buttermere, Newlands, Borrowdale, Great and Little Langdale, at Near Sawrey and over at Eskdale foresters, wardens and footpath teams are actively working to preserve the landscape which so many people take for granted. Not that visitors to the Lakes should be blamed for this. It takes someone like Myrtle Longcake to make people aware of the effort that's gone in to caring for all that surrounds them because like ballerinas, though in this sense only, the people working for the Trust struggle to make it appear that no labour at all has been involved. The National Trust's aesthetic rule for the outdoors is that the landscape should seem untouched by human hands.

Derwentwater

Mike Roulson, the Trust's head warden for Derwentwater, offered to take me through some of the 25,000 acres of countryside in the northern lakes which he manages. We drove up the rocky and wooded approach to the Honister Pass, his rattling Land-Rover making such a racket that I could barely hear his running commentary. Though initially reserved, Roulson soon proved himself a nonstop talker.

Most of the land we could see is owned by the Trust. Where it wasn't the owner, it bought fifteen feet on either side of the road to prevent any widening. Otherwise even now someone could easily come along and declare: 'Well let's have a dual carriageway here.' But because the Trust owns the land on both sides of the road they can't. So this narrow twisting artery remains the only way for a vehicle to get from the Borrowdale over to Buttermere without back-tracking all the way to Keswick.

'On a wet and, windy day this can be a very impressive place to be,' he said as we arrived at the summit of the Honister Pass.

Impressive sounded more like alarming, as he went on with a description. 'Water just pours off down every crack and every crevasse. Huge boulders are moved around as if they were just little marbles. In this sort of landscape we wouldn't do anything. You've got no control over what's going on.'

But on the descent from the Honister we looked out at some of the tens of thousands of acres that Roulson, and other wardens in the region, the foresters, the land agents – and the farmers – work hard to bring under their control.

Mike Roulson, now in his early fifties, worked for a local authority down on the Wirral before going to the National Trust eight years ago. He has no office. His command post is the kitchen table of the cottage where he lives with his wife in the village of Stonethwaite half way up Borrowdale. His territory includes Borrowdale and Newlands Valley and Watendlath.

'I work in the biggest and best National Park,' he says expansively, 'in the best valleys within the National Park. People say "Oh Langdale's nicer than Borrowdale." But Langdale doesn't have a lake; Borrowdale has Derwentwater. It has a river. It has beautiful fells; wooded fell side. When you get to Rosthwaite it all opens out and you've got lovely flat land. I reckon I've the best bits. What more could a man ask for?

'We spend a lot of time working in the valleys on the day-to-day repair jobs,' he says. 'Keeping the place clean and tidy because of the visitor pressures we're now facing.'

To a civilian looking around, the landscape certainly seems in tip-top shape. 'Oh this must be National Trust land,' I find myself saying when a crumbling length of stone walling ends and an immaculate section begins. And there's not a piece of litter any place. Nor are there any litter-bins; to the NT these would be eye-sores. The idea is to create the impression that the only inhabitants of its landscape are birds and butterflies, or in this case sheep. To provide facilities for tourists would spoil the illusion. But of course hundreds of thousands of people visit the Lake District every year. How does the Trust keep the land over which we're bouncing so clean?

'I'm quite keen that we do patrol these roads,' says Roulson. 'Our car parks are looked after seven days a week and litter is cleared every day.' He also visits the local schools.

'If you can talk to five-year-olds and explain why litter is antisocial, that sort of information is retained. They'll go home and tell their parents, hopefully, and say, "You can't throw your cigarette packet away Dad."'

The Lake District is more than a protected landscape, it seems a nature preserve for a species that died out elsewhere in about 1961. While Mike Rouslon's educating country children about litter, elsewhere people are visiting schools trying to convince children that it's antisocial for *them* to smoke – marijuana.

Roulson is conscious of the way the National Trust itself seems to exist in another period.

'We've become too middle class,' he says. In the spirit of the Trust's founders, he'd like the charity to go into the towns and cities and tell people about its work; to arrange for more people who only know urban life to come out into this splendid countryside.

'I've been very happy,' Roulson tells me. 'I've had a great deal of job satisfaction. There's never a day I'm not finding different challenges and things to do. I look forward to the future.'

A few miles along the road from the hamlet of Stonethwaite where the Roulsons live is Bowe Barn sawmill where I met Dave Thomason, a forester. Born in Keswick, he is one of the few local people on the National Trust's staff in the lakes.

I had a quick look at the famous reeving machine at Bowe Barn. Built especially for the National Trust, it cuts with the grain of wood as does sawing by hand and not against the grain as other machines do. The result is that a much stronger length of wood is produced. The noise was awful and I was delighted to learn that, like Myrtle Longcake, Dave Thomason has a spot he feels is ideally suited for showing people what the National Trust does in the Lakes and he drove me to it. It turned out to be a car park about a mile away.

The Great Wood car park has room for fifty to sixty cars. People who use it can either walk down to Derwentwater or, if they head in the opposite direction, they can go up deeper into the woods and then on to the fells. There is none of the manicuring and directional signposting that makes a stroll in Bavaria's Black Forest, say, seem more like a trot through the Chelsea Flower Show. Standing in the Great Wood car park, you feel at the edge of the wilderness.

'I don't believe in signs, if we can help it,' says Thomason. 'If people get lost, well you seem to find the best places when you're lost.'

Borrowdale is a key conservation area and Thomason is host to many visitors as a result. 'This is the place I usually bring everybody to show them what we've done. But I also say,' he continued, 'that if you can't see what we've done, then we've done it right.' (This was an uncanny echo of the words used by Rosamund Griffin, the curator of collections at Waddesdon Manor about the hoped for end-result of the millions spent there on the château's restoration.)

Looking around the Great Wood I reckoned that Thomason and his staff must have done things very right, because I couldn't make out much of anything. It was just a big bunch of trees.

Thomason acknowledges that this car park is surely not a platform from which to view the 'landscape' aspect of his work. Nevertheless he insists it is a very good place to observe almost everything else.

'From this car park you can see the commercial side, the conservation side, access.' Although paradoxically, he adds, its very existence 'is actually detrimental to a lot of the big trees'. Because the ground is paved over, their roots get compacted and they begin to die.

The Trust tried to move the Great Wood car park down into an area mainly planted with conifers. But the County Council wouldn't give its permission because it was felt there'd be problems with access on to the road. So the Trust has adopted a strategy of removing some of the big trees – beeches mostly, because these aren't native to the area.

Recently the Trust's forestry strategy has changed. After years of planting young trees by the thousand, they now pursue a policy called 'Natural Regeneration', which means letting nature do it herself. Obviously this is much cheaper and the end-result, well, if it isn't in keeping, what would be?

If he misses working in the forest, Thomason says he is content to be more of an administrator now. He is not, however, convinced that all the reporting that goes on back and forth between the people in the field and the staff at Regional Office is necessary.

The Trust's wardens, foresters, gardeners, each must have a five-year plan for his property. Jobs are scheduled, budgets worked out. The people to whom they report approve it and then the plan is put into place. Dave Thomason has his too. But he doesn't work to it, exactly. Each year he ends up 'shoving jobs' he wasn't able to do into the next calendar year.

At the Regional Office, this isn't always appreciated. 'They think everything is so cut and dried that you can put it on the computer,' Thomason remarks. One of the land agents, in fact, no doubt thinking this was a winning idea, suggested that Thomason change his strategy and do the jobs in the order noted on his five-year plan; as if he were ticking off items on a shopping list.

'It just doesn't work,' he says. 'What we like to do is to pick and choose the jobs when the weather becomes right for it.' And he goes on to say, 'What difference does it make? If the jobs are there to be done and you get them done, it doesn't matter what order you do them in surely?'

His aim is to understand what needs doing, and then to get on with it. And on the whole he's given this freedom. 'You get to be your own little god in your own little empire,' he beams. 'It's very good. It works beautifully.'

Country Pursuits

Following a series of thefts, from the taking of small souvenirs off the tables of stately homes to carefully planned removal of eighteenth-century garden statues, the National Trust realized it had to protect its possessions better. More than three-quarters of a million pounds were spent on security measures during the early 1990s. But the Lake District did not see much of that money because there was little need for it. Vandalism does exist on its Cumbrian properties but, it too seems to belong to a more innocent time. Take for instance the matter of car parking.

After years of being adamantly against it, the National Trust began charging for the use of its Lake District car parks. The scheme was introduced first in Borrowdale. The reason for it was principally economic.

'So much of the work we do is invisible,' explains regional director Oliver Maurice at the Trust's office on the edge of Grasmere. 'The maintenance of foot paths, of stone walls. You may possibly have seen a new fence going up somewhere. But I wouldn't mind betting that for every hundred people who are standing on the top of Scafell Pike, ninety people wouldn't know that it belongs to the National Trust.' How to make people more aware of what the Trust does while not being 'intrusive' is a problem that has yet to be solved. But he began to tell me of a scheme underway to raise more money to pay for the preservation of this landscape. The cost of employing the 200 or so who work in this very office was not mentioned.

The Trust can hardly erect a fence around its tens of thousands of lakeland acres, and force people to enter through the sort of pay turnstiles used at underground stations. The Duke of Marlborough, albeit on a vastly smaller scale, employs just this method at the entrance to his maze at Blenheim. But as Maurice went on to explain, car parks are 'one of the few areas where we can get something back in order to re-invest it in the maintenance of the landscape'. And since by now most people are used to paying for parking, the Trust judged they wouldn't object.

The NT's charges don't seem extortionate. A pay & display ticket good for four hours costs £1; £2 buys a sticker that allows parking for the day – at any and all of its Lake District car parks. The scheme was extended beyond Borrowdale in 1993.

A driver can stop at the car park at Seatoller and climb up to the top of the pass during the morning, drive on and have a walk alongside Rydal Water near Grasmere; and leave the car at Near Sawrey and have a drink at the Tower Bank Arms all with the same £2 sticker in his car.

The people who didn't take to this programme were mainly local, which is understandable. They are likely to want to park their cars for half an hour, say, go shopping and then return to their homes. And owners of restaurants and tea rooms whose customers use nearby NT car parks didn't welcome the introduction of pay & display. Andrew Lysser, for example, proprietor of the Yew Tree Restaurant about six miles along the road from Bowe Barn says, 'In two years I will have gone from carrying ten fulltime local staff to five. Not by my choice, but by the restrictions that have been placed on the parking in the valley.' He is furious about the loss of business which he attributes to pay parking and about the attitude of the Trust towards him when he's complained. 'They say it's none of my business, it's nothing to do with me. That's their policy and that's what their charging and the hell with me. They said that openly in the public meeting.'

In response to the Trust's new programme acts of vandalism occurred. These too belonged to the time warp. Sticker dispensers were not smashed nor were they broken into for the coins inside.

'People keep pushing stuff in so nobody else can put in any money,' says Dave Thomason. 'It's a form of protest.'

A more esoteric kind of mischief-making which the forester then talked about seemed the work of off-comers entirely. And it's pretty bizarre.

Green thieves

Extraordinarily, in spite of all the fumes from their exhausts, the cars parking at Great Wood have not caused severe air pollution problems.

'These lichens are very good indicators of clean air, which is surprising in a car park,' Thomason drily observed as he showed me some grey-green furry patches on the bark of a tree. 'It's quite well known among lichenologists that this is a very good area,' he continued. But even more surprising was this bit of information: people have been parking at the Great Wood not because they want to walk along the lake or hike up into the hills but because they want to steal the lichen growing there.

Lichen!

'The odd people who know lichens come in collecting.'

A civilian might suppose that the sort of person who 'collects' lichen would be on the environmentally sensitive side rather than environmentally bullying. Surely it is extremely doubtful that there's a market for stolen lichen, however unusual the variety. Nevertheless the thieves come and steal.

'We have big lumps taken out; bark and everything,' Thomason reports. 'I have no idea what they do with it,' he continues. 'Do they put it on trees at home? If they do, it probably wouldn't survive because the special features they need are here not there.' If lichen found any old tree growing in any sort of light and weather just dandy, there'd be no reason to visit the Great Wood in the first place. All kinds of lichen would be growing everywhere.

The land agent for the Derwentwater estate is Fiona Southern, the first woman who's had the job and the first woman land agent in the Lake District. She doesn't attract misogynistic remarks but it is noticeable that there are precious few female names on the roster of Trust employees in the Lake District. Dave

Thomason, in fact, was the only man who even brought the subject up.

'We've tried one or two women foresters,' he says. 'But they don't seem to last long. It's a pity,' he added. 'One of the beauties of having lassies working with the lads is that lassies are really good workers and they work as hard as they possibly can. Of course the lads feel obliged to keep up with them.' And they're more productive. 'It's quite good.'

What is the problem then?

'It's really hard work at forester level,' Thomason replies. 'There's a lot of lifting and carrying. They're not physically strong enough at times.' And when they're not, they ask the men for help.

'That puts the lads backs up,' he notes. 'The lads are having to help them out but they're all getting the same pay.'

The size of the area Fiona Southern is responsible for had recently been increased to include Troutbeck, Ennerdale, Ambleside and Windermere as well as the Derwentwater estate – that added thousands of acres more to her responsibilities. She readily concedes that she doesn't have the time she used to have to visit farms and talk to the tenants.

One of John Workman's observations came back to me when I heard this. Workman was the Trust's first forestry adviser and one of the great mavericks in its earlier more free-wheeling days. When I'd talked with him at his house in Gloucestershire at the edge of the magnificent wood he's given to the NT, he'd told me about an exchange that had taken place about fifteen years before, during a period when the Trust had some difficulty in the Lake District with its foresters there. He offered to go up and meet the men, provided he did it entirely on his own.

'I was prepared to talk frankly,' John Workman recollected. And the foresters had returned his forthrightness with straight talk of their own. "Mr Workman," one began (he broke in to his story here to warn me: 'I'm afraid I'm going to tell you what he did say to me'), "'Mr Workman, the forester said, "the man who owned the property before, he was a right bastard, but at least we saw him!"'

John Workman could sympathize. 'It's the land agents who

are running the woods now,' he says. 'But they are very busy people.'

The son of a timber merchant who turned forester, John Workman joined the National Trust in 1945 when he paid £20 to become a Life Member. In 1952, Lord Bolton, an honorary adviser to the charity, invited him to come on the staff.

'When I started at the Trust,' John Workman recalls, 'one or another of the agents was with me in the woods each day and they said what fun it was. "Come again, we'll spend another day," he would say. They don't have time for that now.'

I repeated the gist of this to Dave Thomason. When I finished, I found I'd touched a tender spot.

'I've been snapped off at one or two meetings', he says, 'for voicing my opinions too frequently. It's just because I do care what's going on. I sometimes get the impression that people up at the very top think we're just here because it's a job. They think the lads, especially down at the bottom, are working because it's a job and they're all getting paid for it. But they all care; they care very much. I don't think that gets through sometimes. I certainly don't.'

Neil Allinson, a gaunt man approaching sixty when we met, looked awkward but he turned out to be entirely charming, though there's nothing of the smoothy about him. He was about to retire from the Trust. 'If I applied to the Trust today for a job I wouldn't get it,' he said candidly. 'I don't have the paper qualifications.' And while the same would apply to quite a few first-rate wardens and no end of gardeners, too, in his case what paper qualifications could they possibly dream up? Neil Allinson gives the following job description:

'I advise the Trust on access issues relating to its great open space properties, particularly upland properties,' he says. He's their man on the mountains. Their footpaths adviser, more informally.

'I've had a lot of jobs,' Allinson says, 'but all of them were getting closer and closer to mountaineering.' He must have had plenty because when he began he was pretty far away from where he's ended up. Allinson started out as a merchant seaman and then became a miner in the Durham coalfields.

Allinson knew he wanted to spend his life mountaineering; when he felt he could actually make a living at it, he moved to the Lake District.

'I'm a professional guide,' he reports. 'I still am. I still hold the qualification to take you to Zermatt and up the Matterhorn, if you pay me sufficiently.' And he's author of several books on mountaineering and adventuring.

By the time he went to work for the Trust he was teaching rock climbing and mountain rescue in the Lakes and was an instructor in outdoor education. He moved from being its chief warden for all the north-west to a regional warden in the Lake District, until at last Allinson came to be paid to concentrate on what his special interest and skill makes him most qualified to do.

His work takes him into the fells two or three times every week, he says. 'Then on the weekends I go back into the mountains as a mountaineer and I go abroad as a mountaineer still.'

It is because he has had such a long and intimate relationship with the fells, that Allinson has been able to contribute so much to solving the very severe problems that the Trust began to have during the period he's worked for it.

'In these last twenty, twenty-five years, more and more people have been realizing the attractions of the great open spaces,' he observes. They've had the money to pursue what has lured them. Equipment improved and so did the skills of ordinary people. When Allinson started working for the Trust maybe ten people a day might follow one of the paths to the summit of a fell; now as he approaches retirement the number might be 200. If each day these 400 feet trampled on steep slopes which received a good deal of rain, paths that were, say, four feet wide two decades ago, ended up being 120 feet wide or more, sometimes much more.

'We always thought these great hills, these great Leviathans up there were indestructible.' And he adds, 'In geological terms they are, of course, but in terms of everyone following the same line, which is what happens in the mountains, they are not.'

Part of the explanation for terrible erosion has to do with the way the Lake District is constructed. Seen from an aeroplane it looks rather like a large wheel; the valleys radiating out like spokes from the centre.

'The hub of the wheel', says Allinson, 'is called Eskhaws. If you're going up Scafell, England's highest mountain, you go from Eskhaws. If you're going up Eskpike you go from Eskhaws, if you're going down to Sty Head Tarn you'd go from Eskhaws.' The same applies if you're going into Wasdale or Eskdale or Borrowdale.

'Perhaps the worst erosion of all in the Lakeland was in Stickle Ghyll in Langdale,' he says. There is a very large car park, always filled, at the bottom. 'It is an immensely popular path that goes up Stickle Ghyll and eventually you end up on the famous Langdale Pikes, one of Lakeland's most famous skylines,' he continues. 'The path turned into an enormous erosion scar almost a third of a mile wide with damaged vegetation, groves, gullies, steep scree that was unstable. Now that's almost totally recovered.'

It was a discovery made by Neil Allinson in 1991 that's led to the long, hard work by teams of men out all the year round in every sort of weather, which has made the recovery and regeneration of the eroded paths through the fells possible. He's delighted that he chanced on 'pitching' and travels Britain encouraging other staff in mountainous areas of the National Trust to use it. 'It is terribly important', he says, 'that the repairs we do are carried out in a way that is sympathetic to the wild land through which the path traverses.' And pitching permits him to do this. 'Nothing would be worse', Allinson continues with great feeling, 'than to go up into these wild mountains and find yourself walking along wooden catwalks or concrete steps or plastic drainage pipe. You've come to the mountains to accept a challenge and to escape from everything that's twentieth century, really. The aesthetic and philosophical aspects of our work have to be paramount.'

The technique Neil Allison came upon that could cure the wounded mountains, though completely unknown when he found it, proved to be a very old one.

'It is only in this last hundred years that man has gone into the mountains for pleasure,' Allinson explains at the start of his tale. 'People who were making these paths five centuries ago were the packhorse drivers; the men and women who were taking perhaps a hundred animals, tied nose to tail with great panniers on their backs, over the hill. They were the trade links between these remote valleys.' All those hooves churned up the terrain and made a terribly, boggy mess. 'So the packhorse traders themselves would throw stones into the ground for their horses to walk on. That was the beginning of pitching.'

In the 1980s, when the results of the modern-day enthusiasm for mountain walking had begun to be so damaging, the people at the Trust were terribly worried about how they were going to be able to preserve the fells. They couldn't seem to find a satisfactory answer. It was on Stag Head that Allinson discovered the solution.

'Coming down the pass there was this very, very wide vertical ribbon of destruction,' he remembers. 'There was barely a blade of grass growing on it; it was just grooves and loose boulders.' He'd walked wide of the scar which was more than 100 feet across. 'I was thinking to myself, "I wonder if we took a path, zig-zagging diagonally through it, would people actually come out this far?"'

Standing deep in bracken he happened to look down. 'At my feet I saw that I was standing on a boulder that was shining with wear. But of course we were quite a long way off the path. I got down on my hands and knees and pulled the sod off. And sure enough there was a polished boulder, and then another polished boulder. And another one and another one. The old path had zig-zagged through there. That was when we discovered pitching.'

They stopped trying to work out how twentieth-century technology could be applied to solve the problem of footpath erosion and they studied the evidence left by traders hundreds of years ago trying to work out how it had been done.

A section of the pitched path was taken apart. They began to teach themselves how to recreate it. It might look as if all they're doing is tossing stones into the earth, but in fact the stones have to be placed in such a way that they stay where they're put and allow water to drain off. Once the technique was worked out, Allinson began teaching teams of footpath workers.

At first, mountain lovers were disturbed by the work being done on the fells, and antagonistic towards it. As the scars have been repaired without blighting the fells, they've been won over.

'They have gained the confidence that we're not going to destroy the mountain by using alien materials and alien techniques,' says Allinson. 'They support us wholeheartedly. Some of the highest funds raised by the Lake District appeal have been specifically for the maintenance of upland footpaths.'

When he's talking about how he and the teams working with him have restored the vegetation to damaged fells, there's no doubting that Neil Allinson feels proud. But there a terrible regret mixed in with it. It's as if a devout homoeopath had learned that the only way he can save a cherished patient is to prescribe steroids.

'I hate the work being done up there,' Allinson bursts out. 'I hate having to do this work. It upsets me that we have to go into the mountains and repair them. I would just rather that we didn't. But in fact we do. So let us at least do it as carefully as we can. That's my main role.'

Neil Allinson is certain that all the erosion caused by the thousands of people now climbing the fells of the Lake District and mountains elsewhere in the National Trust's domain can be repaired – if enough of the bigwigs at the Trust think the work is important enough to pay for. But will they?

'If the same damage was happening to one of our stately houses as is happening up in the mountains – in a dozen places up in the mountains – then not only would there be a great hue and cry about how this has been allowed to develop to this point,' says Allinson, 'there'd be a national emergency fund launched to repair it.'

What does it cost to repair mountain footpaths? The answer to this depends on who is speaking and who the audience is. For instance: when Sir Angus Stirling is talking to the press he may use a figure like £16,000 a metre. Mike Roulson, on the other hand, tells me that £45,000 pays for the annual salary *and* housing of his four-man footpath team. They do a lot more than three metres of pitching a year.

But whatever the figure – and obviously it depends on terrain, weather, and how bad the erosion is to begin with – it's clear to Neil Allinson that the problem in the mountains cannot be solved until more people recognize there is one. And there are those at the NT not in a hurry to come and have a look.

Lord Chorley, an avid mountaineer, and Sir Angus Stirling, an enthusiastic walker, have both climbed up to see what has happened on the fells. But Allinson wails, 'the senior budget movers have never put on a pair of boots, have never been on a mountain and have never seen the problems of these hundred-foot-wide scars.' As a result they are less inclined to write the necessary cheques. That there is another side to these people makes them no more appealing to him.

'I suppose because they've been successful at earning money, they have a degree of aggressiveness,' says Allinson curtly. 'They are prepared to do battle.' His fear is that the people who work on the mountains and in the gardens, on the cliffs and in the woodlands will not be a match for the people who work on the balance sheets.

While he remains convinced that 'there is still no other organization in the world like the NT for dedicated people and for looking after its properties,' he feels a struggle is going on in which the people with the highest aims for the Trust won't be the winners. 'I'm worried that we might be getting to that point,' he says. 'I do worry about it, seriously, for the future.'

He's not alone, of course. The growth of National Trust Enterprises and the 'accountant's mentality' has made many others anxious too.

'There's a great danger from the managers the Trust is bringing in,' says Oliver Maurice. 'These people know nothing of the Trust, have no part in its ethos. The Public Affairs people don't come into the regions, yet this is the grass roots of the Trust.'

Merlin Waterson, regional director for East Anglia and one of the most admired and ambitious figures in the Trust, is shrewdly diplomatic as one would expect from a person who is both intelligent and aspiring. In his office at Blickling he'd said as little to me as he could, without appearing altogether obstructive. Yet when the subject of managers came up, even he risked the apparent indiscretion of saying: 'You go after them, I can't.'

Neil Allinson says that, 'there are people now within the Trust, senior people,' he underscores, 'who've come in from the outside and who have said, "Look you have got to get this beast by the throttle and you have got to make money!"'

Whereas in his first years at the Trust the attitude was, 'Well here is a conservation problem. Let's repair it. Go into the red if need be, but carry out the repair. We'll find the money somehow.' Today the approach could hardly be more different. 'Now,' he says, 'almost the first question that is asked is, "How much is it going to cost?"'

It isn't that Allinson or Maurice or Waterson or the others worrying about the managers having too much control fail to realize how much money the Trust needs to keep going. The concern is about whether they have enough knowledge to make the right judgments about the Trust's priorities.

'People like myself were trained to look at things in a National Trust way,' Allinson recalls. 'Enterprises may say, "If you put a car park here you'll make tens of thousands of pounds." And we might say, "But hang on. If we put a car park in here, then the impact on to the open space is going to be colossal. We'll end up with erosion, with destruction. And we've also got a car park where we don't want a car park to be."'

And while we're on the subject, Neil Allinson is not happy about the decision to charge for parking either.

'We used to believe very strongly', he says, 'that you shouldn't charge in a National Trust car park because people will put money in the money-box anyway. And you might just get a million pounds left in a will because someone liked the Good Old National Trust!' And he still does believe that. But he's not fanatical.

'We do need new ideas and new blood,' Allinson concedes. 'Let them come in with their new ideas; come in and debate the issue of whether we charge money for car parks or not. But they've got to start from the concept of having a deep love for the countryside and the buildings and the foundations on which the National Trust was built. If we take people, just because they are good career people successful in commerce, I think it's weakening, if you like, the purity of what the National Trust has stood for.'

Surrounded by the fells in these Lake District valleys it feels remarkably natural to talk about purity and ideals and to talk about spirit also.

'These hills *are* cathedrals,' Neil Allinson said. And even a city person whose notion of hell is to be on a precipice from which there's a drop of more than twenty feet can feel the same about valleys like Newlands and Buttermere and Langdale.

Neil Allinson's notion of the perfect NT tea room may be a mountain hut with a kettle on a camp stove; some others among us have to force ourselves to tour the house first, before heading straight for the stable-block conversion and the cakes. Yet surely very few people have become members of the National Trust principally because it offers 123 shopping opportunities or because it's not possible to find a decent scone except at one of its more than 200 tea dispensaries.

From its start in 1895, hundreds of thousands, millions of people have joined the National Trust to help save the countryside, the Lake District, pre-eminently. A number of the houses are spectacular, the gardens splendid and special. But surely the countryside has got to be the real bottom line. The difficulty, as it turns out, is not only commercialization, however. It's coming to understand and agree on what saving the countryside means. And that includes understanding its cost, which in the Lake District certainly must include the price paid by local people as well as the millions of pounds off-comers need to go on giving if the work of keeping the Lake District looking as it has for so many hundreds of years is to continue.

A Republic of Shepherds

Poets and painters, philosophers, romantics, trekkers and trippers may have been drawn to the wildness of the Lake District for more than 200 years but a lot that thrilled them on arrival was not wild at all, though they often thought otherwise, and still do.

'The fells are "natural",' Bruce Thompson wrote in his 1947 guide, 'and so are most of the lakes but the rest of the scene is more or less unnatural, artificially tamed.'[1]

The Lake District when it was discovered in the eighteenth century was inhabited by charcoal-burners, slate-quarriers, shepherds, farmers, graphite-miners. And it was an area with a very long history of settlement.[2] There are stone walls standing in Great Langdale today that were used by farmers in the twelfth century. While during the two centuries following that, Cistercians, pursuing profits from the wool trade, used the fells from Windermere to Derwentwater as grazing ground for their sheep. Hawkshead, which now is 'a car park with a town attached', was a grange for Furness Abbey in the fourteenth century. The landscape today looks much as it did in the Middle Ages. The reason for this is that in many ways it is the creation of farmers and their domesticated beasts; methods of farming in the Lake District have little changed. Neither climate nor terrain give them much scope.

It is farmers who have cut down the trees, built the stone walls, cleared the bracken to serve as bedding for their animals.

It's been their cows and even more their doughty sheep, which have always grazed there in far greater numbers, who've nibbled away at the vegetation, making it manageable for the tens of thousands of people who now trek over the fells.

More than one hundred sheep farmers and their families are tenants of the National Trust and have therefore become a part of its Lake District domain too. And if at its stately homes the relationship between landlord and tenant has had more varied rewards and penalties than either side anticipated, pressures on tenants as well as landlords are probably greater still in the Lake District. It helps if a National Trust tenant is rich and/or titled (see Chapter 3). Its lakeland farmers are neither. Yet they are as sure that they know what is best for their land as any lord, and they have a freer spirit than many. It's bred into their bones.

'. . . Many of these humble sons of the hills had a consciousness that the land, which they walked over and tilled, had for more than five hundred years been possessed by men of their name and blood . . .' Wordsworth wrote those words in 1810; all that needs changing to make them up-to-date is to lengthen the tradition by a couple of centuries.

The National Trust as landowner sees itself as the great protector and preserver of the Lake District's landscape; its farmers (and their sheep) are the medium through which many of their strategies are turned into actions. Which means there's a lot more to the arrangement than the usual one between leaseholder and lessee.

A Cumbrian tenant farmer, of course, does not see himself as preservation's paintbrush. Nor does he necessarily believe that what the preservationist wants is so smart. And these farmers have got the confidence that comes when people have lived in one place for a very long time.

That's all background. In the foreground is change. So many people now visit the Lake District, that on busy Bank Holiday weekends it reaches saturation point; there's just no room for any more. Markets have changed because of what people choose to wear and eat and because of competition from abroad. For centuries the main 'crop', indeed the only plausible crop, has been sheep. Nevertheless change has come to these mountains and valleys more slowly than to most other places in the National Trust's empire, not only in outlook but materially, too.

Electricity didn't come up Borrowdale until the early 1960s and it was the late 1970s before the last remote Cumbrian hamlet had electric light. All cable was laid underground, of course, something that Hardwicke Rawnsley was campaigning for when he was elected to the first Cumberland County Council in 1888 and the poles and wires in question were for Borrowdale's telegraph. There are still people who throughout all their long lives have never lived anywhere else but in the same small Westmorland valley. The old world, informed by hundreds of years of tradition and a way of life scarcely altered in that time, is still vivid in the recollections of shepherds who pay their rent to the National Trust; it forms the character of their sons. They may never have been owners of the land but, before the National Trust, these farmers had a freer hand.

The severe climate and extreme terrain with its high fells, cut off valleys and all that wet, had never much appealed to lords of the manor who owned large, wedge-shaped slices of it. (The fat ends of these wedges were the valley bottoms; the thin bits, the fell tops.) As a result, the harsh conditions that made life so hard on its farmers and which made them so tough also brought them an unusual degree of liberty.

Provided the men turned up to serve their lords when a border battle threatened, other demands on them, including rents, were relatively small. And by the end of the sixteen century, when the dissolution of the monasteries had taken place and border battles were over, the fell farmers were able to turn what previously had been relaxed practice in the direction of ongoing rights. They became near-free holders of the farms they worked, which meant they could pass on or sell their tenancies as they wished. Farmers in Cumbria's valleys had more autonomy than farmers almost anywhere else in England. Yet at the same time they worked in a more communal way; their survival depended on that. Weather changed so suddenly and the isolation of the valleys was so extreme that when hay-making had to be done for example, it had to be done especially quickly. There often wasn't time to bring in labour from elsewhere. But there was another reason for their cooperativeness.

Earlier on, each lord of the manor had realized that while his thin strip of fell top would be useless for profitable grazing, if he pooled his land on the high fells with the others, all of them would come out ahead. And the high fells had gone on being shared by all as common grazing land, for the most part.

A patchwork community

When the National Trust acquired Wallington, its first large agricultural estate, it took on 13,000 acres. All the farmers on those acres looked to one man, Sir Charles Trevelyan Bt, as their fathers had looked to his. Much the same pattern had existed at Blickling or Ickworth or Killerton and Holnicote. But the fells were not farmed according to this particular feudal pattern.

In the Lakes there were many independently run small farms. Bits of a farm's land were not always contiguous. Sheep might be set to graze several fields away from the main part of a farmer's holding. And, for example, in Borrowdale the National Trust now has an amount of land equal to what came with the Wallington estate, but its 13,000 acres in this Cumbrian valley were the result of *106* separate acquisitions.[3] On the whole, instead of them all looking to one landowner, each fell farmer tended to look to himself.

Now in place of the relative liberty of times past, the fell farmers have a landlord who wants to decide everything from the colour of the slates on a farmhouse roof to the number of sheep that can be grazed – also the breed – as well as the design of the outbuildings and where the rubbish should be kept.

Many of the big houses owned by the National Trust look as though the decorators had only finished their job the day before the season's opening, instead of, say, 1724, when the decorating was originally done. The farms are much the same.

Everything from the stone walls to barns look as if *Vogue* had been sprucing them up to serve as a backdrop for a ten-page spread on country fashions. Very few owners of big houses and many fewer small farmers have the money and time to pay the same degree of attention to keeping every aspect of their property quite so glossy looking.

As for the National Trust: like the housewife who gets cross when her husband throws his dirty socks on the floor and leaves them there for her to pick up and wash, its staff can get pretty fed up with the farmer who treats his yard as a tip. While to the farmer, this may seem like nagging.

What in the world is the National Trust – a conservation, preservation and public access charity – doing in this obviously complex, enormously demanding, extraordinarily influential, bound to be petty and occasionally extremely awkward situation?

They had been warned. When the opportunity to acquire its first village was presented to the National Trust, Octavia Hill had been against it. 'Imagine the Committee faced with the prospect of turning out a poor widow,' she explained.[4] Unthinkable, really. It wasn't until 1934 that West Wycombe in Buckinghamshire became the first of the villages in the care of the National Trust. But as will soon be seen, by 1934 the Trust had already embarked on the perilous course of life as a landlord to the Lakeland's fell farmers.

And having got into the position of attempting to manage a vast and cherished landscape by trying to manage the spunky people who have farmed it for centuries, has the Trust succeeded in avoiding the difficulties Octavia Hill, with her long experience as a landlord, had argued were bound to be a snare?

It was in 1929 that the National Trust become owner of its first fell farms.

'That was our *annus mirabilis*,' wrote Bruce Thompson.[5] This is a startling remark, since elsewhere in the western world, 1929 is remembered as the year of the Wall Street crash which led to the Great Depression. But it seems to be a true one. 'Until then we'd been acquiring bits of lake shore and woods,' says Laurence Harwood who became regional director for the north-west in 1977 and remained in the post for fourteen years. But in 1929 George Macaulay Trevelyan bought three farmland properties in the Lakes for the National Trust which launched its career as owner of vast amounts of the most marvellous landscape in England and its life as landlord to some of the country's doughtiest farmers.

At the time, G.M. Trevelyan was the Trust's vice-chairman, chairman of its Estates Committee and a member of both the Council and the Executive Committee. The professor, a great walker, had bought a house at Robin Ghyll in Great Langdale and it was in this valley that be began buying up farms. His first gift added up to 400 acres and included not only Stool End and Wall End farms but the Old Dungeon Ghyll Hotel. He tried to buy Millbeck Farm, too, but it was 1935 before he managed to get it. The purchases were handled for Trevelyan by William H. Heelis, a Hawkshead solicitor.

Trevelyan wasn't buying up the farms in his valley to save the old buildings on them, nor the fine trees. He was following a preservation strategy. The idea was to buy up the head of the valley, land which was the most attractive to developers. This would protect the rest which, being higher up, was less desirable for building.

The gift was announced to the public at once. Celebration was mixed with caution. These splendid acres were 'not a public open space which can be used as a recreation ground . . .', people were reminded. 'The farms will remain farms and will not become parks or playgrounds.'[6]

The public would continue to have the right to walk in the Langdale valley, but people must 'respect the rights of farmers and conform to the customs of the country'. Translated this meant: 'Don't forget to close the farm gates behind you.' But to this day, farmers complain that remembering to do this rather elementary task appears to be beyond the intelligence of most people passing through.

While Professor Trevelyan was buying his farms in Langdale, Mrs William Heelis, after many difficult negotiations, succeeded in buying the entire 4,000-acre Monk Coniston estate a few miles away. This enormous and expensive purchase was undertaken with the Trust in mind as its eventual owner. The arrangements between Mrs Heelis and the Trust were complex; some of the land was kept by her and left to the charity in her will; the rest, as had been agreed in advance, was held by her until the Trust could raise the money to buy it by launching an appeal.

As a direct result of her effort – and at the cost to her of a large amount of time, money and attention – more than 6,000 acres of Cumbrian farmland came to the National Trust. Like the actions of Sir Charles Trevelyan and the 2nd Lord Aberconway some years later, the confidence in the National Trust shown by Mrs Heelis's actions inspired others to give Lakeland farms to the Trust. If it could manage Monk Coniston, it could manage anything there. But like the baron and the baronet, Mrs Heelis kept control of running these properties herself. Like them she didn't think the Trust was up to it, just yet.

It may very well be that the best thing Hardwicke Rawnsley ever did for future generations was to befriend the shy, sixteen-year-old daughter of the wealthy, middle-class family which came to spend the summer at Wray Castle in 1882 when he was vicar there. He gave her the confidence to carry on creative work that has delighted millions of people all over the world. And he gave her the conviction that the best way to preserve the countryside in which eventually she made her home, was to buy it and have it declared inalienable by the National Trust. At the age of twenty-seven Beatrix Potter began to publish her tales; twenty years later she married William Heelis and embarked on a career as the Lake District's greatest single benefactor.

Whether or not there were amatory undercurrents for either of them, there's little doubt that an inspired friendship grew up between the thirty-year-old vicar of Wray and the timid, talented teenager. It lasted until he died more than three decades later.

In her twenties Beatrix Potter wrote and illustrated her story about the wilful, danger-loving bunny in a blue blazer. But it was years before she found a publisher.

It was Hardwicke Rawnsley who encouraged Beatrix Potter to send out her manuscript and bucked her up when the rejections came. It was he who urged her to try again. Since Rawnsley himself was a published author – indeed one of his own works, *Moral rhymes for the young*, had found quite a sizeable audience – this must have been particularly heartening for her. But what effect could it have had on her confidence when her friend, feeling he'd come to a dead-end with suggestions, came up with a new idea about how to help her? Mixing generosity with vanity, he rewrote her story in verse, thinking this surely would work.

The Tale of Peter Rabbit was published at last in 1893 – and as just about everyone will know, it appeared as written, drawn and painted by Beatrix Potter's own hand. By the time the National Trust was founded in 1895, the book had gone through two more printings. And with Peter's help, in her thirties, she began to stake her claim to a life of her own.

In 1905, the money she earned from *Peter Rabbit* made it possible for Beatrix Potter to buy Hill Top Farm at Near Sawrey, not far from Lake Windermere. She furnished it with great care and a good eye for the fine, old Cumbrian carved oak furniture being discarded as people modernized. Her bedroom at Hill Top has a splendid seventeenth-century canopied carved oak bed. Beatrix Potter wrote and painted at Hill Top. And when she married in 1913, and moved across the field to Castle Cottage, Hill Top 'was her burrow', as one of her friends expressed it.[7]

Peter Rabbit was more than a quarter of a century old before Beatrix Potter began to have an impact on the National Trust and its role in the Lake District. She was by then Mrs William Heelis, of course, and had settled in to Westmorland life. She'd become a sheep farmer, in fact. Hardwicke Rawnsley had died in 1920; his influence on her certainly had not. Just as he'd been there to help her get started in publishing, he was there as an inspiration when she began farming sheep and acquiring land.

In 1899 the canon had founded the Herdwick Sheep Breeders Association in an attempt to preserve this indigenous breed.

And when Mrs Heelis's eyesight lost its acuity and she felt she could no longer draw to her standard, she concentrated on breeding only one kind of beast: Herdwick sheep.

In 1930, she became the first woman to be made president of the association that Hardwick Rawnsley had founded. By then she'd also begun her career as a benefactress of the canon's National Trust.

With the money earned by *Peter Rabbit* and the tales that followed (quite a few with drawings using Hill Top and its farmyard as their model), she'd begun buying Cumbrian farms. There was Hill Top of course, but the first of the big ones was the 1,500 magnificent acres at Troutbeck Park which became hers in 1924. Yet it wasn't only through acquisitions of land which she bequeathed, gave or sold to the Trust that she made her contribution to the charity. She was active in other ways too.

William Heelis, who had handled G.M. Trevelyan's property transactions, did the same for Beatrix Potter, which is how they'd come to know one another. After they married he became an even better source of information about local properties and people. And she was quick to use this intelligence. When, for instance, Willie told her that GMT had finally managed to buy Millbeck farm in Langdale and was giving it to the National Trust, she knew the perfect tenant to farm it for them. That man was Joseph Greg who, according to Tom Storey, was a 'past master' at handling Herdwicks. And Tom Storey was the wizard who'd brought her years of prize-winning sheep.

Beatrix Heelis had hired Tom Storey as a shepherd for Troutbeck Park in 1926. He became her guide through this new phase of her life. A terrific mutual respect, admiration and affection grew up between them. But it wasn't blind love. Storey always insisted that Mrs Heelis was better at loving animals than at farming or knowing the finer points of judging Herdwicks. That was his speciality, after all. Other people don't agree. But there's no question it was clever of her to have picked him out in the first place. Unquestionably she was a fine judge of character. And if Tom Storey said that Joe

Greg was the best there was with Herdwicks, Joe Greg was the man for Millbeck.

'She knew that father wasn't settled at Eskdale,' his son Vic Greg told me at the house where he now lives in the Langdale hamlet of Chapel Stile. At seventy he has a fine, craggy face; he'd been a lad when the Millbeck tenancy opened up.

'One September afternoon,' he recalls, 'we'd been carting bracken for bedding. It had just come to tea time and we had unloaded a cart,' he recalls. 'My mother said come in and have some tea before you go back again.' The men did.

'We sat in the house having our tea when this car came into the yard. In 1935 if a car came into the yard it was something of a red letter day because even the postman came on a bike,' he laughs. And this car was chauffeur-driven.

'Mrs Heelis came to the door and said could she speak to father privately.'

Mr Greg and Mrs Heelis went into the parlour.

'What she'd come for was to get him to go to Millbeck at Langdale,' says Vic Greg. Early the next morning his father set out to see his banker and the Trust's lawyer and when he came back late in the day, having walked back over the Hardknot Pass, the tenancy at Millbeck was his.

Mrs Heelis's intervention turned out to be good for the Greg family and for the National Trust. The sheep stocked at Millbeck Farm were in better condition when Joe Greg retired in 1954 than those that the Trust had there when he'd begun. And Vic Greg, another man with a good eye for Herdwicks, took over the tenancy of Millbeck Farm from him. But then, when he in turn approached retirement and was ready to pass it on to someone else, landlord–tenant relations began to go badly wrong. And even eight years after he eventually retired, what happened at Millbeck continues to trouble him. The story is disturbing in its own right, and because the attitudes that made certain actions possible seep right the way through the National Trust.

'Beatrix Potter would not have left the farms to the National Trust if she'd known how many of the farmers were going to be treated,' Josephine Banner who knew her insists. And Mrs

Banner, approaching ninety, has been fighting to make it treat them better especially at Millbeck Farm where the Trust has really blundered terribly (as will be seen below).

No one can say with certainty what Beatrix Potter would or would not have felt, of course. But enough is known about her feelings for the Herdwick men, that when the Trust wants to justify some change of strategy in the Lake District, it doesn't cite her as a precedent the way it does elsewhere with Octavia Hill. They wouldn't dare.

'The Trust is a noble thing, and humanly speaking – immortal,' Mrs Heelis had written. But, she added acidly, 'There are some silly mortals connected with it.'[8]

When the sixty-six-year-old Mrs Heelis wrote: 'The National Trust is the only salvation for the Lake District,'[9] she was not being dreamy nor was she being adulatory. This was her realistic estimate, given the alternatives. It was a small, amateurish and inexperienced organization but once it owned the farms, inalienably, they would be safe and the Trust could grow and learn how to look after them. And Mrs Heelis wanted these farms saved; the Herdwicks with them and the people who farmed them.

Vic Greg remembers that when he and his brother were boys their father would take them with him when he went to the various shows for the sheep judging. 'Mrs Heelis would always come to us and give us a copper or two,' he says. 'In those days it was money. She would stop and talk to us, when we were six and seven, well right up to the time when we came back to Langdale,' he adds. 'She'd ask us how we were getting on with learning about what she thought was a marvellous business, I suppose.'

Though he's retired, Vic Greg says he still keeps 'a few sheep'. The day after our talk he was off to judge Herdwicks at the Westmorland County Show. It's not a line of work; it's a way of life. He was born to it; she came to it late.

Greg is clearly aware that Beatrix Potter 'hadn't been used to Herdwicks before she came into this part of the world. Herdwick sheep were the last thing she'd be thinking about when she was young.' But they'd become part of her life too.

'She came to know sheep,' Vic Greg says, clearly more impressed than Tom Storey who helped teach her. Her ewes, says Greg, 'were unbeatable for I should think eight or ten years'. For those who might wonder: it was always ewes and never rams because the grass on her fells was 'too soft' to produce the attributes required for prize-winning males – like his.

It was a condition of Beatrix Heelis's gifts and bequests to the National Trust that Herdwick sheep be grazed on all her fell farms. These short-legged, rough-coated, grey creatures are heafed to those fells. More sheep talk: a heafed sheep knows its patch and will stay on it without needing to be fenced – very handy in such sprawling rugged country. A heafed sheep mustn't be sold to a neighbouring farmer, of course, because it would just walk right back 'home', to the fell where it had been born.

Like their Herdwicks, the fell farmers and their way of life are heafed to these Lakeland valleys. Lose the sheep farms and you lose a race of people, the society they've produced and the landscape they've helped create. Mrs Heelis knew all this and perhaps for her the Herdwick men came first because she knew the landscape could be trusted to come wagging its tail behind them.

Mrs Heelis managed the land she bought for the National Trust, and the land she bought for herself but intended to bequeath to them. Four years after she bought the 1,500-acre Troutbeck Park farm and while she was negotiating for the 4,000-acre Monk Coniston estate she began writing to the National Trust, 'sharing' her thoughts about the proper way to manage hill farms in her part of the world. They needed educating and in 1928 she'd decided to get down to it.

H.B. Heelis, as she often signed herself, wrote literally hundreds of letters addressed to Mr Hamer, secretary of the National Trust, a post he'd taken in 1911. There were periods when Helen Beatrix Heelis wrote S.H. Hamer at least one letter a day.

Mention these letters at the Hollens in Grasmere or at Queen Anne's Gate in London, and the reaction you get is the equivalent of a knowing wink and an elbow in the ribs. What a card! That Mrs Heelis was one old curmudgeon! Her letters to the National Trust have been adorablized by them; just as Beatrix Potter's books are thought to be treacly by those who've never read them. But Mrs Samuel Whiskers was not adorable: and while conciliation and compromise might be fundamental to the National Trust's 'management style' they were not part of H.B. Heelis's.

She could be tender, funny, kind, thoughtful and she could be bossy and as preemptive as Sir Charles Trevelyan or the 2nd Lord Aberconway. But the important thing about this campaign of instruction is that Mrs Heelis was attempting to teach the National Trust how to be competent landlords of fell farms, and that meant that they must become more knowing and wiser about people.

These are the letters written by an experienced sheep farmer, a shrewd countrywoman of exceptional intelligence and imagination to a mind that was on the dull and mediocre side. She leaned a little hard sometimes, she could be amusing, she was aware of what she must seem like to him and, occasionally, as if a curl came tumbling down her forehead from under her usually snug lace cap, she would include in a letter some memory from childhood that for a moment made the exchange suddenly intimate.

In one communiqué she cautioned Samuel Hamer that the Trust must not make the mistake of the typical absentee landlord. Such people hired land agents who had 'the faults of the idle rich with bumptiousness added'. The behaviour of these men had 'made what socialism exists in the countryside'.[10]

Another letter was a lesson in how to judge character: 'To learn the merits of a possible agent to work for them, they must not look to the yachtsmen or tennis players but to the joiners and blacksmiths,' she explained. 'A man's attitude towards his subordinates, and their opinion of him is an acid test . . .'[11] As for that list he had sent on which the names of potential agents had been written. 'Oh dear – oh dear! – Mr Hamer,' she wrote, '*I did hope he would be a gentleman . . .!* Our Westmorland lads are rough,' she admits, 'but you have no idea how sharp they are to reckon up whether a man is a gentleman or not.'[12]

On a spring day in 1930 she is answering a letter from Mr Hamer in which he seems to have been unenthusiastic about one of her previous ideas. 'What a thing it is to have imagination!' she exclaims to a man who might not be expected to know from first-hand experience. 'But', she adds, 'at times it is a trial and anxiety.'

A winter letter signs off with 'depressed but still arguing and spending!'

Other letters were unmitigatedly caustic. 'Did not someone define good taste as the fitness of things?' she asks Mr Hamer after receiving some property signs from the National Trust which she judged looked a 'bonny old muddle'. She then gave her views on how to improve them. Another day she observes, 'It's so kind of you to say my words of wisdom are not useless. Here's a few more. I think you need a better class of man.'[13]

In 1932 Bruce Thompson became the National Trust's first northern area representative; the first fulltime, decision-making employee of the National Trust to be based anywhere outside London. Mrs Heelis retired from fulltime, active duty as their properties manager. She did not retire from giving advice. But now Mr Thompson was often the recipient of her instructions and so he remained until 1943 when she died. She never let up because she felt there was a great deal left to teach – and a great deal for the National Trust to learn.

Bruce Thompson was a disappointment to Mrs Heelis. 'A man cannot help being born dull,' she said, but this was combined with no eye for how things should look and an unreceptive intelligence.

In his writing Bruce Thompson does give an overall idea of the National Trust's approach to managing the landscape. And he wasn't as doltish as she sometimes suggested. He, too, plainly saw that 'the sheep farms are characteristic of the region and so are the men and women who live on them'.[14]

In Borrowdale

Sheep farmers in Cumbria are no longer isolated as they were
for so many hundreds of years and well into the second half
of the twentieth century. Nor, as a consequence of that and
other things as well, is their society as cohesive. But because
the unravelling has only just begun the character, the way
of life of many people born and raised in these valleys,
remains shaped by ways of thinking, seeing and doing that
are traditional. Though the number of people this applies to
is diminishing, a strong sense of community remains. There
were times, listening to those who live in these valleys, when
it sounded almost Biblical.

Chris Bland is tanned from outdoor work. Born and raised
in the village of Stonethwaite, he used to work at the Honister
quarry. Since it was shut down he has been a builder. Bland
built his house at the edge of the village, opposite the church
where we met. It's solid and handsome but doesn't have the
been-here-300 years look of so many of the buildings in these
fell valleys. Yet for all the modernness of the surroundings, as
he talked about the families who were his neighbours when he
was growing up, listening to Chris Bland was like hearing a
Cumbrian version of the begats.

'In Borrowdale,' he began, 'I cite the Longtree Farm and
Yew Tree Farm. When I was a nipper, Yew Tree Farm had
the Bainbridge family. There was Tom Bainbridge and his
wife. They were the seniors. Son Frank worked alongside
his Dad on the farm and brought up two children. John
and Judith in a cottage within the village of Rosthwaite. Jesse,
daughter, and son-in-law Bobby Pearson. . . . Jesse worked the
house for house guests and Bobby was a length man on the
roads. Bachelor son Tom helped in the house with visitors
and accommodation. . . . Longwaithe Farm had Ben Paterson
and Mrs Paterson. Daughters Peggy and Diane and Uncle Jack

as farm man with Auntie Mary living down the valley and four children . . .' Obviously, there were always plenty of hands to help cut the bracken and the hay and to help the others when they needed it; there were plenty of children to fill the Borrowdale school.

'I've worked in the valley all my life,' he says. 'With luck I'll die here and be buried across that road. That makes me the richest person on this planet. I've got everything I want, but it seems the National Trust hierarchy can't believe that we can be trusted with it.'

Bland feels that the Trust's specialists and academics just don't have any confidence in the judgments of local people even though they are bound to know the valleys so much more fully. 'They think we're simple,' he says. 'But', he fervently adds, 'it's simple people who've created what they've got here.' By simple he does not mean slow-witted; he means unpretentious.

The Trust's farmer-tenants, of course, have an almost microscopic knowledge of the way the National Trust does things in the Lake District. As might be expected, there is both unanimity of opinion about some aspects of the Trust's work – and a common attitude – as well as wide differences in experience.

'There are more oak leaves on their vehicles than on the trees,' says Stan Edmondson at Seathwaite. He's a compact, clever man of sixty-seven.

Edmondson was 'born and bred' at Seathwaite; as was his father and grandfather. His son Peter, approaching forty, lives there as does his teenage son Alan, who shows every sign of wanting to stay on and farm Seathwaite himself one day. Stan Edmondson's self-confidence, his shrewdness and the breadth of his vision within an apparently confined space – he is not a man who thinks much of travel – give him the aura of being a local elder statesman.

Many fell farmers, though born in the region, lack the same degree of rootedness to a spot that the Edmondsons have. They may start out working for someone else to gain experience, then move to a small farm which isn't self-supporting and therefore take on work elsewhere to supplement their income, labouring and saving until the tenancy of a bigger farm opens up. And then, one day when they cannot work so hard under such difficult conditions any longer, they give up the tenancy and retire to a house somewhere else in the valleys while a new farmer comes on to the farm. But when, as with Edmondson, you've grown up on land which you're the third generation to farm and know your son will be the fourth and reckon his son will become the fifth, when you know you will live out your life where you were born, a kind of instinctive poise results: you are on your own territory – no matter what a piece of paper may say about freeholds.

Edmondson is only half joking when he talks about how the Trust has taken over the routes through these valleys. 'I often say it's a tussle between the water authority and the National Trust, who has the most vehicles on the road.'

Bobby Cubby, a few miles further up the valley, agrees. Cubby, small and slight with most of his teeth gone, farms at Seatoller opposite the guest house owned by the Trevelyan family. He wears a stiff tweed cap and speaks in a more extreme local dialect than any of the other Herdwick men I met. 'Troost' is the way he pronounces Trust; 'Waaden' for Warden. Rather than 'no' he says 'nay'.

Cubby seems so much of a piece with tradition that he could have been hoisted straight out of the nineteenth century; or the seventeenth for that matter. And it isn't just the way he looks and talks. A row of meat hangs drying from the ceiling above us as we talk in his farmhouse, his lad is outside tending to the cows. But Bobby Cubby is well aware that nowadays farmers like himself have to become adept at dealing with the public. Not only does his wife run a B&B at their farm; he regularly appears on local radio. He's articulate but he's no blowhard.

Three crooks with carved horn tops lean against one wall of his farmhouse. 'I'm not good enough to enter the shows,' he remarks when I compliment him on his work. And he backs away from anything that might look like a personal attack on anyone. 'None of us is perfect,' he says. 'None of us knows everything.' Yet he does not keep his emotions nor his opinions to himself, even when they are critical.

'Look at all these Land-Rovers that ride up and down this road,' Cubby said excitedly. 'It's serious. Every Trust employee is riding about in a Land-Rover. But you can't take a Land-Rover up fell side to do a job. You've got to carry stuff on your back. Why are there so many of them? Big ones as well. Where can they go that a little van couldn't?'

It isn't only the number of Land-Rovers with the National Trust logo on their doors that sets a lot of farmers to grumbling. So do huge number of vehicles crowding into the staff car park at its Regional Office in Grasmere. There's the expense of maintaining this fleet and the feeling that it's all part of a kind of swanning about. And, of course, those cars are a reflection of the Trust's swollen bureaucracy.

Victor Brownlee who farms at Stonethwaite says drily, 'They've all got to justify their existence somehow so they start churning out paperwork.' The Brownlee sheep dogs keep on barking outside as we chat near the Aga.

'You've got four different levels of management before you come to a worker,' Victor Brownlee says ruefully. 'I remember back in Tony Lord's day – he was a grand chap – way back in his day I remember his saying "It's getting out of hand. It's getting too big." (Tony Lord started working in the Lakes in 1958 and became regional director in 1972. Before retiring, he became regional director for Northern Ireland.) 'Since then it's much bigger estatewise,' Brownlee continues. 'And peoplewise it's maybe ten times bigger. They've got to chop a lot of trees down to turn out all these reams of paper.'

In many ways Victor Brownlee is inclined to try to see things from the Trust's point of view. And he believes that 'the Trust have always been fairly good landlords'. Nevertheless he feels they're not terribly efficient. 'Probably too many bosses,' is how he puts it.

The National Trust defends itself against such accusations by mentioning all the experts it has to employ to deal with everything from nature conservation to public relations. And, as is their style, each expert must consult all the others to arrive at a consensus. At the office in Grasmere a staff meeting in the conference hall seems to be going on four days out of every five. Try to reach someone at the National Trust and if the person isn't a secretary, they are nearly always in a meeting or at a conference or on a course. Papers are prepared for these meetings; papers are produced by them; memos are written in reply.

'It's a big business now,' Stan Edmondson says, his voice not overcome with admiration. Today there are more than 200 fulltime staff working out of the Hollens on the edge of Grasmere. When the Trust acquired his farm in 1943 from Marshall's Tanneries, there were two, maybe three.

Edmondson's enterprise is much the same as it was when the National Trust became his landlord. There's no doubting he feels that this is just as it should be. He's tremendously proud of Seathwaite farm. It's 'real traditional', he says, 'and one of the best sheep farms – even though it's a hard one, winterwise. It can be a cruel place,' he admits. And there isn't a wetter one. Some 120 inches fall on the heads of its inhabitants every year. But to Stan Edmondson, 'it's a great farm, Seathwaite.' And he's put his life into keeping it that way.

'We have between twenty-five and thirty miles of stone walls,' he reports. 'All those enclosures were down and I rebuilt them right round. Many finger ends bleeding. But I made it fit. Now we can put sheep in these enclosures when we put the ewes to the rams. It's a big advantage really.'

Edmondson spontaneously recalls the days when he was growing up in the valley: its farmhouses crowded with big families, its rooms heated by coal and lit by candles. 'Anyways, everybody was happy in those days,' he declares. 'It was a slower pace of life, I should think. People went about their work in a quiet sort of way with their horses and ploughing. They made the hay and that; sometimes they didn't because of the bad weather. . . . Oh aye, I can picture it all.' These days it's probably only right after a blizzard that it is ever as quiet in Borrowdale as it was all summer long back then.

It isn't only in retrospect that Edmondson enjoys his spot. 'The end of October it will be absolutely magnificent,' he tells me. 'All the oak trees . . .' Then he laughs. 'I'm talking like this now. Once I would never have dreamt of looking at it!

[321]

The older you get, the more you appreciate your own land. It's beautiful.'

Strangers have been trekking through Seathwaite since before his grandfather's time. Generations of climbers and walkers have passed through the cobbled yard of the farmhouse on their way to the high fells behind it. It's as natural for Stan Edmondson to look out the window and see the public passing by as it is for Nigel Nicolson at Sissinghurst in Kent.

For Edmondson, as for the other farmers who are tenants of the Trust in these valleys where the high fells rise up behind, there's certainly nothing new about having a landlord. What bothers him most about the Trust is not its presence in his life, but curiously, its lack of staying power. The other farmer-tenants I met feel much the same.

'As far as I'm concerned,' says Bobby Cubby, 'this is a very bad fault of the National Trust. You always get changes with agents. They put a young land agent in here, give him four or five years. Then when they're starting to appreciate the problems that we have and they're getting to know the valley and the folk . . . the real ins and out . . . what does the National Trust do? Move them! Then you get another one coming in, maybe right out of college. Of course they want to make a name for themselves.' Which means they make their presence known to the higher-ups by throwing their weight around with the farmers, or, to put it more neutrally, they alter the policies of their predecessor. Very likely, they genuinely believe this will improve things.

'But they don't know the basic principles of our way of life,' Bobby Cubby explains. 'You can sit and look at a colour picture book of the Lake District and you can think it's beautiful,' he continues, his irritation building up. 'We know it's beautiful. We wouldn't live here if we didn't think that! It's not for any money that we make. But', he adds, homing in on his target, 'they come and they start telling us what we should be doing. It isn't right!'

Victor Brownlee observes that 'An agent will be fitted in, start to sort of guide us to the Trust's liking – after we've been here for a lifetime!' And having done that, 'maybe two years later, they'll be moved out to another area. I suppose that maybe they feel they've got to try to be the new brush that sweeps clean.'

Obviously new ideas and attitudes can be beneficial. Maybe there is no such thing as a balance between that and the intimate knowledge of a landscape that can only develop over time, the relationship Mike Freeman, for instance, the Trust's coastal warden at Low Newton-by-the-Sea, talks about having with his stretch of land in Northumberland, having worked there for more than a decade.

The farmers know that management of the sheep farms in the Lake District is a demanding undertaking for the Trust. After all, it's pretty demanding for them and they've been at it for generations.

'Coming into these places and trying to run them is very difficult really,' Stan Edmondson acknowledges. But he's as firm as the others in his belief that 'you've got to live with the people and work with them and get to know them'. Then, too, there is the matter of attitude. A staff member representing the landlord who comes in acting like a know-it-all is bound to cause friction.

From land agents to regional directors, 'they're all alike', Edmondson says. 'It's been my whole life, put it that way. Over the years they do gain experience and begin to understand. But they never get the depth of understanding that they should have. They're pretty dumb, you know,' he lets out. 'I think they are. The agents have got to live and learn like we do.'

And from what the farmers say, very few of the land agents have any first-hand knowledge of what goes into the work they find it so easy to decide needs doing differently.

'A young whiz kid comes in and tries to tell you what the rent should be when they've never farmed a hill,' says Stan Edmondson. 'This is where the trouble is.'

'They're ga good,' says Bobby Cubby who like his neighbours will praise the landlord when they think it's due. 'If it wasn't for the National Trust, I don't know what the hell this area would look like.'

Victor Brownlee has come to agree, though his is a case of

making the best of what could easily have turned to bitterness instead. When his father first became a tenant at Stonethwaite in 1952, it was understood that H.F. Fisher who owned most of the village would bequeath his tenants the chance to buy their freeholds. But, in fact, on his death the property was left to the National Trust. 'It would have been better for us as individuals financially,' Brownlee candidly admits, but he adds, 'not for the area as a whole'. If they'd have been able to become owners, the people then living at Stonethwaite would have sold up to off-comers who wanted their farmhouses, barns and cottages for holiday homes. Victor Brownlee doesn't take to the moral high road about this. Nor do other farmers in the region. What business man doesn't accept the profit motive? But, when the landlord thinking to improve his profits lets a farm to a tenant who is an off-comer, they are absolutely opposed.

'Maybe you get a land agent coming in thinks, "Oh the folks sitting here they think they know everything and I'll show them,"' says Bobby Cubby. 'They bring somebody of another area in. But once you get the wrong tenant, then there's a little bit in the valley that acts like a sore on your arm. It gets bigger and bigger and upsets everything all around as well.'

These farmers can recite each gap in an enclosure, every unhealthy sheep that has been produced as a result of the Trust bringing in outsiders to farm these fells. And it's not only outsiders as farmers that they object to but also the National Trust having so many off-comers on its staff.

'Farmers grumble' is the way the Trust reacts to such criticism. You can't ever hope to please the farmer. But as the farmers see it, everything would work much better were there an in-built sympathy and understanding between the representatives of the landlord and themselves.

'If it was a local fellow and there was a job to do,' says Cubby, 'and you thought they weren't doing it right, you could discuss it with him. He would have his idea of how to do that job. You would have your idea, and you could discuss it. But you can't discuss something with somebody who doesn't understand. If you got to start and explain everything to them.

And they might not pick it up right. The local fellow's done it since he was a boy.'

Much the same point was made by Gareth Roberts who is both a local fellow and the Trust's warden for the Llyn Peninsula. (See Chapter 7.) Obviously the National Trust is capable of understanding the idea. It knows it must have local people on the ground in North Wales. Maybe if Herdwick men had their own language, as well as their own traditions, things would be more agreeable for the farmers in the Lake District.

Bobby Cubby feels it's hopeless. 'If there's, I won't say a dirty job, but a job right at the bottom end of the scale, if there's an odd job like that, they'll maybe consider a local. But there's all these wardens riding up and down this valley, and they won't entertain a local for a job like that. They definitely won't. Ah, people have tried,' he says. 'They've given over trying now because they know they don't stand a chance.'

If the Trust fails to put its confidence in the local people and thinks they're not good enough, the local people feel much the same about the Lake District's biggest landowner. The only positive thing that can be said about it is that it's a fair exchange. But such prejudices are not unbreakable. Herdwick men have been known to accept off-comers and to go even further than that. Beatrix Potter is one example. Cubby Acland who became the National Trust's first trained land agent in the Lake District is another.

'Mr Acland was a gentleman,' says Chris Bland, 'and if one has to say it, from a different plane in the structure. But he was a countryman, so he could talk to a countryman at any level. That seems to have disappeared now.'

'He ran the Lake District,' is how Laurence Harwood portrays Cubby Acland. 'Nobody was going to tell him how to run it from the centre. He was a man who, luckily, was living at a time when you were able to say "Yes" or "No". You couldn't do that today. You'd have to consult 300 people.'

Cuthbert H.D. Acland was the younger brother of Sir Richard Acland who in 1942 gave the Trust his estates at

Killerton and Holnicote. He had become a land agent before the war and went to work for the National Trust when he returned from India. And from 1949 to 1973 he ran the Lake District or, as his official title describes it, he became the National Trust agent for the north-west.

Cubby Acland, a life-long bachelor, appears to have been a chap with a temper to match his panache.

'Cubby Acland, he used to get everybody's back up,' Stan Edmondson remembers. 'There'd be rows about the rents and one thing and another. But he was a good fellow.' And one reason Edmondson thinks so is that, 'he got to know the people. It was funny how he blended in with the hill men, which was a great thing.'

Edna Garlick, fifty-three, who has been a part-time receptionist at the Trust's Regional Office since 1980, came to Cumbria as a young wife and mother in 1968. Her husband had taken a job as the National Trust's first building manager for the region. (She's had a long time to get to know the Trust and she is a sharp-eyed, though good-natured observer. When trying to find out something at the office in the Hollens, she often seems the only person there who knows what's going on. So it's especially galling to hear the way some of the staff there talk to her. Chris Bland isn't exaggerating when he says, 'They think we're simple.' Fortunately for Edna Garlick, she seems a buoyant person.)

'He was a fair and honest man,' Mrs Garlick says about Cubby Acland, 'And thoughtful'. On the day she and her husband arrived at their new home, a National Trust cottage at Loughrigg, there was Mr Acland.

'Cubby came in,' she remembers, 'and put two bottles of wine down on the packing cases. "One is to drink now," he said.' And the three of them set to enjoying it. The other he left for the Garlicks to enjoy on their own.

They'd been promised that their completely unmodernized cottage would be redone and ready for them when they arrived. In fact it remained as it had been: there was no bathroom, no toilet and only a cold-water tap. The couple had three sons under the age of six. She still sounds amazed about it when she says, 'We used to be invited to his home to have a bath. And we did go,' she adds. All five to Cubby Acland's.

'Cubby Acland was here quite a lot of years,' says Stan Edmondson. 'Towards the end he really loved his fell farmers. He got attached to them.' And they were not unmoved by this. When Acland retired, we 'all clubbed together and bought him a horn stick and some tweed to make a suit of'. Woven from Herdwick wool, no need to ask.

'It was a sad time when he retired because things changed after that,' Edmondson continued. 'There's was a new outlook on to farming. There was one or two whiz kid agents, You know what I mean?'

It's not that the Herdwick men think that everything good about the National Trust happened years ago. For instance, a lot of them praise without reservation the Trust's insistence that all its buildings should be preserved using traditional methods and that any new buildings ought to look much the same as the old ones do, at least superficially. If breeze-block is used, it will be faced with local stone, for instance.

'They're doing a good job,' Stan Edmondson. 'It's good that if you have anything built it has to be in stone and all. You don't want an old tin shed in these areas. I know it costs a lot more money to use slate and all that, but I think that's one thing they're good at.'

Ignoring for the moment the implied criticism, the other things they are not quite so good at, he discussed the building works at Seathwaite and other farms nearby. There was a certain amount of chuckling when he got to what had happened when Victor Brownlee needed a new farm building.

Susan Denyer, the National Trust's historic buildings representative for the north-west, had scrutinized the architect's plan for the building that Brownlee was going to get. She then climbed up the fells behind the hamlet to look at the proposed site from above. It was then that she noticed that, as planned, it would be the only structure parallel to another. So she had the plan altered in order that the new building would be 'in keeping', which is to say, she had it set at a slight angle to its neighbours.

[327]

'Ah she's very strict like. Very strict,' Stan Edmondson said as he embarked on a story that was like a send-up of the nursery rhyme, 'In and out the window'.

A farmhouse in the valley had a window that had needed replacing. The Trust's workmen fitted a new one. Susan Denyer came along to inspect it. 'Not quite right,' she decided. Out it came. Back she went. Out it came again. And again. Until, finally, she approved. Two other people told me this tale also. It seems to have provoked equal amounts of hilarity and outrage. To the farmers it was all so finicky and such an extravagance.

Mrs Denyer, when I later said something on the subject to her, wasn't prepared to acknowledge there might be anything in the slightest bit extreme about the way she goes about things. In her forties, she looks both much younger and at the same time old-fashioned. Before being hired by the National Trust, she had established herself as an expert in the mud-hut dwellings of African villages. In some Cumbrian farmhouses, this causes at least as much rueful smiling as the story of that window. To her – and presumably to the people who hired her – the relevance of her specialization to her current work is clear. Her great interest is in vernacular architecture.

Mrs Denyer was wary when we first met. Suspicious. When I asked if I could tape our interview, she replied, 'It depends what you want to ask me.' She simply didn't respond when I mentioned that some of the farmers – that is every farmer I spoke to, though I didn't say so – found her exacting. She just sat there. What could I mean? I gave an example in the form of a question. Why had she thought to climb up and look at Stonethwaite from above when she was considering the plan for Victor Brownlee's new farm building?

'I hope Victor Brownlee says, at the end of the day, it was worth the effort,' Susan Denyer responded. 'On the whole he seems happy with the building.'

But don't the days before that matter? Which is to say, getting back to my actual question, 'Why this almost zealous scrutiny of the site?'

'We now have to add this visual or aesthetic dimension to

what we're doing,' she answered. 'We can't pretend things are just happening the way they were 100 or 200 years ago. We have to size things up, decide what the impact is going to be. Looking at things from the fell tops is extremely important', she continued, 'because that's how a lot of people see a hamlet . . . walking on the footpath and looking down.'

'You should be flexible, shouldn't you?' says Stan Edmondson, speaking as the experienced business man he is. 'If you're doing a deal, you give a bit. Give and take. But she's hard, she won't give an inch, I think. And what she says goes.'

An historic buildings representative's job is to make decisions about the decoration and presentation of the National Trust's houses and gardens, houses particularly. But there are no palaces in the Lake District. And it has extremely few large houses of any kind. In fact Sizergh Castle is it, unless you want to count the Georgian house in Cockermouth where William Wordsworth was born. There is only one garden its own right, Acorn Bank near Penrith. It's a charming two and a half acres.

Both her previous interests and the territory she was given to look after might suggest that Susan Denyer would be a relatively minor figure at the National Trust. But as befits her gifts and her aspirations, Susan Denyer has made it her job to oversee the Trust's other dwellings in the north-west. And that means its 2,000 vernacular buildings. Nor has the absence of gardens kept her indoors. Lacking any, Mrs Denyer has chosen to guide the Trust in its handling of the historic and aesthetic aspects of the landscape instead. The *landscape*: that means more than 155,000 acres; getting on to a third of the entire Lake District; one quarter of all the countryside the National Trust owns in England, Northern Ireland and Wales!

Susan Denyer is knowledgeable, ambitious, hard-working and she has come to have a very great deal of influence.

'She has more power', Stan Edmondson believes, 'than the agents. You can sort them out a bit like, but not with the buildings or any houses. No. No.'

'I've always got on with her,' says Victor Brownlee who is indeed pleased with the building the Trust erected for him, at a slight angle, in Stonethwaite. But he adds, 'she seems to antagonize a lot of people, does Susan'.

If she notices this, she doesn't seem to find it hard to cope with. She has already managed quite a few impressive feats and feels her job offers a lot more scope.

When Susan Denyer was hired in 1981, the National Trust wasn't even sure how many vernacular buildings it owned, never mind how many of them there were in the Lake District. But, she says, 'I felt that first and foremost, I wished to be involved in some way in the restoration and management of those small buildings.' So, as a start, she undertook a survey of their vernacular buildings in the north-west. No such thing had been done anywhere in the Trust's domain. And when she was finished with that one, she organized similar surveys elsewhere. As a result, the Trust now knows that it owns 20,000 vernacular buildings in England, Wales and Northern Ireland and it knows what and where these buildings are.

Next, and again beginning with her own territory, Susan Denyer undertook the first large-scale landscape survey ever done by the Trust. Cross-matching documents with the evidence on the ground, she and her co-workers – staff and volunteers – have been able to map out the position of boundaries, hedgerows, paths, stone walls. 'In many ways,' she says, 'these are what dominated the landscape when you looked down any particular valley; what gave it its particular character.' Again this became a model for surveys being carried out in other regions of the Trust's empire.

Her current project is organizing interviews with local people. The collection of oral histories from residents of the various valleys in the Lake District will be complete in ten or fifteen years. When combined with the results of the buildings and landscape surveys, this will provide an invaluable archive for future study and planning. And the public is to benefit also.

In fifteen years' time, as Susan Denyer sees it, 'people coming to the Lake District can, if they want, read a guidebook to the valleys in the same way they read a guidebook to the houses and have a bit of knowledge about how the landscape's developed and come to look as it does today.'

Susan Denyer is an empire builder every bit as much as Michael Trinick and Cubby Acland were. She fights for her corner as much as the Border Raider Sheila Pettit ever did. But she's got the approach of an academic which none of them had. And it's impossible to imagine her turning up at a cottage with welcoming bottles of wine. People's feelings seem to play the smallest part in the picture she's studying. The stories that follow therefore are not likely to be a part of the National Trust Guide to these valleys. But they do give an idea of how the National Trust as landlord affects the lives, rather than habitats, of their tenants.

A lease gone right, in the end

'It's ten years since I started,' says Bobby Cubby.

Before he was given the tenancy at Seatoller Farm he was a shepherd at three different properties. 'It was always our aim to have a spot of our own,' he says. 'And just because the National Trust was here, we never lost heart. Laurence Harwood, he told us never to give up. "There'll be a spot for you sooner or later," he said.

'The tenant before me at Seatoller died.' But the family went on farming the land until the Trust offered the tenancy to Cubby.

'For all that I had no involvement with it, our first ten months here was hell,' he reports.

It appears that the transition of the previous tenancy to his was a miserable period. These seems to have been bad feeling from the day Bobby Cubby and his wife arrived, starting with the sheep counting.

Each tenanted farm comes with a certain number of sheep. The same number of sheep, in essentially the same sort of condition, must eventually be turned over to the next tenant.

[331]

If there are too few or if the beasts are in far worse condition, the tenant who is leaving has to make good, so counting and evaluating the condition of the beasts, which has to be done each time there's going to be a changeover, is not an idle endeavour. And like many such things, sheep 'livrying', as it's called, has its own rituals.

Two men come in to count for the outgoing tenant; two others for the new man. Two are there to make the final acceptance on behalf of the landlord, the owner of the stock, in this case the National Trust.

'It's always been social,' Bobby Cubby explains. 'Half a day's work in the sheep pens. If they're satisfied, they ask the Trust's two men to look through the sheep. Ninety-nine times out of a 100 it goes off. Everybody knows everybody else.'

Once the counting is done and the landlord accepts that the stock are as they should be for the new tenant, a celebration begins.

'Tradition is', says Cubby, 'that outgoing tenant provides the meal and the incoming tenant provides the drink.'

As this Herdwick man thinks back on that day when at last he became a tenant of a sheep farm, as he'd been wanting to do all his life, tears flow down his cheeks. He doesn't seem even to notice.

'They never ate or drank,' Bobby Cubby recalls. 'All they did was stand outside – and the shouting and the swearing and the carrying on that went on in those sheep folds out there! It was terrible altogether.' The tears continue.

'There was two old fellows who was asked to come and do the livrying, got in their cars and went,' he reports. 'They said they'd never seen or heard of the like of this in their lives before.'

Ten months of acrimony followed. 'I was getting to my wit's end,' he remembers. And as he talks about the men who he feels caused trouble from the day he took on the tenancy, a look of real animal hatred comes over Bobby Cubby's face.

'One day Laurence Harwood came here. He said to me, "What do you want to do?" It was an hour before they were having another meeting here. I said, "Get these buggers off this farm, Mr Harwood. Let me farm it"' He did, Bobby Cubby reports. 'He chased them. And Trust lost money. It wouldn't have been a hell of a lot of money. But Laurence Harwood forgot about that. He'd seen it from our side. What was going on and what was going on in our heads and the people that was coming here and the arguing and the friction and that it was past a joke, like. He saw it from the personal side.'

His gratitude is understandable but not blinding.

'It isn't all bad the Trust,' Bobby Cubby says. 'What they're trying to do preserving the Lake District, it's grand. It is. But in any big organization they must keep turning themselves inside out and have a look. And I don't think they do that often enough.'

A lease gone wrong

Eric Taylforth is the tenant at Millbeck, the farm George Macaulay Trevelyan was finally able to buy for the National Trust in 1935 as part of his attempt to insure that the head of Langdale and the rest of the valley with it would remain unspoilt. It has long been a popular starting-off place with visitors to the Lake District who walk through the farm to climb Stickle Tarn and the Langdale Pikes. The troubles, however, have had nothing to do with the issue of public access versus farming efficiency. 'Things aren't right in Langdale,' as a shepherd in another valley remarked.

Huge white tents were pitched in the vast open fields below the Hardknott Pass. At the sheep pens, each of the Herdwick men was bent forward on his crook. One hand grasped its horn head, the elbow of the other arm, folded, rested on it. They were studying their breed: short-legged, and tough, the

Herdwicks had been gussied up for the judging; their grey wool dusted with a vibrant magenta powder.

Vic Greg was there. He told me that, even for him, getting a lease to farm at Millbeck hadn't been an automatic thing, although his own father had been the retiring tenant. The Trust actually advertised the letting and considered giving tenancy of the 250-acre farm to an outsider for a higher rent. But because he was a local lad, Joe Greg's son and keen to farm at Millbeck, eventually they gave it to him.

It was in the middle 1980s that he felt it was time to retire and he had someone in mind to take it over.

'There's a chap who was working for me,' says Greg, 'Eric Taylforth. He'd worked for me for five years and he applied for the farm.'

Again, the Trust advertised the Millbeck tenancy. And while it considered what it was going to do, the land agent came over to see Greg and talk about the farm's future. The agent told Greg that when it wrote the new lease, the National Trust intended to give some of the land at Millbeck to Middle Fell Farm next door. When the agent described just exactly which land this was, Greg was appalled.

'In that case we needn't go any further,' Vic Greg told the landlord's agent. 'I'll not give up! I'll withdraw my notice and stay on.'

As Vic Greg saw it, the scheme the National Trust proposed was disastrous. In bad weather it would be potentially deadly for his Herdwicks.

No action had been taken on the boundary changes when, in 1985, age finally made Vic Greg give up his tenancy at Millbeck Farm. He recommended that Eric Taylforth be given a lease. The shift in boundaries was debated again, as was Taylforth's tenancy. In the seventy years the National Trust had been a farm landlord in the Lake District, it had never given a temporary lease. But now that is all it would offer Eric Taylforth: five years, a trial lease, rather than one which would see him to his retirement.

Some local people say Taylforth should never have agreed to it. I asked him why he did. Taylforth, in his thirties, had just finished judging Herdwicks at Eskdale when Vic Greg introduced us.

'In talking it over with the National Farmers Union,' Taylforth explained, 'they said, if you make a fight now, they'll say you're a difficult tenant and they were justified in putting this five-year thing on.' He wanted badly to take on Millbeck, so he agreed to the Trust's terms.

At that, it was almost nine months after the Taylforths had moved into Millbeck before the trial lease was actually signed. During that time Vic Greg wrote to the Trust.

'I told them to come and meet me on the fell,' he says. 'That I would explain to them what would happen if they did what they wanted to do. They never came.'

About a year before the five-year trial lease was to end, the National Trust warned Taylforth that they weren't going to renew it; that he should begin making plans to leave.

'I told them they'd have to throw me out,' he says. 'And that I would go to court. I'd take an independent jury's verdict. Or an arbitrator.'

Eric Taylforth went to Bristol to get legal advice. That alone cost him £1,200. The lawyers there reckoned that he wouldn't stand a chance against the National Trust, the biggest landowner in the Lake District National Park, when the case was heard locally, but they felt sure he would win on appeal.

'I told the Trust that nobody would be the winner,' Taylforth says. 'It will cost me £10,000 in legal fees and them the same. It's money that should be spent on the farm.'

The National Trust strives to resolve its disagreements privately. There are several reasons for this; its preference for consensus rather than confrontation among them. However the principal reason for shunning court-room battles must be that it feels this would attract the sort of publicity from which it couldn't gain a thing. But if the charity is prepared for long drawn-out discussions as a way of arriving at a workable agreement, an individual may not be able to afford such dickering. It can be too costly emotionally as well as financially.

'It's been a miserable mess,' Eric Taylforth says. 'We farm

it the best we can in the circumstances, not knowing for the future.'

Eric and Susan Taylforth and their two young sons had been living at Millbeck Farm for eight years, the last three of them without a lease, when we met at the Eskdale show.

Susan Taylforth, who was with her husband at the show, is a blonde woman who operates the very successful B&B at their farm. Though chubby her face looked drawn.

'She's a terrible nice body,' Bobby Cubby later told me. (Cubby considers himself their neighbour though he lives in another valley. His sheep in Borrowdale and Taylforth's in Langdale share some of the same fell-top grazing.) The awful time the Cubbys had during their first year at Seatoller was clearly in his mind.

'The Trust should have give a thought to Eric's wife,' he burst out. 'What that lass has had to live through! Eric – I suppose us fellows, we are different. We're outside. We can sort of get away from it when things aren't just as they should be. But womenfolk are stuck in the house and it's there with them. "Is this going to be mine tomorrow? Is it worth cleaning the floor?" What Eric's wife has had to put up with! It's dragged on far too long.'

What was going on? Is Eric Taylforth such a rotten farmer? 'Eric Taylforth is, by a long way, the best farmer there is in Langdale, I can tell you that,' Vic Greg asserts. A lot of other farmers agree.

'When he had his problem,' Bobby Cubby says, 'the whole of this valley, the farming community, we all got together one night and we pledged our support. We each gave a statement to his solicitor as to our knowledge of Eric and his way of farming. He has some of the best Herdwick sheep in the Lake District,' Cubby adds. 'He put as much into them as ever he can afford.'

Even Laurence Harwood who was the Trust's regional director during the years when most of this misery was taking place says that Eric Taylforth 'was a jolly good farmer, he really was. A good stock man.'

One problem may have been the disagreement about boundary

changes at Millbeck. Taylforth, like Vic Greg, found the Trust's proposals unacceptable. But the big trouble seemed to be a matter of character.

'I think he'd be the first to admit he has a bit of a temper,' Bobby Cubby admits. 'But if you're going to survive around here, you've got to have a bit of spirit. He's a hell of a good neighbour. For the rest, all I know is gossip, and I'd rather not . . .'

And gossip is all that there ever was. No public accusations were ever made against Eric Taylforth. The alleged misbehaviour I did hear falls somewhere between flirting and pawing. But was there any truth to the gossip? Or was it in fact the vicious turn taken in what really was a boundary dispute between neighbours and the landlord?

Josephine Banner heard about the troubles at Millbeck Farm from her friend Ann Taylforth, Eric's cousin. Mrs Banner became one of Eric Taylforth's champions.

'It was wicked,' she says. 'They were trying to destroy a farm which had been given to the National Trust. Oh there was a lot of dirty work . . .'

'If I had the money,' Josephine Banner wrote to Dame Jennifer Jenkins who was then the charity's chairman, midway through her campaign to help Eric Taylforth, 'I would sue the Trust for cold-blooded persecution of an innocent man and wife.'

But still there was no lease forthcoming.

'It's like being on a sentence,' Taylforth says.

Yet none of this turned him against his farm. Nor against his landlord.

'I have nothing against the National Trust,' he told me. 'It's the management that's wrong.'

A gap of a year came in the negotiations between Taylforth's solicitor and the National Trust. For the second time since I began my studies of the Trust, I did more than stick my nose into the story. (The first time was by objecting to the Trust's treatment of Peter Borlase at Lanhydrock.) In the course of a chat with Julian Prideaux, I said I'd like to know what was going on at Millbeck.

[337]

'Progress is being made,' he told me a week later when he'd chased up the latest 'news'.

'Oliver Maurice is very approachable,' says Susan Taylforth. 'He seems to have a real feeling for the farmers.'

Almost a decade after Vic Greg suggested Eric Taylforth as the new tenant to farm at Millbeck, a lease satisfactory to landlord and tenant will be written.

Eric Taylforth was never charged with any crime through all the years of contention about his lease at Millbeck Farm. Never having been accused of anything, there was nothing he could stand up and refute – or try to. He couldn't be found innocent because nobody ever said what he was guilty of. And, in any case, what could the 'crime' have been, to justify such action on the part of the National Trust?

'It's not as if he was discovered running a brothel,' a solicitor in London said when she heard the story.

Who are these people at the National Trust to take to the moral high ground and refuse to budge? Laurence Harwood himself might not have qualified for a National Trust lease using the standards by which he was judging his tenant(s).

One afternoon while entertaining NT colleagues from outside the Lake District, Laurence Harwood invited them to his house. When the group entered the kitchen, they found a note on the blackboard from his wife waiting to greet them. Janet Harwood's message read: 'F*** you National Trust!' And she meant it to stand; written in marker, it had to be painted out.

In 1987, the Harwoods separated. But well before that, Laurence Harwood had begun an affair with the woman he has subsequently married. *All* of this was going on while Eric Taylforth was being judged unfit to farm at Millbeck because of vaguely rumoured hanky-panky.

As Oliver Maurice ever so slowly opened negotiations with Taylforth to arrive at a proper lease that would secure the tenancy of the Langdale farm, across the country in another corner of the Trust's domain, the Marquess of Bristol – in gaol on drug charges – was, finally, being told that his lease for the tenancy at Ickworth House was going to be ended. It was the first time ever that they had made such a move against a donor or a donor's family.

'If you hadn't been through it,' says Eric Taylforth, 'you wouldn't think it was real.' Or happening at the largest richest charity in the land at the close of the twentieth century.

[10]

Fashions in Fantasy

Idealism is 'only a flattering name for romance in politics and morals', George Bernard Shaw wrote in 1898. Idealists, GBS continued, just warming up, promote a 'fictitious morality and fictitious good conduct . . .'[1] He could have, but didn't, single out the National Trust which had been founded only three years before.

Had they happened to see this piece of writing, Octavia Hill, Sir Robert Hunter and Canon Rawnsley – all dedicated idealists – would have found Shaw's remarks neither sympathetic nor accurate. They sincerely believed, along with similarly inclined Victorians, that doing good would bring about a better world, inevitably; and to that end they laboured.

But in time a person need not have been an idealist to support the National Trust, of course. Forty years later Shaw himself left his own house to the charity. And in the same period, far greater gifts came to the Trust on the death of Beatrix Heelis. Her genius was to make art from close observation of what is. As Graham Greene wrote in an admiring essay, the action in her tales 'is described from the outside by an acute and unromantic observer, who never sacrifices truth for an effective gesture'.[2] It was in order to save something true, that Mrs Heelis became a preservationist.

And Shaw's remarks have their application to the National Trust today. In place of the people who so unshakeably believed that they knew what was good for the less fortunate, came the people who knew what was 'good taste'. At first they were only busy saving good things for one another. Now the audience is all the middle class. And as Hollywood producers discovered a long time ago, there's nothing people like better than a good romance.

In their effort to preserve beautiful old things and exquisite landscape, the National Trust has found itself in the business of telling us about the past. How they've chosen to do it – what they highlight and all they leave out – shows how the charity has become a purveyor of fantasies. The research has been thorough and the production values are high; so are the costs. But it's not the past preserved that we find when we follow the brown and white arrow with its oak leaf and acorns. It's an idealized, tightly edited fabrication.

A spring garden? Can't have them any more. They wouldn't draw crowds in July or August. So no matter where it is in the National Trust's domain or how it was originally laid out, a garden must be colourful every single month of the open season. But it is when the Trust presents a person's home to the public that the greatest distortions occur.

Take, for example, Chastleton House, a fragile, barely modernized Jacobean manor in a sleepy if gentrified green and hilly hamlet. Though built of stone it has a delicate beauty.

In the mid-1950s, Alan Clutton-Brock inherited Chastleton from his cousin Irene Whitmore-Jones. He lived there until his death in 1976.

A brilliant boy, Clutton-Brock was a scholar at Eton along with George Orwell. Later, at Kings College, Cambridge he was part of a set that included Anthony Blunt. 'He had this disease of cynicism,' it was said of Cyril Connolly. This seems to have applied as well to Alan Clutton-Brock. 'Everybody else was the stupidest person around,' someone well-acquainted with Clutton-Brock has said.

George Orwell remained a good friend and when Alan Clutton-Brock married and was living in Greenwich with his wife Sheelah, Orwell used to go there, change his clothes and go off tramping. Later he'd come by and change back again. At the time he inherited Chastleton, Clutton-Brock was well known and highly regarded as art critic for *The Times*.

Because of who he was and whom he knew, because of the lovely, other worldliness of the rather neglected house into which he moved, and because of its location too, which put it in the path of lots of people who were spending weekends in the country, quite a few men and women whose opinion and influence counted had stayed at Chastleton and had fallen for it. And even those who weren't insiders could visit.

Barbara, Alan Clutton-Brock's second wife and widow, stayed on at an ever-more delapidated Chastleton, and people who had heard about its specialness could come to see it. They were taken around, often by an elderly figure who, like the interior itself, seemed somehow beyond old-fashionedness. The house was once used in a filmed version of Evelyn Waugh's *Scoop*. As those who know the book will already have imagined, it played the part of Boot Magna.

Chastleton had only the most minimal electrification and heating. Great gaps could be seen in the roof of the stables; bits of roofing felt flapped in the breeze. Birds flew into the house through the broken, diamond-paned windows; much of the glass that remained was 400 years old – still there from when the house was built. In the Long Gallery, which runs for seventy-three feet across the top of the house, pigeons raced under the arching, plaster ceiling with its carved roses, daisies and fleurs-de-lis. It had been a long time since the gallery had seen any other use, and possibly even longer since Chastleton House had had much money spent on its upkeep.

Believing that 'Chastleton is a national asset', Robert Parkinson, who was both architect and conservation officer for the West Oxfordshire District Council in the late 1980s, tried to see that the house got repaired. Because of its importance, the fact that it had admirers in high places, and because Mrs Clutton-Brock had said it would eventually go to the National Trust, English Heritage, most unusually, offered her hundred per cash grants to make critical repairs.

Mrs Clutton-Brock was not inclined to accept grants. It may be that like other independently minded people she didn't care for being told what to do, how to do it and when. But, not irrelevantly, Chastleton House was a Grade I listed building and because of that its owner – Barbara Clutton-Brock – was legally responsible for keeping it sound. The district council, for instance, could have served her with 'an emergency works notice' and then gone in, done the repairs as it saw fit and billed her – or her heirs or beneficiaries – later. The figure could have amounted to more than £100,000, easily. And she knew it. This may only have increased her feeling that she was being ordered about, of course. Chastleton after all was *her* house.

On 2 May 1991, the men of the National Trust (and English Heritage and the West Oxfordshire District Council) opened *Country Life* and saw an advertisement that shook them. Chastleton House in all its leaking, crumbling glory, Chastleton which was going to belong to the National Trust one day where it would be looked after and protected, was now on the market. This may have been the most provocative action connected with Chastleton since 1602 when Robert Catesby sold the estate to Walter Jones and used the £4,000 he got to finance the Gunpowder Plot.

Barbara Clutton-Brock, reclusive, clever and touchy, had changed her mind. Alone in the house, she'd become ill earlier in the year and hadn't been able to get out of bed. 'If I hadn't come by she might have died,' says Ted Townsend, a local farmer. The Townsend's wealth in land grew as the family sold off more and more of their estate to keep Chastleton going. Ted Townsend chose to clip the topiary, as once his grandfather gardened there for wages.

At seventy nine, Barbara Clutton-Brock decided she could no longer go on living in a house that was draughty, damp and cold even for a Jacobean mansion.

Nevertheless, why had she put it on the market? The National Trust would have been delighted to make a snug, roomy flat for her if she'd wanted. She seemed to have turned against the house as if it had become a memento mori. A flat would not do. And it seems certain that she'd turned against the National Trust.

'She despises the National Trust,' one local gossip said in

explanation. Nearby Moreton-in-Marsh was a hotbed of people who agreed.

The reasons Mrs Clutton-Brock had for suddenly taking against the National Trust were partly the reflection of a capricious temperament; but partly she appears to have been reacting against the smugness, complacency and amateurish fumbling of the National Trust.

A year before, because they felt so anxious about the condition of the house, a heritage pow-wow had taken place. Among the chiefs attending were Lord Charteris, as head of the National Heritage Memorial Fund, Dame Jennifer Jenkins, chairman of the owner-to-be the National Trust, Lord Montagu, chairman of English Heritage. There were delays in arranging a meeting with Chastleton's owner, and Julian Prideaux, the Trust's chief agent, decided to help out and 'pop in' when he was in the neighbourhood. He chose to appear unannounced at her door on both Christmas Eve and New Year's Day. Mrs Clutton-Brock was not inclined to forgive such impudence.

He meant well, of course. But Julian Prideaux would not have turned up – uninvited and on Christmas Eve – at the door of Lord Aberconway, for instance, or of the Duchess of Devonshire, or of Lord Gibson the Trust's former chairman, come to that. He'd have known, no question about it, that this was rude. A grandee of course might have appeared not to notice. Mrs Clutton-Brock not only noticed, she rang her estate agent.

Well, Chastleton had fans in high places – among them Lord Charteris at the NHMF. And the NHMF did the negotiating with Mrs Clutton-Brock's agent. Months went by. As fate had it, there was a grave worldwide recession, and few people with the millions required were spending their money on a stately home with no land, severe restrictions on alterations and a future repairs bill that would be colossal.

The money for the house and contents was eventually 'found'. With a £4 million contribution from the NHMF, Chastleton House became a property of the NT in 1991 and an appeal was launched to raise some of the money needed to endow it.

A five-year restoration project was begun within the year, the impossible-to-achieve object of which was to make Chastleton House appear as if nothing had been done to it. The decay of Chastleton had become part of its beauty; to 'save it' that would be destroyed.

Most of the above will not appear in its guidebook. Chastleton House will simply be one more heroic rescue; one more treasure preserved for the nation. Also absent from the guidebook will be this:

The eminent Alan Clutton-Brock, last in his family to be owner of Chastleton House, was a drunkard: a fall-down, under-the-table alcoholic. This is not only a bit of gossip. It has pertinence too.

Chastleton became the property of the National Trust in 1991. But almost as soon as this was publicly announced – before the endless meetings about how it was to be restored had begun, before the scaffolding went up and the furniture was moved out – a relatively minor burglary took place. Some Edwardian dresses, miscellaneous this and that. There was insurance to cover the loss. With the £17,000 the National Trust received, Martin Drury, its historic buildings secretary and deputy director general went in search of the Jacobite glasses which were well known to have been part of the contents of the house for centuries. (The contents of Chastleton had been photographed and written about in *Country Life* as early as 1919; the original seventeenth-century inventory of the house was still in it.)

Drury tracked down the man who had bought four of the glasses and one decanter, when ten of them along with a second decanter had been auctioned at Sotheby's in the early 1960s. The man who had kept them safely in a cupboard all this time eventually agreed to part with them. The cost to the Trust was very near the £17,000 in insurance money Drury had gone shopping with.

Visitors to Chastleton House will see these four prized mid-eighteenth-century glasses and decanter. They are aesthetically and historically precious. Each is decorated with a rose and an oak tree and a motto in Latin praying that Bonnie Prince Charlie shall soon be returned; they are rare examples of Jacobite glass surviving in the house for which it was bought.

'Imagine living in such an extraordinary place,' people will think when they visit Chastleton. 'Imagine the days when they had such splendid things to drink from.'

Alan Clutton-Brock did more than imagine: he drank from – and broke – them. Though no Jacobite glassware was in Chastleton House when the National Trust acquired it, there had been a considerable amount more, not so many, many years before.

In 1962 when Alan Clutton-Brock, in order to try and raise some money, decided to sell the two decanters and ten glasses, he'd also taken a posset cup, when he set off for Sotheby's from Chastleton. This dainty seventeenth-century glass cup had been further embellished with glass squiggles and curlicues – 'the glass equivalent of slipware', as Martin Drury describes it. Like some Venetian glass in its way. On his arrival at Sotheby's, the items were unwrapped. The posset cup was in smithereens. The nonchalant Mr Clutton-Brock hadn't done much to protect it for the journey. But there was more to the story.

The successful bidder on the lot that thirty years later was sold to the National Trust saw that there was no stopper to his Jacobite decanter. He got in touch with the vendor and Alan Clutton-Brock suggested that he come to Chastleton and have a rummage round.

When the man arrived, Alan Clutton-Brock was so drunk he couldn't get up out of his chair. He waved towards a box and told his visitor to have a look. In the box was a mound of old glass; it was filled with stoppers to yet more Jacobean decanters.

Night after night, those who saw him at Chastleton recall, Alan Clutton-Brock sat in a chair and drank. When he drew himself up and stumbled off, any glass that happened to be in his hand might crash to the floor and shatter.

One after another, these rare glasses were destroyed. He didn't hesitate to reach for the next one. There was none of the bourgeois 'save the good glasses for company', nor more strangely, none of the aesthete's cherishing of the beauties of the past.

Alan Clutton-Brock was a man who never cut his fingernails unless he was pressed to do so by someone else. He just didn't care. Fingernails or rare Jacobite glass – he had neglected himself, the enchanting house he'd inherited and the treasures that were in it. It was all the same, and equally inconsequential to him.

This is not what the display of those four glasses and that single decanter will convey to those entering with their National Trust season tickets. A drunken negligent aesthete will not be part of the Chastleton House display.

Well, why should it be? It's hardly an attractive story. Don't people prefer the falsified version better? How can the National Trust know? Has it given people a choice?

When Hollywood favoured glamour in its most synthetic form, even tenements were made to look poignantly attractive. Kitchens might be humble; they were never shabby. No cockroach ever scurried up a wall; paint didn't peel or pipes drip. Every film had a happy ending. Is the National Trust so very different?

'Many of these houses look like Covent Garden stage sets,' says Lord St Levan, who does what he can to keep the Trust from overdoing things at St Michael's Mount where he lives. Or as Sir Roy Strong expresses it: 'They've become Upstairs/Downstairs crossed with Merchant Ivory.'

These houses are filled with real sixteenth-, seventeenth- and eighteenth-century furniture, carpets, tapestries, china of course – though not always bought for the particular mansion in which it is on display. Montacute, which is well furnished today, came to the Trust with nothing in it. Every year the National Trust pays more attention to historical accuracy. The whole operation is done at huge cost, and with such deliberation. But the veracity that its academics go for is so incredibly narrow. Say, for example, that an eighteenth-century mansion, lived in until 1974, then went to the NT, who prepared it for public viewing. It decided that the enormous kitchen would be among the open rooms. Very likely a battery of copper pots and pans would be part of the display; a fish kettle large enough for a fourteen-pound salmon included. It's difficult to think of a single case in which such a kitchen has an electric tea kettle on one of its counters. In most of the National Trust's country houses, the twentieth century never happened. The result has got to be a distortion, not to say a lie.

The natural look

'I'll tell you a story about Hardwick,' Lady Emma Tennant began. She was smiling mischievously.

'Instead of going to the seaside on bucket and spade holidays, we used to go to Hardwick when we were children.'

Young Emma and her brother were sent to this rather high-faluting substitute for Blackpool because it is where their great-grandmother Evelyn, Duchess of Devonshire, lived.

'A lot of people found her very austere and she was a daunting character.' Hardwick was incredibly cold, the kitchen was very far away. 'She didn't notice that sort of thing,' Emma Tenant said. The children obviously did. But they didn't mind because to them Evie, as she was called, was indulgent and they had a very good time.

On the walls of Hardwick are hung sixteenth- and seventeenth-century tapestries. Evie, 'one of Nature's curators', sat at one of the tables in the High Great Chamber and stitched away at mending them. But she wasn't academically minded.

'If something looked dingy,' Lady Emma remembers, 'she would say, "Come on. This looks a bit faded. Why don't you brighten it up?"'

In 1970 Hardwick Hall went to the National Trust when Emma's father Andrew Cavendish became the 11th Duke of Devonshire and was settling his bill for death duties. Since she later on became something of a figure on the committees of the Trust, she has occasionally led parties around it.

During one of these tours she started to feel unsettled. 'Have

I made it up?' she puzzled, 'or do I really remember putting orange paint on some fruit coming out of a cornucopia?'

While she was brooding about this, her Trust colleagues stopped in front of one of Hardwick's celebrated tapestries.

'Oh this is so beautifully preserved,' they were saying. 'Of course. It's never exposed to light.'

'There it was! The cornucopia that my brother and I had gone over with our paints!'

When the National Trust took over Hardwick they set about their form of tidying up.

'They've got a wonderful staff who look after it perfectly beautifully,' said Emma Tennant's mother, Deborah, Duchess of Devonshire, when we talked at Chatsworth.

'They've got the best teas, and the best of kitchens, and all that,' she continued. At Hardwick, 'the teas are in the Kitchen as they were in Granny's day. It's marvellous. But', she added, 'for myself I don't like what they've done with the decoration inside.'

It's hard to think of anybody who could play the part of a Duchess better than Deborah Devonshire. Blue-eyed, white-haired, good-looking, feet up on the table in front of the sofa and never for a second not in command, she wasn't willing to sound as if she were being critical of the National Trust even if her words were. 'That's a purely personal view,' she amended. 'I'm not really educated up to what they do. Because that's not my style. We all have our own style, don't we?'

In fact, the Trust doesn't have a style in that sense. They've got a strategy.

'I loved it when Andrew's granny was there and she had bits of things all over the place,' the Duchess continued. 'And a lot of Victorian furniture. Because Hardwick was always like a repository of things which were out of fashion here. All sorts of things were humped over to Hardwick to get rid of them. They were never sold.

'The National Trust has, according to their lights, put it back, you see, Elizabethan. So there's none of that clutter of peculiar things. There were some marvellous bits of furniture

[349]

there which you don't see any more. Because they're not Elizabethan and that's what the National Trust thought it should be.'

Until the National Trust got busy making Hardwick Hall authentic, it probably hadn't looked Elizabethan since the end of the reign of the first Elizabeth Regina.

'I think,' the Duchess went on, 'if they have a fault – which has to be squeezed out of me because I think what the National Trust do is quite wonderful – I think they are bound by their very being to freeze a house. They're terribly shackled in that way, I consider. Hardwick is frozen in an Elizabethan time.'

It is the policy of Gervase Jackson-Stops, the architectural adviser to the National Trust, that all the state rooms in its houses should be formally presented. The grand rooms should be as they were when originally decorated, all ready for the ambassador or a ball.

'But what about the other rooms?' I asked as we talked in his office at Queen Anne's Gate.

He looked puzzled. Other rooms? Were there other rooms? Plenty, I prompted.

Oh, dairies? laundries? Was that what I meant?

It took a few minutes for Gervase Jackson-Stops to grasp what I had in mind – dining rooms, bedrooms. Not all its big houses are palaces, not every room designed for a state occasion, even when built, though it took a few minutes more before he seemed prepared to concede even this.

I got the feeling that the State Rooms of its mansions might be all that interested Gervase Jackson-Stops and the notion that they had changed over the years as families' lives had changed in them, was something that interested him perhaps only academically. From the point of view of the presentation of the house this was apparently inconsequential, beside the point.

'Think of Calke Abbey,' I said, bringing up the subject of the house the Trust described as 'the place where time stood still', when in the middle 1980s it waged a successful campaign to save it for the nation. In the case of Calke, an eighty-room Derbyshire mansion, this was because for generations the Harpur-Crewes accumulated possessions and no one ever threw anything out. When the house was electrified in 1962, more than fifty of the oil lamps were put in the butler's pantry, just in case. It was this accumulation of possessions from walking sticks to stuffed birds and tin soldiers that made its atmosphere so evocative. I was fortunate to see it after the Trust became its owner in 1985 but before the restoration began. Although, during its four-year-long restoration, the NT had made great efforts to keep Calke as it had been, in fact what they did was leave the cobwebs in the front hall but tastefully tidy up the clutter. 'The magic is gone,' I said.

'No it is not!' Gervase Jackson-Stops retorted. He became fierce in his defence of what the Trust has done at Calke. But he can insist all he wants, the evidence of the way the Harpur-Crewe's lived at Calke has vanished and the magic of the atmosphere went with it. Today Calke Abbey looks like a big, undistinguished house filled with not very remarkable objects which are being very well looked after. The 750-acre park however remains magnificent; its loveliness has not gone.

Lord Scarsdale positively bellows when he starts on the subject of the National Trust and its art history academics.

'Were they alive in the eighteenth century? I wasn't! They say, "Well that's what would have happened. It's known." So then I say, "How do you know that my family weren't an exception?" Plasterers and carvers may have worked to a pattern book, but when they moved into a house, people didn't live by pattern books too.

'What's so sacrosanct about 1766?' Francis Scarsdale would like to know. 'Should we all go around in knee breeches? Take all the wiring out and have only candles?'

In the process of returning them to their stark formality, so much furniture was removed from the state rooms at Kedleston Hall that Lady Scarsdale says, 'Our friends thought we are flogging it!'

In an effort to try to make the Scarsdales happier, to try to 'warm things up a bit', Simon Murray, the historic buildings representative who looks after Kedleston, had an inspiration: a violin case was put on the Music Room floor and opened; across it a fringed white silk scarf was draped.

Presumably this was would give the impression that only a second ago the violinist had rushed in, put down his things but before he'd had a chance to start playing he'd dashed out again: to kiss milady's hand – or blow his nose.

'How silly can you get?' Lord Scarsdale asked.

Lady Trevelyan had similar comments about what the National Trust had done at Wallington; and it was never built as a show place but was a family house from the start. The last Trevelyans to occupy it were a rambunctious lot, or as Helen Trevelyan puts it, 'It was a very natural house.' Catriona, George and Helen's little girl, used to ride her rocking-horse in the Great Hall, the one that Ruskin decorated in part. 'Everyone was very untidy,' Lady Trevelyan recalls. She contributed to this when the runners of the rocking-horse on which little Catriona was riding ripped into one of the painted piers of the Central Hall.

The National Trust duly tidied up at Wallington. And once it had, it set about trying to re-introduce naturalness.

'Spectacles were put down in the library on the chair, as if Sir Charles had just got up,' Lady Trevelyan chuckles. 'And in the bedrooms, the pillows were all dented as if they'd just left it. It's ridiculous.'

In his astute, highly charged and otherwise rewarding 1909 book, *On the Making of Gardens*, Sir George Sitwell wrote: 'The utmost extreme to which artificiality can go is the mock natural.'[3] Maybe the National Trust could put this on a tea towel and give one to everybody on its historic buildings staff, and to the authors of its guidebooks.

'The rich are different from you and me,' F. Scott Fitzgerald famously wrote. He himself, of course, provided a terrible example of what can happen when a person persists in believing that their lives are better than ours and that they alone are exempt from the dictum that everything has its price. Yet isn't this the message communicated by National Trust Productions?

The donors of the National Trust's great houses are portrayed not only as people who were richer and more privileged in everything from their schooling to the stuff of their clothes; not only exposed at an early age to pictures and books and great swathes of countryside to roam in and people who would help them get on when they grew up, but they are portrayed as happier too, less complicated and more protected from distress.

It's not evil of the National Trust to give people the illusion that money and privilege really did bring a better life in every way before nasty old taxation threatened to take most of it from them, but it is surely a kind of romantic corruption.

Life in these often fabulously luxurious and sometimes exquisitely lovely houses was not all hunt balls, lavish dinners and weekend house parties at which Nancy Mitford wickedly teased her fellow guests, or a prime minister got to know an up-and-coming young MP of his party. And I don't just mean that there were usually too few bathrooms and that often it was hideously cold.

Like the decorations and the landscaping, the loneliness in these houses seems to have been on a grand scale too. Maybe most routinely – if misery is ever routine – for the children who were brought up in them. Yet when these houses are opened to the public, the artifacts of childhood – toys and games, a nursery above all – are artfully displayed, and for the rest of us they appear as emblems of the sugar-coated childhood enjoyed by those more privileged than ourselves.

To begin at the beginning, with the very first house that came to the National Trust through its country house scheme: Wightwick Manor outside Wolverhampton in the Midlands.

Mother Goose

Sir Geoffrey Mander had three children with his first wife Florence whom he married in 1905. In 1929 he married Rosalie, twenty-five years his junior, and they had a son and then a baby girl. Anthea, the youngest in the family, was born during the Second World War when Sir Geoffrey was in his early sixties; Wightwick Manor where she grew up had been the property of the National Trust since 1937.

'I thought everybody had people going around their house twice a week,' says Anthea Mander Lahr. And her father, she reports, really felt that once he gave Wightwick, it actually belonged to the nation. When the doorbell rang, they took it in turns to show people around, and if somebody asked Sir Geoffrey about where in the house he lived, he'd even take the person upstairs to have a look at the bedrooms.

Hospitable, funny, highly strung and tiny, Anthea, as she is happy to have me call her, has an upper-class accent and her parents' left-wing point of view. Her extreme thinness also seems to run the family. When at Oxford, her mother, who came from a family that was not well-off, was pleased to be so thin, her daughter says, because she was able to make herself skirts from only a single length of cloth.

As Anthea Mander told this story, she seemed proud of her mother. During our meeting it seemed to be the only memory of her mother Rosalie which she found pleasant.

No. There was one other: to celebrate the hundredth anniversary of the house, the National Trust wanted to throw a party at Wightwick.

'They wanted to have Lord this and Lord that at the reception,' Anthea Mander Lahr reports. 'But my mother, oddly enough, was very good. She completely said "No! Those people have never taken one bit of interest in Wightwick. We're having a party for the guides."'

Relations between Anthea and her mother were poor; Lady Mander's relations with the owner of Wightwick's freehold seem to have been only marginally better. Rosalie Mander collected Pre-Raphaelite paintings and wrote on the subject. She felt she knew and cared more about Wightwick's contents than the Trust's people did – with one or two exceptions.

'One day my father came into the library and found this man with his head in my mother's lap,' Anthea recalls. The chap was one of the Trust's 'artistic representatives'. Sir Geoffrey Mander did not go into a jealous rage.

The Trust's bureaucracy grew and Lady Mander's affection for her landlord decreased more or less in tandem. She left the National Trust £5 in her will, in case they had not previously got her message.

One veteran volunteer guide at Wightwick who first arrived during the time Lady Mander was in residence says that she was a kind woman and generous. Other volunteers agree. None of them held it against her that when she invited them for tea they weren't given cakes and got her favourite burnt toast instead. 'But she was always Lady Mander,' this long-time guide added. 'The only time I saw her as a human being was once when she was in the kitchen talking to Anthea who had come to visit. Then the front was gone.' Lady Mander's vulnerability to her daughter had melted it away.

There never was an end to the friction between mother and daughter. Sir Geoffrey Mander died in 1962, Anthea, who was a teenager, left home. After that she persuaded herself to go back to visit her mother at Wightwick about once every eighteen months or so.

Yet in a way the story has a happy ending – though to call it a posthumous reconciliation would be going too far.

Wightwick Reoccupied

'My mother would say, "You see, Anthea isn't in the least bit interested in Wightwick."' And her mother was right. But to everyone's surprise including perhaps her own, from the August day in 1988 when she received a call to say that Lady Mander had been taken to hospital in a coma, Anthea Mander Lahr became fervently possessive.

The very next day she was on the phone to the National Trust.

'I rang them up and said, "Right. What are we going to do about Wightwick now?"

'They said, "Well ummm . . . your mother isn't dead yet."

'I said, "No, but she's going to be. They say she's not going to recover. We've got to start now."'

'Live, live with me, and thou shalt see; The pleasures I'll prepare for thee . . .' These lines from Herrick's 'To Phyllis' are carved into the gables at Wightwick Manor. Anthea Mander Lahr with predatory practicality set out to make them applicable at last.

Her brother, an alcoholic, had already died. Anthea, as Lady Mander's only remaining child, took charge. Her interest was focused on one thing: she wanted to make sure that there wouldn't be any dispute about what was going to happen to Wightwick. She rushed down to see the National Trust's lawyer.

'He said pious things, like "You know, it's a bit premature, your mother . . ."'

Anthea wasn't having any of the Trust's fastidiousness, nor their well-known torpor.

'Don't be stupid,' she retorted. 'You've got to get this settled.' By 'this' she meant the arrangements governing the tenancy of Wightwick. And she was in a position to get them moving. Her legacy was rather larger than the National Trust's proved to be.

According to his memorandum of wishes, Sir Geoffrey was able to live on at Wightwick and his widow after him. On her death a member of the family would inherit that privilege – and the money from a Trust fund he created. Anthea assumed that the fund probably held something like £25,000. It proved to contain almost three-quarters of a million pounds.

She says she wasn't interested in the money. From the way she lives as well as the way she talks, she probably wasn't. But money buys more than clothes and jewels and fast cars. It is well known that without parting with a penny, the possessor of a large bank account can purchase quite a lot of clout. And it was to gain leverage that Sir Geoffrey's daughter was as interested in the £700,000 as any lover of diamonds could have been.

Anthea was determined to become Wightwick's next tenant. Her own child, Christopher, who was then entering his teens, would become the logical person eventually to succeed her in the house that had been home to her father and his father before him. Christopher is quite well endowed on the paternal front also. The son of John, a fine biographer and theatre critic, his grandfather Bert Lahr was the wonderful rubber-faced American vaudevillian and actor, most famous now for playing the part of the cowardly Lion in *The Wizard of Oz.*

'I told them that they had to settle everything before the memorial service on 17 January in 1989,' Anthea reports. She didn't want to leave time for other claimants to start making complications.

'I rushed it through. I really held a gun to their heads.'

What she rushed through was the adoption of this proposal: with some of the £700,000 a flat would be created upstairs in the house. She would have the right to stay in it and so would the rest of the family, as well as friends and people connected with the Trust. The interest from that £700,000 would also pay for improvements to Wightwick Manor and its grounds. On the day of the memorial service for Lady Mander, anyone who asked about the future plans for Wightwick Manor was told of the new arrangement which was now in place.

Anthea Mander Lahr, the new man in her life, and her son frequently stay in the flat that NT made. And with all the money it now had to spend on restoration, the National Trust began working on opening more rooms for visitors to see at Wightwick Manor. Both its day and night nurseries were refurbished.

'Other people go round and ooh and ahh,' when they visit the nurseries at Wightwick,' says Anthea. 'They like them and that's fine.' But when she goes to stay at Wightwick and acts as a guide during its opening hours, which she routinely does, 'I sit in the library, I won't go into the nurseries. Somebody else can do that. I can see that other people enjoy it. That's enough. Don't ask me to.'

She explained that while the restoration and presenting to the public of a house like Wightwick Manor is 'an artistic exercise with no emotional content', for the historic buildings representative, she found it unnerving when they got to work on the nurseries. 'In many cases, they are putting a room back to a time which is very painful.'

The day and night nurseries had always before been in that small part of the house which was completely private. These rooms had been her home all the years she had lived at Wightwick.

In 1992 she wrote an article in the magazine[4] that goes out to all National Trust members, about growing up in the nurseries. (By that time they had been refurbished and opened to the public.) It was more personal than what normally finds its way into the Trust's literature, more revealing, and a great deal more unsettling. Her tone was cool, but there was passion in her words and what they portrayed.

The atmosphere of the place sounds familiar – life at Wightwick seems to have been very like that at Wallington when it came to such things as temperature and cuisine; the former frigid, the latter revolting.

Wightwick which had been so advanced at the time it was built that it had central heating – and in the servants' wing too – never had the heating system turned on while she lived there, with the exception that, on days when the house was open to the public, the rooms they viewed were given just enough to take the chill off.

Eggs and baked beans seemed to have been the main feature of the meagre, monotonous diet served in the nursery. This wasn't because her parents felt children didn't deserve anything better or wouldn't enjoy variety. Sir Geoffrey and Lady Mander had exactly the same food at their table downstairs. 'Nothing like the menu the Trust has in the dining room now!' Anthea crows.

'No wonder,' she wrote in her piece for the NT magazine, 'that so many of the children from these nurseries found drink more palatable and comforting.'

In her written recollections, Anthea is often alert to psychological meanings, communicated in her dispassionate way. But then, suddenly, her observations crackle with an uninsulated and unmediated electric charge – direct from the generator, as it were. For instance, when purportedly she's only trying to get across the information that the nurseries were filled with the accumulated possessions of decades, what she writes is: 'The family discarded people but not things.'

'Emotions were swept under the linoleum,' she continues. As were facts to which, unavoidably, emotion might have attached themselves. So it was from an entry in a newspaper's diary that she found out Sir Geoffrey Mander, *her father*, was dying. And she adds, 'I found out that I had another brother and two sisters by seeing a letter.' (Were these children of Sir Geoffrey and Florence among the discarded people to whom she'd earlier referred?)

Visitors to Wightwick enjoy the nurseries. The rooms are like delightful illustrations from old-fashioned story books, only better because they are real. And like the drawing rooms of stately homes with their carvings by Grinling Gibbons and their Robert Adam furniture, the day and night nurseries at Wightwick are filled with pint-sized treasures. There are wicker chairs and tea sets for tots; picture tiles illustrate the days of the week; Snow White lives on the curtains and a cut-out, painted wooden terrier is guardian of the book cases. There is Teddy of course, and a William Morris rendition of Brer Rabbit, a tale Sir Geoffrey had a weakness for. He saw it an allegory 'of slavery and its opposite, Socialism', his daughter says.

And what was her childhood behind those curtains an allegory for?

'The golden age of the nurseries has now come,' Anthea wrote in the NT magazine, concluding her account of her life in the day and night nurseries of Wightwick. 'Through the enjoyment of visitors, their happier memories and their appreciation, these rooms are being transformed.'

Rubbish I'd felt when I first read those words. Double rubbish, I thought when I'd met their author. Anthea Mander Lahr makes it plain that she can't bear going into either one of the rooms because of the misery that still clings to their walls. As for the rest of us, what she calls the Golden Age of the nurseries is in fact the Golden Age of National Trust fabrication, juvenile division.

Croeso y Gymru[5]

Dame Jennifer Jenkins was chairman of the National Trust from 1986 to 1991. Serious, forceful, competent and of the type called no-nonsense, Dame Jennifer was from the decorous side of the left wing and solidly established. Not only had she previously headed the Consumers' Association, the Historic Buildings Council and the Ancient Monuments Society, she had been honoured for it; her husband Lord Jenkins had been chancellor of the exchequer, a founder of the Social Democratic Party and president of the European Community.

The old guard needn't feel too alarmed by the appointment of Dame Jennifer, while others could feel encouraged because she seemed to look out at a wider world. For example, it was Dame Jennifer who, not surprisingly, had the perspicacity to take the National Trust to Brussels and initiate its dealings with the EC. And unlike her post-war predecessors whose preoccupations were often aesthetic, Dame Jennifer seemed more concerned with the public and its use of properties. Predictably, to sanctify, as it were, this shift in emphasis, comparisons were made with Octavia Hill. 'It is tempting to think of a reincarnation,' said John Gaze's 1988 official NT history.[6]

When Cragside was offered, Dame Jennifer was not put off by the big ugly Victorian house in Northumberland, though many others were. The Duke of Grafton, for instance, took one look and said, 'I can't think what the Trust is coming to. This is Virginia Water, no better than that.'[7]

Perhaps. But Lord Armstrong for whom it was built had been an inventive engineer as well as a successful industrialist and Cragside's hydro-electric and hydraulic machinery (as well as its 1,000-acre park) were bound to make it appealing to visitors. And Dame Jennifer on that account thought it was a good thing. So it has proved to be. More than 80,000 people visit Cragside House and Country Park each year.

Many of the staff who worked with her seem to have thought Dame Jennifer herself to be a good thing. And like Lord Armstrong she too was something of an engineer; though more in the social than the mechanical department.

In 1989, the National Trust paid £400,000 for a row of terraced houses in the hamlet of Cwmdu in Dyfed, Wales. This was almost 'home territory' for her, Roy Jenkins being the son of a Welsh coal-miner. She, presumably, knew first hand how greatly local people feared the break-up of their villages and wanted to do something about it.

For local people there was a great temptation to make a substantial profit and move out. The same has been true in the Lake District and other beauty spots. The attractiveness of the landscape and the lack of economic vigour in the communities are the climatic conditions that set a familiar tornado whirling.

A house goes on the market; local people can't pay the asking price which has been driven up by outside demand. More outsiders move in; the area becomes gentrified and even more attractive to others who live elsewhere. Prices rise still higher, making the temptation for locals to sell at yet greater prices, and the spiral continues until no one native to the place is left.

This has been happening all over Britain. On the south coast of Dorset, for example, 'you can rent a farm for half, a quarter, the cost of renting just the farmhouse,' says George Elliott, the warden on the Trust's Golden Cap estate there.

In a Welsh-speaking hamlet like Cwmdu, the high price of housing meant not only the exodus of local people but the end to the cohesiveness that had allowed their language and culture to survive.

'It worries us to see the way things are changing in Wales,' Richard Keen, the Trust's historic buildings representative at the time said. 'This project is a measure of our concern.'

But wasn't the National Trust chairman's acquisition of cottages in Cwmdu the Fabian equivalent of that Hameau a French queen had made for herself at Versailles?

While it's nice to think that the grocery will continue to sell tea bags and the post office stamps in Cwmdu, the hamlet isn't exactly a place of historic nor aesthetic importance. And £400,000 is quite a lot of money for a charity to spend in order, in effect to take out an advertisement alerting the British people to the dangers of gentrification.

Why should the National Trust not be thinking next of buying up the centre of say, Bury St Edmunds in Suffolk or Ludlow in Shropshire or Evesham in Gloucestershire? All of them are charming, still functioning market towns. Such purchases would show the National Trust's 'concern' for the way they are being threatened by superstores on their outskirts. The Trust's members would then get free admission to a genuine local butcher and a cobbler who still mends shoes by hand. Would the Golden Age of market-town life be added to the Golden Age of nurseries and State Rooms in the artificial world the National Trust is so ambitiously creating? Where is it going to end – certainly not with a row of terraced houses in Wales.

'In the old days,' says Laurence Harwood, formerly regional director in the Lake District, 'you could get quite a good return for your farm, and in return the farmer managed it, looked after the landscape moderately well – if he was kept an eye on by the land agent. So we had the farm, some income, put some capital in here and there. But the actual business of maintaining the landscape was worth while for the farmer because he had as a product something that was valuable.'

And today?

I put the question to Victor Brownlee, the Trust's tenant at Stonethwaite, and his wife (See Chapter 9). Mrs Brownlee runs a Bed & Breakfast as do many other wives of National Trust farm tenants in the Lakes. She is an intelligent woman with a mind of her own and doesn't shirk from speaking it.

'They're doing a good job with the farmland, with the walls and fencing,' Mrs B. says of their landlord. 'And they've tried various ways for the wool and the meat. They've investigated the avenues. But I've said to Victor, "If a manufacturer was producing something that nobody wanted, they would have to go out of business." If Herdwick sheep wool isn't the product the general public wants,' she continued, 'what do you do? You can't force people to want it. However hard the marketing is.'

Mr Brownlee wasn't hearing this for the first time. And as far as he was concerned he had an unanswerable reply. 'We couldn't change over to another breed,' he explains. 'It's so wet on the tops of the fells and there's so little to eat. It's only the Herdwick we can have on there.'

The farmers as well as the National Trust are trying to see if a market can be created for Herdwick chops. The Trust is already involved with those manufacturing Herdwick-it-never-wears-out-carpet. But it seems probable that unless there is a drastic change, what will be needed to continue sustaining these fell communities is subsidies. Whatever the lingo – setaside, Sites of Special Scientific Interest, Environmentally Sensitive Areas – grants of this kind are the only answer for the moment. And that means tax-payers' money. Both the Brownlees are aware that other working people may come to see the farmers as petitioners for an unending hand-out.

'The general public has to be made aware that it has to be a social thing,' says Mrs Brownlee, 'rather than the farmers up in the Lake District having their living handed to them. The attitudes would have to change, wouldn't they?'

The farmers have had to change theirs. 'I think we realize, we all do,' says Victor Brownlee, 'that to a certain extent we're here to keep the area as it is – if that's what the general public require.' For a farmer to shift from thinking always in terms of productivity, this is a major alteration in outlook. The public's thinking will have to change at least as much.

If visitors want to find the landscape as it now is when they go to the Lake District, then Herdwicks will have to continue grazing on the fell tops and tax money may have to pay for it (along with subscriptions to the National Trust). And even then there is reason to think this may not be possible.

The fell valleys as working communities are already well into decline. In many hamlets the houses have been sold to off-comers and sit empty half the year, only to open during holiday times. Chris Bland and Bobby Cubby work hard trying to raise the sum of almost £10,000 needed to keep the school open in Borrowdale so that their children can be educated in the valley and not bused to Keswick. Vic Greg, in Langdale, says that only one of the six houses that form a row at the base of the village is now actually lived in fulltime. The school he went to has only a third of the pupils now that it had in the late 1920s when he was a pupil. It wouldn't even have that many if the Great and Little Langdale schools hadn't combined.

Vic Greg looks back and says, 'My wife and I when we were in our twenties and were coming down to dances in the village here, we knew that if we got to the bottom of the lane about half past seven or a quarter to eight, there'd be the whole gang coming down on their bikes. We'd all go together and many times go home together. Fourteen or fifteen of us. Now if there was a dance in the village, there'd be nobody there. It's sad.'

This decline affects more than hill farmers. It applies at least equally to the farms on the big estates which the National Trust began to acquire when it introduced its Country Houses Scheme. The income from farms, which once went to support the life of men like Sir Charles Trevelyan and Sir Richard

Acland, was to pay the upkeep of their houses when they went to the National Trust. But in all but a few cases it doesn't.

Sir Francis Dashwood is one of many landowners who believes that the grave agricultural depression that began in 1875 and lasted for decades has recurred. 'I see it all happening again,' he says. If this is true the consequences can be expected to be of more than local interest. They were before.

When England's nineteenth-century agricultural depression occurred as a result of poor harvests and competition from the opening of America's prairies to 'mass producing' grain, the result was the 'overthrow of the British landed aristocracy', according to G.M. Trevelyan. Indeed by the 1930s very few large estates were as in as sound financial shape as was his brother's at Wallington. To him the far worse effect of this depression was that it destroyed the intimate relationship between Englishmen and nature which for so long had formed the national character. Another such depression threatens the relationship between the English and their landscape. Without farmers the countryside would change dramatically.

Certainly the National Trust has become aware of the problem. Though perhaps it is not taking as large a view of the potential for disaster as it might. Lord Chorley for example wonders if, in future, the Trust will have to demand an endowment before it agrees to accept a farm – an endowment in stocks and shares. Just as it does when large houses are offered. He fears the answer is yes. And if so, the taking-on of farms by the National Trust, like the accepting of grand houses, may have come as close as it can to crossing the finishing line without actually officially doing so.

The fate of the farms it already owns remains in doubt.

'It may not be long before mountain sheep are valued as park-keepers rather than as producers of mutton and wool!' Cubby Acland said decades ago. Today Laurence Harwood puts it like this:

'I can foresee a situation,' he says, 'where we put our own people into farms; almost our own wardens and pay them a wage. They might have a certain number of stock but the rest of the time they would be holding it together, maintaining the infrastructure – as if they were park managers or park keepers. It would be sad,' he reflects. 'The individuality of the places would be lost.'

It would certainly be very sad. And it is already happening.

Small farms have been put together to make larger, more economic, ones. The redundant farmhouses become available for staff or as rentals to local people or as holiday lets. In Beatrix Potter's village, Near Sawrey, half the houses – including her own – belong to the National Trust. This has successfully prevented Near Sawrey from becoming a fiesta for Pottermaniacs. But the village has the feel of a place that's been injected with formaldehyde.

'I love the National Trust,' James Lees-Milne had told me. And then, with a plaintive smile, he added: 'It's an awful thing to be saying about something one's worked for all one's life, but it's the kiss of death, really. Isn't it?'

Surely the National Trust was not founded to preserve the landscape and historically or aesthetically important buildings from destruction only to turn everything it touches – farms, villages, country houses – into a stage set, a romance, a cadaver or a museum?

AN EDWARDIAN REGATTA

Sir Francis Dashwood, and the National Trust, invited the public to a fund-raising Fête Champêtre at West Wycombe Park. There was a choice of three July nights; the first of them proved to be very cold for July and raining. Nevertheless the fields near the gate to the estate were packed with cars.

The lawn between the swan-shaped lake and the Palladian mansion was crowded with people, many of them in Edwardian costume, others in whatever sort of fancy dress appealed to them more. Uniforms had been unpacked and aired; the wrinkles shaken out of Granny's evening dress. There were old people and children, though most of the guests seemed to be between thirty and fifty.

The veteran picnickers came with plastic rain shelters and poles to keep them aloft. Obviously there were people who'd arranged to come with groups of friends; some had set up proper tables inside their tents with candlesticks and champagne flutes. There was even a public school version of a lager lout, dressed in a loud black and white striped jacket and possessed of a voice louder still, who hooted out his comments on other people's clothes as they passed by.

The idea was to have a good time and people seemed to be enjoying themselves. Imagination and effort had gone into helping them do so.

A trad jazz dance band played on the terrace. (Sir Francis, on trumpet, had a band at Eton.) A tight-rope walker, dressed in a jersey covered in colourful diamond shapes, like a Commedia dell'arte character, swayed his way back and forth between two poles set up near the house. A man on stilts walked through the crowd; a jester dressed as a tramp shuffled up to revellers and joked.

At about ten o'clock, when most people had finished eating, the entertainment reached its most ambitious stage. From a powerful sound system set up near the lakeshore in a tent of its own, came the score of an operetta. No one could have missed hearing it however strong the wind.

In the distance there was much rushing about as a couple of dozen children, some of them dressed as pirates, carried on. It didn't take too long to realize that these boys and girls were not doing the actual singing. The voices came from the sound tent. Their turn finished, two gondolas appeared on the lake. Two tenors and a soprano emoted their song, courtesy of the sound tent again. This was a very slick enterprise with none of the homeliness, humour or warmth there might have been if something less than the standard set by Placido Domingo had been attempted.

The audience was engaged and having a fine time, weather apart. And Commander Rawnsley would have been proud to see the wholehearted response of the public once these aristocratic preserves became more welcoming. Though about the next phase of the entertainment he may have been more doubtful – for all its embodiment of the fête's nautical theme.

Over the loudspeakers came a man's voice with the news: 'Sir Francis and Lady Dashwood will be arriving from around the bend of the lake.'

In the far distance a spotlight played on the otherwise inky water. Elgar's *Pomp and Circumstance* exploded from the music tent. Tension was given time to build.

Finally, and very, very slowly, a yacht could be seen. It was soon obvious that in fact this was not an Edwardian yacht at all but, literally, stage craft. Like Sir Francis's most recent proud possession – the gigantic equestrian statue high up on a hill which was made of fibreglass and came to him from Pinewood Studios in exchange for a case of champagne – a dinghy had been transformed to create an effect.

Sir Francis in splendid uniform, his svelte Lady in a large feathered hat and long flowing gown, stood on the forward deck. Edward VII and Queen Alexandra: they stood motionless and together, like decorations on a waterborne wedding cake.

Elgar played, the dinghy/yacht slowly headed to a bit of shore where a ramp was waiting to allow them to disembark gracefully.

Had Sir Francis and Lady Dashwood not taken in that even today's Royal family could not get away with such a performance any more. Who did they think they were? And who did they think was sitting on the shore?

Most people weren't even looking at the Dashwoods as they stood with straight backs on the prow of their mock yacht. There was no applause as they went past. At least the couple forbore from handing out penny pieces to the boys and girls as they disembarked. They vanished into 'the finest Palladian Villa in England' as soon as the boat had docked.

'This is the real National Trust,' said Warren Davis, the press relations officer who's worked for the charity since the day when Commander Rawnsley had sent his balloon up at Saltram in Plymouth.

Did Davis mean the bizarre and blush-making, if heartfelt, charade performed by Sir Francis and his wife? Or all the middle-class men and women having such a fine time in the extravagant park the aristocratic Dashwoods had made hundreds of years earlier and the current Dashwood was keeping up, for the benefit of himself of course, but also for the nation? I like parties and picnics myself. But the real National Trust?

Every bit as much as the use of the gauzy filter as an aid to selective forgetting and the carefully mixed, well-researched, high-quality embalming fluids, ambiguity of just this kind is routinely employed backstage at NT Productions. And really it's all in a good cause, isn't it? This was a fund-raising event, wasn't it?

The Edwardian Regatta at West Wycombe Park raised £2,000 for the National Trust. 'The weather wasn't kind to us,' said the Thames & Chilterns Regional public relations officer.

Juggernaut

'Jekyll remains unaware of Hyde's existence,' Robin Fedden, the Trust's deputy director general wrote in 1968. The government's relationship to the countryside is what he had in mind and he observed that while it showed 'increasing concern for the preservation of open spaces many of their undertakings are calculated to destroy them'.[1] Since 1968, both Dr Jekyll and Mr Hyde have expanded their territory.

Today everybody is crazy about the environment; there's not a politician who would campaign against preservation of the landscape. But the Department of Transport . . .

I rang the DoT to ask about a planned 'upgrading' of the A35 which would cut through National Trust land, inalienably owned land, belonging to the nation. 'Hate the country; want more roads,' said the man on the other end chirpily.

Continuing my search for information about the route, I rang a Mr Mick Campbell, a spokesman for the DoT in Bristol. I was not disappointed. When pressed for details about the comparative cost to a driver using the already existing road and the proposed new one he cackled, 'It's not the Himalayas we're talking about you know!'

The bypass in question was in Dorset. The countryside it threatened was the National Trust's Golden Cap estate; and a stunning seven and a half miles of coastal land it happens to be. Thirty separate land purchases and gifts were pieced together to form this estate; the Golden Cap could not be a better illustration of Enterprise Neptune's success. It is part of a tradition that's been inspiring people since 1897 when the Trust acquired its first piece of coast.

Not far from the castle in Cornwall where it's alleged King Arthur lived is a headland called Barras Head. This cliff was bought with money raised by public subscription. It had 'thus become in a new and very real sense the Common Land of England', said Octavia Hill. 'It is the very first which has been, not given by one far-sighted and generous donor, but purchased by the combined help of many – rich and poor, near and far, American and English – giving each in their measure to buy a bit of England as the common playground, study, resting place, vantage ground for seeing the holy things of nature.'²

All this applies as well to the Golden Cap.

Its tawny, heaving cliffs, among them the highest one in southern England, the balding, ochre Golden Cap itself drop to the sea which looks positively Caribbean on a sunny day. There's even a touch of blue in it when it rains. Ponies graze on some fields, cows in others. Each beast chomps differently according to his species and this, in turn, encourages the regeneration of different kinds of wild vegetation. Hedgerows carve out the boundaries of half hidden farms, fields of yellow gorse are cut across by dark green shadows.

This is an undulating landscape. The tracks that cross the 2,000-acre estate hugging the sea to the south of the A35 rise steeply and then bucket down again. It is a long and narrow stretch of countryside – most of it is only about half a mile wide and some of it only a few yards across in places. But because the terrain is so varied and so lovely, because there's so much dipping down and climbing up again and because of its great salty silence, the Golden Cap estate seems a vast and private world as well as a majestic one.

There's even a twelfth-century chapel (with Elizabethan additions) high up on the Golden Cap cliff at the hamlet of St Gabriel's. Nearby is the now overgrown lane that once served as the main route for horse-drawn coaches travelling between Dorchester and Exeter. George Elliott, the coastal warden for the estate, has overseen its restoration. Still intact at the beginning of the twentieth-century, there were photographs to guide him. Elliott went to Exeter Cathedral to learn about the source of the stone that had been used in building the chapel and he found bits of its Gothic arched doorway in a nearby stream. George Elliott, dark-haired, bearded and middle-aged, could hardly put more of himself than he already does into bringing out the best of the Golden Cap.

Elliott lives with his wife Alison and their two sons down an unpaved road on a remote farm, with a view that sweeps across the fields out to sea. He is bright, good-humoured and committed: a loyal servant of the National Trust, but not slavishly so.

'The Trust has been going for a hundred years; it accumulates habits, not always the best of habits,' he says. Like many of the men who work directly on the land he is not afraid of speaking his mind. But he is well aware that, 'if anyone rocks the boat, he falls out'. There is, therefore, a certain amount of holding back. He is not planning to jump overboard.

Elliott says he 'wouldn't mind the money rangers earn'. And understandably; the *starting* salary for a Council ranger is a thousand pounds a year more than the £14,000 or thereabouts he earns as the Trust's head warden at the glorious Golden Cap. But he feels that, 'the Trust is too good an organization and its properties are too important to be down in the dumps'.

The normal routine of his job is demanding. In overseeing an estate that has a budget of more than £60,000 a year, he must look after the conservation of its insect life and the plants; there is a camp site and a base camp for volunteers. Then, too, because the Golden Cap is made up of so many small fields (the average size is six acres), there are more fences, stiles and gates to repair than there would be on an estate with fields of thirty acres or more. There's woodland too, ancient and replanted; and footpaths to maintain, as well as relations with the public and his employer, of course. But besides all this, George Elliott has become a master hedge-builder in order to be a better teacher for the volunteers who turn out to help replace the hedgerows. And he reconverted a farmhouse into four holiday cottages which are let almost every week all year round. He is not a National Trust staff member who is anti-commerce; the profit from these cottages goes back into the estate. There's the work he's done on the chapel at St Gabriel's of course and the experiments with grazing different kind of animals to see what results it has on improving the native fauna. He's led a team of volunteers rebuilding the stables and sheds on one of the estate's farms, demonstrating to the Trust just how much can be done by Acorn camp and YTS volunteers. Slides showing the work-in-progress are now used by the National Trust's head office to demonstrate the initiatives it takes in making use of young people's labour.

George Elliott, himself once a farm manager, worries about finding the right tenants when vacancies come up. There's no lack of applicants; what concerns him is the shortage of people with the dedication, the experience and enough money. During the property boom that followed the end of the last great agricultural depression, men of his age were priced out of the farm market. The pool of experienced farmers, therefore, is smaller than it might be. And the particular parcel he was anxious about when we met was suitable for about seventy-five cows while one would need twice that number to make the farm economic.

But with all his interests, his dedication, his studies and his keenness for the Golden Cap estate, one subject dominates George Elliott's talk and his thoughts: the Morecombelake bypass. It has been bedevilling him for a long time. From the first public announcement of the proposal in 1987 to the public enquiry alone took seven years. However the details are altered by events occurring after this account goes to press, the struggle over protecting the Golden Cap will remain illustrative of a devastating, widespread problem and the need to find a better solution to it than the National Trust has managed.

In 1987 the Department of Transport's original plan was to improve the existing A35 simply by bypassing the village of Chideock. Now the bypass it proposes will involve transforming the A35 into a dual carriageway on an embankment fifty feet high, with the steepest gradient the law allows.

'This is always the problem,' says David Bett, the Trust's

regional director for Wessex. 'Once the foot's in the door, the thing gets bigger.'

The Trust had anticipated that one day there might be such a danger to the Golden Cap and tried to head it off. Had the DoT kept to a modest proposal for a road to skirt the nearby village of Chideock, the charity's strategy would have worked.

'Some years ago, when acquiring land in the area,' Bett reports, the National Trust 'set aside a corridor of land close to the village which was not declared inalienable in order to accommodate the sort of bypass which was then in vogue. We'd taken that precaution; but the road scheme now being proposed couldn't possibly be accommodated within that land.'

As now drawn up, the three-and-a-half-mile stretch of road will cost the government £24 million – just to build. Added to that is whatever they have to pay out for compensation and purchases of land, enquiries and so on. But the cost to taxpayers will be immeasurably more – however many millions the scheme adds up to. And that amount will be added to by every generation, because the Morcombelake bypass will cause everlasting damage to the Golden Cap estate. The tranquillity of the Golden Cap would be lost; exchanged for a saving of seventeen minutes on the drive from Bournemouth to Exeter.

'It slices through our land,' George Elliott forthrightly says. 'It's going to be very visible from Morecombelake. But it's not just the visual impact,' he adds. Nor is it only the pollution and the smell of petrol and diesel fumes. 'It will also increase the speed of traffic and that will be heard on the estate.' Everywhere.

'They asked if we could win if we fought it,' George Elliot says of his bosses at the National Trust. 'I told them you've *got* to fight this. It's morally the only choice you've got.' To him this is not an example of rocking the boat, but of keeping it on course.

Were the Morecombelake bypass built, anyone walking the estate's twenty miles of footpaths would no longer feel alone with sound of the waves and the wind; a person sitting on a rock at the St Gabriel's chapel could no longer let himself drift back through time and imagine what life might have been like on the Golden Cap when it was built; a child would not be able to fancy she hears the sound of hooves as the Dorchester to Exeter coach approaches – all that will be overwhelmed by that hideous, unrelenting, mind-wearying, unvarying hum. A person might as well take a seat at the edge of the M25.

This of course is most certainly not a new problem. The danger to the countryside from those desiring to build more and more railways; the hopelessness of having to fight the battle anew each time there was another threat (as well as the pressures from developers) had led Hill, Hunter and Rawnsley to set up the National Trust in the first place. And the charity gained supporters when, later on, the hazard became motorized char-a-bancs, then even bigger coaches and cars.

'Since the full development of motor traffic and its consequences, the National Trust has come to be regarded by lovers of nature as an ark of refuge and a bulwark in the days of trouble,' G.M. Trevelyan wrote in 1929.[3] And he was right; many people did hope that the National Trust would save the countryside from being entirely sliced up by roads. But he certainly was wrong about motor traffic having reached its 'full development'.

Navigation of the ark has become a good deal more demanding, as a result. In fact it sometimes appears as if the ark is endlessly shooting the rapids.

There were about a million vehicles on Britain's roads in 1929. At the time of the public enquiry into the proposed Morecombelake bypass there were more than 20 million. By a curious coincidence, the land holdings of the National Trust have grown by much the same factor. There were 33,000 acres in 1929; there are 600,000 today. Tourism meanwhile has become one of Britain's major sources of income, contributing £30 billion to the Exchequer of which it is reckoned almost £200 million is spent at 'heritage sites'. Many of the 10 million people who pay to visit NT properties start their explorations from an NT car park (Pay & Display or otherwise).

Most school children know that more cars mean more roads; more roads attract more cars and so on. Nor is it only that new roads are required; old ones have to be made wider. Towns and villages like Chideock must be protected from all this traffic by bypasses. Because the National Trust is the largest private landowner in Britain, some of its property was bound to be in the path of all this motorized expansion. The kind of activity that led to its foundation is occurring all over again. And in spite of the Act of Parliament of 1907 – though it was drafted to protect its holdings from just this sort of attack – the National Trust's inalienable land no longer looks as secure as it should. In 1968, Robin Fedden was writing about road building as a threat to inalienability. That was the year the Trust went to Parliament to try and stop the A38, a six-lane carriageway, from cutting through its eighteenth park at Saltram in Devon. It badly fumbled the handling of its objections and lost.

The proposed dual carriageway circumventing the village of Chideock in Dorset and cutting across the Golden Cap estate at Morecombelake is 'is one of the road schemes that is causing us most concern at the moment', says Sir Angus Stirling. 'If it goes ahead as planned it will eat into that marvellous landscape.' The A35 bypass is not the only assault on the protection to the landscape provided by the National Trust. 'You've got so many – forty odd – situations at any one time of the Trust's inalienable land being affected by road schemes,' Lord Chorley reports.

'Nobody thought through the environmental consequences on a landscape at the outset before starting a road scheme,' says Sir Angus when commenting on the Department of Transport's approach. 'If they don't do that in the future, we are going to have this situation again and again.'

Forty or so such situations would seem to be more than enough already.

'You've got to become concerned with how the Department of Transport goes about preparing a particular scheme,' says Lord Chorley. 'You've got to talk to the transport secretary, too. We will try to get across the philosophy of them trying to get the environmental consideration built in right at the start of the process. Roads is a case where we are in a semi-campaigning mode because we're so directly affected.'

To be semi-campaigning is perhaps not unlike being a little

bit pregnant. Either you campaign if you want to win, or you don't.

In 1992 the Trust, which had chosen to be a non-campaigning organization for half a century, 'refined its strategy for responding to the threat of road schemes', according to the director general in that year's Annual Report. What this meant was that press conferences were called to announce the danger to various properties from proposed roads. In addition, the National Trust was going to provide 'a training programme for management staff faced with threats of roads', and the chairman and director general were going to meet ministers and officials of the DoT. Four times that year a Roads Advisory Group gave 'expert advice at a national level'. It was chaired by Ian Kennaway, previously the regional director for North Wales and then the NT's director of regions (a new, let's get coordinated, management position).

Sir Angus and Lord Chorley went on talking to ministers. Further press conferences were called. The Roads Advisory Group held its meetings. Ian Wilson, the Trust's policy research coordinator, extended his responsibilites to include roads. 'What are the objectives of a transport strategy?' he asks. His answer is that the National Trust can develop one 'academically, here in-house without being a campaigning organization'. But if it adopts an academic stance who is going to pay any attention to its 'strategy'?

Talk about priorities . . . The National Trust was taking the programme for its Centenary a lot more seriously than the threat to its properties from roads. Staff were mobilized from end to end of its empire planning events that would celebrate this great anniversary and help raise money. A special team was gathered and given office space; a new member of staff hired to oversee all the activity. All this was both understandable and even, in a general sort of way, sympathetic.

But why was no one hired to devise an 'inalienability strategy' for the National Trust, to coordinate the battle against threats to its properties from road schemes? Why was no one on the staff creating a programme to educate the Trust's members and the larger public about the piecemeal assault

[377]

on the landscape which people, wrongly it seems, assumed was safe?

Think what the National Trust has been able to accomplish since 1987, when Angus Stirling took the initiative and decided it was time for the charity to change its attitude towards the education of young people. There had always been people connected with the Trust who behaved as if children didn't exist – or shouldn't; that they were best ignored if adults insisted on carting them along. As did some donors: at Waddesdon Manor until Lord Rothschild – the first in the line of its inhabitants to be a parent – re-opened the château in 1994, children were barred.

In 1988, Patricia Lankester was hired by the Trust as its first education manager. She now oversees a staff of thirty people, though not all of them are fulltime. The job she set herself was to encourage teachers to see the National Trust's properties as a place they could use to help educate young people; somewhere that might be fascinating for them and fun as well as instructive. Her annual budget is about £300,000, some of which is spent on head office staff, some of which is given to the regions. And more comes from corporate sponsors too. Barclays Bank, for instance, provided £350,000 between 1989 and 1994 (and for the Centenary year alone gave a gift of £100,000) in order to support the Young National Trust Theatre.

Sir Angus can be an innovator. He can be firm.

'He has been consistently strong in making people aware that education should be an integral part of the Trust's work rather than a bolt on,' Tricia Lankester says of her boss.

Then why for heaven's sake have a bolt-on transport strategy? If only Sir Angus were half as consistent or half as strong in his prosecution of the so-called campaign to get the Department of Transport to consider preserving outstandingly beautiful landscape a necessity, before it embarks on its plans for building roads, and to acknowledge that inalienable land is off-limits.

Oh, the Trust is doing *something*. In advance of the public hearing on the Morecombelake bypass, it hired a firm of engineering consultants to investigate possible alternatives and to scrutinize the ministry's figures and their engineer's reports. To George Elliott's great relief, 'a panel of experts will be putting the Trust's case before the public enquiry'. But he concedes that the Trust has gone 'about this skirmish in a very amateurish way'. It certainly looks that way. Even more crucially the Trust ought not to be skirmishing. It was for the purpose of stopping this wasteful, exhausting, expensive and, therefore, frequently ineffective way of operating, that the National Trust was founded.

Telephone Queen Anne's Gate for information about the current status of any of the major 'situations' in which land held in trust for the nation may be spoiled by a proposed road, and what you are told is: 'Ring the region, they'll know.'[4]

Usually the region doesn't know much more than the road's number and the parcel that is in jeopardy. They recommend ringing the particular property if more information is needed. And that means the warden.

'When the Trust says, "we're not a campaigning body," that horrifies me,' says George Elliott. 'If something is wrong, you must campaign.' Yet routinely that is just what the Trust does assert, as if this were written in its Constitution. In much the same way, people at Queen Anne's Gate describe the National Trust as 'a safety net', the idea being that the charity was created as something that would just lie there, in case of emergency. The purpose of both assertions is to justify the National Trust's passivity. But it wasn't at all passive at the start. For example, in 1900 when C.R. Ashbee mentioned some wooded property in Ruislip he hoped the National Trust would buy, Octavia Hill's interested reply was, 'I happen to be on the look out for an open space to preserve.'[5]

It is not necessary to use a Ouija board to know with certainty that Octavia Hill, Hardwicke Rawnsley and Sir Robert Hunter would think that the warden of the Golden Cap estate was stating the obvious. They were campaigners all their lives.

'You have to have a very long view about the National Trust don't you?' Lord Rothschild cautioned when I'd revealed how exercised I was about the fainthearted way it was being run.

'It is one of this country's unique and sensitive institutions. Although it may at times be tempting to seek radical change, I would recommend a very careful and organic approach.'

Jacob Rothschild's view is sensible, possibly also wise. Intuitively it is shared by thousands of members of the National Trust. Undoubtedly one reason that, though the huge majority of subscribers play no part in the voting, as many as 50,000 people give the chairman their proxies to use as he sees fit. By doing so they are providing ballast for the ark; to help it stay steady and keep its cargo safe no matter how tumultuous the voyage. But caution and the inevitable conservatism of an organization whose business is conservation surely is not the same thing as cowardice.

'What does the future hold unless there is some sort of restriction as the price of protecting the environment?' asks David Bett, the Trust's regional director for Wessex during one of our conversations about the Golden Cap. Sir Angus and Lord Chorley seem to think this question too political for the National Trust to ask.

'We must be very careful about what we say on the subject of transport because many of our members favour roads and won't like it,' the director general of the National Trust informed me when I pressed him about the fate of the Golden Cap.

'A great national gallery of the landscape,' Canon Rawnsley called America's Trustees of the Reservations on which the National Trust patterned itself.[6] How can the National Trust's director general, while someone is poised and ready to draw a moustache on the Mona Lisa and paint out the face on Rembrandt's self-portrait, just stand there, murmuring, 'But some of our supporters like graffiti.'

Fear as well as power corrupts. This very great charity sometimes appears so terribly defensive, secretive and timid. We and the properties deserve better than that.

There may be no single group of individuals more resistant to having their mobility restricted than drivers of cars. I certainly loathe the idea. But surely I am not the only car owner who would rather crawl along the A35 than see the Golden Cap spoiled for ever.

The idea that roads cannot for ever go on being widened, and new ones built, is not controversial. Nor is it contentious that some more coherent thought has to be given to how all of us are going to get from Bournemouth to Exeter or from Cardiff to Conway without destroying everything in our path and the very things we are travelling to see. The answers may be debated, politically charged, difficult to find. But the questions by now are commonplace – though evidently not at Queen Anne's Gate.

If only the National Trust, created as a solution to the problems mass transport was causing, would raise its head above the parapet again, think of the leadership it might provide! And think, if it doesn't, of all that is being risked. By not being seen to stand up for its properties, the Trust may soon begin to lose ground.

It's said sometimes that when Sir Henry Benson advised the National Trust to increase its membership dramatically, he was abetting in the creation of a monster. The people running the National Trust often act as if this is what has happened. And with at least a third of its annual income coming from its more than 2 million subscribers, the Trust would be in big trouble if people decided to give their pounds and pennies to a Donkey Sanctuary instead.

But the membership does not act like a monster. It could hardly be more benign in fact. Two million people are content enough to let the Trust get on with things as it chooses. As for the tiny minority that isn't content: doesn't the smell of fear excite aggression in those who might be inclined to take a bite or two? Doesn't failure to act, failure to be open, to answer questions, doesn't this actually invite trouble instead of warding it off? And doesn't smugness and complacency inflame those who simply wish to be heard?

And in any case, where a threat to its properties comes from planned roads, there is no need for the National Trust to campaign *against* the use of cars. That needn't be the message at all – not yet in any case and perhaps never. What it needs to do is to help people understand that land of outstanding natural beauty held in trust for them and their heirs is going to be blighted permanently if the DoT doesn't alter its methods.

In the spring of 1994 the DoT announced a change in its roads policy. It was going to concentrate its limited resources on improvements to motorways. And even the DoT acknowledged that in future roads were to be only one of the methods of transport it would be considering. However, those plans for roads which are not motorways, and which had already been announced, were put into various categories that, loosely, suggested the order in which their construction would begin. Some planned roads were cancelled outright: in this group were three that would have affected National Trust land. This left thirty-seven others, among them the A35 at the Golden Cap.

'We are still blighted,' says Ian Wilson at Queen Anne's Gate. The planned roads remain 'a threat to our properties and their management'. Which means skirmish after skirmish must be prepared for and then fought when the DoT gets around to a particular road at an as yet unspecified future date.

Lord Rothschild refers to the Trust's membership as the 'largest private army in the country'. What more sympathetic and concerned group can there be when it comes to the preservation of the countryside and how untapped is its good will.

People with intelligence and drive, imagination and courage, acquired the properties now held in Trust for the nation. There were romantics among them and there were pragmatists also. They were willing to experiment even if that always brings with it the risk of failing. The National Trust will have to find such qualities again if we are going to keep our possessions and discover what we want to do with them, what we want them to do for us.

To take one example: is there a policy governing the Trust's acquisition of houses? Apparently not. While Martin Drury, the deputy director general and historic buildings secretary disagrees, some of his staff and numerous outside supporters believe the National Trust should be amassing a portfolio of houses or creating a kind of architectural smorgasbord. Nigel Nicolson, for instance, would like the Trust to acquire a

Lutyens house complete with a Jekyll-designed garden. Perhaps it was in response to critics who say it doesn't have enough from the twentieth century that the charity decided to open Mr Straw's House to the public in 1992. Certainly Mr Straw himself had never imagined this would be the result when he left the house and its contents to the Trust.

When William Straw died in 1990 at the age of ninety-three, he left the charity £1.5 million as well as his early twentieth-century semi-detached villa and everything that was in it. His thought was that the Trust would sell the house, add that money to the rest of his bequest and use it for one of its preservation projects. Some of the contents might go to the local history museum, he thought, and with that in mind he labelled everything he felt was of any interest or importance. There was a lot to sort through. Since his widowed mother's death in 1939 nothing had been thrown out. But what the National Trust did instead was to declare that this house on the edge of Worksop in Nottinghamshire was another one of its 'time capsules' and it used William Straw's legacy to endow the house so that it could be opened to the public. Mr Straw's House is so small it can only hold four visitors at a time. It is not of historic or architectural importance nor even an illustration of how people lived in a particular period. It is merely the not especially attractive suburban home of a cranky bachelor who hated to throw things out.

A la Ronde, which was bought in 1991 with help from the National Heritage Memorial Fund and the launch of an appeal by the Trust for £500,000 to go towards its restoration, initially seems a more plausible acquisition. It is a charming sixteen-sided, eighteenth-century house in South Devon built for two spinster cousins and imaginatively decorated with their own handiwork. Jane and Mary Parminter elaborately embellished the interior with extraordinary mosaics made from shells and feathers and glass. Their triumph is the magnificent shell gallery which lines a gallery thirty feet above the central hall. It proved to be so fragile, however, and the stairway leading up to it so narrow, the balcony that rings it so shallow that when the house opened in 1993 visitors to A la Ronde found that to view its shell gallery they must remain on the first floor and look at a video! What is the point? For whom has A la Ronde been saved at great cost?

The NTs houses open to the public are owned inalienably. They cannot be sold, mortgaged or given away. But they can be let. Why not close some of the large, unoccupied houses that are not in the Kedleston Hall category? Have the grounds open to the public, if they are attractive, but find tenants for the houses themselves. As for the smaller houses from which the public can scarcely benefit, perhaps it is time for the Trust to think harder before it acquires.

Maybe what the National Trust needs today is a James Lees-Milne in reverse; someone to go around England, Wales and Northern Ireland making an inventory of country houses not worth the cost of opening to the public. I am not alone in having candidates for such a list.

There are so many other matters that need to be more openly and carefully considered. Among them these:

Doesn't there need to be a shift in where its money goes so that the countryside properties, and the people who give themselves to preserving them, receive more support? For example, should there be a cap placed on how much is spent at mansions which are costing hundreds of thousands of pounds more to run than they bring in each year? Why should absolutely everything in a house be looked after as if it were a priceless treasure simply because the Trust owns the property for ever? And why are such treasures as the paintings and books in the houses not properly catalogued so that members and the public are aware that they exist? How can people benefit from such gifts to the nation if they don't know they're there? Hasn't the Trust become too keen on professionalism by demanding paper qualifications from gardeners and wardens when its own experience shows the advantages of choosing the right person rather than the right piece of paper? And hasn't it remained too devoted to amateurism when it comes to the administrative staff? The bureaucracy should be put on a very strict diet: 6,000 fulltime office staff is surely too many. And the Trust could only gain if the staff remaining were of higher calibre. Isn't it time to rewrite radically the Constitution of the National Trust so that it will have a system of checks and balances that works, and its highest ranking officers will be answerable to people other than themselves? Why not use the AGM as the occasion for wardens, gardeners, foresters, administrators of houses, housekeepers and conservation staff to give seminars to members about the work that goes on throughout the year? Or variations on the theme of *Gardeners' Question Time*? Staff and members would gain from having such an exchange. AGMs would be less dreary and the emphasis on voting, which only encourages people to have the illusion that members are shareholders making policy-decisions, would be diluted. It should be, since constitutionally they are not. Would it be practical for NT tenants to form an association that would help put them on a more equal footing with their landlord? Will computer cottages replace sheep pens in the hill farms of Yorkshire, Wales and the Lake District, or are we prepared to start eating a lot of premium priced rack of Herdwick? All these are matters that should be addressed, and not only behind closed doors at the National Trust.

'It will be preserved in its present loveliness,' Octavia Hill promised in a speech after the 108 acres of Brandelhow Park became the National Trust's first property in the Lake District in 1902. 'And it belongs to you all and to every landless man, woman and child in England.'[7]

There is much to celebrate: 600,000 acres so far, 531 miles of coastline and more than 230 houses and gardens, among them the most wonderful in England, Wales and the six counties.

There is much to question.

Notes

Unless otherwise attributed, all direct quotes in the text are from interviews conducted by the author. If the source is not identified by name it is because he or she asked to remain anonymous. The abbreviation NT refers to the National Trust archive.

Chapter 1: In the Nick of Time

1 Canon Rawnsley, letter, 2 February 1883, NT.
2 Octavia Hill, letter, 22 March 1897, NT.
3 Gillian Darley, *Octavia Hill* (1990).
4 The main sources for the biographical information that follows are Darley (see note 3); Graham Murphy *The Founders of the National Trust* (1987); John Gaze *Figures in a Landscape* (1988) and the National Trust archive.
5 C.R. Ashbee's diary, 16 November 1900. Ashbee Journals. King's College, Cambridge.
6 Osbert Sitwell, *Left Hand, Right Hand!* (1949).
7 G.M. Young, *Portrait of an Age* (1986) p.37.
8 Thomas Southwood Smith, *The Philosophy of Health* (1865).
9 Paul Thompson, *The Life of William Morris* (1967).
10 NT.
11 J.C. Loudon, 'Breathing spaces for the Metropolis,' in the *Gardener's Magazine*, 5 (1829)
12 Alessandra Ponte, 'Public parks in Great Britain and the United States', in *The History of Garden Design* (1991). Background source for information about Loudon and Paxton which follows.
13 Frederick Law Olmsted, Speech given before the American Social Science Association (1870).
14 E.S. Maurice, *Octavia Hill: Early Ideals* (1928) p.10.
15 John Ruskin, 'General Statement explaining the Nature and Purposes

of St George's Guild'. (1882).

16 James S. Dearden (ed.) *The Professor: Arthur Severn's Memoir of John Ruskin.* (1967).

17 Graham Murphy. *Founders of the National Trust.* (1991).

18 Letter from Octavia Hill to Robert Hunter, February 1885, NT.

19 Hardwicke Rawnsley, 'A national benefactor. Sir Robert Hunter' in *Cornhill Magazine*, February 1914.

20 NT.

21 Duke of Westminster, letter, 10 November 1900, NT.

22 Octavia Hill, letter, 25 November 1900, NT.

23 H.D. Rawnsley, *A Nation's Heritage* (1920).

24 C. Edmund Maurice (ed.) *Life of Octavia Hill: as told in her letters* (1913).

25 Vita Sackville-West, *English Country Houses* (1947), p.7.

Chapter 2: Gentlemen's Agreements

1 Ashbee Journals. June 1901.

2 Earl of Wharncliffe, letter, 2 June 1896, NT.

3 For the purposes of this book the terms inheritance tax and death duties are used interchangeably.

4 Michael Astor, *Tribal Feeling* (1964).

5 David Cannadine, *G.M. Trevelyan: A Life in History* (1992)

6 Interview with Sir George Trevelyan.

7 Cannadine (as note 5).

8 In time the National Trust began to feel it had a duty, indeed that it was bound by its Act of Parliament, to preserve everything from curtains to bicycles in such a way that they will last 'for ever'. As a result it often seems as if the same exacting conservation standards that a museum would apply to the treasures on display are now being used by the Trust for virtually everything in its care. This is expensive, shows a lack of proportion – not everything is a treasure after all, indeed a great deal is not – and contributes to removing any sense of human occupation from its houses.

9 Lady Anne Acland, *NT Guide to Killerton* 2nd ed. (1978).

10 H.R. Rawnsley, *A Nation's Heritage* (1920).

11 James Lees-Milne, *People and Places* (1992).

12 David Cannadine. *The Decline and Fall of the British Aristocracy* (1990).

13 Paul Thompson, *The World of William Morris* (1967).

14 James Lees-Milne, *Midway on the Waves* (1985).

15 Gillian Darley, *Octavia Hill* (1990).
16 Vita Sackville-West, *English Country Houses* (1947).
17 James Lees-Milne, *Another Self* (1970).
18 James Lees-Milne (as note 17).
19 James Lees-Milne, *Prophesying Peace* (1986).
20 James Lees-Milne, *Caves of Ice* (1986).
21 James Lees-Milne, *Ancestral Voices* (1987).

Chapter 3: Squires in Wonderland

1 Osbert Sitwell, *Left Hand, Right Hand!* (1949).
2 Caroline Davidson, *A Woman's Work is Never Done* (1986).
3 NT.
4 James Lees-Milne, *People and Places* (1992)
5 Arthur Jones, *Britain's Heritage* (Weidenfeld & Nicolson, London 1985). This book gives the history of the events leading up to the creation of the NHMF. Following the loss of Mentmore, Mr Jones was the MP who chaired the sub-committee investigating the way the Land Fund functioned and the way the Treasury apparently did not – at least when it came to spending already allocated money on art, architecture or the landscape.
6 Compton Mackenzie, *I Took a Journey* (1951).
7 Following a programme mapped out by Helen Lloyd, the NT's chief housekeeper, the charity's staff arranges the contents of almost all its country houses at the end of the visiting season each year so that objects and furnishings can rest over the winter. At many properties this is also the period when major conservation projects are carried out because there will be little interference from – and inconvenience to – visitors.

Chapter 4: A Poisoned Trident

1 Commander Rawnsley's Archives. All quotes from his correspondence with the NT are from this source.
2 G.M. Trevelyan, 'Amenities and the State', in *Britain and the Beast*, edited by Clough Williams-Ellis (1937), p.183.
3 Graham Murphy, *Founders of the National Trust* (1987), p.90.

4 Phrase used by Warren Davis, press and public relations manager to describe the NT at the time.

5 Rawnsley Archive.

6 NT.

7 The owner of a property can create a legally binding document that places restrictions on what can be done to the land or buildings. These covenants can be made over to the National Trust, which retains them even if the property is subsequently sold. While covenants are a useful tool for protecting properties, they are a relatively weak one because they are difficult to police and expensive for an organization like the National Trust to enforce if people fail to comply with them.

8 Josselyn Hennessy, 'Preservation and Progress – An Economist looks at the National Trust'. *Lloyds Bank Review* April 1964. p.49

9 Rawnsley Archive.

10 *Observer*, 6 November 1966.

Chapter 5: How to Build an Oak

1 Though only an interpretation of events, this account of how it was that Angus Stirling left the Arts Council and went to the NT has been repeated by many observers. Sir Angus, however, reports that when he was offered the post he was not sure he should accept and spent a year deliberating about it before he decided to leave the Arts Council and agree to become director general of the Trust.

2 Letter from William Morris to Hardwicke Rawnsley, 10 February 1896. NT

3 It wasn't until the Hornby Working Party's report was presented to the Trust the following year that the Trust was advised to alter its 'chain of command' so that its salaried staff in the regions would report directly to its headquarters and the role of the various Regional Committees would become advisory. This was adopted. There continues to be confusion in the minds of a number of the volunteers who serve on the Trust's Regional Committees, however, who think that it is they and not the NT's staff who make the important decisions affecting the properties.

4 The fact that it's almost impossible to get rid of a volunteer who wants to serve is one arguement used by those who are opposed to the NT relying on ever more voluntary help.

Chapter 6: Pretty as a Picture

1 James Lees-Milne, *Midway on the Waves* (1987).
2 Letters, NT.
3 NT.
4 The MacMillan Nurses who work with cancer patients are the principal beneficiaries of money raised through the NGS.
5 NT.
6 Letter from Vita Sackville-West to Harold Nicolson published in his diaries.

Chapter 7: A Mixed Bouquet

1 In the case of Ham House and Osterley Park, two mansions set in vast parks on the edge of London, the Trust accepted far less than the Chorley Formula. The formula produced a figure of £22 million for both; the NT accepted £14.5 million. They did so because they said the threats to both properties were great and the sum offered was the best they could hope to get and if they refused it, eventually their financial liability would be far worse, as would the condition of both properties. The Trust had been the owner of the freehold of both houses since 1948 but because they had been given with no endowment the government had a ninety-nine year lease on them and had put them in the care of the Victoria and Albert Museum to manage. By 1989 the government had come to feel that these properties were too expensive to keep up, while the NT felt that the government hadn't been spending enough on their upkeep and they were deteriorating. The government offered to buy itself out of the remaining fifty years of its lease for £14.5 million. The Trust is putting that towards endowment and restoration of both Ham and Osterley.

Chapter 8: Strangers in Paradise

1 Robin Fedden, *The Continuing Purpose* (1968).
2 'Havoc' by E.M. Forster, in *Britain and the Beast*, edited by Clough Williams-Ellis (1937).
3 Susan Denyer, *Traditional Buildings & Life in the Lake District* (1991). This book by Mrs Denyer and interviews with her provided much invaluable information about the history of the region.
4 Arthur Young, *A Six Month Tour through the North of England* (1770).
5 Bruce Logan Thompson, *The National Trust Properties in the Lake District* (1930).
6 G.M. Trevelyan, 'The White Peril', in *Nineteenth Century* (1901).
7 W. Wordsworth, *A Guide through the District of the Lakes* (1951 ed.),
8 Wordsworth (as note 7).

Chapter 9: A Republic of Shepherds

1 B.L. Thompson, *The National Trust in the Lake District* (1946).
2 Interviews with Susan Denyer and her book *Traditional Buildings & Life in the Lake District* were invaluable sources of historical information.
3 Observation made by Laurence Harwood, the NT's former regional director for the north-west, in an interview.
4 Gillian Darley, *Octavia Hill* (1990).
5 B.L. Thompson (as note 1).
6 NT.
7 Interview with Josephine Banner.
8 'This Quixotic Venture', by Susan Denyer, in *So I Shall Tell you a Story* (1993).
9 NT.
10 Susan Denyer (as note 8).
11 *Beatrix Potter's Letters*, edited by Judy Taylor (1989).
12 Susan Denyer (as note 8).
13 Judy Taylor (ed.) (as note 11).

14 B.L. Thompson (as note 1).

Chapter 10: Fashions in Fantasy

1 George Bernard Shaw, *Plays Pleasant and Unpleasant*. vol. II. (Grant Richards, London 1898).
2 Graham Greene, 'Beatrix Potter: A critical estimate', in *Collected Essays* (1969).
3 Sir George Sitwell, Bt, *An Essay on the Making of Gardens* (1909).
4 Anthea Mander Lahr, 'Under the Linoleum', in *The National Trust Magazine*, no.66, summer 1992.
5 Welcome to Wales.
6 John Gaze, *Figures in a Landscape*. (1988).
7 Interview with Major Peter Orde.
8 G.M. Trevelyan, *English Social History* (3rd edn., 1946).

Juggernaut

1 Robin Fedden, *The Continuing Purpose* (1968).
2 E. Moberly Bell, *Octavia Hill* (1942).
3 G.M. Trevelyan. 'Must England's Beauty Perish? A plea on behalf of the National Trust'. Pamphlet (1929).
4 The National Trust Regional press staff has the job of keeping local people informed about the Trust's work and providing local newspapers with press releases and information of other kinds. The headquarters in London, in an attempt to implement its policy of decentralization, frequently refers journalists working on national or overseas papers and magazines to the appropriate regional press office. With extremely few exceptions this results in frustration on both sides. The regional staff seem to feel pressured, they don't know the journalists ringing up, they don't understand why they should be asked to return calls quickly, etc. Instead of creating a more efficient system, 'ring the region' often acts as a barrier.
5 Ashbee Journals. King's College, Cambridge
6 NT.
7 Gillian Darley. *Octavia Hill* (1990).

Select Bibliography

Astor, Michael, *Tribal Feeling* (John Murray, London 1964)

Bell, E. Moberly, *Octavia Hill. A biography* (Constable, London 1942)

Cannadine, David, *The Decline and Fall of the British Aristocracy* (Yale University Press, New Haven and London 1990)

—— *G.M. Trevelyan. A life in history* (HarperCollins, London 1992)

Cornforth, John, *The Inspiration of the Past* (Viking, London 1985)

Crawford, Alan, *C.R. Ashbee* (Yale University Press, New Haven and London 1985)

Darley, Gillian, *Octavia Hill* (Constable, London 1990)

Dashwood, Sir Francis, *The Dashwoods of West Wycombe* (Aurum Press, London 1987)

Davidson, Caroline, *A Woman's Work is Never Done. A history of housework in the British Isles 1650–1950* (Chatto & Windus, London 1986)

Denyer, Susan, *Traditional Buildings & Life in the Lake District* (Victor Gollancz/Peter Crawley in association with the National Trust, London 1991)

Fedden, Robin, *The Continuing Purpose. A History of the National Trust, its Aims and Work* (Longmans, London 1968)

—— *The National Trust Past and Present* (Jonathan Cape, London 1974)

Fedden, Robin, and Joekes, Rosemary, *The National Trust Guide* rev. ed. (Jonathan Cape, London 1979)

Gaze, John, *Figures in a Landscape: A history of the National Trust* (Barrie & Jenkins in association with the National Trust, London 1988)

Hewison, Robert, *The Heritage Industry* (Methuen, London 1987)

Hunter, Sir Robert, *The Preservation of Open Spaces and of Footpaths and other Rights of Way: a practical treatise on the law of the subject* (Eyre & Spottiswoode, London 1902)

Lane, Margaret, *The Tale of Beatrix Potter* (Penguin Books, London 1962)

Lees-Milne, James, *Ancestral Voices* (Faber & Faber, London & Boston 1987)

—— *Another Self* (Hamish Hamilton, London 1970)

—— *Caves of Ice* (Faber & Faber, London & Boston 1986)

—— *Harold Nicolson. A biography* vol. 2. *1930–1968* (Chatto & Windus, London 1981)

—— *Midway on the Waves* (Faber & Faber London & Boston 1987)

—— *People and Places. Country House Donors and the National Trust* (John Murray, London 1992)

—— *Prophesying Peace* (Faber & Faber, London & Boston 1986)

Lees-Milne, James (ed.), *The National Trust: a record of fifty years' achievement* (Batsford, London 1946)

Legg, Rodney, *Open Space Society Bulletin*. Spring 1991. vol. 23. no. 10.

Mackenzie, Compton, *I Took a Journey* (Published for the National Trust by the Naldret Press, London 1951)

Maurice, C. Edmund (ed.), *Life of Octavia Hill: as told in her letters* (Macmillan, London 1913)

Morley, Edith J. (ed.), 'John Ruskin and social ethics', the Fabian Society (undated)

Mosser, Monique, and Tyessot, George (eds), *The History of Garden Design* (Thames & Hudson, London 1991)

Murphy, Graham, *Founders of the National Trust* (Christopher Helm, London 1987)

Nicolson, Harold, *Diary and Letters. 1945–1962*, Nigel Nicolson (ed.) vol.3. (Collins, London 1968)

Olmsted, Frederick Law, 'Public parks and the enlargement of towns', American Social Science Association (The Riverside Press, Cambridge, Mass 1870)

Rawnsley, Rev., H.D. *Literary Associations of the English Lakes*, vols. I and II (James MacLehouse, Glasgow 1894)

—— *A Nation's Heritage* (George Allen & Unwin, London 1920)

Sackville-West, V., *English Country Houses* (Collins, London 1947)

Seebohm, Caroline, *The Country House. A wartime history, 1939–45* (Weidenfield & Nicolson, London 1989)

Sitwell, Sir George, *On the Making of Gardens* (John Murray, London 1909)

Sitwell, Osbert, *Left Hand, Right Hand!* (Macmillan, London 1949)

Smith, Thomas Southwood, *The Philosophy of Health* (Longman, Green, Longman, Roberts & Green, London 1865)

Strong, Roy, Harris, John, Binney, Marcus, *Destruction of the Country House* (Thames & Hudson, London 1974)

Taylor, Judy, *Beatrix Potter: Artist, Storyteller and Countrywoman* (Frederick Warne, London 1986)

Taylor, Judy (ed.), *Beatrix Potter's Letters* (Frederick Warne, London 1989)

Thomas, Graham Stewart, *Gardens of the National Trust* (Weidenfeld & Nicolson, London 1979)

Thompson, Bruce Logan, *The National Trust Properties in the Lake*

District (Titus Wilson, Kenda 1930)
—— *The Lake District and the National Trust* (Titus Wilson, Kendal 1946)
Thompson, Paul, *The Work of William Morris* (Heinemann, London 1967)
Tinniswood, Adrian, *A History of Country House Visiting: five centuries of tourism and taste* (Basil Blackwood and the National Trust, Oxford 1989)
—— *Historic Houses of the National Trust* (National Trust, London 1991)
Treveylan, G.M., *English Social History* (Longmans, Green, 3rd edn., London 1946)
Williams-Ellis, Clough (ed.) *Britain and the Beast* (J.M. Dent, London 1937)
Woolf, Leonard, *Sowing. Autobiography of the years 1880–1904* (Hogarth Press, London 1962)
Wordsworth, Dorothy, *Journals of Dorothy Wordsworth* Mary Moorman (ed) second ed (Oxford University Press, Oxford New York 1983)
Wordsworth, William, *A Guide through the District of the Lakes in the North of England* (Rupert Hart-Davis, London 1951)
Wright, Patrick, *A Journey through Ruins* (Radius, London 1991)
Young, Arthur, *A Six Month Tour through the North of England*. 4 vols (W. Strahan, London 1770)
Young, G.M., *Portrait of an Age. Victorian England* (Oxford University Press, Oxford & New York 1986)

Index

INDEX

Johnstone, Major Lawrence, 200, 211–12, 224
Jones, Sir Roderick, 70
Jones, Walter, 343

Keating sisters, 265
Kedleston Hall, Derbyshire, 106–10, 118, 351–2; fountain removed, 110–11
Keen, Lady Mary, 228
Keen, Richard, 362
Kennaway, Ian, 237–8, 377
Kent, William, 70
Kentish, Mavis, 156
Keswick, Cumbria, 26
Keswick Footpath and Commons Society, 26
Killerton estate, Devon, 60, 61–2, 73, 168, 325; training at, 251
Kingston Lacy, Dorset, 118, 270
Knole House, Kent, 48, 85–6, 91, 199, 243
Kyrle Society, 22–3, 31

Lacock Abbey, Wiltshire, 62
Lahr, Anthea Mander, 354–60
Lahr, Bert, 357
Lahr, Christopher, 357
Lahr, John, 357
Lake District: proposed railways for, 26, 278; Wordsworth warns of dangers to, 64, 280; NT properties and land in, 112, 273–5, 281, 284–8, 306–9, 313, 324; discovery and idealization of, 275–9, 302, 303; numbers of visitors, 278–9, 304; trees and forestry, 280, 293–4; as National Park, 281; recruiting in, 282–6; car parking, 289, 291–2, 301; landscape preservation, 291, 296–7, 302, 329–30; footpath erosion and pitching repair, 296–300; farmers and farming in, 303–9, 311–14, 316–28, 331–3, 363–4; electricity supply, 305; non-local officials in, 323–5; vernacular buildings in, 327–30; social change in, 364
Lake District Defence Society, 26
Land Fund see National Heritage Memorial Fund
Landmark Trust, 131
landscape gardening: and city life, 17–18
Langdale, Cumbria, 333–6, 364
Lanhydrock, Cornwall: garden, 199, 209; gardener's accommodation, 242–4, 337
Lankester, Patricia, Lady, 378
Latham, Robert, 149
Leconfield estate, 278
Lees-Milne, James: on Killerton, 62; social attitudes, 66, 68; visits Gawthorpe Hall, 66; works as secretary to Country Houses Committee, 70–4; at Wallington House, 73, 277–8; upholds squirearchy, 76–7, 80; and potential donors, 82, 90, 93, 98, 207, 384; and access to West Wycombe Park, 87; on life-style of NT property

occupants, 99; stipend from NT, 127; retained as adviser, 142; collaborates with Nichols, 169; dislikes Bodnant, 201, 218; on 2nd Lord Aberconway., 213; on effect of NT, 366
Legg, Rodney, 132, 156
Leighton, Frederic, Baron, 167
lichen: theft of, 292
Lilleshall Hall, Shropshire, 206
Lindisfarne Castle, Northumberland, 171; garden, 232
Lindsay, Norah, 224
Llandudno see Annual General Meeting (1990)
Llyn (Lleyn) Peninsula, Gwynedd, 265–8, 325
Lodore Falls (Lake District), 29
Londesborough, William Henry Forester, 1st Earl of, 78
London: parks and open spaces, 17–18; population, 17
Londonderry, Edith, Marchioness of, 207
Long Crendon Courthouse, Buckinghamshire, 37–9
Longcake, Myrtle, 282–6
Lord, Tony, 320
Lothian, Philip Kerr, 11th Marquess of, 41–4, 46, 49, 57, 59, 63–4, 69, 75
Loudon, John Claudius, 17–18
Louise, Princess, 181, 192
Low Newton-by-the-Sea, Northumberland, 262–3, 323
Lutyens, Sir Edwin, 224, 383
Lysser, Andrew, 292

MacDonald, Ramsay, 51
Mack, Terence, 246
McKennall, John, 270
Mackenzie, Sir Compton, 112
MacNeice, Emma, 246
Man, Isle of, 19, 35
Mander, Sir Geoffrey, 46, 67, 354–5, 357, 359–60
Mander, Rosalie, Lady, 47, 67–8, 73, 91, 354–7, 359
Mariner's Hill, Kent, 66
Marlborough, John George Spencer-Churchill, 11th Duke of, 248, 291
Marshall, Jim, 252
Martineau, Anthony A., 126
Mason, Dave, 250–4, 269, 271–2
Matheson, Donald MacLeod, 69
Matheson, Hilda, 69–70
Maurice, Oliver, 291, 300–1, 338
Melford Hall, Suffolk, 217–18
Memorandum of Wishes, 51
Messel, Lt Colonel L.C.R., 204
Meyric, Dick, 243–4
Michalak, Jan, 245–9, 271
Middle Fell Farm, Cumbria, 334

[403]

INDEX

Thomas, Graham Stuart: at Melford Hall, 217–18; visits Bodnant, 217; succeeded by Sale, 220; *Gardens of the National Trust*, 201, 235

Thomason, Dave, 288–90, 292–5

Thompson, Bruce, 278, 303, 307, 316

Thorneycroft, Peter, Baron, 104

Thorpe, Jeremy, 149

Thring, Edward, 24–5

Times, The, 32, 59

Tooley, Professor Michael, 232

Townsend, Ted, 343

Toynbee, Arnold, 24

trees and forestry, 280, 293–4

Trelissick, Cornwall, 242

Trevelyan family, 44, 277–8, 319

Trevelyan, Catriona, 56, 352

Trevelyan, Sir Charles, 3rd Baronet: transfers Wallington to NT, 43–6, 50–5, 57–60, 63–4, 68, 112, 202–3, 309; retains management of Wallington, 58–9, 211, 306; Lees-Milne on, 73; farm income, 364

Trevelyan, Editha Helen, Lady, 56–7, 352

Trevelyan, Geoffrey, 54–5

Trevelyan, Sir George, 4th Baronet, 53–8

Trevelyan, George Macaulay: idealises country life, 35–6, 278; on Trevelyan family values, 44; and Wallington estate, 45; devises Memorandum of Wishes, 51; and appointment to Country House Committee secretaryship, 71; and coastline properties, 121, 134; proposes membership increase, 181; outdoor games in Lake District, 278; buys Lakeland farmland properties for NT, 308, 311, 333; on social effect of agricultural depression, 365; and motor traffic, 375

Trevelyan, Mary, Lady, 44, 48, 53, 73–4, 81

Trevelyan, Pauline, Lady, 44–5

Trevelyan, Sir Walter, 44

Trinick, Michael: on Antony (Cornwall), 89–90; regional administration in Cornwall, 133, 168–9, 266, 331; and Crawford, 172; on aristocratic network, 173; on devolution, 181; defends Borlase, 243–4

Troutbeck Park, Cumbria, 311, 314

Trustees of the Public Reservations (USA), 165–6, 380

Tyn-y-Fynnon, near Barmouth, 33

Uhlman, Diana, 96–9

United States of America: conservation in, 165–6, 380

Vaughan Williams, Ralph, 278

Victoria, Queen, 22

Waddesdon Manor, Buckinghamshire: author visits, 4; acquired by NT, 47, 94–5; open to public, 94, 96; management, 95–6, 104–5, 199; restoration, 95, 289; admission charge and rebate, 96, 217; children barred, 378

Wall End farm, Cumbria, 308

Wallington (estate), Northumberland: given to NT, 43–6, 50, 52–3, 55, 57–60, 112, 171, 306; NT improvements, 53–4; management, 58–9, 74; Lees-Milne visits, 73, 277–8; training at, 270; preservation, 352

Walton, John, 269

Ward, Mrs Humphry, 167

Washington Old Hall, County Durham (Tyne and Wear), 171

Waterson, Merlin, 135, 241, 301

Watson, Philip, 258–61, 262

Waugh, Evelyn: *Scoop*, 342

Wembley *see* Annual General Meeting (1993)

West Penrith, 270

West Wycombe Park, Buckinghamshire: transferred to NT, 62, 80–1; limited public access to, 87–8; upkeep, 90; contents, 101–2; park and landscape, 219–20; Edwardian regatta, 366–9

West Wycombe (village), Buckinghamshire, 307

Westbury, Wiltshire: NT office in, 181

Westminster, Hugh Lupus Grosvenor, 1st Duke of, 30–2, 167

Wey & Godalming Navigation, Surrey, 184–8

Wharncliffe, Edward Montagu Stuart Granville, 1st Earl of, 39

Whitmore-Jones, Irene, 341

Wight, Isle of, 270

Wightwick Manor, near Wolverhampton: reluctant acceptance by NT, 46–50, 68, 93; tenancy, 67, 356–7; garden, 200; NT management and restoration of, 354–5, 358, 360; Trust fund, 357; family life in, 358–60

Wilde, Oscar, 12, 24

Wilkinsyke Farm, Cumbria, 284

Wilson, Ian, 377, 382

Windemere, Cumbria, 278

women: as foresters, 293–4

Wordsworth, Dorothy, 280

Wordsworth, William, 64, 275–8, 280, 304, 329; *Guide to the Lakes*, 276, 280

Workman, John, 220–1, 294–5

Works & General Purposes Committee (NT), 168

Worksop, Nottinghamshire, 383

Worsley, Sir Marcus, 171

Wray Castle, Cumbria, 25, 309

Wright, Tom, 228

[407]